MULTIPLE OBJECTIVE DECISION METHODS
AND REGIONAL PLANNING

Studies in Regional Science and Urban Economics

Editors

ÅKE ANDERSSON
WALTER ISARD

Volume 7

NORTH-HOLLAND PUBLISHING COMPANY – AMSTERDAM • NEW YORK • OXFORD

Multiple Objective Decision Methods and Regional Planning

PIET RIETVELD

Department of Economics
Free University, Amsterdam

1980

NORTH-HOLLAND PUBLISHING COMPANY – AMSTERDAM • NEW YORK • OXFORD

ISBN: 0 444 86001 0

Publishers:
NORTH-HOLLAND PUBLISHING COMPANY
AMSTERDAM • NEW YORK • OXFORD

Distributors for the U.S.A. and Canada:
ELSEVIER NORTH-HOLLAND, INC.
52 VANDERBILT AVENUE
NEW YORK, N.Y. 10017

Library of Congress Cataloging in Publication Data

Rietveld, Piet.
    Multiple objective decision methods and regional
planning.

    (Studies in regional science and urban
economics ; v. 7)
    Bibliography: p.
    Includes indexes.
    1. Regional planning--Decision making.
I. Title.
HT391.R56   361.6'1   80-14405
ISBN 0-444-86001-0

PRINTED IN THE NETHERLANDS

1-12-85

INTRODUCTION TO THE SERIES

Regional Science and Urban Economics are two interrelated fields of research which have developed very rapidly in the last three decades. The main theoretical foundation of these fields comes from economics but in recent years the interdisciplinary character has become more pronounced. The editors desire to have the interdisciplinary character of regional science as well as the development of spatial aspects of theoretical economics fully reflected in this book series. Material presented in this book series will fall in three different groups:

– interdisciplinary textbooks at the advanced level,
– monographs reflecting theoretical or applied work in spatial analysis,
– proceedings reflecting the advancement of the frontiers of regional science and urban economics.

In order to ensure homogeneity in this interdisciplinary field, books published in this series will:

– be theoretically oriented, i.e., analyse problems with a large degree of generality,
– employ formal methods from mathematics, econometrics, operations research and related fields, and
– focus on immediate or potential uses for regional and urban forecasting, planning and policy.

The Editors

CONTENTS

x   Contents

CHAPTER 1

INTRODUCTION

1.1 Multiplicity of Objectives

This study is based on the fundamental idea that deliberate
decision-making generally requires that the decision-maker
takes into consideration various points of view. Thus, when
evaluating the set of possible actions, the decision-maker
should try to do justice to a multiplicity of objectives or
options.

This starting point can be illustrated by means of numerous
examples such as:

a. A consumer buying a car will pay attention to a series of
    attributes of a car such as safety, capacity, size and
    price.

b. A family looking for a house will strive for a favourable
    combination of variables like distance to schools and one's
    working place, comfort of the dwelling, and presence of a
    pleasant environment.

c. An unemployed person seeking work will take into consider-
    ation many job characteristics such as salary, working
    place, career prospects, etc.

d. An employer trying to fill a vacancy will be in an analo-
    gous position when appraising the characteristics of the
    applicants.

e. A local community confronted with planning public invest-
    ments will take into account various aspects of these in-
    vestments including accessibility, costs, and social bene-
    fits.

f. Planning committees composed of different interest groups
    will have different priorities with respect to the elements
    of plans to be decided upon.

g. A national government judging alternative locations of a
    large industrial complex has not only to consider the pros
    and cons for the economic and environmental development of
    a certain candidate region, but also the spill-over effects
    upon other regions.

1

These examples vary substantially with regard to the quantity of information required, the scope of the decisions, or
the way in which the decision-makers usually take their decisions. They share, however, the characteristic that various
objectives are pursued and that these objectives are in conflict
with each other. It appears to be impossible to find an alternative in which all objectives are realized to a maximum extent.
A maximum result for one certain objective generally implies
poor performances for other objectives.

This conflict may arise due to intrapersonal and interpersonal reasons. The illustrations a, c and d are examples of intrapersonal conflict; the illustrations b, e, f and g are examples of mixed situations reflecting conflicts within family members or committee members as well as among them. Because of
these conflictual elements, the choice of a good alternative
may be a difficult task to accomplish. Consequently, there is
a basic need for methods to solve the conflicts among objectives
in order to reach acceptable compromises.

One should note that, although a multiplicity of objectives
is a general feature of decision problems, it is especially pertinent to western culture, which is characterized by a high
technical and economic development. Two examples may illustrate
this statement.

Consumer behaviour in a welfare state is mainly determined
by a high share of discretionary income, so that a level is attainable which is far above the subsistence level. People have
many resources for choosing freely consumptive activities; they
are very mobile and have much information about choice possibilities. Consequently, the set of feasible consumption patterns
is large and many needs have to be weighed against each other.

In the field of regional planning, the economic development
resulted in a highly interwoven system of social, economic, in-
frastructural and environmental components. The mutual depen-
dency of these components hampers an independent execution of
policies for these components separately, since this would yield
unintended impacts on other fields. Consequently, regional
planning aims at integrating these diverse policies. Clearly,
this entails the necessity of weighing the importance of the objectives formulated for these fields.

This first chapter will be devoted to a brief exposition of
multiobjective problems in regional planning. This chapter is
organized as follows. Sections 1.2 and 1.3 are devoted to a
general description of regional planning and of methods for
helping (regional) decision-makers confronted with various objectives respectively. Section 1.4 contains the formulation of
the central research questions of this study and the procedure
used to answer these questions. Section 1.5 presents a guide
to the reader, while in Section 1.6 some methodological aspects
of the research questions are clarified.

1.2   An Outline of Regional Planning

The term "region" in regional planning may be used in various ways. It refers to a spatial entity which is marked out according to classification principles such as homogeneity, functional intradependence or administrative purposes (cf. Paelinck and Nijkamp [1976]). The scale of a region may vary from a district to an entire country or even a group of countries.

The term "planning" refers to preparing and implementing decisions to achieve certain goals by appropriate means (cf. Chapter 2).

In consequence, regional planning is oriented to attaining goals formulated for a certain spatial entity. The precise goals formulated in regional planning will depend among others on political priorities and on the stage of development of a certain region. Generally speaking, goals will pertain to one of the following facets:

- economic (income, wealth, differentiation of economic structure);
- social (quantitative and qualitative aspects of the labour market);
- spatial (location patterns, occupation rates, transport networks);
- services (education, health, cultural services);
- environmental (ecological quality, pollution, noise, quantity of natural areas).

Regional planning aims at integrating the various facet policies. This means that attention has to be paid to:

1) conflicts between facet policies; for example, a policy aiming at environmental protection may have a negative impact on the economic performance of a region;

2) spill-over effects; the decision taken in one region may have (unintended) impacts on surrounding regions.

An important aspect of regional planning discussed in Chapter 2 is that many actors may be involved (national, regional and local authorities, private and public enterprises, families etc.). Since their preferences and decisions are often unknown during the plan preparation, they form a major source of uncertainty for the planners.

The instruments in regional planning are, in general, diverse. Examples are:

- the imposition of standards (norms for the emission of pollution, e.g.);
- the formulation of prescriptions concerning land use (zoning, e.g.);
- the provision of infrastructure (roads, schools, industrial

      estates, e.g.);

    - price instruments (investment subsidies, subsidies for pub-
      lic transport, charges on emission, e.g.);

    - locational decisions for governmental agencies (for exam-
      ple, the creation of employment in peripheral regions).

    This brief description of regional planning implies that
many types of problem situations fall within its scope. In
certain situations, planning is focused on an integrated approach of a <u>problem region</u>. Stilwell [1972] distinguishes
several types of problem regions: depressed, underdeveloped
and congested ones, each demanding a special type of policy.
In other situations, regional planning is concentrated on bottle-necks in certain facets. Examples are transportation
planning, regional economic planning, the planning of the urban
quality of life and of social structure.

    In the following section an outline of multiple objective
decision methods will be given. It will be shown that these
methods form a good framework for an integrated regional
planning.

1.3   An Outline of Multiple Objective Decision Models

    In the preceding sections we have exposed that there are
many decision problems in which persons and organizations face
several conflicting objectives. Fortunately, many people have
attained a certain skill in solving these decision problems,
depending on the scope and the frequency of occurrence of these
problems. Sometimes immediately, or sometimes after a period
of information collection and deliberation, they are able to
make a (sometimes intuitive) decision which is satisfactory to
them.

    There are, however, also decision problems which are more
difficult to solve intuitively. This may be due to the complexity of the problem at hand which may hamper obtaining immediate and adequate insight into the structure of the problem.
Another reason may be that the criteria used in the decision
are incommensurable, so that they can hardly be used simultaneously in the evaluation of alternatives. An example of both
reasons is the decision about the optimal location of a danger-
ous terminal of liquified, natural gas with a whole series of
positive economic impacts. In such cases, one certainly needs
information of experts, because the problem involves many technical elements. In addition, the criteria used are very diverse; regional economic effects, risk of a catastrophe, damage
to natural environment, and others.

    Given the above-mentioned reasons, several scientific meth-
ods have been developed to aid decision-makers facing complex
decision problems involving multiple conflicting objectives.
These methods have been called multiple objective decision
methods (abbreviated as MOD methods).

The first contributions to MOD methods date back to the early fifties, in a period when also management science and operations research started their development. Until the late sixties, however, the number of contributions remained small. Only since the beginning of the seventies has a large stream of studies been published on this subject (1). Nowadays, researchers from entirely different disciplines are working in this field, including economics, urban and physical planning, regional science, and business economics. Zeleny [1976a] presents a bibliography on MOD methods with no less than 450 contributions.

Despite a considerable diversity in these contributions, it is not difficult to present some general features which are shared by all methods:

1. A decision-maker (DM) faces a certain choice problem.

2. The DM is assisted by an analyst who has the task of providing scientific assistance.

3. The DM evaluates the alternatives by means of a certain set of objectives he wishes to achieve.

4. The analyst has at his disposal information about the instruments to realize the objectives as well as the impacts of the decision instruments on the objectives.

5. The objectives and instruments have been operationally defined. The objectives are at least ordinally measurable (2).

These characteristics are not different from those which are typical for single objective decision methods as dealt with in micro-economics and macro-economics. The only difference is that in single objective decision methods, the additional assumption has been made that the number of objectives is equal to one. In this case, the co-operation of DM and analyst can easily be structured, as illustrated in Figure 1.1. Once the DM has stated the objective aimed at, he can passively wait for the optimal choice to be determined by the analyst.

This pattern changes substantially when the DM aims at attaining several conflicting objectives. Then an unambiguous optimal solution cannot be provided by the analyst unless the DM has accurately stated his priorities concerning the objectives. Alternatively, when the DM is unable to list priorities, the analyst can generate a number of relevant alternatives from which the DM, after a certain deliberation phase, may select the desired one. These possibilities have been illustrated in Figure 1.2.

This figure indicates that in the case of multiple objectives, the DM's part in the activities of the decision process is substantial. The DM can choose in which phase of the process he will accomplish the main part of his activities; i.e. at the beginning or at the end. If he decides to do the first (for example, by specifying ex ante a utility function with the objectives as arguments), the deliberation phase at the end will be short, since the analyst can directly compute the optimal

Actor   Activity

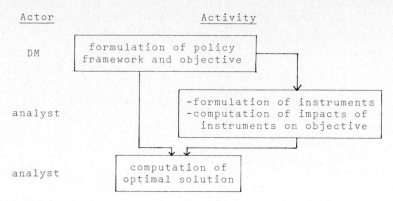

DM

analyst

analyst

Fig. 1.1.   Activities to solve a single objective decision
                          problem

alternative. Obviously, the disadvantage of this approach is
that it is very difficult to formulate one's priorities before
one knows the relevant alternatives. If the DM does not specify any priorities at the beginning of the process, he will
bear the full weight of the deliberation activities at the end
of the process, which may be very heavy since the number of
relevant alternatives generated is usually large.

Of course, the DM can also <u>partly</u> formulate his priorities
at the beginning of the process. This will reduce the range of
relevant alternatives to be produced by the analyst; and hence,
the deliberation phase at the end of the process will be easier.

Actor   Activity

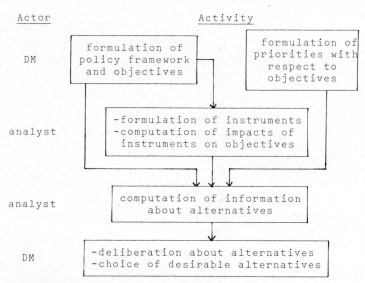

DM

analyst

analyst

DM

Fig. 1.2.   Activities to solve an MOD problem

Another more appropriate way to avoid the negative aspects
of the two extreme options is the introduction of a possible
feed-back for the DM into Figure 1.2. This would mean that the
DM is allowed to refine his provisional formulation of priorities on the basis of information about the alternatives computed by the analyst. After each revision, the analyst computes additional information about relevant alternatives. The
process only ends if the DM feels no further need to refine
his former statements of priorities (see Figure 1.3.).

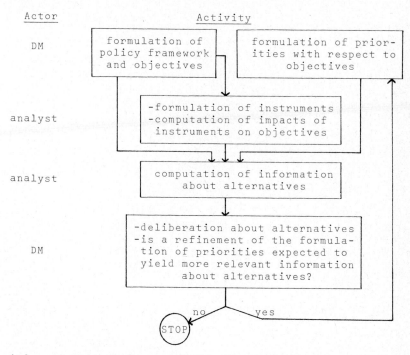

Actor   Activity

DM   formulation of   formulation of prior-
          policy framework   ities with respect to
          and objectives   objectives

analyst   -formulation of instruments
          -computation of impacts of
           instruments on objectives

analyst   computation of information
          about alternatives

DM   -deliberation about alternatives
          -is a refinement of the formula-
           tion of priorities expected to
           yield more relevant information
           about alternatives?

                              no   yes

                        STOP

Fig. 1.3.   A general framework for MOD-making.

This figure shows a communication scheme with a continuous
exchange of information between the analyst and the DM. Both
parties discount the information produced by the partner in a
subsequent statement of new information. The analyst produces
information about possibilities, the DM about desirabilities.
Convergence of the communication means that finally the possibilities and desirabilities have been led to an agreement.

The framework in Figure 1.3. was called "general" because it
includes the non-interactive MOD methods (Figure 1.2.) as well
as the single objective decision methods (Figure 1.1.) as special cases. Figure 1.3. does not indicate that all MOD methods
include all activities mentioned in it. Some methods only concentrate on a part of the activities.

It is easy to see that MOD methods may be valuable in

regional planning. Regional planning aims at integrating various facet policies (each with its own objectives) taking account of interregional interdependencies and conflicts. Consequently, the way in which preferences among objectives are
modelled is a crucial part of the planning process. The framework for MOD problems presented in Figure 1.3. is adequate for
this modelling since it explicitly recognizes the occurrence of
a multiplicity of objectives. Besides, it allows a large flexibility in dealing with priorities among objectives.

By means of this framework, it is also possible to pose a
number of questions on which research concerning MOD methods
can be concentrated:

1. In which forms can priorities be formulated?

2. Which types of information about alternatives are relevant
    to the DM?

3. How can this information be attained?

4. Which rules should the DM obey in refining priority formu-
    lations to achieve a convergent interaction?

In the following sections we will present the plan followed in
this book to study these questions.

1.4   Formulation of the Problem

In the preceding section, we saw that dropping the assumption
that only one objective will be regarded by the DM gives rise
to considerable changes in decision processes. The idea of only one choice possibility (the optimal one) is no longer relevant; more feasible alternatives must be considered. Besides,
the role of the DM has become far more active. It is he who
has to weigh the importance of the various objectives.

These changes are substantial, but one may wonder whether in
this way the critics on single objective decision methods can be
satisfied completely. The general nature of the criticism (cf.
Simon [1976]) is that this rational model of decision-making may
have interesting theoretical properties, but that it is incapa-
ble of serving DMs in most real world problems because of its
stringent assumptions. Examples of such criticisms are:

1. The objectives are only vaguely defined.

2. The set of instruments is only partially known.

3. The effects of decisions are stochastic in nature.

4. The number of decision-makers is larger than one.

As an illustration of such a real world problem one may use
the selection of a certain land reclamation project by a coun-
ty council. Objectives such as "beauty of the landscape" or
"ecological quality" are certainly relevant, but their meaning
will probably be rather obscure for the council members. The
effects of a certain choice cannot be evaluated with certainty.
For example, changes in prices in the future may influence the
costs and benefits of the projects and, hence, their relative

attractiveness. An unpredictable spring-tide in the next year
may supersede all calculations.

As will be shown later, it is certainly possible to adapt
the rational decision model to meet, to a certain extent, the
objections mentioned above. Yet these objections are important
enough to keep in mind when one is evaluating MOD methods,
since no definite conclusion has been drawn up to now about the
value of MOD methods for real world problems. The main reason
is that the number of real applications of MOD methods has been
limited so far (3). Consequently, the need for a critical
evaluation of MOD methods is obvious. Such an evaluation will
be one of the main points of this book.

The central questions which will guide the course of this book
are:

1. Which criteria must be met by MOD methods in order to en-
    sure a fruitful application to real decision problems?

2. What are the results of an evaluation of MOD methods by
    means of these criteria?

1.5   Organization of the book - A Guide to the Reader

The outline of the book implied by the foregoing research
questions is as follows:

1. Confrontation of the MOD framework with a number of dis-
    ciplines related to the subject of MOD methods (Chapters
    2-5). These disciplines are:

    - planning theory (studying the nature of decision prob-
      lems as well as decision-making in organizations);

    - psychology (studying problem-solving behaviour);

    - economics (studying choice behaviour and the modelling
      of preferences);

    - philosophy (studying the relationships between disci-
      plines and the multidimensional character of reality).

2. Survey and development of various types of MOD methods
    (Chapters 6-9).

3. Evaluation of MOD methods by means of relevant judgement
    criteria (Chapter 10).

4. Illustrative applications of the methods to regional plan-
    ning problems (Chapters 11-13).

In light of the scope of this book, it is obviously impossible to give a full account of the relationships between the MOD
framework and the disciplines mentioned above. Therefore, only
a selection of the most relevant points of contact will be presented.

The reader who is only interested in MOD methods as such and
not in the confrontation with other disciplines may omit
Chapters 2-5.

Chapters 6-9 give mainly an abstract presentation of the methods. Illustrative and empirical examples are scarce, but the
reader who experiences trouble in understanding these methods
can find numerical applications in Chapters 11-13.

The applications in Chapters 11-13 and most of the examples
used in the text have been derived from the field of regional
planning. The methods and criteria are however applicable to
any other field of policy-making.

For the reader already acquainted with the subject of MOD
methods, it may be helpful to know which parts of the book
contain new elements. It should be noted that the aim of this
study is not to provide a completely new and unambiguous method,
but rather to synthesize the existing body of knowledge in a
new way and to show its relevance for regional planning. As
such, this study does not aim at drastically shifting the frontiers of research in the field of MOD methods. It does, however, contain various new theoretical views, concepts and methods which may be fruitful for the further development of the
field of research.

The effort of finding relevant elements of other disciplines
with regard to MOD methods is not new. It has already been undertaken in a comprehensive way by Johnsen [1968]. The emphasis in Johnsen's study is different, however, since he looks
for arguments in favour of MOD methods, while in this book the
search is oriented to finding criteria for MOD methods in order
to judge their performance (4). The resulting evaluation of MOD
methods aims at being more systematic and comprehensive than
the evaluations presented up to now (Chapter 10).

In this study, new concepts have been defined in Sections
6.4 - 6.6 and 7.2 (compromise solutions, measures of conflict,
half-compromises and measures of information). These concepts
appear to be useful for the development of several methods.

New methods can be found in Section 6.7 ("determination of
a set of minimum levels associated to a certain facet") and in
Sections 9.7 - 9.9 (interactive methods for discrete problems
for the attainment of ranges and for multiple DMs). The methods suggested in Section 8.10, to reduce the number of objectives, are not new as such, but their application in the field
of MOD methods is certainly new.

1.6   Some Concluding Remarks

A closer look at the research questions reveals that they
do not bear any resemblance with the standard research question: "Is hypothesis A true?". This has far-reaching consequences. If a hypothesis is testable, the inferences drawn
from the investigation will, to a certain extent, be unambiguous. Of course, there always remains a possibility of a certain disagreement concerning the conclusiveness of tests of
hypotheses (for example, because of the stochastic nature of
the phenomena involved), but once a hypothesis has been formu-

lated in an adequate way, this disagreement will only have a
limited range.

Obviously, the above-mentioned research questions do not
have a sharp demarcation of testable statements, so that they
do not guarantee such a low measure of disagreement. The formulation of the desired characteristics of an object, method or
theory allows the researcher much more freedom to express personal opinions then the formal testing of a sharply defined
hypothesis.

This does not imply that the research questions fall outside
the realm of pure science. Similar research questions are
raised, for example, in methodology - "Which criteria should a
certain scientific method satisfy in order to yield acceptable
results?". These questions are inherent to any systematic attempt to develop new instruments and techniques or to judge
scientific efforts.

The second research question, viz. the judgement of MOD
methods, involves an interesting problem. This actually implies the problem of selecting an MOD method, taking into consideration several criteria. Obviously, this is an MOD problem
itself! Strictly speaking, this MOD problem cannot be solved
by means of any of the MOD methods to be evaluated, because
there is no firm base for the use of any specific method (unless all MOD methods are judged by means of all MOD methods simultaneously). Consequently, intuitive and pre-scientific reasoning will have to play a certain role in the evaluation.

The conclusion is that, although the research questions are
legitimate in the realm of science, they leave the researcher a
considerable amount of space to express his own opinions and
tastes. In this respect, a purely objective scientific analysis does not exist: personal convictions, historical factors
and political views play a role in any scientific analysis and
hence also in the present study.

Therefore, it may be important for the reader to understand
something of the background and opinions of the present author.
I graduated in Econometrics from Erasmus University in
Rotterdam. Following graduation, I worked for four years in
the field of regional science at the Free University in
Amsterdam, where I became interested in MOD methods. In my
view, up to now the policy aspects of MOD methods have received
too little attention compared to the mathematical aspects.
This study therefore aims at bridging this existing gap with a
particular emphasis on regional planning, although I am aware
that the attainment of a balanced equilibrium between formal
and policy aspects for MOD methods is very difficult to realize.

MOD methods have become for me an attractive object of research for at least three different reasons.

1.   In a theoretical sense, MOD methods are interesting since
      they aim at bridging the gap between normative (rational)

and descriptive (behavioural) theories of decision-making.

2.   MOD methods imply a view of a free, active and responsible
     decison-maker, which is a refreshing alternative to many
     traditional deterministic economic approaches (see
     Chapter 5).

3.   MOD methods contain a valuable approach to improve the
     generally weak communication processes between research
     and policy-making.

   I do hope that this book will enlarge the interest for MOD
ideas in the theory and practice of decision-making.

Footnotes

1.   See Keen [1977] and Starr and Zeleny [1977] for a more
     detailed discussion of the development of MOD methods.

2.   See for a definition of ordinal measurability Section 4.3.

3.   MOD methods can be divided into five classes with respect
     to the measure in which they have been applied to real
     world problems.
     1. Methods which have only been dealt with in abstract
        symbols in order to prove general properties such as
        consistency.
     2. Methods which have been applied to an imaginary deci-
        sion problem.
     3. Methods which have been applied to a real decision
        problem but without the participation of DMs.
     4. Methods which have been applied to a real decision
        problem with a participating DM but not in a real de-
        cision-making context.
     5. Methods applied to real decision problems with a par-
        ticipating DM and in a real decision-making context.
     The difference between the fourth and fifth case is that
     in the former case, the DM may conceive of the MOD meth-
     od as a play which may yield interesting information, but
     which does not produce binding results. In the latter
     case, this little engaged attitude is ruled out.
     Up to now, only a small part of MOD methods belongs to
     class 5, which implies that only a few methods have real-
     ly been tested with respect to their applicability to real
     world problems.

4.   This difference in emphasis clearly reflects the differ-
     ence in the state of MOD methods. In 1968 they were only
     in the first stages of development, and research in this
     field still needed legitimation. At present, the methods
     have been elaborated in many directions. Reflection is
     necessary now in order to judge whether we created what we
     needed.

PART A

MULTIPLE OBJECTIVE DECISION-MAKING IN
A MULTIDISCIPLINARY CONTEXT

Chapters 2-5 of this study will be devoted to a concise survey of the most important parts of several relevant disciplines for MOD methods: planning theory; psychology; economics and philosophy.

The kind of contributions of these successive disciplines varies substantially. In our view, two pairs of categories can be distinguished, viz. descriptive versus normative contributions and analytical versus structural contributions. The first pair of categories concerns the presence or absence of an evaluative directedness:
- <u>Descriptive</u> contributions try to answer questions like: "how does decision-making take place?".
- <u>Normative</u> contributions deal with such questions as: "in which way should decision-making take place in order to attain certain ends?".
The other pair of categories can be used to indicate the scope of a contribution:
- <u>Analytical</u> contributions aim at formalizing certain aspects of decision-making such as the specification of preferences.
- <u>Structural</u> contributions aim at providing a framework for decision-making by indicating the overall structure of decisions. This can be done by mentioning the elements involved in decision processes and the relationships between these elements.

How can the contributions of the various disciplines be characterized on the basis of these categories? An unambiguous classification is difficult to achieve, since research in these disciplines is heterogeneous and, furthermore, in certain cases, research in different disciplines overlaps. Given this fact, we will not try to characterize the contributions of the various disciplines in general, but only the <u>main</u> emphasis of the contributions as they will be presented in this study (see Table A.1).

As set out in Section 1.5, the focus of the forthcoming chapters will be on deriving criteria or desiderata with regard to the contents and the use of MOD methods.
- <u>Descriptive</u> contributions may be useful to derive such desiderata, since these contributions may yield insight into the bottle-necks that the participants experience in deci-

	type of contribution			
	I		II	
	descriptive	normative	analytical	structural
planning theory	x	x		x
psychology	x		x	x
economics		x	x	
philosophy		x		x

Table A.1.   Types of contributions of various disciplines to
MOD methods

sion processes; avoiding these bottle-necks may then be a
meaningful desideratum in the use of MOD methods. For example, for many DMs their limited information processing capacity is a bottle-neck in complex decision problems. This
result gives rise to the desideratum to avoid an excessive
claim upon this capacity.
- Normative contributions yield desiderata by definition.
- Analytical contributions give rise among other things to desiderata to avoid ambiguous, unnecessarily specific or inconsistent statements.
- Structural contributions yield desiderata with regard to the
  scope and the framework of MOD problems.
Chapters 2-5 each conclude with the formulation of several desiderata which provide the judgement framework for MOD methods
in Chapter 10, where an evaluation of MOD methods will be performed.

Obviously, it is impossible to derive desiderata with respect to MOD methods without some guiding principles concerning
decision-making. For the author the following considerations
have been crucial in Chapters 2-5. People with all their analytical and decision-making skills have the responsibility to
their Creator of contributing to a harmonious development of the
world. Given the present state of decision-making in many
fields (regional planning being one of these fields), at least
two bottle-necks in decision-making processes can be mentioned
which hinder such a harmonious development. These bottle-necks
pertain to: a) the role of science in decision making and b)
the range of the effects of decisions which are taken into account. They can be expounded as follows (cf. also Section 5.4).
- For decisions concerning complex problems, in general scientific knowledge is indispensable. Therefore the aim should
  be to reach a balanced contribution of analytical and evaluative skills in decision processes. In many situations,
  however, such a balance does not occur. On the one extreme,
  scientific reasoning may dominate the course of decision
  processes, for example when decisions are simply taken on
  the basis of experts' judgements without critical reconsid-

eration of the value of such scientific contributions. In this technocratic manner of decision-making, scientists especially determine the decision to be made. The information they provide is not sufficiently linked up with the knowledge and skills of other people involved in the decision process (for example through public participation). The other extreme is that purely political considerations dominate the outcome of the decision process in such a way that scientific contributions to the problem are entirely ignored. A harmonious development of the world means that an absolutization of certain facets must be avoided. For example, when in regional planning only the economic facet is of importance, other facets (for example the environmental facets) may suffer. Therefore, the range of the effects taken into account should be as broad as possible - given the decision framework - and the conflicts between various policy objectives should be carefully studied. Another way to avoid one-sided decisions is to make a final decision only after deliberating on various representative alternatives.

CHAPTER 2

PLANNING THEORY AND MULTIPLE OBJECTIVE DECISION-MAKING

2.1   Introduction

Deliberate decision-making involves the explicit consideration of instruments and objectives as described in Section
1.3. It appears that the concept of planning is closely related to this deliberate decision-making. For example, Dror
[1963] defines planning as follows: "Planning is the process
of preparing a set of decisions for action in the future, directed at achieving goals by preferable means " (p. 51). Of
course, other definitions are possible. Dror himself quotes
more than ten of them, but they do not differ substantially.

Planning may be performed by individuals as well as by organizations. One should realize that until the Industrial
Revolution, relatively few larger organizations existed: the
army, the Roman Catholic Church, and some trading companies are
examples of these. Therefore, it is not surprising that only
in the twentieth century organizational planning received
scientific attention.

Planning has been directed to many different subjects. One
of the earliest examples was economic planning such as the well-
known Five Year Plans in the U.S.S.R.   Afterwards other fields
were covered by planning, which gave rise to e.g. physical planning, town planning and regional planning.

During the first decades of planning, planners felt little
need for theoretical reflection on their activities. One was
generally convinced that planning was important to solve problems. In the course of time, however, planning itself became
a problem. In many cases planning appeared to be unsuccessful,
and this gave rise to research which indicated that planning
must be structured in order to be successful. It became more
widely accepted that every subject of planning does not need another specific kind of theory. Therefore, much work has been devoted to the development of conceptual frameworks as a way of
studying planning phenomena in general. No generally accepted
theory of planning has been developed so far, however.

At present, theorists disagree on a number of important questions. For example, Galloway and Mahayni [1977] suggest that
the present confusion about planning theory is due to a paradigm change. The old ideal of planning was the construction of

detailed blueprints for the future. The impossibility to im-
plement the blueprints led to another orientation of planning.
Galloway and Mahayni [1977] point at the following responses:

1. Planning is conceptualized as a process;

2. Planning is conceptualized as an activity, independent of
    the subject matter;

3. Conceptual schemes are developed for planning.

    Other contributions to planning theory stress that planning
is rational decision-making. Hence, such views primarily describe planning problems by means of concepts derived from the
field of economics (cf. Davidoff and Reiner [1962] and Faludi
[1973])(1). Goals and means are the central concepts being
used here. On the other hand, others pose that uncertainty is
such an essential element of planning situations that it is
useless to require a rational planning process (Gillingwater
[1975]).

    Such a controversy clearly indicates that planning theory
has many normative aspects. It does not only deal with the
description of planning activities as they actually are performed, but also with the prescription of the way in which
planning has to be performed (cf. Kornai [1970] and Boyce
[1975]).

    The confrontation of MOD models with planning theory will
be performed on the basis of four viewpoints:

1. Relationships between analyst and DM;

2. Input of the planning process: problem formulation;

3. Throughput of the planning process: modes of planning;

4. Output of the planning process: implementation.

2.2   Partners in the Decision Process

    Planning theory considers planning as a process with at
least four phases (Faludi [1973]):

1. The recognition of a problem;

2. The generation of alternatives to meet the problem;

3. The choice of an alternative;

4. The implementation of the alternative chosen.

Various actors may be involved in this process. A very common
distinction is that between planner and politician. The politician is the person who is formally held responsible for the
choice of a certain alternative as well as its implementation.
The planner has the task of providing scientific assistance to
the politician during all phases of the planning process (cf.
Friend and Jessop [1969]).

    This description leaves open a great number of possible la-
bour divisions between planner and politician. One extreme is
that the politician performs no real part in any of the four

phases. He is only formally responsible for the outcome of the
planning process. An example may be the government official
who does not have time to be involved in the many day-to-day
routine decisions made in this department. The other extreme
is the politician who makes decisions without anyone's assistance. For example, this may be the case when the council of
a small town designs the location pattern of schools without
any professional help.

Less extreme variants imply a shared commitment in some of
the four phases. The politician may be engaged in problem recognition and selecting alternatives, while the planners take
charge of the remaining activities. Of course, they may also
be simultaneously engaged in some activity. This means that
81 (3^4) types of labour divisions may exist in planning processes. Some examples have been presented in Table 2.1.

activity	involvement of actors						
	1	2	3	4	5	6	7
recognition of problems	P	P,PL	P,PL	P	P	PL	PL
generation of alternatives	P	P,PL	PL	PL	PL	PL	PL
choice of an alternative	P	P	P	P	PL	P.	PL
imple- mentation	P	PL	PL	PL	PL	PL	PL

Table 2.1.   Some types of labour division between planner
             (PL) and politician (P).

Table 2.1. implies that in general there are no special activities in decision processes which are the exclusive concern
of either the politician or the planner. Basically the difference between them is not related to the activities they perform,
but to the responsibilities they bear. The politician carries
the formal authority for the selection and the implementation.
Hence, he is held responsible for mistakes or one-sidedness.
He is the "decision-taker" who must defend his work and that of
his co-operators in political forums (Friend et al. [1974]).
These co-operators have been called planners. The term "planner" is thus a collective term for the actor involved in one or
more of the various elements of planning - from preparation to
execution.

It is interesting to confront the conceptual pair (i.e. pol-
itician-planner) with the pair introduced earlier (i.e. DM-ana-
lyst). Are these pairs based on the same distinction, or are
other elements involved? A closer look teaches that these
pairs are to a certain extent related, but it is certainly not
possible to place identity signs between them.

The first difference is that the actors in MOD-making are
only concerned with the second and third phases of the planning
process. The phases of problem formulation as well as implementation remain outside the range of vision. This means that
the second pair of concepts has been used in a narrower context than the first pair.

We can also see that other divisions of tasks between analyst and DM different from those discussed in Section 1.3. are
not possible. For example, it is unthinkable that a DM would
calculate the impact of instruments, whereas an analyst would
deliberate about choice possibilities. This means that the
terms DM and analyst do not indicate actors in decision processes, but rather <u>roles</u> of actors.

How can these roles be described? It may be illuminating to
place them in the context of Friedman's [1953] distinction between normative and positive statements and Tinbergen's [1956]
distinction between analytical aspects of decision problems and
preferential aspects. The role of the analyst is to study the
relationship between means and ends and to provide information
about it. The DM is concerned with the specification of preferences among ends.

These two differences teach us two lessons:

1. MOD methods deal only with a part of the planning process.

2. Planners and politicians can be conceived of as different
    actors in planning processes. DMs and analysts can be con-
    ceived as roles of actors (see Table 2.2.).

actors / roles	planner	politician
DM	A	B
analyst	C	D

Table 2.2.   Combinations of actors and roles of actors
                      in planning.

The above table shows that both the planner and the politician
may function in the process as decision-maker or analyst. Examples can be presented by means of the seven illustrative labour divisions presented in Table 2.1. Examples of cases A, B,
C and D can be found in the variants 5, 3, 6 and 1 of Table
2.1., respectively.

This interchangeability does not alter the fact that politicians will generally be inclined to perform decision-making activities, while leaving the analytical tasks to the planners.
The formal responsibility of the politician for the outcome of
the planning process makes it desirable that he is

engaged in the normative stages. In this way, the probability
is higher that an alternative can be chosen which is defendable.
However, many circumstances may hinder this "ideal" division of
labour. For example, lack of time, understanding, and/or interest on the politician's side may give rise to a situation
where planners put their stamp upon the outcomes. On the other
hand, planners, unable to provide relevant information, may
cause the politicians to decide on only intuitive grounds.

What is the advantage of the distinction between the two
conceptual pairs? The advantage is that the decision-making
scheme developed so far can be maintained irrespective of the
special division of labour prevailing in a certain situation.
There is no need to adjust it when a planner accidentally assumes a task formerly performed by a politician. One should
realize, however, that this distinction does not solve the
real issue; i.e. how can persons performing analytical and decision-making tasks co-operate in order to reach satisfactory
solutions of problems?

Friedmann and Abonyi [1976] discuss decision problems when
objectives are ambiguous or in conflict, or where the impacts
are highly uncertain.They present different institutional frameworks for co-operation between planner and politician. We will
present here two typical representatives; a market model and a
bureaucratic model.

1. The market model assumes the existence of a market of in-
    formation. Research units are able to provide it, and pol-
    iticians demand it. For a certain price, the politician
    tries to contact a research unit to provide the information
    necessary to solve a problem. Of course, the planning unit
    is free to reject the order.

2. The bureaucratic model arises when the research unit is an
    element of a bureaucracy formally controlled by the politi-
    cian. In this case, the unit is continuously connected to
    the politician. It can neither reject nor accept orders at
    one's own discretion.

According to Friedmann and Abonyi, both models must tackle
a very basic problem, since in their opinion the politician's
view of the world differs essentially from the researcher's
view. The politician's world "is characterized by tight decision deadlines, short time horizons, complex political pres-
sures, critical pay-offs, and the hierarchical constraints of
bureaucratic management. The policy maker's criterion for accepting or rejecting new information is an essentially pragmat-
ic one: will it lead to a workable solution?" (p. 6). On the
other hand, the researcher's world is characterized by attempts
to answer very narrowly defined questions. The criteria for
accepting or rejecting answers in this case circles around concepts such as statistical adequacy and logical consistency.

This divergence of worlds means a very wide communication
barrier. In the market model it may give rise to the provision
of answers the politicians consider to be unusable. The bureau-

cratic model entails another difficulty. Here it is quite possible that the planners are able to communicate with the politicians, but they may have lost their scientific standards,
which may lead in the long run to ineffective policies.

   The conclusion drawn from this section is clear - a communication gap is probable between a politician and planner. This
gap may make its presence felt in all phases of the planning
process. It may also hinder, therefore, a fruitful accomplish-
ment of the activities included in the MOD model. It may be
expected that the fewer people involved in the planning, the
less the communication difficulties. An extreme case is variant 1 in Table 2.1. where only one person acts. This means a
minimal chance of misunderstanding between analyst and DM.
When analytical and decision-making activities are performed by
different persons, however, many difficulties may arise. Variant 2 is a good example of this.

   One should be aware that in many situations neither the
planner nor the politician are single persons. Many policy
problems are so complex that they can only be tackled by units
consisting of various persons. Besides, various units may be
involved in the course of planning. For example, administrative units are not always the units which have to prepare decisions. Even at the level of the same planning phase, different units may operate. Faludi [1973] discusses this by citing
the advantages of the creation of multi-planning agencies for
the phase of generating alternatives. This allows a far
greater measure of specialization than normally is the case.

   The same type of examples may be given for the politician.
The politician will often be a set of persons, e.g. a committee
or council. Besides, many decisions imply a shared responsibility between a number of councils. Therefore, often a number
of bodies at various levels (i.e. national, regional and local)
must be given room to influence the outcome of the planning
process (cf. Friend et al. [1974]).

   Hence, complex problems may entail that the planning process
is characterized by a considerable number of planning agencies
and political bodies. Within and between these units, huge
communication streams have to be created to ensure satisfactory
planning results. Gillingwater [1977] stresses the importance
of communication by suggesting that one of the possible views
one may have on planning is that planning equals communication.

   With respect to the central research questions of our study,
the following results can be inferred.
1. In order to make MOD methods applicable they must be placed
    in the broader context of planning processes.
2. MOD methods should regard the possibility that various de-
    cision-making bodies are involved in the decision.
3. Potential communication problems between various agencies
    should be recognized and handled adequately.

2.3   Problem Recognition

Planning processes are cyclical in nature. They entail a
continuous leaping over from one phase to another. Therefore,
it is actually impossible to indicate a starting point in planning. For ease of presentation, however, it is certainly possible to use as a starting point the phase of problem recognition.

Faludi [1973] defines a problem as "a state of tension between the ends pursued by a subject and his image of the environment" (p. 82). This definition implies a close relationship
between the concept of objectives and planning. Planning may
start when a subject recognizes a certain present or future
situation as unsatisfactory in light of some objectives he
wishes to pursue.

This definition of a problem implies that basically two different causes can be mentioned for the emergence of problems.
Problems may occur because (a) subjects have changed their
minds about satisfactory outcomes for objectives or (b) the
subject's images of the environment have changed.

When a certain problem arises, it is in its first recognition phase normally ill-defined. The subject who perceives it
does not have a clear picture of all the elements involved. He
has only vague ideas about objectives, instruments, impacts and
priorities. Friend and Jessop [1969] distinguish three basic
uncertainties which play a part in the perception of problems:

a. Uncertainties concerning the operative environment (this
    category includes the uncertainties about the potential
    instruments as well as their impact on objectives and un-
    certain developments of exogenous variables (2));

b. Uncertainties concerning related choices (an example of
    this category is the lack of knowledge experienced by a
    subject about decisions which other subjects must make and
    which will influence the pertaining problem);

c. Uncertainties of policy (this class embraces the vagueness
    attached to the objectives to be pursued as well as the
    priorities to be given to them).

These uncertainties are fundamental for many problems. It is
therefore necessary to confront them with the MOD scheme developed in Section 1.3. The important question is whether the
scheme does justice to these uncertainties. It is clear that
it has been devised to capture problems around the third category. Has it been a successful attempt and is it also possible
to deal with the other two problems?

Another important characteristic of problems is that they
may be dynamic (Gillingwater [1975]), i.e. they may change during the phases of preparation and implementation of plans.
These changes are closely related to the various types of uncertainty in problems - new information about exogenous variables may be obtained, other political bodies may take crucial

decisions and/or new objectives may be recognized as important.

   Furthermore, Rittel and Webber [1973] call planning problems
"wicked". They sum up ten reasons why this is so:

1. No definitive formulation can be found for them;

2. They have no stopping rule;

3. Solutions to these problems are not true-or-false, but good-
    or-bad;

4. There is no immediate and no ultimate test of a solution to
    such a problem;

5. Every solution is a "one-shot operation", because there is
    no opportunity to learn by trial and error - every attempt
    counts significantly;

6. These problems do not have an innumerable (or an exhaus-
    tively describable) set of potential solutions, nor is
    there a well-described set of permissible operations that
    may be incorporated into the plan;

7. Every wicked problem is essentially unique;

8. Every wicked problem can be considered to be a symptom of
    another problem;

9. The existence of a wicked problem can be explained in nu-
    merous ways - the choice of explanation determines the na-
    ture of the problem's resolution;

10. The planner has no right to be wrong.

   Rittle and Webber's conclusion is: "...the formulation of a
wicked problem is the problem" (p. 161). They state that it is
more difficult to arrive at a satisfactory formulation of a
problem than to find an optimal solution for this formulated
problem (3).

   We may learn from this that as to MOD models, attention
should also be paid to the phases of the procedures themselves
as well as to the preceding phases of formulation of the con-
stitutive variables.

   Returning to Faludi's definition of a problem, one may wonder who the subject is that recognizes a certain situation as a
problem. Is it the planner or the politician? At first, one
would say that it is the politician, since he is responsible
for the way in which problems are solved (or not solved).
Faludi [1973] argues, however, that this view on the politician
is unrealistic. There are a number of reasons why politicians
are not so intensely involved in decisive phases of the planning process. Therefore, the role division of the politician
as the master and the planner as the servant will not do. There
will be many cases where the planners play a very important
role in the formulation of decision problems. Also in the preceding phase, i.e. the problem recognition, they may be active.

   This modesty on the politician's side can be attributed to
three factors:

1.   Politicians are not hyperactive; they have restricted time
     and energy;

2.   Politicians are not trained to formulate objectives; there
     is a tendency to formulate objectives only once a choice
     has been made;

3.   The master-servant type of bureaucracy is only adequate for
     the solution of routine problems; when new types of prob-
     lems arise, planners themselves have to structure them in
     order to solve them.

   This active participation of planners in the problem formulation may give rise to communication problems as previously
mentioned.   An example may be the question of whether certain
problems are related or not.

| | | politician considers two problems to be: | |
		related	independent
planner considers two problems to be:	related	A	B
	independent	C	D

Table 2.3.   Perception of relatedness of problems.

Table 2.3. presents four possible combinations of opinions on
the relatedness of problems.   Cases A and D present no difficulties because here planner and politician agree.   Disagreement may arise in the other cases.   Case C refers to a situation where two problems are in a technical sense independent.
For the politician, they are related in the case when the same
pressure group is involved in both problems, for example, when
environmental protectionists raise objections to two independent land reclamation projects.   Case B describes the reverse.
Here the politician does not see a relation between the problems, whereas the planner is of the opinion that the decision
taken for one problem will influence the other, for example,
when the policies for congested regions will have impacts on
depressed regions and vice versa.

2.4   Modes of Planning

   Planning has been applied in a great number of fields and under various circumstances.   It is not astonishing, therefore,
that various types of planning have evolved.   Faludi [1973]
distinguishes three pairs of ideal types of planning:

1.   Blueprint versus process mode;

2.   Rational comprehensive versus disjointed incrementalist
     mode;

3.   Normative versus functional mode.

We will first try to supply these terms with a meaning.

(1) Planners come from various disciplines, including geography,

economics, and sociology. In certain fields, engineers have
been active also. For example, the designs of buildings, dams,
or water resource systems have been their task. From these
types of problems a certain type of planning came into existence, which has become known as the blueprint type. The important characteristic of this planning mode is that a plan is
produced which is, with certainty, considered to be practicable
(Faludi [1973]).

Indeed, the pertaining types of problems are characterized
by low degrees of the various kinds of uncertainty. Take, for
example, the dam. There are little relevant exogenous variables of which future developments are uncertain. At best, one
might think of calamities like earthquakes. There are also few
uncertainties concerning other persons whose activities might influence the pertaining problem. Finally, the objective(s) are
generally clear. In this case, given the dam's capacity and
some safety requirements, one may try to minimize its construction costs.

These circumstances allow a straightforward performance of
the planning process; the phases follow each other properly.
Preparation, decision and execution are carried out consecu-
tively. At a certain point in time, a decision is taken about
a plan which contains all information for the implementation
phase. Because of the low probability of unforeseen events,
there is generally no need to revise the plans during the implementation. This mode of planning has also been applied to
non-engineering types of problems, such as town and country
planning. An example is the Second Memorandum on Physical
Planning in the Netherlands [1966] which designed a blueprint-
like settlement pattern for the year 2000. This type of attempt has however often been unsuccessful, leading to the proposal of another ideal planning type - process planning.

Process planning tries to recognize the uncertainties mentioned above as much as possible. Because of these uncertainties, it is impossible to get through the planning phases
straightforwardly. In many cases, it appears to be unwise to
take decisions concerning uncertain problems at only one point
in time. Instead, it is sensible to spread the decision-making
over a period of time.

As to the first type of uncertainty, it is thus possible to
make corrections when certain decisions do not have the intended impact. There is also more room to tackle changes in exogenous variables. Besides, the dynamic character of problems
can be better dealt with.

The second aspect of uncertainty can be dealt with more sim-
plicitly because in process planning, the question of when decisions are made is important. It is possible, for example, to
study the postponement of decisions until other actors have
made decisions concerning related problems.

This way of planning, finally, also regards uncertainty

about priorities. It is possible, for example, to take into
account future changes in priorities. By process planning, no
plans need to be implemented which are clearly conflicting with
present priorities. It allows a certain measure of flexibility
to change directions during the implementation phase when in-
sights have altered.

Which of the two modes of planning should be preferred? The
answer depends upon the type of problem to be solved. It is of
little use to apply process planning to a well-defined and con-
trolled decision problem. Likewise, the application of blueprint planning to highly uncertain problems is of restricted
value.

Another important question is with which of the two planning
modes are the MOD methods best matching? Clearly, MOD methods
can easily be integrated into blueprint planning procedures.
They may have the potential to be applied in process planning
as well.

(2) The second pair of modes is the rational comprehensive type
versus the disjointed incremental one. The characteristic used
to distinguish the modes is the scope of the plans produced.

In rational comprehensive planning, in principle, all feasible alternatives are judged against all formulated objectives.
It is "rational" in the sense that alternatives are evaluated
by means of objectives.

Lindblom [1965] criticizes the ideal of rational comprehen-
sivity in a sharp way. In his opinion, it is not adapted to:

1. Man's limited intellectual capacities;

2. Inadequacy of information;

3. Costliness of analysis;

4. Difficulties experienced when one tries to construct a set
    of objectives;

5. The closeness of observed relationship between fact and
    value in policy-making;

6. The openness of systems of variables with which it must
    contend;

7. The diverse forms in which policy problems actually arise.

These objections are indeed radical. Lindblom, therefore, proposes to drop the ideals of rationality and comprehensiveness.
In his opinion, the desirable alternative is "disjointed incrementalism". Faludi [1973] describes it as a mode of planning
"where the programmes considered by any one planning agency are
limited to a few which deliberately do not exhaust the available action space, and where that action space is itself ill-
defined" (p. 155). It is termed "incremental" because planning
decisions are judged only by means of the marginal changes they
are supposed to produce with respect to the status quo. The
term "disjointed" stems from Lindblom's view on the number of
planning agencies involved in planning. Planning decisions are

made at a large number of small power centres. Each centre has
only a small amount of control over the problems. The result
of all the actions is certainly not coherent, but instead, the
actions are disjointed.

Again, we may wonder which of the two modes should be preferred. It should be clear that disjointed incrementalism prevails in the solution of many day-to-day problems. In many
cases, that may be satisfactory, but there are still important
exceptions. For the solution of more fundamental problems and
when agencies have obtained strong competence, the ideal of rational comprehensiveness looks more attractive. Faludi [1973]
argues that a number of Lindblom's objections can be shown to
be wrong. Gillingwater [1975] does not agree with Faludi, however. He maintains that disjointed incrementalism is a better
way to deal with some essential features of approaches to problem-solving. In his opinion it recognizes the dynamic uncertain character of problems better than the rational comprehensive mode. Besides, it is more process-oriented than the comprehensive mode.

When we compare MOD methods with the modes being discussed
here, it is clear that they are adequate for a rational comprehensive attack on problems. Both deal with a systematic investigation of feasible actions and their consequences, and both
entail an explicit distinction between instruments and objectives. These elements can certainly not be integrated in a
disjointed incremental planning mode.

(3) The third pair of ideal types is the normative-functional
one. In this case, the distinguishing feature is the extent to
which planners are active in the formulation of objectives.
Faludi [1973] indicates that functional planning is a mode
where planners only study how certain desired levels of objectives (being fixed by politicians) can be attained by an adequate combination of instruments. In normative planning, however, the objectives are not fully prescribed to the planner.
He has, to a certain extent, the possibility of including his
own or other people's views into the analysis.

The functional form of planning is closely related to Weber's
concept of bureaucracy. The planner's role is that of a bureaucrat (Beckman [1964]). He has been appointed in order to
plan and to execute according to the directions given by the
politician. The way of organization is completely hierarchical;
the politician is at the top - he controls all processes in the
bureaucracy.

The opposite extreme is the normative form of planning.
Here, the place of the planner in the organization is characterized by a considerable degree of autonomy. He has the possibility to stress aspects commonly not recognized by politicians. By doing so, he becomes involved in political spheres.
Thus, the planner's role may become that of an advocate of minority groups and/or their views (Davidoff [1965]). As to
Davidoff, this is the way to introduce the pluralism of society

into planning processes.

Which of the two forms should be preferred? Faludi [1973] argues that the modes are complementary rather than substitutive. In his opinion, planning should give room to creative inventions. These are more probable to arise in normative than functional planning contexts, because in the latter, the problems are too predefined.

Planning problems are generally so complicated, however, that it would be impossible to study them as a whole. Various departments of a planning agency may specialize in certain facets. It is even possible that various planning agencies become involved in the planning process. In such a case, a normative mode of planning for each of the planning agencies would result in an unco-ordinated list of programmes. The necessary co-ordination can be achieved when a strategic planning agency is established.

Strategic planning agencies may play a central role in a fruitful combination of normative and functional planning modes. Over against the responsible political body, a strategic planning agency has a considerable amount of autonomy, enabling it to adopt a normative planning mode. Over against a subordinate planning agency, it has a considerable amount of authority, so that the subordinate planning agency has to adopt functional planning modes. As to Faludi [1973], this design of planning activities may resolve the conflict between creativity and co-ordination.

To which mode of planning are MOD methods most related, the normative or the functional one? The answer is obvious - multiple objective decision methods are closely related to normative planning styles. An important common element is that a number of desired outcomes of objectives is not specified before the beginning of the planning process. On the contrary, MOD methods try to present the whole spectrum of alternatives. They indicate how stressing certain objectives will entail disappointing values for other objectives.

The following table summarizes the results of the confrontation of the three pairs of planning modes with the idea of MOD making.

Mode of planning	Are MOD methods useful?
Blueprint	yes
Process	maybe
Rational comprehensive	yes
Disjointed incrementalism	no
Normative	yes
Functional	no

Table 2.4.   Usefulness of MOD methods for various types
of planning

2.5   Implementation

The main attention in planning theory has been devoted to
the preparation of plans rather than the implementation or ex
post evaluation. There is one planning mode, however, for
which this does not hold true: process planning. In process
planning the results of implementation in phase n have effects
on the preparations for subsequent phases. Consequently, feedback is possible when more information has been attained about
the sources of uncertainty, mentioned in Section 2.3. An important element of process planning is flexibility in plan
formulations. The more options one reserves for the future
phases, the greater the opportunity to adapt to unexpected developments.

The theoretical and practical interest in ex post evaluations is small in regional planning (cf. Van Lohuizen [1979]).
The reason may be that neither the planner nor the politician
wants to be reminded of his possible failures in the past. As
indicated in Section 3.3, people have the tendency to experience every decision problem as essentially unique. Consequently, the gains of ex post evaluations (learning-by-doing)
are in danger of being underestimated.

2.6   MOD Methods in a Planning Theoretical Framework

The crucial question dealt with in this study is what may
be the value of MOD methods for real decision problems. One of
the conclusions reached thus far was that the scheme described
in Figure 1.3. is not complete enough to provide a framework
for an answer. It should be extended in order to give room to
the problem-solving character of decision-making. Such an extension can be found in Figure 2.1. It explicitly mentions
three new phases in the decision-making process; (a) problem
recognition and formulation, (b) choice of an adequate planning
procedure, and (c) implementation.

The recognition and formulation (in intuitive terms) of
problems is clearly an activity fitting to a decision-making
role. Here a field is indicated on which the entailing activities should be directed. As mentioned above, the first formulation of a problem is necessarily vague. The subsequent phase
is, therefore, equally fraught with uncertainties.

In this phase of procedural choice, the various ways to
tackle the problem must be evaluated. It is interesting to
note that this implies a multiple objective problem itself,
because procedures can be judged by means of multiple characteristics such as speed, costs, simplicity, and/or comprehensiveness. Indeed, we find here the two activities which are
also present in the final decision-making phases (activities
6 and 7). The analyst presents information about alternative
procedures and the DM makes a choice. This choice involves
among others the planning mode, the distribution of tasks, the
consultation of other decision-makers, and the time scheme.
Of course, not all these choices need to be done consciously.

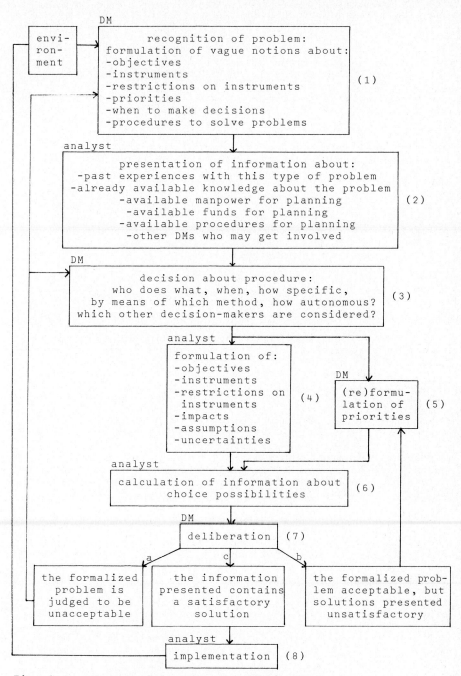

Fig. 2.1. An extended scheme for MOD-making

Especially in generic problems such choices may be routine affairs. One of the choices is also whether or not to adopt MOD
methods.

What may be the reasons when DMs sometimes seem to be reluc-
tant to adopt such methods? Two different reasons may be mentioned. The first one arises at the analyst's side. He may
simply omit them when presenting the various alternatives. He
may do so because (a) he is not acquainted with these methods;
(b) he is well up in the subject matter but he himself prefers
other methods (such as cost-benefit analysis); and/or (c) he
may also expect in advance that the DM will consider them to be
unsatisfactory, although he himself is convinced of their qual-
ities. The second source of disuse may be the DM's point of
view. He may be content with other approaches so that he does
not feel the need to try something new. Another reason may be
that he has had disappointing experiences with them. One
should also not forget the tendency on the DM's side to distrust
scientific contributions to decision-making problems (cf. Vink
[1977]). In any case, rightly or wrongly the conclusion is
that there may be many reasons for disuse of MOD methods (4).

Another respect in which Figure 2.1 and Figure 1.3 differ
is the possibility of feedback for the DM. Figure 1.3 only
allows the DM to give more precise specifications of his priorities between objectives. In the new scheme, however, the
feedback may concern more far-reaching activities. The outcomes of the problem analysis may, for example, cause the DM
to revise his original image of the problem. Another possibility is that the DM may be inclined to modify elements of the
decision procedure agreed upon. It may also be that the DM
concludes that the analyst's formulation of the decision problem is unsatisfactory. The objectives may be too abstract, the
restrictions too binding, etc.

A last and very important feedback distinguished in this
scheme is the impact of the implementation of plans on the environment. It may cause new problems and also the pertaining
problem may be changed. The planning phases may be carried out
at another time when it is found that the planned actions did
not have the intended impact (cf. Gillingwater [1975]).

Figure 2.1 contains a number of important planning activities when MOD methods are used. Of course, this scheme is not
complete; not all aspects of planning have been dealt with.
For example, the scheme does not indicate all possible feed-
backs. Instead, only the important ones are stressed. Further,
no attention has been paid to the participation of other actors
during planning and also the actual distribution of tasks between planners and politicians has not been handled. On the
other hand, two important aspects of planning have been empha-
sized: multiple objective decision-making has been placed in a
(a) problem solving and (b) process-oriented planning framework.

2.7 Conclusion

Most of the planning theoretic notions mentioned in this chapter also apply to regional planning. Regional planning problems are in general so complex that many decision-making bodies and agencies performing analytical tasks are involved (Section 2.2). The three basic types of uncertainty are present (Section 2.3):

a. uncertainty concerning the operative environment (for example: lack of knowledge about the effects of a regional investment subsidy);

b. uncertainties concerning related choices (these arise, for example, when a new town must be planned, while no decision at that time has been taken about a railway connection for that town);

c. uncertainties of policy (this is present for example when there is no clear way to trade-off the economic and environmental impacts of a new industrial site).

All the modes of planning discussed in Section 2.4 arise in regional planning. Examples of blueprint as well as process planning can be found in the planning of human settlement patterns. The ideal of rational planning is often held for example when decisions are made about the location of new airports. In the implementation of house-building programmes, disjointed incrementalism is often the result of decisions taken by many independent communities. Normative as well as functional planning styles are present in the preparation of integral structure plans for certain regions.

With regard to MOD methods, planning theory gives rise to the following general desiderata:

- it should conform to the DM's skills (i.e. analytical, communicative, evaluative);

- it should conform to the analyst's skills (i.e. analytical, communicative, evaluative);

- it should conform to the problem's characteristics (i.e. uncertain, dynamic);

- it should conform to the available resources.

These general requirements or desiderata can be elaborated for the various activities in Figure 2.1.

1. The objectives should be clearly defined; they should be intelligible for the DM and in accordance with the intuitive formulation in phase 1.

2. The instruments should be clearly defined; they should be intelligible and operational and in accordance with the dynamic character of problems. Moreover they should be in agreement with the intuitive notions in phase 1.

3. The restrictions on instruments should be adequate, neither unnecessarily limiting the action space, nor allowing obviously infeasible actions; they should recognize the existence

of uncertainty.

4. The impacts should be theoretically sound; they should recognize the existence of uncertainty.

5. The assumptions made should be adequate; they should not restrict the problem so that it would become unrecognizable
to the DM (see phase 4).

6. The priorities should be specified in accordance with the
DM's vague ideas.

7. The calculated information should be of such a quantity and
quality that it enables the DM to make a deliberate choice
for any of the three options.

8. The rules for the DM's feedback with respect to priorities
should lead to a converging communication and should be manageable for the DM. They should recognize the possibility
of multiple DMs involved in decision-making.

9. The activities should entail amounts of time, money, manpow-
er and computer capacity which are as small as possible.

It is obvious that these requirements are to a certain extent conflicting. For example, the analyst faces the difficult
task of regarding two entirely different points of view in
problem formulation. On the one hand, he must formulate it in
agreement with the DM's vague statements about it in order to
be able to produce recognizable results to the DM. On the other hand, he must formulate it in agreement with the rigorous
rules of theoretical research in order to obtain valid results.
Another example of conflict arises between the aim to reach a
sufficiently comprehensive formulation (5) and the aim to restrict the costs of planning (9).

Of course, not all requirements and desiderata are equally
important for various types of problems. For example, for many
problems uncertainty is an essential characteristic; hence, the
requirements (3) and (4). For other problems, uncertainty only
plays a minor role. In such cases, these requirements can be
judged to be less important. Therefore, the conclusion may be
that, according to the type of problem, certain MOD methods can
be chosen which comply best with the prevailing requirements.

The conflict between some requirements implies that not all
requirements can be met simultaneously. There is another reason why it can be maintained that not all requirements need to
be satisfied immediately at the beginning of the decision process. In the planning scheme of Figure 2.1., the possibility
that certain activities have not been accomplished satisfacto-
rily is taken into account. In such situations, a feedback of
type (a) may bring about a better outcome.

The formulation of the requirements has been rather loose
so far. To enable a sensible application (see Chapter 10), it
must be made more exact. For that purpose, various other fields
of research may be helpful. Psychology may be of special importance, because here human problem-solving approaches and capac-

ities are studied. Therefore, the next chapter is devoted to
the contribution of psychology to the theory of MOD-making.

Footnotes

1.   Important parts of this chapter are based on Faludi [1973].

2.   An example of uncertainties concerning the impacts of in-
     struments on objectives is the lack of information about
     the effect of subsidies on industrial investments. An
     example of uncertainties about exogenous variables is the
     lack of insight into the development of the population
     size or the energy prices. Smit [1979] argues for the
     area of traffic planning that uncertainties of the latter
     type may strongly influence the reliability of the traffic
     forecasts.

3.   Buit [1977] points at another important aspect of the
     transformation of ill-defined problems into well-defined
     ones. He remarks that in the literature of planning the-
     ory a number of recommendations can be found for the ex-
     plicit formulation of objectives; inter alia:
     - assign a certain priority to each objective;
     - avoid vague, multi-interpretable objectives;
     - construct a hierarchy of objectives;
     - avoid conflicting objectives;
     - consider only objectives affected by the decisions to be
       taken.

     According to Buit, it is striking, however, that in the
     literature also the opposite recommendations occur. Obvi-
     ously, there are many ways to model a certain decision
     problem. The way in which one proposes to achieve the
     modelling of a decision problem may reflect one's views on
     the decision-making process, one's interests or one's in-
     tentions.

4.   One should realize that there is still a third category of
     actors which may try to influence the choice of evaluation
     methods: action or pressure groups such as environmental
     protectionists. It cannot be said in general whether
     these groups will favour MOD approaches in planning. It
     depends on their power and willingness to consider compro-
     mises. For example, when a group has reasons to doubt
     that its special interests will attain sufficient atten-
     tion, it may urge the necessity of an impartial analysis
     of all relevant consequences of the actions to be under-
     taken. This obviously would be a plea for MOD methods.
     On the other hand, action groups using the conflict model
     often will not be interested in scientific research (and
     hence MOD methods) at all, since they may already have an
     opinion on the "best" alternative beforehand.

CHAPTER 3

PSYCHOLOGY AND MULTIPLE OBJECTIVE DECISION-MAKING

3.1   Introduction

Psychology aims at describing and explaining human behaviour
and attitudes. It studies topics such as thinking, language,
motivation, problem-solving, perception and memory. For various fields of decision-making behaviour, psychological analyses
have been performed. Examples include consumer choice behaviour (Hansen [1972]) and managerial decision processes (Johnsen
[1968]). Obviously, these results may be of interest for the
study of MOD problems in regional planning. We will concentrate
on the question of which abilities man has for performing planning activities and which disabilities may obviate successful
planning. In the framework of our study the following subjects
will be dealt with:

- problem perception;
- problem-solving;
- aspiration levels;
- judgement of alternatives.

3.2   Perception of Problems

People are often able to digest a large number of sensory inputs. How do they treat a wide variety of such stimuli? Bruner
et al. [1956] have formulated a theory to answer this question.
People do not perceive all sensory input as being a new experience; they have the capacity to relate it with already available information. New information is categorized by means of a
certain coding system. The basic elements of this system are
called concepts. The conceptual system acts as a selector (cf.
Faludi [1973]); only the inputs which are recognizable in terms
of concepts are perceived.

These concepts are not only used in perception, but also in
thinking itself and in communication. Hansen [1972] distinguishes three important attributes of concepts:

1. They enable man to define things. For example, a certain
   vehicle is perceived as a car rather than a bicycle, or a
   certain expenditure is an "investment" rather than a "consumption".

2. Many concepts are evaluated more or less negatively or positively. For example, the concept of "stagnation" may arouse

negative feelings.

3. Each concept is related to other concepts. For example, the
   concept of "unemployment" arouses the concepts "total demand" and "wage level".

A conceptual system leads to a conservative perception. Entirely new facts can only be digested with difficulty. Conceptual systems are not however entirely static. They are change-
able. Piaget [1936] has described how children's cognitive development involves the accommodation of the conceptual system
to new information. Thus, new concepts may arise, old concepts
may change, evaluative attributes may interchange and new relations may be found.

In Section 2.3. we discussed the difficulty in formulating
decision problems adequately. What can be said about this difficulty in terms of the psychological theory of conceptual systems?

Basically, two types of problems have been distinguished.
The first type is termed·ill-defined, unstructured or wicked.
These problems have the attribute that the essential variables
are not numerical, but rather symbolic or verbal; the objectives are vague and non-quantitative. The second type is
termed well-defined, well-structured, tame or benign. These
problems are definable and separable; solutions can be found
(Rittel and Webber [1973]). The goals are well-defined, the
essential variables are measurable. These problems can be
solved by known and feasible computational techniques. With
each well-defined problem there is also some systematic approach
to find out whether a proposed solution is acceptable (Reitman
[1964]). Examples of the first type are many real-world and
planning problems. Most formal problems are of the second type.

The perception of these two types of problems may differ essentially. As to unstructured problems, it is obvious that the
actor will not have a clear image of them. The characteristics
of the problem are so extraordinary for him that he is not able
to integrate it fully into his conceptual system. Some objectives for which he strives, some feasible ways of action, and
some impacts may be clear to him. The actor cannot, however,
oversee the problem as a whole. His conceptual systems falls
short of digesting the problem in a holistic way.

Some reasons for this state of affairs may be suggested.
The relevant concepts may be weakly developed so that the actor
cannot apply them adequately. Moreover, the actor's concepts
may only be poorly related to each other so that he overlooks
important connections. Another reason is that people may evaluate certain concepts before they develop an adequate perception
of the problem.

One may wonder how people perceive well-defined problems.
Table 3.1 suggests distinguishing between analytically trained
and not analytically trained persons. Both can be assumed to
have difficulties in comprehending unstructured problems (cases

perceptor		type of problem	
		well-defined	ill-defined
	ANALYST	A	B
	DM	C	D

Table 3.1.   Perceptors of problems

B and D). Cases A and C, however, which deal with well-structured problems, may give rise to a divorce between analyst and
DM. Actors, specially equipped with analytical skills, may
have little trouble in perceiving and solving well-structured
problems. Their conceptual structure is very well adapted to
this type of problem. This cannot be said of DMs in general.
Many well-structured problems, especially formal problems, involve elements which the DM is completely unable to absorb.
His conceptual system is not developed for it.

    As Rittel and Webber [1973] stated, planning problems are
ill-defined. The preceding discussion yielded that some well-
defined problems may be perceived and solved by some actors.
Unstructured problems, however, cannot even be perceived clearly. Therefore, the question arises as to how this type of problem can be solved.

3.3   Problem-Solving

    Once one is aware of a problem, the question arises as to
whether one wants to solve it (1). Hansen [1972] points to the
fact that this depends upon the optimal arousal level of the
actor. This arousal level is the mental activity which the actor feels to be best. When the problem perceived seems to be
too complicated, actors may be inclined to change their perception, which may in turn result in a neglect of certain problems.

    Let us assume that an actor does not avoid the problem.
Then, according to Skull et al. [1970], essentially two different approaches are possible, adaptation and innovation. The
appropriate approach depends on the type of problem. Steiss
[1972] presents a taxonomy of problems (2):

1. The first occurrence of a generic problem;

2. A recurrent generic problem;

3. A non-recurrent generic problem;

4. A truly unique problem.

Steiss stresses that many problems are of the second type. They
may pass, however, for new problems and be treated accordingly.
The second and third types of problems imply the possibility of

taking recourse to former experiences. An adaptive response is
therefore appropriate. The actor may, for example, adopt a
previously experienced behavioural pattern, a previously employed problem-solving process, or a previously tried search
process. The first and fourth type of problem, however, cannot
be solved in an adaptive way. Here an innovative response is
needed. A new search process for a solution must be started
(cf. Skull et al. [1970]).

In Table 3.2, the two problem-solving responses (adaptive-
innovative) have been confronted with the two problem types
(well-structured-unstructured). Examples of the four cases
arising from the relationship of the two variables include:

A. A linear programming approach applied to a regional input-
    output model.

B. The application of a rule of thumb for granting a licence
    to open a new business which appeared satisfactory in for-
    mer real world problems.

C. The introduction of multiple objective programming ap-
    proaches to models concerning interregional externalities.

D. Measures to tackle the problems proceeding from the oil
    crisis of 1973.

Because so many planning problems are unstructured, the question arises as to how cases B and D can be mastered.

| type of | type of problem | |
response	well-structured	unstructured
adaptive	A	B
innovative	C	D

Table 3.2.   Types of problems and responses

First, case D will be dealt with, because this is the most
intricate one. Skull et al. [1970] indicated that people en-
gage themselves in search when trying to solve new, unstructured problems. This search, however, is not entirely at random. Krech et al. [1974] describe problem-solving as a process
in which the actor formulates the problem, as well as possible
solutions, in an increasingly specific way. He begins with a
very general statement of the problem in order to indicate directions for search after more specific solutions. In subsequent phases, these directions are worked through, resulting in
a more specific formulation of the problem and a narrowing of
the range of possible solutions. There is no guarantee that
the search will lead to an acceptable solution. The search may
enter a deadlock in a certain direction. Then the actor has to
return to a more general level of problem formulation and try
out other directions.

Reitman [1964] presents a related view on problem-solving
processes. He suggests that the actor may impose constraints
on his originally formulated problem. In this way, as a matter of fact, the actor structures the problem; he creates variables and fixes them at certain levels. Various combinations
of constraints are tried out successively. When they do not
seem to allow scope for an acceptable solution, other constraints may be formulated.

These views on problem-solving stress some common elements.
They describe problem-solving as a search process for feasible
solutions. They point at the existence of feedback when search
in a certain direction is fruitless. Both views imply that
during the search, the problem becomes formulated in an increasingly exact and structured way. Feedback may arise on
numerical values of certain variables as well as on the content of the variables themselves.

Not much attention has been paid to the question of how the
actor, during the search, discounts the information attained by
his preceding attempts. It would be interesting to know, for
example, how the actor digests the information already gained
in the search process when he must select a certain direction
for the device of another alternative. Another related example is the question as to on which grounds the actor decides
to stop searching. This type of question will be dealt in
Sections 3.4 and 3.5.

Once a structure has been delineated for an innovative response to unstructured problems, elements of an adaptive response (type B) follow straightforwardly. The actor will start
with the conceptualization of the problem he used on former oc-
casions. Disappointments about former outcomes as well as
ideas about changed circumstances may induce him to change the
formulation of the problem to a certain extent; some constraints may be added or removed, the values of some variables
may be changed. New search processes may be induced but on a
far more moderate scale than in innovative responses.

3.4   Aspiration levels

The concept of aspiration level has been devised to deal
with goal-oriented behaviour (cf. Johnsen [1968]). It was
first formulated in the field of psychology (Lewin [1936]).
Later on, however, it received the attention of economists. Examples are: Katona [1951], Simon [1957], Kornai [1971], and
Admiraal [1976]. Kornai [1971] defines it as a vector of outcomes of the various objectives, arising at the beginning of a
decision-making process. "It expresses the first ideas of the
decision-maker about the decision to be taken at the end of the
process and takes into account his wishes and internal expectation....Attainment of the aspiration level is not excluded in
principle...." (p. 157). Katona [1951] distinguishes the concept explicitly from the concepts of an ideal level and a realized level. The ideal level is the best outcome one can imag-
ine, irrespective of the constraints. One may expect that the

aspiration level is somewhere between the ideal and the realized levels. This is not always the case, of course, since
some elements of the aspiration level may, in retrospect, appear to have been too pessimistic.

Katona [1960] formulates a number of generalizations concerning aspiration levels:

"1. Aspirations are not static; they are not established once
    for all time.

 2. Aspirations tend to grow with achievement and decline with
    failure.

 3. Aspirations are influenced by the performance of other mem-
    bers of the group to which a person belongs and by that of
    reference groups.

 4. Aspirations are reality-oriented; most commonly they are
    slightly higher or slightly lower than the level of accom-
    plishment rather than greatly different from it." (p. 130).

Lewin et al. [1944] suggest a number of determinants of the
aspiration level (3). Some of them include:

- past experiences in similar problems;

- situational factors (e.g., when the actor has just accomplished an easy activity, he tends to set a high aspiration
  level for the following activity);

- cultural factors (e.g., group standards);

- reality levels (e.g., the attitude of actors may vary from
  "realistic" to wishful);

- personality characteristics.

Most applications of the theory of aspiration levels deal
with repetitive problems. It has thus been treated mainly in
adaptive contexts of problem-solving. An anchor point is already available in these situations as outcomes of past decisions are known. If this is the case, it will not be so difficult to establish aspiration levels. More difficulties may be
experienced when innovative responses are needed. Then the
task to fix aspiration levels will be difficult to accomplish.

3.5   Evaluation and Choice

In Section 3.3 it was indicated that problem-solving implies
search for solutions. An important question now arises as to
how solutions are evaluated. This question will be dealt with
now.

A general finding in psychological literature (4) is that
conflicts may arise from evaluation and choice. This conflict
can be described in terms of the conceptual system of the actor. The perception of a problem arouses a number of cognitive
elements. Since concepts are related, the aroused concepts will
activate again other concepts. The aroused concepts form together the salient conceptual system. This salient conceptual

system is only a small part of the total, latent, conceptual
system.

Salient conceptual systems can be characterized by the measure in which they are balanced. A salient conceptual system,
consisting of two elements, is balanced when both elements are
evaluated positively or negatively, and when a positive relationship exists between them. The salient system consisting of
the concepts employment and national income, for example, is
balanced when the concepts are considered to be positively related. An unbalanced system arises when a positively evaluated
concept is positively related with a negatively evaluated concept. An example of this case is a system consisting of the
concepts healing and operation.

More extensive systems cannot be characterized by simply
saying that they are balanced or unbalanced. Some parts of a
system may be in equilibrium, while others are not. In this
case, it is appropriate to use the term "degree of balance".
Hansen [1972] poses that there is a clear relationship between
the degree of balance in a salient conceptual system and the
degree of conflict experienced in this situation. In many decision problems the conflict arises from two different sources:

- the alternatives perceived are not satisfactory; they are
  too far removed from the aspiration level;

- the alternatives perceived seem to be equally attractive.

How do people deal with problems they experience as conflicting? Hansen [1972] suggests that people can be ascribed
an optimal level of conflict. They tend to adapt the level of
conflict, aroused by the problem, to this optimal level. When,
for example, the problem induces a very unbalanced structure,
people try to reduce the level of conflict by:

- seeking new, more satisfactory alternatives;

- seeking more information per alternative;

- changing the salient conceptual structure.

Obviously, these responses depend on the source of conflict.
The search for new alternatives is an adequate response when
the alternatives found thus far are unsatisfactory. In the
same way, the second information searching response is related
to the situation when some alternatives seem to be equally attractive. Changing the conceptual structure may imply that the
actor neglects certain concepts, evaluates them in another way,
or assumes other relationships.

Thus, it seems that the search will continue until the experienced conflict is equal to the optimal level of conflict.
Then the actor can safely make his decision. According to
Hansen [1972], this is not that simple since another source of
conflict is connected to continued search: the conflict arising
from endured search.

Figure 3.1 makes clear that there are cases where the con-

flict arising from the endured search may become greater than
the conflict of the problem itself. In this case, the actor
will make a decision as soon as possible, even though the conflict connected to it is greater than the optimal level of conflict. This means in terms of aspiration levels that these
levels are not satisfied. The actor may learn from this experience by lowering his level for the next problem, so that the
optimal level of conflict will be increased.

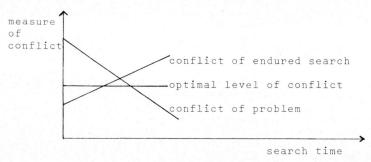

Fig. 3.1. Conflict and search time

There is also another response to this possibility. In consumer theory (cf. for example Walster [1964]), a number of
studies has been devoted to so-called "post-choice processes".
A general finding is that once a choice has been made, people
may feel very uneasy about it. It often happens that the alternative selected suddenly seems less attractive after the
choice itself. A number of theories, mainly based on
Festinger's [1957] ideas about cognitive dissonance, have also
been developed. Many studies indeed indicated that in post-
choice situations, people change their salient conceptual
structure of the problem in order to reduce the conflict.

Of course, the findings depend on the question of whether
decisions are reversible or not. If one can revoke a decision,
it is also possible that post-choice conflict results in the
choice of another alternative. In this case, reduction of conflict after choice may simply mean the deliberation about a
certain alternative before another one is actually chosen.
Shepard [1964] puts forward the following point (5):

   "I suggest....that one device that people use to resolve
   the conflict and to consummate the decision is to try out
   various frames of mind until they find one whose associated subjective weights give one alternative the clearest
   advantage over its competitors....Festinger argues that
   the change of attitudinal state occurs subsequent to the
   actual decision and serves to reconcile the individual
   with a choice already made; I am proposing that the change
   of state precedes the decision and serves to render the
   decision possible" (p. 277).

Shepard [1964] presents an excellent summary of a number of investigations about man's capacities to deal with MOD problems. One of the results is the finding "that there are rather severe limitations on the number of conceptual units that can be handled at any one time" (p. 263). Miller [1956], for example, mentions the "magical" number seven as the maximum which appears to prevail for very different types of problems. People, trained in handling certain types of problems, may have higher maximum levels. In most situations, however, even the number seven appears too high. Shepard observes that "there seems to be an overweening tendency to collapse all dimensions into a single 'good versus bad' dimension with an attendant loss in detailed information about the configuration or pattern of attributes unique to any one object" (p. 264).

Meehl [1954] performed a very interesting study concerning man's capacity to combine various attributes in evaluation and prediction. One of his topics was the prediction of study success for college students in relation to a number of attributes of the students and former accomplishments in school. He obtained predictions in two entirely different ways. One way was the intuitive judgement of educational specialists. The other way was a computational procedure. The amazing result was that the computer made better predictions than the specialists. Shepard [1964] and Dawes [1980] quote additional results which imply that people can take account of only a very limited number of criteria in making an evaluative judgement. Another result is that people are not always aware of the very restrictive view they hold of evaluation problems. They often pretend to take more criteria into consideration than they actually do. Einhorn [1970] observed a tendency that actors evaluate alternatives mainly in terms of best or worst attributes.

Hollnagel [1977] and Pitz [1977] stress that a simultaneous comparison of all alternatives according to all relevant attributes is, in general, impossible due to the limited capacity of the cognitive information processing system. A way out of this problem has already been mentioned: concentration on the salient attributes of alternatives. Tversky [1972] elaborates this idea into the direction of sequential choice. His "elimination by aspects" strategy means that sequentially alternatives are eliminated according to their performance for certain attributes. The imposition of new side-conditions on the performance levels of attributes continues until all alternatives but one have been eliminated. Tversky interprets his findings as follows:

"When faced with an important decision, people appear to search for an analysis of the situation and a compelling principle of choice which will resolve the decision problem by a clear cut choice without relying on estimates of relative weights or on numerical computations. ....people seem to have more confidence in the rationality of their decisions than in the validity of their intuitive estimates..." (pp. 297-298).

The conclusion is that people often prefer a sequential evaluation of multi-attribute alternatives above a simultaneous one. This conclusion is in accordance with research in other fields of psychology where sometimes a hierarchy of objectives is assumed. Maslow [1954], for example, has assumed a hierarchy of needs. In each phase of psychological development, a certain need dominates the others. For choice situations, this implies that actors first consider the most urgent objective. The second objective will only play a part when some alternatives are equally evaluated according to the first objective (cf. Sections 4.3 and 7.5).

The finding that people have very limited capacities to handle problems in which multiple attributes are involved leads to still another conclusion. Psychologists recommend the use of computers for these types of problems (cf. Shepard [1964]) (6). Computers may assist man in performing the activities of a decision-making process for which he is least adequately equipped.

Limitations in man's evaluative abilities have also been found in the field of consistency of choice. May [1954] finds that people violate the rule of transitivity in many circumstances (cf. Section 4.2). This rule states that when alternative A is preferred to B, and alternative B to C, then alternative A is preferred to C. Kornai [1971] cites a number of studies about consistency of consumers' decisions. The general conclusion is that consumers sometimes take inconsistent choices. Kornai argues, however, that one should not maintain a too restricted view on consistency. When a broader view is taken, such as giving room to search for information, many so-called "inconsistencies may appear as examples of clever behaviour" (p. 148).

3.6   Conclusions

Comparing psychological contributions to our subject with planning theoretical ones, it is striking that the latter are far more normative in nature than the former. Implicit in a number of planning theoretical contributions is the question: how should planning proceed in order to achieve good decisions? Psychology, on the other hand, concentrates on the question: how do people actually behave when involved in decision-making?

The decision-making model described in Section 2.6 is in accordance with psychological findings in a number of important points:

- problems induce search processes for alternatives;

- problem-solving implies the structuring of the problem;

- problem-solving entails a learning of aspiration levels;

- feedback on account of unsatisfactory results is an important element of problem solving;

- for certain activities involved in decision-making, computers may prove to be useful.

The findings also suggest a number of bottle-necks when the
planning scheme is applied. Therefore, the following requirements concerning the way in which the planning activities are
performed can be stated.

1. The formulation of the objectives and instruments should be
   performed in such a way that they are digestable in the DM's
   conceptual system; (a) the DM should be able to identify the
   problem by means of it; (b) the DM should be able to relate
   the concepts to each other; and (c) the DM should be able to
   evaluate the concepts.

2. The number of objectives should be restricted as far as possible.

3. The evaluation process of alternatives should be structured
   such that it corresponds to the DM's ability to produce
   priority statements. It seems to be easier for DMs to specify side-conditions for the performance levels of objectives
   than to indicate relative weights.

Once the DM is engaged in problem-solving, he will experience conflicts. As he must co-operate with other people during the decision-making process, it may be difficult to reduce
the conflict. For example, it is less easy to neglect the
problem or to change its conceptual structure because others
(notably the planners) may not agree with him. When this method of conflict reduction is only restrictedly available, the
other method of conflict reduction (i.e. information acquisition) gains importance.

To improve the DM's willingness to co-operate, the following
additional points should be stressed:

4. Information acquisition should be performed when the DM asks
   for it;

5. When the DM suggests adapting the problem formulation, it
   should be carried out as far as possible.

6. Given the many signs of inconsistent or intransitive behaviour of DMs, the DM should be given room to revise former
   statements about priorities.

The desiderata will be used in Chapter 10, where a comprehensive evaluation of MOD methods will be given.

Footnotes

1.   Many of the concepts used in this section and subsequent
     ones are also discussed in Yu [1979].

2.   Cited in Gillingwater [1975].

3.   Cited in Johnsen [1968].

4.   The first part of this section is mainly based on Hansen
     [1972].

5.   By means of similar concepts, Zeleny [1976b] presents the

view that lowering one's aspiration levels induces a
transformation of pre-choice conflict into post-choice
conflict.

6.   It should be noted that this division of labour is in ac-
      cordance with the distinction between decision-making and
      analytical tasks, presented in Chapter 2. This division
      of labour is fundamental for the entire study. Its most
      consequent elaboration can be found in Chapter 9.

CHAPTER 4

ECONOMICS AND MULTIPLE OBJECTIVE DECISON-MAKING

4.1   Introduction

   One of the main points of interest in economics has been the
choice behaviour of people. The utility concept has played a
central role in this theory of choice. If a person's preferences can be represented by a utility function, we are able to
predict his selection of alternatives. We will discuss the assumptions underlying the utility functions in relation to our
MOD analysis. In Sections 4.2 - 4.4 various ways of defining
utility functions will be considered, as well as the consequences for the scale of measurement (e.g. ordinal, cardinal).
We will show, among others, that in cost-benefit analysis a
utility function is employed which is measured on an unnecessarily specific scale for certain purposes. In Section 4.5 we
will pay special attention to a property of certain preference
relations: incompleteness. This concept enables one to develop
utility theories even when certain alternatives appear to be
incomparable. In Sections 4.6 - 4.8 we show that the MOD philosophy is in agreement with a number of ideas which arose in
economics during the last decades: activity analysis (Koopmans),
new theories of consumer demand (Lancaster) and procedural rationality (Simon). For certain economists the recent attention
for multi-dimensional phenomena even has the character of paradigm change (cf. Abele [1971] and Nijkamp [1979]).

   Several concepts introduced in this chapter will be used in
the following chapters. For example, the concept of ordinal
measurement will be used in Chapter 8; the concept of efficiency is central in Chapter 6; the incompleteness property will be
used in Section 9.5.

4.2   A Concept for Utility

   Fundamental areas of economics are based on the utility concept. For example, consumer theory and welfare economics draw
heavily upon it. As we shall see later, the concept has been
used in many different situations and for many different ends.
Hence, a careful definition is necessary.

   Our point of departure is the state space X. This space is
the set of all possible alternatives which a certain person can
choose. For consumer theory the space X may be conceived of as
the set of all possible combinations of goods that can be con-

sumed. If it is assumed that people do not choose arbitrarily, it
is fruitful to introduce for a pair of alternatives x and y $\in$ X
the term x "is preferred to" y. This will be denoted by
x $\geq$ y. For this preference relation $\geq$ on X, various potential properties may be devised. Three of them have been proposed frequently:

a. Reflexivity : x $\geq$ x $\forall$ x $\in$ X

b. Transitivity: x $\geq$ y and y $\geq$ z imply x $\geq$ z, where
                  x, y, z $\in$ X

c. Completeness: $\forall$ x, y $\in$ X where x$\neq$y, either x $\geq$ y or
                  y $\geq$ x.

ad a. The reflexivity property implies that x $\geq$ y can be
interpreted as: x is equivalent or preferred to y. There is a
related preference relation on X which is reflexive when $\geq$
is reflexive, i.e. the indifference relation $=$. This relation can be defined as follows:

        x $=$ y if {x $\geq$ y and y $\geq$ x} $\forall$ x, y $\in$ X.

It can easily be seen that when $\geq$ is reflexive, $=$ is also reflexive. Another closely related preference relation on x is not
reflexive when $\geq$ is reflexive. To show this, we can define
the relation "is strictly preferred to", indicated by $>$ as
follows:

        x $>$ y if {x $\geq$ y and not y $\geq$ x} $\forall$ x, y $\in$ X.

It is obvious that $>$ is not reflexive, otherwise {x $>$ x and
not x $\geq$ x} $\forall$ x $\in$ X, which is, of course, a contradiction.

ad b. The transitivity property is a very important one in
consumer theory. In Section 3.5 it has already been indicated
that in some cases consumer's preference relations have been
found to miss this property. Intransitivity may form a serious
problem. For example, when x $\geq$ y, y $\geq$ z and z $\geq$ x, the
alternative which will be chosen depends on the order in which
the alternatives are compared. A well-known example of intransitivity arises in Arrow's voting paradox. Arrow [1951] shows
how a pairwise majority voting procedure may produce an intransitivity in the preference relation of the pertaining collective.

ad c. The completeness property of a preference relation on X
has far-reaching consequences. It means that the individual is
able to compare each arbitrary pair of elements of X. In
Section 4.5, this property will be discussed in more detail.

    A preference relation which is reflexive, transitive, and
complete will be termed a total quasi ordering (cf. Takayama
[1974]).

Until now, nothing has been said about utility. The concept
of utility can be defined by means of the primitive concept X:
a utility function is a function U: X → R (1). Therefore, by
means of a utility function, each alternative x ∈ X is assigned
a real number. It is useful to introduce an additional requirement on a utility function, such that it reveals something of
the preference relations on X. This can be formulated as follows:

$$x \;\gtrsim\; y, \text{ if and only if } U(x) \geq U(y)$$

$$x \;\succ\; y, \text{ if and only if } U(x) > U(y)$$

$$x \;\doteq\; y, \text{ if and only if } U(x) = U(y)$$

A utility function defined in the above way is said to give a
"faithful representation" of a preference relation on X (cf.
Aumann [1964]). When x is preferred to y, the utility function
indicates a higher value for x than for y. Inversely, when the
utility function shows a higher value for x than for y, alternative x is preferred to y. So a utility function is simply a
very concise way of representing a **preference** relation on a certain set of alternatives X.

Since utility functions may thus be a very efficient way to
describe a preference relation, one may wonder whether each
preference relation can be represented by means of a utility
function. A short examination teaches us that preference relations have to satisfy certain requirements to allow their representation by a utility function. For example, a preference
relation which is not complete cannot be represented in a
faithful way by a utility function. In the discussion about
the representability of a preference relation the properties of
reflexivity, completeness and transitivity play an important
role. Debreu [1959] has shown that these properties are not
sufficient to warrant the representability of a preference relation in general. For example, the lexicographic ordering
(see Section 7.6) is a total quasi ordering, but a utility indicator does not exist for it. It appears that the additional
property of continuity has to be stated for a preference relation before representability can be proved.

d. Continuity: ∀ x' ∈ X the two sets {x|x ∈ X, x $\gtrsim$ x'}

   and   {x|x ∈ X, x' $\succ$ x} are closed.

Roughly speaking, continuity means that any alternative x which
is very close to an alternative y that is preferred to some
given alternative x' must be preferred to x' (cf. Quirk and
Saposnik [1968]).

For a very general class (2) of state spaces X, the following
theorem holds:

<u>Theorem 1.</u> Let X be a connected subset of R^m and let $\succ$ be a
continuous total quasi ordering on X. Then there exists a continuous utility function on X for $\gtrsim$.

See Debreu [1959] for a proof.

Theorem 1 plays a crucial role in utility theory. It bases the utility concept on the preference relation $\geqslant$. It says that when $\geqslant$ satisfies certain requirements, a utility function can be derived.

   Theorem 1 gives rise to a number of interesting questions:

1. Is the utility function unique?

2. Which properties can be derived for the utility function?

3. What are the effects upon the utility function when the assumptions concerning $\geqslant$ would be relaxed?

4. What are the effects upon the utility function when stronger conditions than in Theorem 1 can be imposed on $\geqslant$?

These questions will be dealt with in the following three sections.

4.3   Utility and the Theory of Measurement

   It will appear fruitful to associate the questions asked in the previous section with some elements of the theory of measurement (cf. Roberts [1972]). Measuring can generally be defined as imputing a number to an object or state x by means of a function g(x). So, assigning a utility value to a state is an example of measurement. Various forms of measurement have been suggested in the literature. These forms, called scales, can be characterized by means of the function g. In this context, four well-known scales will be discussed (cf. Torgerson [1958]):

a. Nominal scale.

b. Ordinal scale.

c. Interval scale.

d. Ratio scale.

ad a. A nominal scale is used to classify the elements of the space X. Each member of a certain category is assigned the same number. For example, consider the countries Holland, Switzerland, and France. Suppose that the function g is defined in such a way that E.E.C. countries are denoted by the number 1 and other countries by the number 2. Then the image of the list of these countries produced by g is (1,2,1). Notice that in order to classify, letters or other symbols can be used equally well as figures. Figures have the advantage, however, of making data accessible to computers. The function g is certainly not unique. Each function h obeying h(x) = h(y), if and only if g(x) = g(y) is also suitable to make a classification.

ad b. For ordinal scales another restriction on the function h is introduced. The function h is suitable to measure the same property as g when the following conditions hold:

$$h(x) > h(y), \text{ if and only if } g(x) > g(y)$$
$$h(x) = h(y), \text{ if and only if } g(x) = g(y).$$

In the nominal scale the expression g(x) > g(y) simply means
that x and y belong to different classes. It does not necessarily say that x possesses more of a certain property than y.
Ordinal scales, however, have been devised to measure properties for which it is significant to know both (1) whether an
object is different from another and (2) whether an object possesses more of the property than the other. An example of a
property measured on an ordinal scale is the beauty of the
landscape in a region. In one region, the landscape will be
more pleasant than in the other. Other examples can be found
in Chapter 8.

ad c. The next scale discussed is the <u>interval</u> scale. Just as
the ordinal scale is a special case of the nominal scale, is
the interval scale a special case of the ordinal scale. For
the function h this means that an extra condition is imposed.

Consider, therefore, the ratio $\frac{h(x) - h(y)}{g(x) - g(y)}$, where $g(x) \neq g(y)$.

In the nominal case, this ratio may attain all positive and negative real values. In the ordinal case, the ratio should be
positive. In the interval case the following condition must be
fulfilled:

$$\frac{h(x) - h(y)}{g(x) - g(y)} = \frac{h(v) - h(w)}{g(v) - g(w)}$$

for all x, y, v, w $\in$ X. Therefore, g and h measure the same
property on an interval scale when the ratio of the intervals
between two pairs of objectives are equal. This interval measurement is suitable for properties where it is not only important to know (1) <u>that</u> x is ordered higher than y, but also
(2) <u>how much</u> higher <u>it is</u> ordered. A well-known example of a
property measured on an interval scale is temperature.

ad d. The <u>ratio</u> scale is a special case of the interval scale.
The functions h and g measure the same property on the ratio
scale when:

$$\frac{h(x)}{g(x)} = \frac{h(y)}{g(y)} \ .$$

In this case, both the ratio of the intervals and the ratio of
the measurement values are equal. This scale is adequate when
a property is measured for which it is important to know the
distance to a certain fixed zero-point. An example of such a
property is the energy consumption of a town.

   This enumeration of scales gives rise to three important
conclusions.

1. Each scale is a special case of the preceding scales; e.g.
   the ratio scale is a special case of the nominal scale.

2. The choice of a scale for a certain property depends on the
   ends for which one wants to use the property at hand. For
   example, if one wants to find the region with the worst
   physical infrastructure, an ordinal scale of the quality of

infrastructure would be sufficient, but if one wants to dis-
tribute funds among regions in order to improve infrastructure, an interval scale is more appropriate.

3. There is no scale for which the function g measuring a property is unique. There are always other functions h measuring the same property equally well. However, for each following scale, the freedom to select a certain function h is
increasingly restricted. If g is a function measuring a
property, the function h measures the same property when
(cf. Torgerson [1958]):

nominal scale : $h(x) = h(y)$, if and only if
$$g(x) = g(y) \; \forall x, y \in X;$$

ordinal scale : h is a monotone increasing transformation of
$$g \text{ (e.g. } h = a + be^g; \; b > 0)$$

interval scale: $h = a + bg, \; b > 0$;

ratio scale   : $h = bg, \; b > 0$.

What are the implications of the theory of measurement for
the utility concept? We draw the following conclusions.

1. A utility function is never a unique representation of a
preference relation.

2. The utility function defined in the preceding section is a
function implying an ordinal scale of measurement, because
each monotone increasing transformation of U is also able to
represent the preference relation.

3. U can also be defined such that it implies a measurement on
the other scales. The common element in each definition of
utility is that it is a function mapping X into R. The definitions diverge in the way they require an adequate representation of the preference relation on X:

a. $U : X \rightarrow R$ is measurable on the <u>nominal</u> scale when
$\forall x, y \in X$, $x \ominus y$, if and only if $U(x) = U(y)$.

b. $U : X \rightarrow R$ is <u>ordinal</u> measurable when $\forall x, y \in X$
$x \oslash y$, if and only if $U(x) > U(y)$
$x \ominus y$, if and only if $U(x) = U(y)$.

c. $U : X \rightarrow R$ is measurable on the <u>interval</u> scale when
$\forall x, y, v, w \in X$
$(x - y) \oslash (v - w)$, if and only if
$U(x) - U(y) > U(v) - U(w)$ (3)
$(x - y) \ominus (v - w)$, if and only if
$U(x) - U(y) = U(v) - U(w)$

d. $U : X \rightarrow R$ is measurable on the <u>ratio</u> scale when
$\forall x, y, v, w \in X$
$(x - y) \oslash (v - w)$, if and only if
$U(x) - U(y) > U(v) - U(w)$
$(x - y) \ominus (v - w)$, if and only if
$U(x) - U(y) = U(v) - U(w)$
$\exists x_o$ with $U(x_o) = 0$.

4. The choice for a certain utility concept depends essentially
   on two factors: (a) the information available about the preference relation on X; (b) the ends for which one wants to
   use this concept.

   Especially the last conclusion is remarkable. An analyst is
free to choose a scale, but he has to take into account his
knowledge about the preference relation and the purpose for
which he wants to use it. The first factor has already been
discussed for the ordinal measurable utility function U.
Theorem 1 states a set of conditions to be imposed on the preference relation $\geq$ which is sufficient to guarantee the existence of an ordinal utility function (4). For the other scales
of measurement, similar sets of conditions can be found. Kapteyn
[1977], for example, presents several sets of conditions for
preference relations which are sufficient to warrant the existence of a utility function, measured on the interval scale.
The second factor played a very interesting role in the development of utility theory in the last two centuries. This will
be dealt with in the next section.

4.4   The Need of a Cardinal or Ordinal Utility

   Many debates about the scale of utility have taken place in
the field of economics. One group (for example, Samuelson and
Hicks) maintains that the appropriate scale is ordinal, the
other group (for example, Von Neumann and Morgenstern [1944] and
Kapteyn [1977]) argues that the appropriate scale of utility is
cardinal (the cardinal scale is equivalent to the interval or
ratio scale). A choice in favour of one of these parties is
difficult to make. The approach in the preceding section suggests taking into account the ends for which a utility function is defined. Some ends may imply heavier requirements on
the scale of the utility function than others. This will be
illustrated for several fields in economics:

a. demand theory;

b. decision-making under uncertainty;

c. welfare economics;

d. cost-benefit analysis.

For each of these fields we will discuss the appropriate scale
of utility. Especially the discussion about the scale employed
in cost-benefit analysis is important in the context of this
study, since this evaluation method is closely related to certain MOD methods.

ad a. One of the questions dealt with in demand theory is: how
to find a form basis for the demand function. This base has
been sought in the direction of utility theory. Needless to
mention that one does not necessarily need a utility theory to
analyze demand. For example, Adam Smith implicitly assumed the
existence of demand functions, but had no well-developed utility theory at all (cf. Stigler [1950]). Cassel even explicitly
proposed to start demand theory with the demand function, without basing it on a utility concept. The standard approach
which has almost generally been accepted, however, is to base

the concept of the demand function on that of utility. This
can be carried out as follows:

Assume that $X \subset R^n$. Each element of X is a bundle of n commodities which are evaluated by a consumer. The prices of the
commodities x_i are known and equal to p_i. The consumer has at
his disposal an income of Y. Then his decision problem is:

$$\max! \quad U = U(x_1, \ldots, x_n) \tag{4.1}$$

$$\text{subject to } \sum_i p_i x_i = Y \tag{4.2}$$

The solution to the problem is the following set of first order
conditions:

$$\frac{\frac{\partial U}{\partial x_2}}{\frac{\partial U}{\partial x_1}} = \frac{p_2}{p_1}, \ldots, \frac{\frac{\partial U}{\partial x_n}}{\frac{\partial U}{\partial x_1}} = \frac{p_n}{p_1} \tag{4.3}$$

Equations (4.2) and (4.3) describe implicitly a set of demand
functions for the n commodities. They point at the importance
of the concept of marginal utility instead of utility as such.
Especially the ratios of marginal utilities play a central
role. These ratios have a special property. They are insensitive to monotone increasing transformation of the utility function (5). Therefore, each monotone increasing transformation
of U yields exactly the same system of demand functions. Hence,
an ordinal utility concept is sufficient to derive demand functions. Cardinality is simply superfluous in this context. This
conclusion, however, has not been drawn from the beginning.
Gossen, for example, assumed that utility was measurable on a
cardinal scale. Prior to Fisher and Pareto, this conclusion
had not been made explicit (cf. Stigler [1950]).

ad b. The experiences in demand theory have led many economists
to the conviction that cardinal utility was an unnecessary element of economics. There is, however, another subject in economics for which this conviction would be very disagreeable.
This subject is decision-making under uncertainty. The treatment of this class of problems has very deep roots. It actually dates back to Bernouilli [1738]. The type of question
dealt with by Bernouilli and the founders of the modern decision theory under uncertainty, Von Neumann and Morgenstern
[1944], was as follows: Given the set of possible states of X
and given J vectors $\underline{p}'_j = (p_{j1}, \ldots, p_{ji}, \ldots)$, $\sum_i p_{ji} = 1$, with probabilities p_{ji} for each $x_i \in X$, we find the probability vector
$\underline{p}_j$ which produces the most desirable results. So, ignoring the
utility of gambling, solve:

$$\max_{j} \sum_{i} p_{ji} \ U(x_i) \ . \tag{4.4}$$

We can draw the conclusion from this formulation that it assumes a cardinal scale for utility. The choice for a probability vector $\underline{p}_j$ is in general sensitive to a monotone transformation in U (6). Or stated otherwise: if utility is measured on
an ordinal scale, the selection of a certain strategy j depends
on the specific way in which the preference relation has been
represented by a utility function. If one wants to avoid this
arbitrariness, utility should be measurable on a cardinal
scale.

ad c. Welfare economics includes such questions as: (1) which
amounts of commodities should be produced and how should they
be distributed to yield a desirable economic state from a desirable economic state from a social point of view, and (2) how
can the desirable pattern of production and distribution be realized? (cf. Bator [1957]). The reasoning in welfare economics
is as follows. Given certain amounts of production factors and
given production functions, it is possible to derive a contract
curve by means of an Edgeworth-box type of analysis. The contract curve can be transformed into a production possibility
curve. Given this curve and the utility functions of the persons (i=1,...,n) concerned, a utility possibility curve
$P(U_1,...,U_n) = 0$ can be derived similarly. This curve depicts
the set of all feasible distributions of utility for the n persons. What does one need to know to be able to select the most
desirable distribution? To answer this question, one should
introduce interpersonal utility comparisons.

A social welfare function $W = W(U_1,...,U_n)$ implies interpersonal utility comparisons (cf. Bergson [1938] and Samuelson
[1953]). The problem of how to find the most desirable utility
distribution can be formalized as:

$$\max! \quad W = W(U_1,...,U_n) \tag{4.5}$$

$$\text{s.t.} \quad P(U_1,...,U_n) = 0 \tag{4.6}$$

The solution is:

$$\frac{\frac{\partial W}{\partial U_i}}{\frac{\partial W}{\partial U_1}} = \frac{\frac{\partial P}{\partial U_i}}{\frac{\partial P}{\partial U_1}} \quad i=2,...,n \tag{4.7}$$

This result is very similar to (4.3). We find in a similar way
that an ordinal welfare function W is sufficient to derive the

optimum. What about the scale of U_i ? A closer look at (4.7)
reveals that it is insensitive to an arbitrary monotone transformation $V_i = V_i(U_i)$ (7). Consequently an ordinal scale of
measurement is appropriate in this context.

ad d. Cost-benefit analysis (CBA) has been designed to answer
the questions of whether an investment project should be undertaken and which project out of a set of alternatives should be
selected (Mishan [1971]). To do this, in principle all effects
of the projects on a whole society have to be listed. This
list contains in general private costs and benefits which will
be paid for by the people, but also external effects which are
not paid for but which yet have to be evaluated.

   In terms of the theory of measurement, CBA aims at assigning
a number $U(x)$ to an alternative x indicating the value of benefits minus costs (if necessary after applying an appropriate
rate of discount to future costs and benefits). This is done
by translating all benefits and costs into a common denominator
(usually money) after which $U(x)$ can be computed as the difference between the sum of all benefits and the sum of all costs,
both measured in the common units. When $U(x) > 0$, the net benefits of a project x are positive, which means that the project
is acceptable. In CBA, utility is measured on a ratio scale:
it assumes the existence of a natural zero-point and ratios of
utility values can be interpreted in a meaningful way; if, for
example, two projects x_1 and x_2 give rise to net benefits $U(x_1)$
and $U(x_2)$ where $U(x_2) = 2U(x_1)$, it is meaningful to say that x_2
is twice as attractive as x_1.

   Does the ratio scale of measurement follow directly from the
purposes for which CBA has been designed? The first mentioned
purpose - determining whether the benefits of a project out-
weigh the costs - indeed requires that the utility of a project
is measured on a scale with a fixed zero-point. A positive
value for $U(x)$ means that executing the project x is better
than doing nothing. The same conclusion cannot be drawn, however, for the second purpose - selecting the most attractive
project from a set of alternatives. Obviously, for this purpose an ordinal scale of measurement (which is less specific
than a ratio scale) is adequate. When CBA is only used for the
second purpose, the utility of a project is measured in an unnecessarily specific way (9). This may be one of the backgrounds of the criticisms expressed against CBA (cf. Van Delft
and Nijkamp [1977] and Nijkamp [1977]).

   The conclusion which can be drawn from these illustrations
is that different ends of analysis may imply different scales
of measurement of utility. Neglect of this conclusion may give
rise to the use of unnecessarily specific scales of measurement.
Consequently, a flexible attitude concerning the definition of
utility is appropriate. This will be helpful for the following
section, where two definitions of utility will be introduced
which have a special relationship with MOD methods.

4.5   The Completeness Condition

The previous section was devoted to the question of ordinal
or cardinal scales of utility in the light of a given aim of
the analysis. No attention has been paid to the question of
whether such scales can actually be constructed. The aim of
this section is therefore, the discussion of some of the difficulties inherent in the measurement of utility.

One may wonder how much information is needed about a person's preference relations to be able to derive an ordinal or
cardinal utility function. Theorem 1 mentions a number of conditions for preference relations which are sufficient to warrant
the existence of an ordinal utility function. In many situations however these conditions for ordinal utility may appear
problematic. This implies that the base for both ordinal and
cardinal utility is weak. The difficulties are related to two
conditions: transitivity and completeness. In Section 3.5
we discussed the fact that the transitivity condition is not
always valid. We will concentrate here on the completeness
condition because by means of this condition a fundamental aspect of MOD-making can be illustrated (see also Section 9.5).

The completeness property of the preference relation implies
that all alternatives in X are comparable: for all x and y ∈ X
either x is preferred to y, or y to x. It seems a very trivial
condition, but it certainly is not. The completeness property
would imply that the decision-maker does not worry about one of
the three basic sources of uncertainty in decision-making mentioned in Section 2.3 (i.e., the uncertainty of policy). It
assumes that decision-makers do not experience difficulties
when they are comparing the attractiveness of various alternatives (cf. Grover [1974]).

In the light of Chapters 2 and 3 this assumption is unrealistic for many fields of decision-making, among them regional
planning. It is clear from Fig.2.1 that incomplete preference
relations are an essential ingredient of MOD methods. A complete preference relation would imply the absence of incompara-
bility of alternatives due to conflicting multiple objectives.

Consequently, it is important to know for MOD methods whether a theory of choice can be retained when the completeness
condition is abandoned. Is it possible to maintain a utility
concept after such a reduction of conditions has been imposed
on preference relations? We will show that also when the completeness assumption is abandoned a meaningful utility concept
can be maintained. One should realize that the removal of the
completeness property does not imply that all alternatives are
necessarily incomparable. It only means that one is no longer
sure that all alternatives are necessarily pairwise comparable.
Many pairs of alternatives may simply remain comparable.
Recall the definition of utility. It is a function $U: X \rightarrow R$
under an "if and only if" condition: i.e. for all x and y in
x, x $\textcircled{>}$ y or x $\textcircled{=}$ y imply $U(x) > U(y)$ or $U(x) = U(y)$, respectively, and $U(x) > U(y)$ or $U(x) = U(y)$ imply x $\textcircled{>}$ y or x $\textcircled{=}$ y, respective-

ly. The first part of the definition is not hurt by an omis-
sion of the completeness condition. However, this is not the
case for the second part. In the set of real numbers R, we
know that either $U(x) \geq U(y)$ or $U(y) \geq U(x)$. This property
cannot be mapped into the space X, because it is not sure that
for each x, y either $x \circledgt y$ or $y \circledgt x$.

These remarks lead to the conclusion that for incomplete
preference relations an adapted utility concept has to be defined. Therefore, the term partially representing utility
function is introduced. It is defined as follows (cf. Aumann
[1964]): A partially representing utility function U_{pr} is a
function $U_{pr} : X \to R$ so that $\forall$ x, y $\in$ X:

$$x \circledgt y \quad \text{implies} \quad U_{pr}(x) > U_{pr}(y)$$

$$x \circledeq y \quad \text{implies} \quad U_{pr}(x) = U_{pr}(y).$$

Partially representing utility functions (10) should be treated
carefully. One may never conclude that if $U_{pr}(x) \geq U_{pr}(y)$,
then $x \circledgt y$. The reverse may be equally true.

Concerning the relationship between faithfully and partially
representing utility functions, it is clear that every utility
function faithfully representing a preference relation is also
partially representing the same preference relation. Therefore,
the set of utility functions faithfully representing $\circledgt$ is a
subset of the set of partially representing functions. A computational example may clarify this statement. Let X contain
four alternatives {w, x, y, z}:

$$\left\{ \begin{matrix} 0 & 100 & 75 & 25 \\ 100 & 0 & 75 & 100 \end{matrix} \right\}$$

A transitive and complete set of preference statements is:

$$y \circledgt x \circledgt z \circledgt w \tag{4.8}$$

Let us restrict the set of utility functions to a linear form:

$$U(v) = \lambda_1 v_1 + \lambda_2 v_2 \tag{4.9}$$

where v_1 and v_2 denote the values obtained by the first and the
second attribute of alternative v, respectively, and where
$\lambda_1 \geq 0$ and $\lambda_2 \geq 0$ are the corresponding weights. Then (4.8)
implies:

$$\frac{1}{3} \leq \frac{\lambda_2}{\lambda_1} \leq \frac{3}{4} \tag{4.10}$$

Consider now a case for which the preference statements are not
complete, so assume that we only know:

$$y \circledgt w \tag{4.11}$$

This implies:

$$0 \leq \frac{\lambda_2}{\lambda_1} \leq 3 \qquad (4.12)$$

Comparing (4.10) and (4.12), we conclude that the set of linear utility functions representing the complete ordering is a subset of the set of utility functions representing the incomplete ordering. Statement (4.12) leaves room for no less than five complete orderings, (4.8) being one of them:

$$\begin{cases} z \circledgt y \circledgt w \circledgt x \\ y \circledgt z \circledgt w \circledgt x \\ y \circledgt z \circledgt x \circledgt w \\ y \circledgt x \circledgt z \circledgt w \\ x \circledgt y \circledgt z \circledgt w \end{cases} \qquad (4.13)$$

Statement (4.10) only allows preference ordering (4.8).

This example shows that the less we know about the ordering of alternatives, the more scope there is for utility functions to give a partial representation of the preference relation. An extreme case arises when all pairs of alternatives are incomparable. Then every function $U:X \rightarrow R$ is partially representing the preference relation on X. For an illustration of the use of partially representing utility functions in interactive decision making, we refer to Section 9.5.

Roberts [1972] proposes another way to maintain a utility concept for an incomplete preference relation. He defines utility as a vector-valued function: $U_v:X \rightarrow R^K$. The scalar valued utility functon U, defined in Section (4.2) is obviously a special case of U_v, viz. when K = 1. The complete definition of vector utility runs as follows (11):

A vector utility function is a function $U_v:X \rightarrow R$ so that $\forall \, x, y \in X$

$$x \circledgt y \quad \text{if and only if} \quad \underline{U}_v(x) \geq \underline{U}_v(y)$$

$$x \circledeq y \quad \text{if and only if} \quad \underline{U}_v(x) = \underline{U}_v(y).$$

The example given above may illustrate this concept. As $z_1 > w_1$ and $z_2 = w_2$, we find that $z \circledgt w$ when we may assume that both elements of the alternatives are evaluated positively. A vector utility function representing this incomplete set of preferences is $U_v(\underline{x}) = \underline{x}$, i.e., $U_{v1}(\underline{x}) = x_1$ and $U_{v2}(\underline{x}) = x_2$.

In this special case, the dimension of the order K is equal to the dimension of X. In general, K is equal to or less than the dimension of X (cf. Section 8.10).

We conclude that it is essential for MOD methods that incom-

plete preference relations have a place in it. The discussions
about partially representing and vector utility functions have
shown that also for incomplete preference relations, appropriate
utility concepts can be developed. In the next section we will
show that vector utility functions are closely related to the
economic concepts of Pareto-optimality and efficiency.

4.6   Efficiency

Traditionally, economists assumed the existence of complete
preference relations. Hence, they did not need vector or
partial representing utility functions. For some problems,
however, incompleteness has been introduced, e.g., in welfare
economics and in activity analysis.

In welfare economics, Pareto argued that a social welfare
function such as (4.5) does not exist. This would imply interpersonal utility comparisons, which was judged by Pareto to be
impossible. In his opinion, economists reach the border of
their profession when they derive a utility possibility function. The choice of a certain social optimum should not be
studied by economists; this analysis belongs to the field of
sociology (cf. Tarascio [1968]). These ideas have led to the
introduction of a new and weaker optimality concept: Pareto
optimality. This roughly means that a certain distribution of
goods is Pareto optimal when it is impossible to improve a giv-
en person's utility performance without making other people
worse off. It should be noted that Pareto optimality is defined completely independent from such a concept as a social
welfare function.

Approximately half a century later, Koopmans [1951] introduced a similar concept in activity analysis. The subject of
his study was the selection of production processes. Special
attention has been devoted to the question of whether it is
possible to make a certain selection without any information
about the prices of inputs and outputs. Indeed, it is possible
to discriminate between efficient and inefficient processes.
The latter will never be chosen, whatever the prices of inputs
and outputs may be.

Let the inputs of a certain activity be $a_1,\ldots a_n$ and the
outputs $b_1,\ldots b_m$. Then an activity or process is defined by
the vector $(a_1,\ldots a_n, b_1,\ldots b_m)$. A process is called efficient
when no other process exists which produces more outputs with
less inputs.

A formal definition of efficiency reads as follows:

Let $X \subset R^J$ be the set of feasible alternatives. $\underline{x} \in X$ is called an efficient point of X if there does not exist an $\hat{\underline{x}} \in X$,
$\hat{\underline{x}} \neq \underline{x}$, such that $\hat{x}_j \geq x_j \ \forall \ j = 1\ldots.J$ (cf. Section 6.3).

An implicit assumption in this definition is that the J dimensions of X have been formulated in such a way that more is
preferred to less.

In Figure 4.1 the efficiency concept is illustrated.

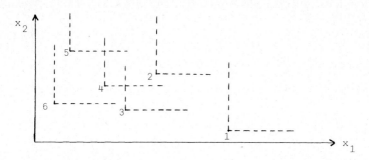

Fig. 4.1 Efficiency in the two-dimensional case.

   In this two-dimensional case, X contains six alternatives.
Three of them are efficient. However, the alternatives 3, 4
and 6 are not efficient. The latter, for example, is dominated
by the alternatives 2, 4 and 5.

   Efficiency is a very important concept in MOD methods, because it has been defined completely independent from the ordinary utility concept. It allows one to reduce the set of relevant feasible alternatives even before anything is known about
the preference relations on X. In Chapter 6 it will be shown
how the efficiency concept can play a central role in the information provision by the analyst to the DM as sketched in
Fig. 1.3.

4.7   Lancaster's Theory of Consumer Demand

   In the preceding section we established that there is a close
link between activity analysis and MOD methods. During the last
decades also other theories and concepts have been developed in
economics which are related to the MOD approach, namely
Lancaster's [1971] theory of consumer demand and the concept of
procedural rationality (see Simon [1976]). In the present section we will deal with Lancaster's theory, while Simon's theory
of procedural rationality will be discussed in the next section.

   Lancaster developed his theory as an extension of the traditional demand theory as sketched in Section 4.4. One of the
weaker points of the traditional theory is its lack of opera-
tionality in gauging the effects of introducing a new product
on the market. The reason is that the utility function (4.1)
only depends on the quantities consumed of the products, but not
on the characteristics of the products. Instead of this utility
function $U(x_1,\ldots x_n)$, Lancaster states that the utility function
depends on the characteristics (attributes) of the goods. Let
b_{ji} denote the quantity of the j-th characteristic per unit of
the i-th good and let z_j be the total quantity of the j-th characteristic, then - given the quantities $x_1,\ldots x_n$ consumed -
the amount of characteristic j consumed is:

$$z_j = \sum_i b_{ji} x_i \quad \text{for } j = 1, \ldots J$$

Thus according to Lancaster's theory, the decision problem of the consumer is:

$$\begin{cases} \text{max!} \quad U = U(z_1, \ldots z_J) & (4.14) \\[2mm] \text{s.t.} \quad z_j = \sum_i b_{ji} x_i \quad j=1, \ldots, J \\[2mm] \sum_i p_i x_i = Y \\[2mm] x_i \geq 0 \end{cases}$$

Although the operationalization of this theory is not easy, because the characteristics may be difficult to assess, this approach has attractive properties. One is that Lancaster's theory enables one to analyze the prospects for new products on the market as soon as their consumption technology coefficients b_{ji} are known. The new approach may also be helpful to remove the artificial boundaries between micro-economics and methods of marketing analysis. Another attractive property is that Lancaster's theory enables one to determine whether or not two goods are close substitutes, irrespective of the fact that the preferences of the actors may be known.

The value of Lancaster's theory is that it makes explicit that an actor bases his decisions on the values of a multiplicity of attributes of alternatives. Consequently, this theory is in accordance with one of the basic assumptions underlying MOD methods. Another interesting consequence of this theory pertains to the relationship between economics and psychology. Lancaster's theory implies that psychological research concerning the perception of attributes of products can be directly linked up with the economic theory of consumer demand. In the following section we will see that until now such a direct relationship between economics and psychology has often been strived after but that it has seldom been reached.

4.8   Economics and Psychology

In this section we will deal with the relationships between economics and psychology and the importance of these relationships for MOD methods. Given the subject matter of economics and psychology, one may expect strong links between these disciplines; for example, that certain results of research in psychology will be used in economics as assumptions taken for granted. Although certain attempts (12) to establish these links are known, it is clear, however, that an output-input relation between psychology and economics has not been reached. Most assumptions in economics are not based on psychology. For example, the assumption that subjects maximize utility or long run profits is certainly not borrowed from psychology.

This state of economic theory did not win everybody's approval. Coats [1976] describes that during the last hundred years an undercurrent in economic thought has often stressed

the importance of a closer link between the two disciplines.
He summarizes the critique on the established theory in a list
of nine proposals, made by the unorthodox economists. We quote
the most important ones (pp. 49, 50):

(ii)   Adopt 'realistic' fundamental assumptions, i.e., assumptions compatible with observed behaviour or consistent with the
findings of other scientific disciplines (especially psychology).

(iii) Derive assumptions from the study of psychology (and
other disciplines) and empirical research into the actual behaviour and motivations of consumers.

(iv)   Abandon efforts to formulate abstract, general theories
and concentrate on the development of more specific, low or
middle-level, empirically grounded theories.

(vi)   Undertake systematic empirical studies (and draw upon
any relevant studies undertaken by scholars in related disciplines) as a basis for formulating sound empirical generalizations and for testing and, if necessary, reformulating established theories.

(vii) Wherever possible, replace static theories by empirically grounded dynamic theories (e.g. to take account of changes
of income, tastes, new commodities, etc.).

(viii) Broaden the scope of economic theory to take account of
the social forces influencing economic behaviour (e.g. habit,
custom, social emulation, advertising, etc.).

(ix)   Go beyond prices and exchange values to examine the influence of market and non-market forces on economic and social
welfare.

In Coats' opinion, however, the critics have not been very successful in elaborating their proposals. They have not been
able to change substantially the scope and method of economics.
Apparently, an integration of psychology and economics is difficult to achieve.

   An important dimension in which economics and psychology diverge has been analyzed by Haan [1975]. He argues that the behavioural postulates in economics, such as rationality, do not
function as premises but as principles. Hence, economists
study behaviour in a normative way. They concentrate on the
question: how should people behave in order to meet certain
criteria? As we have seen in Chapter 3, psychologists, on the
other hand, are devoted to the question of how people actually
do behave. Simon [1976] adds a related point concerning the
relationships between economics and psychology, viz. the distinction between procedural and substantive rationality. Psychologists generally adopt the concept of procedural rationality: behaviour is conceived of as procedurally rational when
it is the outcome of appropriate deliberation. Psychological
research is not focused on the outcomes of decisions as such,
but on the processes by means of which these outcomes are

reached: learning, problem solving and concept attainment. Economists, on the other hand, traditionally adopt the concept of <u>substantive rationality</u>: behaviour is substantively rational when it is appropriate to the achievement of given objectives within the limits imposed by given conditions and constraints. As a result, most economic research is focused on the outcomes of decisions and not on the way in which these outcomes are reached (13).

Simon [1976] indicates that in several fields of economics the beginnings of a shift from substantive rationality to procedural rationality can be perceived. Examples are the theory of business policy (satisficing versus maximizing behaviour), theories about imperfect competition and the theory of decision-making under uncertainty. This tendency of "psychologizing" of economics has also been illustrated in the present chapter. The ordinary utility concept as dealt with in Sections 4.2 - 4.4 reflects the idea of substantive rationality: the optimal solution can be determined by means of some mathematical programming algorithm. Sections 4.5 - 4.7 are more compatible with the concept of procedural rationality, however. For example, partially representing or vector utility functions indicate the need to devise search and learning procedures to reach decisions. Lancaster's theory of consumer demand may serve as another example since it points to the fact that information has to be collected about the attributes of products before decisions can be taken.

The development of MOD methods can be interpreted as a good example of the shift from substantive to procedural rationality in economics. In the MOD methods the traditional body of concepts and assumptions of economic theory has been modified in such a way that procedural activities (search, learning, information collecting) have become an integral element of decision-making. Consequently, MOD methods form one of the bridges between economics and psychology.

4.9   Conclusion

Economics appears to deal with subjects which are intimately related to the problems in MOD making. A number of activities mentioned in Figure 2.1 receive attention in the field of economics. The way in which preferences can be formulated has been especially an object of study in economics. To represent preferences, utility functions can be used. As to the representation, the following statements can be made:

1. an adequate scale of measurement for utility has to be used (cf. Section 4.4);

2. MOD methods should leave room for preference relations which are incomplete and intransitive;

3. partially representing utility and vector utility are useful in representing incomplete preference solutions;

4. MOD methods should contain a test for efficiency of alternatives;

5. Also in the latter stages of MOD-making processes (stages
    4 through 8 in Fig. 2.1), MOD-making should be directed at
    designing acceptable procedures rather than attaining cer-
    tain outcomes.

Footnotes

1. R is the set of real numbers.

2. The theorem holds when X is a connected set. A connected
    set can be defined as follows (cf. Apostol[1971]): a con-
    nected set X is one that cannot be covered by two open
    sets whose intersections with X are non-empty disjoint
    sets.

3. The expression $(x - y) \geq (v - w)$ is a preference relation
    on pairs of elements of X. It indicates that x is more
    preferred to y than v is to w.

4. This is not a set of necessary conditions, however.
    Takayama [1974] indicates that the transitivity property
    can be relaxed.

5. Let V be a continuous monotone increasing transformation
    of U. Then:

    $$\frac{\partial V}{\partial x_i} = \frac{\partial V}{\partial U} \cdot \frac{\partial U}{\partial x_i} \quad \text{so that}$$

    $$\frac{\frac{\partial V}{\partial x_i}}{\frac{\partial V}{\partial x_j}} = \frac{\frac{\partial U}{\partial x_i}}{\frac{\partial U}{\partial x_j}}$$

    V should be a monotone increasing transformation of U to
    satisfy the second order conditions of a maximum.

6. The following example may serve as an illustration.
    The expressions:

    $$\text{Max!} \ \sum_j \sum_i p_{ij} U(x_i) \quad \text{and} \quad \text{Max!} \ \sum_j \sum_i p_{ij} \{a + bU^2(x_i)\}$$

    will in general not lead to the same outcome for j, though
    $a + bU^2$ is a monotone increasing transformation of U for
    $b > 0$. The linear transformation for U: $a + bU$ ($b > 0$)
    produces identical outcomes, however. This can easily be
    shown as follows:

    $$\sum_i p_{ij} \{a + bU(x_i)\} = a + b \sum_i p_{ij} U(x_i)$$

So, in order to build a theory of choice under uncertainty, the utility function should be measurable on an interval scale.

7. When $V_i = V_i(U_i)$ is a monotonically increasing function, we find:

$$\frac{\frac{\partial W}{\partial V_i}}{\frac{\partial W}{\partial V_1}} \Bigg/ \frac{\frac{\partial P}{\partial V_i}}{\frac{\partial P}{\partial V_1}} = \frac{\frac{\partial W}{\partial U_i} \cdot \frac{\partial U_i}{\partial V_i}}{\frac{\partial W}{\partial U_1} \cdot \frac{\partial U_1}{\partial V_1}} \Bigg/ \frac{\frac{\partial P}{\partial U_i} \cdot \frac{\partial U_i}{\partial V_i}}{\frac{\partial P}{\partial U_1} \cdot \frac{\partial U_1}{\partial V_1}} = \frac{\frac{\partial W}{\partial U_i}}{\frac{\partial W}{\partial U_1}} \Bigg/ \frac{\frac{\partial P}{\partial U_i}}{\frac{\partial P}{\partial U_1}}$$

So (4.12) is not sensitive with regard to a monotone transformation $V_i = V_i(U_i)$.

8. It is interesting to note that for certain welfare-economic problems (for example, the determination of an optimal pattern of taxation), an ordinal utility function is not sufficient to provide meaningful results (cf. Stigler [1950] who quoted Edgeworth [1897]). For the theory of taxation, utility should be measured on an interval scale and in some model formulations even on a ratio scale.

9. Sinden and Worrell [1979] make a similar point when discussing the need of a monetary valuation of project effects for decision-making. Note that when utility is measured on a ratio scale the selection of a certain alternative should be preferred to "doing nothing" if the utility of that alternative is larger than zero. This statement does not hold true when utility is measured on an ordinal or interval scale. Consequently, if one of these scales were to be employed, it would only be possible to know whether selecting a certain alternative should be preferred to "doing nothing", if "doing nothing" were included explicitly in the set of alternatives.

10. The partially representing utility function as it has been defined in Section 4.5 is measured on an ordinal scale, because each monotone increasing transformation of the utility function is also able to represent the preference relation.

11. $\underline{U}_v(x) \geq \underline{U}_v(y)$ is defined as:

    $U_{vk}(x) \geq U_{vk}(y) \quad \forall k = 1,\ldots K.$

12. One of the attempts to establish a direct link between economics and psychology has been based on the Weber - Fechner law concerning the responses to external stimuli. This law has been employed to obtain a specification for a utility function of income (cf. Stigler [1950]).

13. As an example of the implicit use of substantive rationality, may serve Friedman's [1953] "as if-hypothesis".

This hypothesis says that entrepreneurs behave as if they maximize profits. Consequently, only the outcomes of entrepreneurial decisions are relevant. The preceding steps fall outside the scope of the analysis.

CHAPTER 5

PHILOSOPHY AND MULTIPLE OBJECTIVE DECISION-MAKING

5.1 Introduction

The preceding chapters have shown close links with several disciplines. However, these disciplines (i.e. planning theory, psychology and economics) are not the only ones related to MOD methods. The list of relevant disciplines can be further extended in two directions: 1) disciplines studying aspects of decision problems as such and 2) disciplines studying procedures to solve problems.

ad 1. For the formulation of the structure of the decision problem, a number of disciplines will contain indispensable information. For the study of impacts of instruments on objectives, one must rely upon disciplines such as economics, engineering, biology, ecology, chemistry, and physics.

ad 2. In the process of making a decision, elements of several disciplines are involved:

- planning theory: provides a background of how to make consistent decisions in organizations;
- psychology: gives insight into problem-solving behaviour;
- economics: considers choice-behaviour and the modelling of preferences;
- mathematics, operations research, management science: focuses on the formulation of decision problems;
- ethics, anthropology: studies the idea of responsible behaviour.

The conclusion is that MOD methods transcend the boundaries of only one discipline. Since philosophy studies among others the relationships between disciplines, this is obviously an impetus for a philosophical discussion of MOD methods.

We will start our discussion with a concise presentation of systems theory which is proposed by some scientists as a unifying framework for research. Indeed, the conclusion is that a certain kinship exists between systems theory and MOD methods (Section 5.2). The next section will be devoted to the formulation of methodological rules to be satisfied by systems in general and by systems used in MOD procedures in particular. Section 5.4 contains a philosophical discussion of multi-dimen-

sionality of reality, which is the origin of MOD methods. By
means of this, it is also possible to deal with questions concerning the relationship between MOD methods and responsible
behaviour and the range of scientific knowledge with respect to
decision-making. The last section will be devoted to some conclusions.

5.2   Systems Theory

Systems theory is a branch of science which has mainly been
developed since the last three decades (1). The founder, Von
Bertalanffy, was originally a biologist. He developed systems
theory by extrapolating theories about the functioning of or-
ganisms to systems in general.

In an abstract sense, a system can be defined as the combination of two sets:

1. a set of elements identified with some variable attribute of
   objects;

2. a set of relationships between the attributes of objects.

A system defined in this way is a mathematical abstraction; it
can be analyzed independent of a certain operational interpretation of its elements and relationships. It is an interesting
property of systems that the elements of a system can be conceived of as (sub)systems themselves. Consequently, systems
theory allows the construction of hierarchies of systems. As
to the second part of the definition, several types of relationships can be distinguished. An example, which is well-known in
the context of cybernetics, is the feedback relationship.

The development of systems theory has mainly been performed
in three directions; (1) mathematics, (2) methodology and
philosophy, and (3) empirical research.

(1) The mathematical approach to systems theory has been directed to the elaboration of properties of systems. Mathematics can be used, for example, to analyze the stability of systems when certain external variables change. Mathematics can
also be used to analyze the syntactical analogy of systems applied to certain problems. In particular cases, it has been
possible to show the syntactical identity (isomorphy) of systems used in entirely different situations (2).

(2) Systems theory has also been employed with respect to methodology and philosophy. For example, an important impact of
systems theory on philosophy concerns the idea of the unity of
science. The link between the two is based on the observation
that the elements of systems can be conceived of as systems.
Consequently, it may be useful for the study of a certain overall system to divide it into a number of subsystems, each being
the object of study of a certain discipline. Systems theory
forms a stimulus to integrate the knowledge in various fields
of research to be able to understand the structure of the whole.
Thus, systems theory clearly suggests an interdisciplinary approach to research.

Some proponents of systems theory go even further by saying that systems theory provides an essential complement to the scientific method (cf. Landry and Malouin [1977]). In the opinion of Landry and Malouin, the scientific method is still largely dependent on the ideal developed by Descartes. Descartes proposes the decomposition of complex realities into such simple parts that their understanding will become evident. The knowledge of the "whole" can then be obtained by the aggregation of the knowledge of the parts. Landry and Malouin indicate that the weak point in this approach is the lack of a clear frame of reference for the aggregation process. This results in numerous unsuccessful attempts to find relationships between the parts. The authors propose, therefore, the use of systems theory for obtaining a frame of reference.

Hence, systems theory is considered valuable for the first phase of research where the researcher's experience and intuition also play an important role. It forces the researcher to identify the global structure of the phenomenon studied. It may serve as a generator of theories and hypotheses. However, in the second phase of research when the specification of the relationships generated by the systems theory must be identified, the scientific method is helpful (3).

This point of view gives rise to some questions concerning the status of systems theory. Is it, in fact, possible at all to grasp the "whole" of a phenomenon by scientific means as systems theorists propose? What is the role of intuition in the construction of systems (see also Schuurman [1977])? These types of questions will be discussed in Section 5.4.

(3) The third use of systems theory has been in empirical research. Well-known examples of the explicit application of systems theory to dynamic problems are Forrester's Urban Dynamics [1969] and World Dynamics [1971].

Polenske [1980] identifies the following stages in the construction of an empirical model of a system: (4)

- define precise problem;

- determine objectives;

- determine boundaries;

- choose pertinent variables;

- formulate hypotheses of the interaction of the variables;

- select suitable parameters and go through several iterations of the simulation;

- make exploratory policy tests.

The third stage deserves some additional comments. When one carries out an empirical application of systems theory, one must explicate which variables are determined in the system and which are not. The latter can be conceived of as the environment of the system. All variables determined in the system are inside the boundaries of the system. The other variables are

outside the boundaries. A system is called <u>closed</u> when there
is no interaction between the variables inside and outside the
boundaries (5). Otherwise, a system is called open.

The relationship between systems theory and MOD methods becomes obvious when one compares the seven stages cited above
with the MOD-making scheme in Figure 2.1. Essentially, they
require the same activities. For both systems theory and MOD
methods the recognition of the multidimensional character of
phenomena is essential. Both are problem-oriented and both deserve the combination of knowledge from various disciplines.
The difference between the two is that systems theory concentrates on the structuring side of problems, whereas MOD methods
focus on the decision side of problems.

Having established the relationships between MOD methods and
systems theory, we note that systems theory has also certain
links with regional planning. It appears that several elements
of systems theory are directly applicable to regional planning.
For example, regions can be conceived of as subsystems of a
larger system. To present another example: the various facet
policies which play a role in regional planning (see Section
1.2) can be reflected by various subsystems (which are more or
less independent), such as an economic system, a spatial system
and an environmental system.

This section on systems theory serves as a point of departure in two directions. The first direction concerns the practical aspects of system building. It deals with the rules to
be obeyed in systems modelling (Section 5.3). The second direction concerns a philosophical discussion of the multidimensional character of reality as reflected by systems theory and
the MOD methods (Section 5.4).

5.3   <u>Rules for the Construction of Empirical Models of Systems</u>

In this section we will first deal briefly with some rules
to be obeyed in the construction of system models. We will
then discuss in detail the requirements that arise when these
models are used in an MOD context.

An excellent treatment of the requirements to be satisfied
by the relationships in a mathematical model can be found in
Somermeyer [1967]. He lists four classes of requirements: logical, theoretical, methodological, and practical.

<u>Logical</u> requirements imply that it should be impossible to
draw inconsistent conclusions from the relationships in a model. An example of the violation of this requirement is a model which does not guarantee that the sum of the parts is equal
to the whole (6). Another example is a model which may yield
negative values for variables which are positive by definition
(for example, regional consumption).

<u>Theoretical</u> requirements concern the foundations of rela-
tionships in a model. Relationships should be based on theory,

if available, rather than on ad hoc considerations. Theory
indicates which causal relationships are to elaborated. It may
suggest the format of the relationship: additive or multiplicative. It may provide information whether certain coefficients are positive or negative.

Methodological requirements concern the flexibility and uniformity of the specification of relationships. The flexibility
requirement states that the form of a specification should be
sufficiently general. The uniformity requirement states that
similar relationships should be specified in a similar way.

Practical requirements pertain to the manageability and simplicity of relationships. Simplicity refers to the number of
variables in a relationship. The manageability of a relationship refers to the number of operations which should be performed to estimate coefficients or to calculate impacts (7).

These four classes of requirements mainly refer to the specification of the relationships of a model, not to its estimation. With respect to the estimation, two additional sets of
requirements arise. One concerns the statistical quality of
the estimation of the model. The other set of requirements
concerns the operational definition of the elements of the system which would be established in order to obtain measurable
variables.

The former set of requirements is well-known. It consists
of a number of statistical tests of the significance of the estimated coefficients and the quality of the model's predictions.

The latter set of requirements is often neglected and will
be discussed in more detail, especially since it also serves as
an introduction to the discussion of specific requirements because of the use of models in MOD procedures. These requirements have their origin in the fact that theories can never be
tested or applied directly. Only when the concepts used in
theories have been supplied with an operational definition can
a theory be testable and applicable. Without such an operational definition a concept is not a measurable variable, which
means that it cannot be used in an empirical model.

Possibly in some disciplines the operationalization of concepts is a more delicate problem than in other disciplines, but
in social research it certainly arises (see Forcese and Richer
[1973]). Hence, it can be also expected to play a role in MOD
models. Two basic criteria have been formulated that such an
operationalization should satisfy; viz. validity and reliability. An operationalization is valid if a variable is measuring
the concept it is intended to measure. An operationalization
is reliable if a certain variable can be used repeatedly by the
same or different researchers and the same results will be obtained. Some examples may illustrate the meaning of these concepts.

(a) The regional consumption of natural gas can be measured in
    principle in a reliable and valid way by examining the book-

keeping of a number of gasworks.

(b) When the rules to measure the capital stock in a region
    have not been fully specified, different researchers may
    arrive at different outcomes. Hence the operationalization
    is not reliable, though it may be valid.

(c) When the ecological quality of a region is measured by the
    number of species of animals found in the region, this mea-
    sure may be reliable, but it is only partially valid since
    it only registers one aspect of the ecological quality.

It is important to realize that when a model is used in an
MOD procedure, some additional requirements may arise with respect to the variables incorporated in it. The variables ap-
pearing in the final information produced for the DM should be
transparent (see Section 3.6). This may be a strong requirement in some cases. When, for example, one of the objectives
of regional policy is the minimization of regional inequality
of income, many valid measures of income inequality will not
meet the requirement of transparency, because their structure
is too complex to be explained to outsiders. Obviously, the
precise way in which the transparency requirement is worked out
depends on the skills of the DM and also on other desiderata
with respect to MOD methods, as enumerated in Section 2.7.

Next to the transparency requirement, another requirement
should be mentioned which is a consequence of the use of models
for policy preparation: operationalizations of policy instruments should satisfy institutional constraints. For example,
the possibilities to elaborate the concept of a subsidy on environmental investments in an operational way may be severly
limited by supranational agreements concerning this instrument.

Neglect of the above-mentioned requirements for model building and concept formation may hinder the successful application
of MOD methods.

5.4   A Philosophical Discussion of the Multi-Dimensionality
      of Reality

It is disappointing to find that philosophers have not
dealt very extensively with the fact that so many scientific
disciplines have been evolved and that multi-dimensionality is
an essential characteristic of so many decision problems. There
is at least one exception, however. The Dutch philosopher
Dooyeweerd has developed a philosophy in which the multi-dimensional character of reality has a central role (8).

A basic distinction of his philosophy is the one he makes
between entities (i.e. things, persons, events) and modes of
being (i.e. aspects which function in entities). The entities
are most directly accessible to our naive experience. Human
beings have the ability to distinguish several types of entities. People also have an intuitive notion of entities of higher and lower order. These distinctions and order are due to the
aspects functioning in all entities. After an extensive study,

Dooyeweerd distinguished 15 aspects in reality (9) (see Table
5.1). Each aspect is characterized by a kernel which cannot be
reduced to the kernel of any other aspect. The aspects are
presented in a deliberate, specific order; each aspect presupposes the existence of its predecessors and lays the foundation
for the following aspects. For example, the lingual aspect
presupposes the existence of human formative power (the historical aspect). It is also a necessary condition for the existence of the social aspect.

ASPECT	KERNEL
15. Pistic	Faith, firm assurance
14. Moral	Love
13. Juridical	Retribution (recompensing)
12. Aesthetic	Harmony
11. Economic	Frugality in managing scarce goods
10. Social	Social intercourse
9. Lingual	Symbolic meaning
8. Historical	Formative power
7. Analytical	Distinction
6. Psychical	Feeling
5. Biotic	Vitality
4. Physical	Energy
3. Kinematic	Motion
2. Spatial	Continuous extension
1. Arithmetical	Discrete quantity

Table 5.1.   Aspects of reality

   In principle all aspects operate in a certain entity. Every
entity has its own structure; certain aspects are more important in it than other aspects. It seems possible to distinguish
a qualifying aspect for every entity - this is the dominant aspect.

   This series of aspects is represented in the division of
sciences. Most of the sciences are devoted to the study of
phenomena under a certain aspect (e.g. biology, economics, etc.).
Only a minority of sciences concentrate on entities (e.g. med-
ical science).

   It is important to go somewhat deeper into the meaning of
the modes of being (aspects). Another term used for these is
"law sphere". Indeed, aspects are connected with the idea of

laws. The laws of law spheres 1-5 are natural, since they hold
without human recognition. The laws of law spheres 6-15 demand,
however, human recognition and are called norm laws.

The laws originate from God's creation of the world as an
ordered whole with all things having their own fundamental
properties (10). Man is required to recognize these laws.
His mission is to develop the created world, while at the same
time obeying these laws. He is responsible to all laws. Consequently, he must uphold all of them simultaneously rather
than making one or more of them all important.

For MOD-making, this view has the following implications.
Decision-making about problems for which MOD methods are relevant is qualified by the economic aspect. Given restricted re-
cources, one wants to select the most attractive alternative.
The preceding aspects all play a certain role in these decision
problems. For example, the numerical aspect functions in the
number of alternatives; the analytical aspect functions in the
research after the impacts of alternatives; the historical aspect appears because the problem is conceived of as a management problem which must be resolved.

However, the objectives according to which decisions must be
taken cannot be established by the first 11 law spheres. For
that purpose we need an "opening process" to the higher law
spheres. This implies that decisions also have to satisfy the
laws of the spheres 12-15.   Consequently, the idea of law
spheres gives rise to the statement that decisions should not
ultimately be judged according to purely economic norms, i.e.
that one has to make use of scarce resources in an efficient
way. Other norms must also be respected. The juridical aspect,
for example, does not only refer to juridical affairs in a formal sense, but also to any situation in which a balanced harmo-
nization of a multiplicity of individual and social interests
occurs.

The general traits of MOD methods are related to the idea of
responsible behaviour described above as aiming at a simultaneous realization of norms (see also Van der Kooy [1978]). Of
course, the use of MOD methods does not guarantee that decisions
are made which are good from the point of view of ethics or
justice. This qualification depends on the way in which MOD
methods are used. Yet, MOD methods have an important advantage
compared to unidimensional methods; they make explicit the need
to regard other norms, next to norms which are qualified by the
economic aspect. Furthermore, MOD methods stress that the selection of a best alternative can not be arrived at in a technical way which can best be performed by an expert (analyst).
Instead of this, it presents the picture of a responsible decision-maker, carefully weighing the pros and cons of alternatives from all relevant points of view.

So far, the conclusion is that MOD methods may be helpful in
avoiding an absolutization of the economic aspect in decision-
making. There is another problem concerning the absolutization

of a certain aspect in decison-making in which MOD methods play
an important role. It is the problem of the character of scientific knowledge with respect to the character of human decisions.

It is not difficult to characterize the nature of scientific
knowledge. It is knowledge obtained by the use of the filter
of the logical reasoning and analytical distinction. Consequently, it is knowledge qualified by the analytical aspect.
Obviously, this is not the only type of knowledge. Personal
experiences and intuition are other forms of knowledge. They
are, in fact, the basis of scientific knowledge. Problems may
arise when the scientific knowledge is used in practice. Because of its dependence on the analytical aspect, scientific
knowledge is one-sided. When scientific knowledge is used in
practice without due regard of its limited scope, the danger of
absolutizing the analytical aspect is real. Indeed, the belief
that only science can help us in solving problems is very
strong in the western world. It results in the "scientification" of the culture (see Schuurman [1977]).

How can this absolutization of scientific knowledge be
avoided? Consider Figure 5.1. The problem of scientification
can be avoided when the scientific knowledge is integrated into
the naive experience of people before it is applied to make decisions. This integration is an essential step in decision-
making. It may be difficult to accomplish, however, when the
complexity of the problem is large. As Figure 5.1. suggests,
MOD methods may be helpful in reaching the integration, since
they aim at presenting information about complex decision problems in a transparent way for non-insiders.

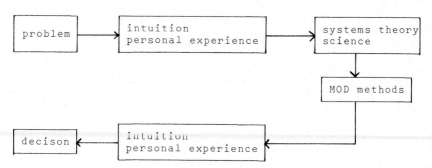

Fig. 5.1. The relationship between decision-making and
science

5.5   Conclusion

MOD methods show a certain kinship with ideas in systems
theory. Both imply the necessity to combine information from
various disciplines. They are complementary rather than substitutes.

The <u>relationships</u> in models should satisfy the following
types of requirements: logical, theoretical, methodological,
practical, and statistical. As to the <u>variables</u> used in models, the following criteria apply: reliability and validity.
When models are used for MOD-making, two additional criteria
can be stated:

- the objectives should be <u>transparent</u> to the DM and

- the instruments should <u>satisfy institutional constraints</u>.

The results of a confrontation of MOD methods with
Dooyeweerd's philosophy yields the conclusion that MOD methods
may serve as means to avoid (1) absolutization of one aspect
in decision-making and (2) scientification of decision-making.

<u>Footnotes</u>

1.   See for an introduction to systems theory Harvey [1969],
      Chapter 23. Keuning [1973] contains a survey of the lit-
      erature concerning systems theory. One should be careful
      in judging the relevance and range of systems theory. Sys-
      tems theory forms a special language in science. Many re-
      sults of research outside the realm of systems theory can
      be interpreted in terms of the concepts of systems theory.

2.   See for example Harvey [1969].

3.   In the terminology of Rudner [1966], systems theory oper-
      ates in the context of discovery, and the scientific meth-
      od in the context of validation.

4.   See for a similar list of activities Naylor [1971].

5.   Forrester's World Dynamics [1971] is an example of a
      closed system.

6.   It is remarkable that there are many allocation models
      which do not satisfy the additivity requirement. An exam-
      ple is the gravity model which has often been estimated
      without the side-condition that the sum of the flows going
      from i to all j is equal to the total outflow out of i.

7.   When a model is used in an MOD context, this forms an ad-
      ditional argument to regard the requirements of simplicity
      and manageability. The more a model satisfies these re-
      quirements, the more accessible the model will be to the
      DM, which may improve his willingness to co-operate with
      an analyst in MOD procedures.

8.   See Dooyeweerd [1953]. Introductions to Dooyeweerd's phi-
      losophy can be found in Kalsbeek [1975], Van Riessen [1970]
      and Spier [1966].

9.   One should of course realize that this series of aspects
      is provisional and subject to debate.

10. See the pertaining parts of Genesis 1 and Psalm 104 of the Bible.

11. Hills [1974] presents a similar confrontation of land-scape planning with the philosophy of Dooyeweerd.

PART B

CONCEPTS AND METHODS IN MULTIPLE OBJECTIVE DECISION-MAKING

In Part A (Chapters 2-5) we treated the links between MOD methods and four different disciplines. These disciplines (planning theory, psychology, economics, and philosophy) shed light on the broader framework in which MOD methods may function and on some backgrounds of these methods. Each chapter concluded with the formulation of desiderata to be met by MOD methods.

In Chapters 6-9 we will discuss the MOD methods themselves. The starting point is Chapter 6, where we show that many concepts and methods are available to characterize relevant aspects of the set of feasible alternatives, even when no data are available about the DM's priorities among objectives. Meaningful information can be generated to enable the DM to understand the structure of a decision problem. In Chapter 7 we will discuss the various ways in which a DM can express his priorities and how an analyst can use this information.

In Chapter 8 we will deal with discrete problems (problems in which the values of instruments or objectives do not vary continuously but only attain certain discrete levels). This feature may give rise to difficulties, such as problems where only ordinal information is available about the alternatives and problems with a small number of alternatives. For these kinds of problems, special evaluation methods have been developed . Chapter 9 is, to a certain extent, a synthesis of the preceding chapters, since it deals with interactive decision methods in which both the analyst and the DM play an important role. It appears possible to develop a communication structure for a DM and an analyst which guarantees a convergence of opinions about desirabilities and possibilities, as long as the rules of the communication are obeyed.

When we confront the MOD methods in Part B (and especially the interactive methods) with the contents of Part A, we conclude that MOD methods can be characterized as an effort to bridge the gap between normative and descriptive contributions to the theory of decision-making. Normative contributions focus on the substantive rationality of decisions. They imply a large task for analysts to ensure this rationality, and consequently give a passive image of the DM. In descriptive contributions it is exactly vice versa. Here dominates the image of an active DM who is involved in search and problem-solving.

Table B.1. Links between the sections in Parts B and C

Substantive rationality does not play an important role in descriptive contributions. MOD methods aim at a balance between these extreme points of view. The methods in Chapter 9, elaborating a well-defined communication structure between the analyst and the DM, can be seen as the most far-reaching effort to arrive at this aim (cf. Nijkamp and Rietveld [1978]).

It is important to note an essential assumption underlying all methods in Part B, namely that at the beginning of an MOD procedure the necessary data concerning the decision problem are available. Consequently, it is of importance to know in advance whether these data are reliable. To that end we presented in Section 5.3 a number of general rules for research in order to ensure reliable results. Nijkamp [1979] mentions, in addition, a number of criteria for an appropriate analysis of spatial systems. In Part B we will not question the reliability of scientific results for planning purposes in general, although we realize that in certain cases this reliability may be debatable. There is, however, one aspect of the limited possibilities of scientific research to which the necessary attention will be devoted, namely that for many attributes of alternatives no exact values can be obtained in a meaningful or reliable way. As will be shown in Chapter 8, the use of ordinal data may solve this problem.

Chapters 6-9 present a survey of existing MOD methods and also of some new approaches in this field. Given this survey character, many links exist between the sections in this part of the study. The most pertinent links have been made visible in Table B.1. The symbol x in column n and row n' of the table indicates that Section n is (partly) based on the contents of Section n'. The table also indicates in which sections of Chapters 11-13 the concepts and methods developed in Part B have been applied.

In Chapter 10, which concludes Part B, the MOD methods presented in Chapters 6-9 are confronted with the desiderata formulated in Part A. As may be expected, no definite method superior to all other methods can be selected, but within certain subsets of criteria or methods more definite inferences can be drawn.

CHAPTER 6

ANALYSIS OF CONFLICTS AND COMPROMISES

6.1   Introduction

   MOD methods focus mainly upon only some of the activities
described in the general decision-making scheme Figure 2.1.
They deal with the provision of information by the analyst
(activity 6) and the formulation of priorities by the DM (activity 5). The preceding stage of formulating the problem and
the following stage of deliberation receive much less attention.
Therefore, the point of departure for MOD methods is a decision
problem of which the structure is assumed to be known in most
respects.

   The following type of decision problems has received much
attention in MOD literature:
- there is one DM;
- the DM has at his disposal I instruments: $\underline{x}' = (x_1 \ldots x_I)$;
- the vector of instruments $\underline{x}$ is an element of a convex set K,
  being a subset of R^I ($\underline{x} \in \overline{K} \subset R^I$);
- the DM considers J objectives: $\underline{\omega}' = (\omega_1, \ldots, \omega_J)$ which he wants
  to maximize (1);
- for each combination of instruments $\underline{x}$, the effects on the set
  of objectives $\underline{\omega}$ can be determined with certainty. Hence, a
  set of J concave objective functions $\underline{\omega} = (\omega_1, \ldots, \omega_J)'$ is assumed
  to exist, each mapping $\underline{x} \in R^I$ to $\omega_j \in R^1$.
A look at these components of a decision problem which are often taken for granted teaches us that they imply a clear definition of a major part of the choice problem. One crucial
piece of information is lacking, however; i.e. the weighing of
the objectives.

   The basic question with which we shall deal in this chapter
is: which channels are open to an analyst to provide relevant
information about the feasible solutions and their implicit
trade-offs to the DM. As the DM's priorities are unknown, it
will appear that the answer to the question is not straightforward. We start with a discussion about the generation of
extreme options (Section 6.2), which is followed by a presentation of the concept of efficient solutions (Section 6.3).
Subsequently we introduce several conceptualizations of compromise solutions and so-called "half-compromise solutions"
(Sections 6.4 and 6.6). Section 6.5 is devoted to the development of conceptualizations of measures of conflicts among the
objectives in an MOD problem. Finally, Section 6.7 deals with

the special features of linear MOD problems.

Most of the concepts and methods discussed will be applied
in Chapters 11 and 12.

6.2   The Pay-off Matrix

The consequence of the assumption concerning the absence of
information about the DM's priorities is that a conventional
economic analysis cannot be applied by the analyst. The only
exception to this rule is the degenerate MOD case, when only
one objective (say j) has to be considered. Then the analyst
has to solve the mathematical programming problem:

$$\begin{cases} \max! \ \omega_j(\underline{x}) \quad \text{for a certain j} \\ \\ \text{subject to } \underline{x} \in K \end{cases} \qquad (6.1)$$

In this case the only relevant information for the DM is the
optimal set of instruments $\overset{*}{\underline{x}}_j$ and the corresponding value of
the objective $\omega_j(\overset{*}{\underline{x}}_j)$.

It is clear that this approach fails as soon as two or more
objectives are considered, because normally the diverse objectives are conflicting. In other words, a successive solution
of (6.1) for j = 1,....J leads to a series of different optimal
solution vectors $\overset{*}{\underline{x}}_1,\ldots,\overset{*}{\underline{x}}_J$. The conflicting nature of the decision problem can be illustrated by means of the pay-off ma-
trix P of order J x J of which J successive columns show the
effects of the J instrument vectors $\overset{*}{\underline{x}}_j$ on the objectives (2):

$$P = \underline{\omega}(\overset{*}{\underline{x}}_1),\ldots\ldots, \underline{\omega}(\overset{*}{\underline{x}}_J) \qquad (6.2)$$

For example, the element $p_{jj'}$ indicates the value of the j-th
objective function which results if the j'-th objective were to
be maximized (See also Table 6.1).

	objectives: max! $\omega_1(\underline{x})$	max! $\omega_2(\underline{x})$.	. max! $\omega_J(\underline{x})$
outcome for:ω_1	P_{11}	P_{12} · · ·	· P_{1J}
ω_2	P_{21}	P_{22} · · ·	· P_{2J}
·	·	·	·
·	·	·	·
ω_J	P_{J1}	P_{J2} · · ·	· P_{JJ} ·

Table 6.1   The Pay-off matrix.

Let $\overset{*}{\underline{\omega}}$ be the main diagonal of P. Then $\overset{*}{\underline{\omega}}$ contains the maximum
attainable values of the J respective objectives. In a similar
way, $\underline{\omega}$ can be defined as the vector with minimum attainable
values for the J objectives, i.e.:

$$\bar{\omega}_j = \min_{j'} (p_{jj'}) \qquad\qquad (6.3)$$

The three concepts defined above play an important role in
the further development of MOD methods. They enable the DM to
form an impression of some essential elements of the decision
problem. The matrix P may be conceived of as a concise description of J scenarios which focus on J different objectives.
Each column of P presents the values for the relevant objective functions when a policy is chosen that aims at realizing
a maximum value for only one objective. Thus, each column of P
shows the consequences for all objectives of a policy, focusing
on the maximization of only one objective and neglecting the
other J-1 ones.

P owes its name to its similarity with the pay-off matrix
defined in the theory of games. It will be discussed in this
context in Section 6.4. P has been introduced in MOD theory
among others by Benayoun et al. [1970, 1971], Belenson and

Kapur [1973] and Fandel [1972]. The two other concepts $\overset{*}{\underline{\omega}}$ and
$\underline{\omega}$ are derived from P. They indicate between which bounds the
ultimate solution will be realized (3). Each policy feasible
within the framework of the model will result in an outcome $\underline{\omega}$,

obeying $\underline{\omega} \leq \overset{*}{\underline{\omega}}$. Thus, $\overset{*}{\underline{\omega}}$ dominates all feasible solutions. It
has therefore been given the name ideal solution. It has re-
ceived extensive attention in the literature (see among others
Benayoun et al. [1970, 1971], Zeleny [1973, 1976b], Nijkamp and
Rietveld [1977], and Starr and Zeleny [1977]).

In certain cases, P may have some special features:
a. it may have identical columns;
b. certain columns may be non-unique.
ad. a. When columns j and j' are identical, this indicates
that there is no conflict between the objectives j and j'. It
may be sensible to delete one of the objectives in this case (4).
ad. b. Non-uniqueness of certain elements j' of a column j
means that with the attainment of the maximum value of objective j, the values of the objectives j' are not yet fully determined. This is an indication of a relative independence be-
tween $\omega_{j'}$ and $\omega_{j'}$, and it may be wise to check whether the decision problem can be separated in two independent subproblems.
In a formal sense, separability can be defined as follows:
an MOD problem is separable if the set of objectives can be di-
vided into two non-empty subsets S_j and $S_{j'}$, $(S_j \cap S_{j'} = \emptyset$,
$S_j \cup S_{j'} = \{1,....J\}$ such that the outcome for the j-th objective $(j \in S_j)$ in:

$$
\begin{cases}
\text{max!} \quad \omega_j(\underline{x}) \quad \text{for some } j \in S_j \\
\text{s.t.} \quad \underline{x} \in K \\
\omega_{j'}(\underline{x}) \geq \tilde{\omega}_{j'} \quad \text{for all } j' \in S_j,
\end{cases}
$$

does not vary with different values of $\tilde{\omega}_j$, leaving the set of feasible solutions non-empty (5). Obviously, from an analytical point of view, it is preferable to solve independent sub-problems separately.

The information contained in matrix P can be used to define a certain measure of conflict among objectives. It is intuitively clear that the conflict between objectives j and j' is greater, as the difference between a certain ω_j^* and a certain $p_{jj'}$ is larger. This idea can be formalized as follows. Let Q, the normalized version of the pay-off matrix P, be

$$
Q = (\overset{*}{\omega} - \overline{\omega})^{-1}(P - \underline{\omega}\underline{\imath}') \tag{6.4}
$$

where $\underline{\imath}$ indicates a vector with unit elements and the symbol $\hat{a}$ a diagonal matrix with the vector $\underline{a}$ on the main diagonal. It can be safely assumed that $\omega_j^* \neq \overline{\omega}_j$ for any j, otherwise the j-th objective would be irrelevant for the decision problem. The normalization has been executed such that all elements of Q are non-negative and smaller than or equal to 1. The main diagonal of Q contains unit elements. Any row of Q contains at least a zero element. Note, that there are also other methods to normalize matrices (cf. Section 7.4).

The larger the sum of the elements of Q, $(\underline{\imath}'Q\underline{\imath})$, the smaller the conflict among the objectives. Therefore, a meaningful aggregate measure of conflict is:

$$
\gamma_1 = \frac{J^2 - \underline{\imath}'Q\underline{\imath}}{J^2 - J} \quad J \geq 2 \tag{6.5}
$$

which has been defined such that:

$$
0 \leq \gamma_1 \leq 1 \tag{6.6}
$$

A value of γ_1 close to 1 indicates a high degree of conflict; a value of γ_1 close to 0 reflects the opposite case.

6.3   Efficient Solutions

So far we have only concentrated on some extreme scenarios of the decision problem as reflected by the matrix P. It is, however, also useful to provide information about intermediate solutions reflecting certain compromises among objectives. In this respect, the concept of an efficient solution, already mentioned in Section 4.6, will prove to be useful. Efficient solutions are non-dominated solutions, and hence deserve special attention.

In a completely non-stochastic and non-fuzzy context, we are sure that any solution which is not efficient is dominated by a feasible solution which is efficient. Therefore, Fandel and Wilhelm [1976] require explicitly that MOD methods should only generate efficient solutions. We will follow this requirement (6), although one should realize that in practice many inefficient decisions seem to be made (cf. Leibenstein [1976]).

Efficiency is defined in the above context as follows:
$\underline{x} \in K$ is an _efficient solution_ if there does not exist another feasible solution $\underline{x}^o \in K$ such that:

$$
\begin{cases}
\omega_j(\underline{x}^o) \geq \omega_j(\underline{x}) & j = 1,\ldots.J \\
\text{and} \\
\omega_j(\underline{x}^o) \neq \omega_j(\underline{x}) & \text{for at least one } j
\end{cases}
\qquad (6.7)
$$

For certain purposes (cf. Theorem 2) it is easy to introduce another efficiency concept, i.e. proper efficiency, which is slightly more restrictive:(7)
$\underline{x} \in K$ is a _properly efficient solution_ if
a. $\underline{x}$ is efficient and
b. a scalar $M > 0$ exists, such that for each j an l exists with

$$
\frac{\omega_j(\underline{x}^o) - \omega_j(\underline{x})}{\omega_l(\underline{x}) - \omega_l(\underline{x}^o)} \leq M
$$

for all $\underline{x}^o \in K$ for which $\omega_j(\underline{x}^o) > \omega_j(\underline{x})$ and $\omega_l(\underline{x}^o) < \omega_l(\underline{x})$.

The problem of identifying efficient solutions has been called the _vector maximum problem_. Early formulations of it can be found in Kuhn and Tucker [1951] and Karlin [1959]. A formal representation of the problem is:

$$
\begin{cases}
\max! \; \underline{\omega}(\underline{x}) \\
\text{s.t. } \underline{x} \in K
\end{cases}
\qquad (6.8)
$$

The general conclusion from the literature on vector maximization is that there are two different approaches to identify (properly) efficient points (cf. Cohon and Marks [1975]); i.e. by means of _weights_ and by means of _side-conditions_.

The foundation of the first method is Theorem 2, proved by Geoffrion [1968].

Theorem 2.
$\underline{x}^p$ is properly efficient with respect to K (convex) and $\underline{\omega}$ (concave) if and only if there exists a vector of weights $\underline{\lambda}(\overline{\lambda} > \underline{0}, \underline{1}' \, \underline{\lambda} = 1)$ so that $\underline{x}^p$ is optimal for the programming problem:

$$\begin{cases} \text{max!} \quad \lambda'\omega(\underline{x}) \\ \text{s.t.} \quad \underline{x} \in K \end{cases} \tag{6.9}$$

This theorem enables the analyst in principle to identify the set of properly efficient solutions by solving (6.9) through varying repeatedly and systematically the values of λ. An example for $J = 3$ of such a parametric programming operation would be to solve (6.9) for the following series of weight vectors: (.8 .1 .1), (.7 .2 .1), (.6 .3 .1),........,(.1 .2 .7), (.1 .1 .8). Although in this way only a small subset of the set of efficient solutions will be generated, this subset may be useful to obtain an impression of the whole set of efficient solutions. Another important implication of Theorem 2 is that once a certain properly efficient solution has been selected, this solution can be interpreted in terms of a certain combination of weights $\underline{\lambda}$.

The second method, which is based on side-conditions, has been elaborated by Haimes et al. [1975]. It is based on the next theorem (cf. Cohon [1978]).

Theorem 3.

Let K be defined as:

$$K = \{\underline{x} \mid g_n(\underline{x}) \le 0 \quad \text{for } n = 1,.....N, \ \underline{x} \ge \underline{0}\}$$

where the functions g_n are convex and continuously differentiable, then $\overset{\circ}{\underline{x}}$ is efficient with respect to K and $\underline{\omega}$ (concave and continuously differentiable) if and only if for a certain j there exists a vector of constraint values $\underline{\omega}$ so that $\overset{\circ}{\underline{x}}$ is optimal for the programming problem:

$$\begin{cases} \text{max!} \quad \omega_j(\underline{x}) \\ \text{s.t.} \quad \underline{x} \in K \\ \underline{\omega} \ge \underline{\tilde{\omega}} \end{cases} \tag{6.10}$$

Thus, by varying the side-conditions it is in principle possible to identify all efficient solutions by means of (6.10). An advantage(8) of (6.10) with respect to (6.9) is that one is also able to capture certain problems with non-convex sets K by means of (6.10) (cf. Haimes et al. [1975]).

Theorem 3 has not been formulated in terms of weights such as Theorem 2, but it is possible to interpret it in this way, given the values of the shadow-prices of the side-conditions $\underline{\omega} \ge \underline{\tilde{\omega}}$. Cohon and Marks [1973], Haimes and Hall [1974] and Miller and Byers [1973] utilized this possiblity in their studies of water resource systems. Haimes and Hall [1974] also attempted to estimate trade-off functions describing the relationship between the constraint values $\tilde{\omega}_{j}$, (for a certain j') and the values of the corresponding dual variable.

The two methods to generate efficient solutions may become

problematic if the number of objectives J is larger than say three or four. First, the computational efforts may become very (computer) time-consuming. Second, even if it appears to be possible to calculate a representative subset of efficient points, it is doubtful whether this procedure is useful for the DM because of his limited information digesting capacity. In some cases, linear MOD problems may be exceptions to these above rules. These will be discussed in Section 6.7. The next section will be devoted to a special subset of efficient solutions, namely compromise solutions.

6.4   Compromise Solutions

The preceding discussion about the generation of efficient points reveals an interesting problem concerning the amount of information to be produced by the analyst.
a. It should be enough so that it presents a good overview of the choice possibilities, but
b. not too much so that the situation is avoided where the DM "cannot see the woods for the trees".

As the methods discussed before imply, in general, a large number of alternatives to be generated, it is worthwhile to consider the possibility of calculating some efficient solutions with special characteristics. An example of such a type of solution may be a so-called compromise solution.

There are various ways to operationalize the idea of a compromise solution. At least three conditions can be formulated which should be satisfied by compromise solutions.
1. a compromise solution should be based on the notion that all J objectives are judged to be equally important;
2. a compromise solution is efficient;
3. extreme solutions such as the elements of P should not, as a compromise solution, receive more consideration than other intermediate solutions.

At first glance, the following solutions seem to be reasonable candidates to merit the adjective "compromise":
a. Find the solution $\underline{x}^a$ which dominates the greatest number of feasible solutions; i.e. solve:

$$\begin{cases} \text{max!} \quad \prod_{j=1}^{J} \{\omega_j(\underline{x}) - \bar{\omega}_j\} \\ \\ \text{s.t.} \quad \underline{x} \in K \end{cases} \qquad (6.11)$$

b. Find the solution $\underline{x}^b$ which is dominated by the smallest number of alternatives in the hyper-cube defined by the opposite corner-points $\overset{*}{\underline{\omega}}$ and $\bar{\underline{\omega}}$; i.e. solve:

$$\begin{cases} \text{min!} \quad \prod_{j=1}^{J} \{\overset{*}{\omega}_j - \omega_j(\underline{x})\} \\ \\ \text{s.t.} \quad \underline{x} \in K \end{cases} \qquad (6.12)$$

c. Find the solution $\underline{x}^c$ which has a minimum distance with respect to the ideal solution $\underline{\omega}^*$. This idea requires normalization
(see (6.4)) of the objective functions and an appropriate
choice of a distance metric. A frequently used distance metric
is the Minkovsky metric:

$$d = \sum_{j=1}^{J} (\omega_j^* - \bar{\omega}_j)^p \qquad\qquad p \geq 1 \tag{6.13}$$

which can be interpreted as a measure of distance (cf. Beckenbach and Bellman [1961]; see also Van Delft and Nijkamp [1977].
For example, if $p = 1$ and $p = 2$, the following successive pro-
gramming problems with solutions $\underline{x}^{c1}$ and $\underline{x}^{c2}$ are obtained:

$$\begin{cases} \min! \quad \underline{\imath}'(\underline{\omega}^* - \bar{\omega})^{-1} \{\underline{\omega}^* - \underline{\omega}(\underline{x})\} \\[2mm] s.t. \quad \underline{x} \in K \end{cases} \tag{6.14}$$

and

$$\begin{cases} \min! \quad \{\underline{\omega}^* - \underline{\omega}(\underline{x})\}' \{\underline{\omega}^* - \bar{\omega}\}^{-2} \{\underline{\omega}^* - \underline{\omega}(\underline{x})\} \\[2mm] s.t. \quad \underline{x} \in K \end{cases} \tag{6.15}$$

For $p \to \infty$ only the objective function with the dimension show-
ing the largest difference appears to be important. Then the
corresponding programming problem is:

$$\begin{cases} \min! \quad \max_j \left(\dfrac{\omega_j^* - \omega_j(\underline{x})}{\omega_j^* - \bar{\omega}_j} \right) \\[4mm] s.t. \quad \underline{x} \in K \end{cases} \tag{6.16}$$

The solution of (6.16) is denoted by $\underline{x}^{c3}$.

d. Find the solution $\underline{x}^d$ which is as far as possible from the
minimum solution $\bar{\omega}$:

$$\begin{cases} \max! \quad \sqrt[p]{\sum_j \left(\dfrac{\omega_j(\underline{x}) - \bar{\omega}_j}{\omega_j^* - \bar{\omega}_j} \right)^p} \qquad p \geq 1 \\[4mm] s.t. \quad \underline{x} \in K \end{cases} \tag{6.17}$$

e. Find the solution $\underline{x}^e$ which is optimal with respect to a set
of weights refecting a compromise in some way. There are various ways to attain such a compromise vector. If, for example,
all objectives are given the same weight, the programming problem (taking into account the different scales of measurement)
will be:

$$\begin{cases} \text{max!} \quad \{\frac{1}{J} \, \underline{1}'(\overset{*}{\omega} - \overset{\wedge}{\overline{\omega}})^{-1}\} \, \underline{\omega}(\underline{x}) \\ \text{s.t.} \quad \underline{x} \in K \end{cases} \qquad (6.18)$$

The solution and corresponding weights of (6.18) are denoted by $\underline{x}^{e}1$ and $\underline{\lambda}_1$. Another way to find a compromise vector is to derive the weights according to which all extreme solutions of the P matrix are valued equally (cf. Fandel [1972], Nijkamp and Rietveld [1976 a,b] and Nijkamp [1977]):

$$\begin{cases} P' \, \underline{\lambda}_2 = c\underline{1} \\ \underline{1}' \, \underline{\lambda}_2 = 1 \end{cases} \qquad (6.19)$$

$\underline{\lambda}_2$ can clearly be conceived of as a combination of compromise weights, as (6.19) expresses no special interest for any of the J extreme solutions. The solution of (6.19) is:

$$\begin{cases} \underline{\lambda}_2 = \dfrac{(P')^{-1}\underline{1}}{\underline{1}'(P')^{-1}\underline{1}} \\ \\ c = \dfrac{1}{\underline{1}'(P')^{-1}\underline{1}} \end{cases} \qquad (6.20)$$

provided P is non-singular. In this case, the programming problem is to find the solution $\underline{x}^{e}2$ of:

$$\begin{cases} \text{max!} \quad \dfrac{(P')^{-1}\underline{1}}{\underline{1}'(P')^{-1}\underline{1}} \, \underline{\omega}(\underline{x}) \\ \\ \text{s.t.} \quad \underline{x} \in K \end{cases} \qquad (6.21)$$

As will be shown in Appendix I, it is a disadvantage of $\underline{\lambda}_2$ that in certain cases it may have negative elements. In this appendix another compromise weight vector $\underline{\lambda}_3$ is also discussed which is based on a game theoretic interpretation of the pay-off matrix P and which can be shown to have non-negative elements.

There is still another way to derive compromise weights, as is shown by Theil [1964]. First P is transformed into a loss matrix Q with elements $q_{jj'} = \overset{*}{\omega}_j - p_{jj'}$, which denote the loss for objective j with respect to the highest attainable level when objective j' is maximized. Obviously $q_{jj'} \geq 0$ and $q_{jj} = 0$. Theil proposes to compute compromise weights λ in such a way that the matrix $\overset{\wedge}{\lambda}Q$ is (approximately) symmetric, where $\overset{\wedge}{\lambda}$ is the diagonal matrix with $\underline{\lambda}$ as main diagonal. This symmetry condition $\lambda_j q_{jj'} = \lambda_{j'} q_{j'j}$ means that the weighted loss for object-

ive j caused by the maximization of objective j' is equal to
the weighted loss for objective j' when objective j is maximized. Since the number of symmetry conditions $(\frac{1}{2}J(J - 1))$ is
larger than the number of unknowns $(J - 1)$, exact symmetry cannot in general be reached. Theil shows that making the corresponding row and column sums of λQ pairwise equal:

$$\sum_j \lambda_j q_{jj'} = \sum_j \lambda_{j'} q_{j'j} \qquad \text{for } j' = 1,....J,$$

yields values for the λ_j's which approximate symmetry. This
outcome for $\underline{\lambda}$, which will be denoted by $\underline{\lambda}_4$, has the attractive
property that it is positive and proof against scale transfor-
mations in the objectives.

f. Find the solution $\underline{x}^f$ such that the side-conditions imposed
on $\underline{\omega}$ are as high as possible. Hence solve the problem:

$$\begin{cases} \min! \quad \delta \\ \text{s.t.} \quad \underline{\omega}(\underline{x}) \geq \delta \, \bar{\underline{\omega}} + (1 - \delta) \, \overset{*}{\underline{\omega}} \\ \quad \underline{x} \in K \end{cases} \qquad (6.22)$$

Figure 6.1 illustrates the various compromise measures in the
case of two dimensions (ignoring the scaling problem). To
avoid confusion, the compromises have been depicted in two
identical figures. The outcomes for the objectives, resulting
from $(\underline{x}^a,....\underline{x}^f)$ have been called $(\underline{\omega}^a,....\underline{\omega}^f)$, respectively.

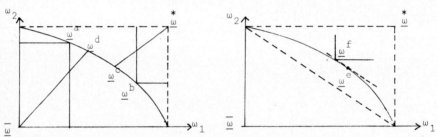

Figure 6.1   Compromise concepts in a two-dimensional
              decision problem.

   Note that the six types of compromise concepts have been developed systematically. For example, $\underline{x}^b$ is a natural continua-
tion of $\underline{x}^a$, the only difference being that the point of refer-
ence is no longer $\bar{\underline{\omega}}$, but $\overset{*}{\underline{\omega}}$: The same holds true for $\underline{x}^c$ and $\underline{x}^d$.
The pair $\underline{x}^e$ and $\underline{x}^f$ reflect the two basic ways to generate effi-
cient points, dealt with in Section 6.3.

   Do these six suggested concepts for compromise solutions satisfy the criteria formulated for this type of solutions? As
to the first criterion, it is clear that the six variants imply
impartiality among objectives. The efficiency criterion, however, causes some trouble. The efficiency is not guaranteed
for all concepts proposed, although for most of them no problems

arise. For $\underline{x}^{c1}$ the efficiency property will be proved in a formal way.

Theorem 4

The solution $\underline{x}^{c1}$ of (6.14) is an efficient solution of (6.8).

Proof

Consider the case that $\underline{x}^{c1}$ is not an efficient solution. Then, there exists another vector $\underline{\tilde{x}} \in K$, satisfying:

$$\begin{cases} \omega_j(\underline{\tilde{x}}) \geq \omega_j(\underline{x}^{c1}) & \text{for all } j \\[2mm] \omega_j(\underline{\tilde{x}}) > \omega_j(\underline{x}^{c1}) & \text{for at least one } j \end{cases} \qquad (6.23)$$

Condition (6.23) implies that:

$$\begin{cases} \omega_j(\underline{\tilde{x}}) - \bar{\omega}_j \geq \omega_j(\underline{x}^{c1}) - \bar{\omega}_j \geq 0 & \text{for all } j \qquad (6.24) \\[2mm] \omega_j(\underline{\tilde{x}}) - \bar{\omega}_j > \omega_j(\underline{x}^{c1}) - \bar{\omega}_j \geq 0 & \text{for at least one } j \end{cases}$$

The latter expression gives rise to the following result:

$$\sum_j \frac{\omega_j(\underline{\tilde{x}}) - \bar{\omega}_j}{\omega_j^* - \bar{\omega}_j} > \sum_j \frac{\omega_j(\underline{x}^{c1}) - \bar{\omega}_j}{\omega_j^* - \bar{\omega}_j} \qquad (6.25)$$

From (6.25) we may draw the conclusion that $\underline{x}^{c1}$ cannot be the optimal solution of (6.14), because there exists another $\underline{x} \in K$ with a better performance. Hence we proved by contradiction that $\underline{x}^{c1}$ is efficient. Q.E.D.

In a similar way, it can be proved that the other compromise concepts $\underline{x}^a$, .. $\underline{x}^d$ are also efficient (see for example Huang [1972]). However, for $p \to 0$, $\underline{x}^c$ and $\underline{x}^d$ produce a minor difficulty. It can be proved that if (6.16) or (6.17) have only one optimal solution, it is an efficient one. When they have multiple optima, it can be proved that one of them is efficient. For a more detailed discussion of the above, see Appendix II. In this appendix, one also finds a proof that a reformulation of (6.16) in a lexicographic way is sufficient to satisfy the efficiency criterion. This concept is denoted by $\underline{x}^{c4}$.

The compromise concept $\underline{x}^{e2}$ is neither completely immune to inefficiency. As detailed in Appendix I, if the number of objectives $J \geq 3$, the compromise weight vector λ_2 may contain negative elements. Theorem 2, however, only deals with the relationship between non-negative weight vectors and efficient solutions. There is no guarantee that a weight vector with a negative element will yield an efficient solution. The weight vector λ_3 derived from the game theoretic approach in Appendix I and the vectors λ_1 and λ_4 should be preferred to λ_2, because they contain only non-negative elements. The last compromise concept $\underline{x}^f$ has the same problems with efficiency as $\underline{x}^{c3}$.

It can be proved that $\underline{x}^f$ and $\underline{x}^{c3}$ are identical. This will be
discussed later in this section.

The last condition which should be tested before $\underline{x}^a, \ldots \underline{x}^f$
can be called compromise solutions is the non-extremity require-
ment. The compromise principles should produce solutions which
are in some respect central in the set of efficient solutions.
A tendency to select solutions strongly favourable for only one
objective is, in general, less permissible. This condition is
violated by $\underline{x}^b$ and some of the $\underline{x}^d$'s. For $\underline{x}^b$ this is evident:
(6.12) attains its minimum zero when $\underline{x}^b$ is equal to one of the
extreme instrumental vectors $\bar{\underline{x}}._.$, underlying the pay-off matrix
P. That $\underline{x}^d$ is a suspicious candidate is most obvious for $\underline{x}^{d3}$,
because (6.17) attains its maximum value 1 for $p \to \infty$, when $\underline{x}^{d3}$
is equal to one of the $\overset{*}{\underline{x}}._.$. The same tendency can be perceived
for $\underline{x}^{d2}$ and $\underline{x}^{d4}$. Only $\overline{\underline{x}}^{d1}$ does not show this pattern because
of the linear structure of the utility function.

Table 6.2 contains a summary of the evaluation of the six
types of compromise concepts.

concept condition	a b c_1 c_2 c_3 c_4 d_i d_2 d_3 d_4 e_1 e_2 e_3 e_4 f
impartiality	
efficiency	$\quad\quad\quad\quad\quad\quad$ x $\quad\quad\quad$ x $\quad\quad\quad$ x $\quad\quad\quad\quad$ x
non-extremity	x$^{(1)}$ $\quad\quad\quad\quad\quad\quad\quad\quad$ x x x

(1) x means violation

Table 6.2   Fourteen compromise concepts evaluated by
            means of three conditions.

The six compromise principles, giving rise to 15 variants which
are at first glance reasonable candidates for compromise solutions, ultimately produce eight variants which do simultaneously satisfy the three conditions. This number becomes even
smaller when we realize that not all variants are different.
The same variant may be based on different principles.

A quick look teaches immediately that $\underline{x}^{c1} = \underline{x}^{d1} = \underline{x}^{e1}$. It can
also be shown that $\underline{x}^{c3} = \underline{x}^f$. The proof of the latter statement
reads as follows:

if

$$\underline{\omega}(\underline{x}) \geq \delta\bar{\underline{\omega}} + (1 - \delta)\overset{*}{\underline{\omega}} \tag{6.26}$$

then

$$\overset{*}{\underline{\omega}} - \underline{\omega}(\underline{x}) \leq \delta(\overset{*}{\underline{\omega}} - \bar{\underline{\omega}}) \tag{6.27}$$

so that

$$\delta \geq \frac{\overset{*}{\omega_j} - \omega_j(\underline{x})}{\overset{*}{\omega_j} - \bar{\omega}_j} \qquad \text{for } j = 1, \ldots J \tag{6.28}$$

The equivalence of (6.26) - (6.28) implies that (6.14) and
(6.22) are identical, hence $\underline{x}^c 3 = \underline{x}^f$. In Appendix II, it is
shown that under certain conditions $\underline{x}^{e}2 = \underline{x}^{e}3$. It is especial-
ly interesting that when $J = 2$, we find $\underline{x}^{e}1 = \underline{x}^{e}2 = \underline{x}^{e}3 = \underline{x}^{e}4$
because then $\underline{\lambda}_1 = \underline{\lambda}_2 = \underline{\lambda}_3 = \underline{\lambda}_4$ (9).

The result of the preceding discussion is that six different
compromise solutions have been developed which satisfy the necessary conditions. Some additional desiderata can be used for
a further evaluation of these compromise solutions ($\underline{x}^a$, $\underline{x}^c1$,
$\underline{x}^{c}2$, $\underline{x}^{c}4$, $\underline{x}^{e}3$, $\underline{x}^{e}4$):

1. Does it entail a scaling procedure of the data?
2. How much information does it require?
3. Can it be calculated easily?

As to the first desideratum, $\underline{x}^a$, $\underline{x}^{e}3$ and $\underline{x}^{e}4$ have the advantage that no scaling procedure is needed (a scaling procedure
would imply a certain arbitrariness; cf. Miller and Starr
[1960]). The solutions $\underline{x}^{e}3$ and $\underline{x}^{e}4$ have the additional advantage that the decision criterion has been based on more infor-
mation than on ω and $\overset{*}{\omega}$ only. The third desideratum concerning
computational feasibility is favourable for $\underline{x}^c1$, $\underline{x}^{e}3$ and $\underline{x}^{e}4$
because these concepts are based on linear criteria, which has
computational advantages. We conclude that the compromise concepts e_3 and e_4 are attractive according to all desiderata. ·

Of course, this list of compromise solutions can be extended.
For example, a straightforward expansion is the inclusion of
variants in which a distance metric is used with values for p,
which are unequal to 1 or 2. One can also devise mixtures of
the six solutions developed here. These additional variants do
not contain new ideas and we will therefore concentrate on the
six compromise concepts developed above.

The concept of a compromise solution proves to be very useful in MOD models. It contains fruitful information for a DM
who has only vague notions about his priorities. It plays a
crucial role in many interactive decision methods to be discussed later. Finally, it gives rise to a number of indicators
for the measure of conflict among the various objectives. The
next section is devoted to this elaboration of the conflict concept.

6.5   Measures of Conflict.

In Section 6.2, we mentioned the possibility of constructing
operational measures for the conflict in a decision problem.
γ_1, as defined in (6.3), is an example of it. However, there
are several additional ways to operationalize the notion of
conflict. It is interesting that each of the compromise concepts developed suggests a certain measure of conflict.

Consider, for example, the compromise solution $\underline{x}^a$. It is
reasonable to say that the more feasible solutions are dominated by $\underline{x}^a$ the less difficult it is to make a choice and the

less conflict there is among the objectives. This means for Figure 6.2(a)

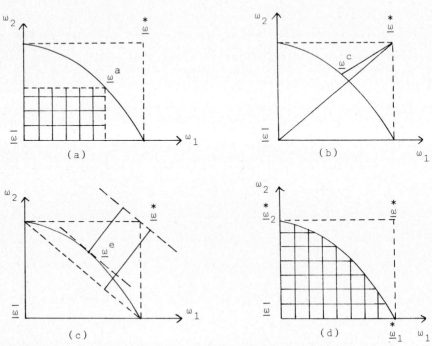

Figure 6.2   Illustration of four conflict measures.

that the bigger the proportion of the sizes of the rectangles with cornerpoints $(\underline{\omega}^a, \overline{\omega})$ and $(\overset{*}{\underline{\omega}}, \overline{\omega})$, the smaller the conflict between ω_1 and ω_2. The formalization of this idea gives rise to the following measure γ_2, obeying $0 \leq \gamma_2 \leq 1$:

$$\gamma_2 = \left[1 - \frac{\prod\limits_j (\omega_j(\underline{x}^a) - \overline{\omega}_j)}{\prod\limits_j (\overset{*}{\omega}_j - \overline{\omega}_j)} \right] \cdot \left(\frac{1}{1 - (\frac{1}{J})^J} \right) \qquad (6.29)$$

Note that the factors $\prod\limits_j (\omega_j(\underline{x}^a) - \overline{\omega}_j)$ and $\prod\limits_j (\overset{*}{\omega}_j - \overline{\omega}_j)$ represent the volumes of the hyper-cubes generated by the pairs of vectors $\{\underline{\omega}(\underline{x}^a), \overline{\omega}\}$ and $\{\overset{*}{\underline{\omega}}, \overline{\omega}\}$, respectively. When the compromise $\underline{\omega}^a$ is equal to $\overset{*}{\underline{\omega}}$ according to (6.29) a minimum of conflict arises, viz. $\gamma_2 = 0$. The conflict attains its maximum value 1 when $\underline{\omega}^a = \frac{1}{J} \overset{*}{\underline{\omega}} + \frac{J-1}{J} \overline{\underline{\omega}}$.

The conflict measures, connected with $\underline{x}^c$ and $\underline{x}^e$ can also be graphically illustrated for J = 2. Figure 6.2(b) indicates that a minimum of conflict is attained when the ratio of the distances between $(\overset{*}{\underline{\omega}}, \underline{\omega}^c)$ and $(\overset{*}{\underline{\omega}}, \overline{\underline{\omega}})$ is at its minimum. Figure 6.2(c) suggests comparing the difference between the values of the utility function in $\overset{*}{\underline{\omega}}$ and $\underline{\omega}^e$ with the difference between these values in $\overset{*}{\underline{\omega}}$ and $\underline{\omega}(\overset{*}{\underline{x}}_j)$. After normalization (in order to guarantee that $0 \le \gamma \le 1$), the entailing measures are:

$$\gamma_3 = \sqrt[p]{\sum_j \left(\frac{\overset{*}{\omega}_j - \omega_j(\underline{x}^c)}{\overset{*}{\omega}_j - \overline{\omega}_j} \right)^p} \bigg/ J(\frac{J-1}{J})^p \qquad p \ge 1 \qquad (6.30)$$

$$\gamma_3 = \max_j \frac{\overset{*}{\omega}_j - \omega_j(\underline{x}^c)}{\overset{*}{\omega}_j - \overline{\omega}_j} \bigg/ \frac{J-1}{J} \qquad p \to \infty . \qquad (6.31)$$

$$\gamma_4 = \frac{\underline{\lambda}'[\overset{*}{\underline{\omega}} - \underline{\omega}(\underline{x}^e)]}{\max_j \underline{\lambda}'[\overset{*}{\underline{\omega}} - \underline{\omega}(\overset{*}{\underline{x}}_j)]} \qquad (6.32)$$

It is interesting to note that for J = 2, $\gamma_4 = \gamma_3(p = 1)$ (10).

Each measure provides some information on a compromise solution with regard to the ideal solution. One might wonder if it is possible to define additional measures which do not consider one $(\gamma_2, \gamma_3, \gamma_4)$ or some (γ_1) efficient points but all efficient points. Such a measure might be the analogue of the Gini coefficient as a measure of inequality in the field of income distributions (11). If J = 2, this measure indicates the fraction of the triangle $\overset{*}{\underline{\omega}}_1, \overset{*}{\underline{\omega}}_2, \overset{*}{\underline{\omega}}$ which is not feasible (cf. Figure 6.2(d)). Hence, if a functional expression for the possibility frontier $(\omega_2 = f(\omega_1))$ could be found, this measure of conflict could be formalized as:

$$\gamma_5 = 2 \left[1 - \int_{\omega_1}^{\overset{*}{\omega}_1} f(\omega_1) \, d\omega_1 \cdot \frac{1}{(\overset{*}{\omega}_1 - \overline{\omega}_1)(\overset{*}{\omega}_2 - \overline{\omega}_2)} \right] \qquad (6.33)$$

When K is convex, it can be shown (12) that $\gamma_5 \le \gamma_2$.

It is worthwhile to note that these measures can be used to describe the conflict among all J objectives as well as among various subsets of objectives. Thus it is possible to identify the most crucial conflict elements of the decision problem.

6.6   Half-Compromise Solutions

This chapter is devoted to the problem of how to produce relevant information for DMs concerning alternatives in intricate
decision problems. Thus far we have discussed:

- the extreme alternatives $\underline{x}_1^*, \ldots \underline{x}_J^*$ underlying P (Section 6.2);

- the compromise alternatives $\underline{x}^a$, $\underline{x}^c$, $\underline{x}^e$ (Section 6.4);

- the conflict measures $\gamma_1, \ldots \gamma_5$ (Section 6.5).

Hence, Sections 6.2 and 6.4 give rise to J + 1 solutions to be
presented to the DM. It is questionable, however, whether this
set will enable the DM to come to an understanding of the trade-
offs involved in the problems. Therefore, it is worthwhile to
consider the question of whether more efficient solutions can
be generated without confusing the DM with too much information.

A parametric approach, based on Theorem 2 or 3, does not
meet the last requirement. One runs the risk that too many alternatives are generated. When for example in (6.10) each
side-condition can attain K values, J^K alternatives will be generated. This number is large even for small values of J and K.
When for example J = K = 4, 256 alternatives will be calculated.

Another way to find a small number of additional alternatives containing relevant information is to concentrate on solutions which are (in some sense) half-way a compromise solution and an extreme solution. Is it possible to operationalize
this notion of a half-compromise? We will find that each of
the compromise concepts elaborated in Section 6.4 also suggests
a half-compromise concept. In each case, a half-compromise is
a compromise between the original compromise solution
($\underline{x}^a$, $\underline{x}^c$, or $\underline{x}^e$) and an extreme solution $\underline{x}_j^*$. Thus, J half-compromises $\underline{y}_j$ (j = 1, ...J) can be constructed. Consider the com-
promise concept $\underline{x}^a$. It is the solution of

$$\begin{cases} \max! & \prod_j \{\omega_j(\underline{x}) - \overline{\omega}_j\}^{q_j} \\ \text{s.t.} & \underline{x} \in K \end{cases} \qquad (6.34)$$

where the series of powers $\underline{q}$ is equal to:

$$\underline{q} = (q_1, \ldots q_J)' = \underline{\iota} \qquad (6.35)$$

We may conclude, therefore, that (6.11) is based on equal
powers for all factors $(\omega_j(\underline{x}) - \overline{\omega}_j)$. The extreme solutions $\underline{x}_j^*$
(j = 1,...J) can be found by means of (6.34) when

$$\underline{q} = J \cdot \underline{\varepsilon}_j \qquad (6.36)$$

Therefore, a reasonable way to calculate a half-compromise $\underline{y}_j^a$

by means of (6.34) is to base it on a series of power vectors $\underline{q}_j$ so that:

$$\underline{q}_j = \frac{1}{2}\underline{1} + \frac{1}{2}(J.\underline{\epsilon}_j) \tag{6.37}$$

For $\underline{x}^c$ and $\underline{x}^e$ similar results can be obtained. The compromise $\underline{x}^c$ is the solution of:

$$\begin{cases} \min! & \sqrt[p]{\sum_j q_j \left(\dfrac{\overset{*}{\omega}_j - \omega_j(\underline{x})}{\overset{*}{\omega}_j - \bar{\omega}_j}\right)^p} \\ \text{s.t.} & \underline{x} \in K \end{cases} \tag{6.38}$$

with

$$\underline{q} = \underline{1} \tag{6.39}$$

Along the same lines of reasoning as above, a half-compromise $\underline{y}_j^c$ can be obtained by means of (6.38), when $\underline{q}_j$ is set equal to:

$$\underline{q}_j = \frac{1}{2}\underline{1} + \frac{1}{2}(J.\underline{\epsilon}_j) \tag{6.40}$$

Thus, for both $\underline{x}^{c1}$ and $\underline{x}^{c2}$ corresponding half-compromises can be obtained (13).

The compromise concept $\underline{x}^e$ is interesting, because it even suggests two different half-compromises. It is the solution of:

$$\begin{cases} \max! & \underline{q}'\underline{\omega}(\underline{x}) \\ \text{s.t.} & \underline{x} \in K \end{cases} \tag{6.41}$$

where:

$$\underline{q} = \lambda \tag{6.42}$$

A half-compromise $\underline{y}_j$ can be obtained after substitution into (6.41) of:

$$\underline{q}_j = \frac{1}{2}\underline{\lambda} + \frac{1}{2}\underline{\epsilon}_j \tag{6.43}$$

An alternative way to construct a half-compromise set of weights is to base $\underline{q}_j$ on the "half-compromise pay-off matrix" P_j, defined as:

$$P_j = \{\underline{\omega}(\overset{*}{\underline{x}}_1),\ldots,\underline{\omega}(\overset{*}{\underline{x}}_{j-1}), \underline{\omega}(\underline{x}^{e3}), \underline{\omega}(\overset{*}{\underline{x}}_{j+1}),\ldots,\underline{\omega}(\overset{*}{\underline{x}}_J)\} \tag{6.44}$$

Along the lines described in Appendix I, it is possible to find the pertaining weights (cf. Belenson and Kapur [1973]). There is no guarantee that the two half-compromises based on $\underline{x}^e$ are equal to each other. A similar result is that the equality of $\underline{x}^{c1}$ and $\underline{x}^{e3}$ for J = 2 does not have its counterpart for $\underline{y}_j^{c1}$ and $\underline{y}_j^{e3}$, as implied by (6.43) (14).

The result of this section is that next to the J + 1 alternatives already defined, another set consisting of J alternatives has been developed, which may contain vital information. Thus a set of 2J + 1 alternatives (15) is found which can be expected to present a good survey of the decision problem.

There is still another context in which the half-compromise solutions can be useful. It appears that half-compromises play an important role in the two interactive decision algorithms, discussed in Sections 9.8 and 9.9. These algorithms can deal with the derivation of a range of satisfactory alternatives and with multi-person decision making, respectively. In these algorithms a more flexible definition of a half-compromise is used, which is based on a generalization of (6.37), (6.40) and (6.43):

$$\underline{q}_j^h = \frac{1}{1 + h} \underline{\lambda} + \frac{h}{1 + h} \ {}^J\underline{\varepsilon}_j \qquad (h \geq 0) \qquad \left\{ \begin{array}{c} (6.37') \\ (6.40') \end{array} \right.$$

$$\underline{q}_j^h = \frac{1}{1 + h} \underline{\lambda} + \frac{h}{1 + h} \underline{\varepsilon}_j \qquad (h \geq 0) \qquad (6.43')$$

When h = 1, the new expressions are identical to the original ones. When h is small, the half-compromise $\underline{y}_j^h$ will tend to the compromise solution; when h is large, $\underline{y}_j^h$ will tend to the corresponding extreme solution. The values of the objectives corresponding to the solution $\underline{y}_j^h$ will be denoted by $\overset{o}{\underline{\omega}}{}_j^h$. As will appear in Sections 9.8 and 9.9, the flexibility of the half-compromises implied by (6.37'), (6.40') and (6.43') is crucial for the convergence of the interactive decision procedures dealt with in these sections.

6.7   Linear Multiple-Objective Decision Problems

Thus far the only assumptions about K and $\underline{\omega}$ have been that the former is convex and the latter concave. If linearity can be assumed, some especially useful results can be attained. Therefore, we pose:

$$\left\{ \begin{array}{l} K = \{\underline{x} \mid A\underline{x} \leq \underline{b}, \ \underline{x} \geq \underline{0}\} \\ \\ \underline{\omega}(\underline{x}) = C\underline{x} \end{array} \right. \qquad\qquad (6.45)$$

Where A is an N x I matrix, $\underline{b}$ an N vector and C a J x I matrix.

The set K defined in (6.45) is a convex polyhedral set. A convex polyhedron can be described by means of a finite number of points $\underline{x}^{+r}$ and directions $\underline{v}^s$ (cf. Rockafellar [1970])(16):

$$K = \{\underline{x} \mid \underline{x} = \Sigma_r \eta_r \underline{x}^{+r} + \Sigma_s \xi_s \underline{v}^s, \; \eta_r \geq 0 \;,\; \xi_s \geq 0 \;,\; \Sigma_r \eta_r = 1\}$$

This property that K is "finitely generated" is useful when one tries to generate the set of efficient solutions since it enables one to describe this set by means of a limited number of points and directions. Hence, considerable efforts have been made to develop algorithms for the determination of the points $\underline{x}^{+r}$ (and the directions $\underline{v}^s$).

Before paying some attention to these algorithms, it is useful to introduce some geometric concepts. A supporting hyperplane H of K can be defined as follows: let $\overset{o}{\underline{x}} \in K$ and let there be a hyperplane $H = \{\underline{x} \mid \underline{a}'\underline{x} = c\}$ such that $\overset{o}{\underline{x}} \in H$ and $\underline{a}'\underline{x} \leq c$ for all $\underline{x} \in K$. Then H is a <u>supporting hyperplane</u> of K. A face of K is defined as the intersection of a supporting hyperplane of K and K. A face may be of all dimensions, varying from 0 to I - 1, where I is the dimension of K. Special names have been reserved for faces of certain dimensions. When the dimension equals zero, a face is called a <u>vertex</u>; when it is equal to one, a face is called an <u>edge</u>; when it equals I - 1, a face is called a <u>facet</u>. In Fig. 6.3 for example, $\underline{x}_1, \ldots \underline{x}_4$ are vertices; the lines $(\underline{x}_1, \underline{x}_2)$, $(\underline{x}_2, \underline{x}_3)$, $(\underline{x}_3, \underline{x}_4)$ are edges and facets simultaneously, since I = 2.

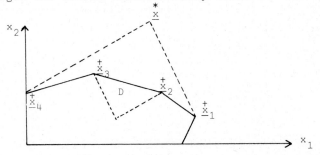

Figure 6.3   The set of feasible solutions as a convex polyhedron.

We turn now to the multiple objective linear programming (MOLP) algorithms which have been developed to find the efficient points of K. In general, two phases can be distinguished in the algorithms. In the first phase the set of efficient vertices of K is determined (see for example Philip [1972], Evans and Steuer [1973] and Zeleny [1974]). Starting with an initial efficient vertex, the adjacent vertices can be generated by means of a multi-objective simplex tableau. Several non-dominance tests have to be applied to decide which of the new vertices are efficient. When the procedure is repeated for the new efficient vertices, finally the whole set of efficient

vertices can be determined. In the second phase the whole set
of efficient solutions is determined by generating the efficient faces of various dimensions $(1,\ldots, I - 1)$. (see for example Gal [1976] and Winkels [1979b]. A drawback of all methods is that computational efforts rise rapidly with the size
of the problem. Therefore, Steuer [1976] proposes to consider
only a part of the set of efficient solutions, namely only those
solutions which satisfy some a priori restrictions on the weights
of a linear utility function.

Fig. 6.3 suggests two important characteristics of MOLP problems:

1. There are many combinations of weights $\underline{\lambda}$ leading to one
   efficient vertex $\underline{x}_1^+$;

2. There is one combination of weights $\underline{\lambda}$ yielding equal utility
   for all points on a facet

The first statement implies that the solution of an LP problem is relatively insensitive to small changes in the weights
$\underline{\lambda}$. This may facilitate the DM's task when he has to express
his priorities. Even when he is not completely certain about
the weights to be attached to the objectives, it may be that in
all cases the same solution results. Ordinary primal-dual relationships suffice in determining the range of insensitivity
to changes in $\underline{\lambda}$, as can be seen by the proof of the following
theorem.

Theorem 5.

The set of weights $\Lambda(\underline{x}_1^+)$ leading to an efficient corner-solution is a convex polyhedron.

Proof.   Consider the LP problem:

$$\begin{cases} \text{max!} & \underline{\lambda}'C\underline{x} \\ \text{s.t.} & A\underline{x} \leq \underline{b} \\ & \underline{x} \geq \underline{0} \end{cases} \qquad (6.46)$$

The dual of this LP problem reads:

$$\begin{cases} \text{min!} & \underline{b}'\underline{y} \\ \text{s.t.} & A'\underline{y} \geq C'\underline{\lambda} \\ & \underline{y} \geq \underline{0} \end{cases} \qquad (6.47)$$

The duality theorem of linear programming (cf. Zionts [1974])
says that $\underline{x}_1^+$ is the optimal solution of (6.46) if and only if
(6.47) has a feasible solution $\underline{\overset{\circ}{y}}$ such that

$$\underline{\lambda}'C\underline{x}_1^+ = \underline{b}'\underline{y}^\circ \qquad (6.48)$$

From (6.48) we may conclude that different values of $\underline{\lambda}$ give rise to different values of the shadow-prices y^o. Moreover, we can see that $\overset{+}{\underline{x}}_1$ is optimal if and only if $\underline{\lambda}$ satisfies

$$\begin{cases} \underline{\lambda}'C\overset{+}{\underline{x}}_1 = \underline{b}'\underline{y}^o \\ A'\underline{y}^o \geq C'\underline{\lambda} \\ \underline{y}^o, \underline{\lambda} \geq \underline{0} \\ \underline{\iota}'\underline{\lambda} = 1 \end{cases} \qquad (6.49)$$

The equalities and inequalities of (6.49) form a convex po-lyhedral set of $\underline{\lambda}$ and $\underline{y}^o$. Hence the set $\Lambda(\underline{x}_1)$ is a convex po-lyhedron.   Q.E.D.

Sengupta et al. [1973], Kornbluth [1974] and Werczberger [1978] have elaborated this subject. Sengupta et al. and Werc-Werczberger introduce the concept of the probability of a cor-nersolution $\overset{+}{\underline{x}}_1$, defined as the ratio of the hypervolume of $\Lambda(\overset{+}{\underline{x}}_1)$ and the hypervolume of $\Lambda(\overset{+}{\underline{x}}_1)\cup....\cup\Lambda(\overset{+}{\underline{x}}_L)$, which will be denoted by $p(\overset{+}{\underline{x}}_1)$. This concept can be conceived of as a mea-sure of sensitivity of the solution of (6.46) for variations in in $\underline{\lambda}$. The larger the probability of a vertex, the smaller its sensitivity to changes of weights (17).

It is important to note a complication in the calculation of $p(\overset{+}{\underline{x}}_1)$, which seems to be overlooked by some of the authors on this subject. It appears that $p(\overset{+}{\underline{x}}_1)$ depends on the scale of measurement of the objectives. Consider for example the follo-wing vector maximum problem:

$$\begin{cases} \text{max!} \quad \omega_1, \omega_2 \\ \text{s.t.} \quad \omega_1 = ax_1 \qquad (a > 0) \\ \qquad \omega_2 = x_2 \\ \qquad x_1 + x_2 \leq 1 \\ \qquad x_1, x_2 \geq 0 \end{cases} \qquad (6.50)$$

The efficient vertices are: $\overset{+}{\underline{x}}_1 = (1,0)'$, $\overset{+}{\underline{x}}_2 = (0,1)'$.
The corresponding sets are:

$$\Lambda(\overset{+}{\underline{x}}_1) = \{\underline{\lambda} \mid \lambda_1 \geq \frac{1}{1 + a}; \lambda_1 + \lambda_2 = 1; \lambda_1, \lambda_2 \geq 0\}$$

and:

$$\Lambda(\overset{+}{\underline{x}}_2) = \{\underline{\lambda} \mid \lambda_1 \leq \frac{1}{1 + a}; \lambda_1 + \lambda_2 = 1; \lambda_1, \lambda_2 \geq 0\}$$

Consequently, we find for the probabilities:

$p(\overset{+}{\underline{x}}_1) = \dfrac{a}{1 + a}$ and $p(\overset{+}{\underline{x}}_2) = \dfrac{1}{1 + a}$. Thus the probabilities depend on the scale of measurement of the objectives. This means
for example that when x_1 denotes the employment measured in the
number of man years, the probability $p(\overset{+}{\underline{x}}_1)$ is sensitive to
changes in a so that when ω_1 is measured in thousands of man
years a larger probability will be found than when ω_1 is measured in units of man years. This sensitivity can be avoided
when the objectives are normalized before the sets $\Lambda(\overset{+}{\underline{x}}_1)$ are
computed. In Section 7.4 more attention will be paid to this
normalization process.

    Charnetski [1976] and Werczberger [1978] have pointed to the
fact that when the number of objectives J is large, it will be
very time-consuming to calculate the hyper-volume of $\Lambda(\overset{+}{\underline{x}}_1)$ in
the traditional way (namely by decomposition of $\Lambda(\overset{+}{\underline{x}}_1)$ into
a series of pyramids). Therefore Charnetski has developed a
numerical method to approximate the hyper-volume of $\Lambda(\overset{+}{\underline{x}}_1)$.

    Let us turn now to the second characteristic of MOLP-pro-
blems suggested above. There is one combination of weights $\underline{\lambda}$
yielding equal utility for all points on a facet. If the overall utility structure is linear, the facets of the problem are
rather uninteresting, because a non-vertex solution to (6.46)
is exceptional. When the overall utility structure is non-
linear, however, the facets deserve more attention, because interior points of facets are candidates for the final solution.
For ease of presentation we will concentrate on the facets in
the space of objectives. Thus let $S = \{\overset{+}{\underline{\omega}}_1 | \overset{+}{\underline{\omega}}_1 = C\overset{+}{\underline{x}}_1, \ l=1,..L\}$
be the set of efficient vertices in the objective space. Then
a facet F_m is the J - 1 dimensional intersection of a suppor-
ting hyperplane defined by $\underline{\lambda}'_m\underline{\omega} = c_m$ and the set of feasible
outcomes. Obviously, all convex combinations of the vertices
of a facet are elements of that facet.
Thus when $(\overset{+}{\underline{\omega}}_{m_1}, \overset{+}{\underline{\omega}}_{m_2}, ...\overset{+}{\underline{\omega}}_{m_k})$ are the extreme points of the facet
F_m, then

$$F_m = \{\underline{\omega} \mid \underline{\omega} = \sum_k \eta_k \overset{+}{\underline{\omega}}_{m_k} ; \sum_k \eta_k = 1, \ \eta_k \geq 0\}$$

    It is tempting to state that when the vertices of a facet
are efficient, all interior points of that facet are efficient.
This statement does not hold true in general, however, as can
be shown by the following example.
Let the vertices be:

$$\overset{+}{\underline{\omega}}_1, \ \overset{+}{\underline{\omega}}_2, \ \overset{+}{\underline{\omega}}_3 \ = \ \begin{pmatrix} 100 \\ 75 \\ 40 \end{pmatrix}, \ \begin{pmatrix} 0 \\ 100 \\ 0 \end{pmatrix}, \ \begin{pmatrix} 0 \\ 0 \\ 100 \end{pmatrix} \tag{6.51}$$

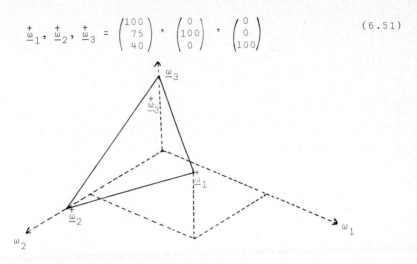

Figure 6.4   A two-dimensional facet.

Figure 6.4 shows the three corner-solutions of the example.
Due to the relatively dominating position of $\overset{+}{\underline{\omega}}_1$, we find that
every interior point of the facet, including the elements on
the edge $(\overset{+}{\underline{\omega}}_2, \ \overset{+}{\underline{\omega}}_3)$ is dominated by a point on one of the edges
$(\overset{+}{\underline{\omega}}_1, \ \overset{+}{\underline{\omega}}_2)$ or $(\overset{+}{\underline{\omega}}_1, \ \overset{+}{\underline{\omega}}_3)$.   For example, the point $(0, 70, 30)$,
on the edge $(\overset{+}{\underline{\omega}}_2, \ \overset{+}{\underline{\omega}}_3)$ is dominated by $\overset{+}{\underline{\omega}}_1 = (100, 75, 40)'$.

The reason for this difficulty is that one element of $\underline{\lambda}_m$ is
non-positive.   The outcome for $\underline{\lambda}_m$ is (cf. Appendix I):

$$\underline{\lambda}_m = (\ - \ \frac{3}{37}, \ \frac{20}{37}, \ \frac{20}{37} \ )' \tag{6.52}$$

From Theorem 2 we learn that when $\underline{\lambda}_m > \underline{0}$ the corresponding optimal solutions are efficient.   Hence, we have to define the
statement rejected above by imposing the additional constraint
that $\underline{\lambda}_m > \underline{0}$.   Thus we find when the vertices of a facet F_m
are efficient and when $\underline{\lambda}_m > \underline{0}$, then all interior points of the
facet are efficient.

There is another aspect of facets that deserves our attention.   It appears that in certain respects there is a striking
similarity between vertices and facets.   Compare the following
statements: the former having been proved earlier in this section and the latter yet to be proved.

1. To each corner-solution $\overset{+}{\underline{x}}_1$ a set of weights $\Lambda(\overset{+}{\underline{x}}_1)$ can be as-

signed. Λ is a convex polyhedron.

2. To each facet F_m, a set of minimum requirements $\Omega(F_m)$ can be assigned. Ω is a convex polyhedron.

The set $\Omega(F_m)$ is defined in the following way:

Definition.

$\Omega(F_m)$ is the set of all minimum requirements $\underline{\omega}_m^{min}$ such that all efficient points satisfying

$$
\begin{cases}
\text{max!} \quad \underline{\omega} = C\underline{x} \\
\text{s.t.} \quad A\underline{x} \leq \underline{b} \\
\qquad \underline{x} \geq \underline{0} \\
\qquad \underline{\omega} \geq \underline{\omega}_m^{min}
\end{cases}
\qquad (6.53)
$$

are elements of the facet F_m. Figure 6.3 presents an example of the newly defined concept. As to the facet determined by $\underline{x}_2^+$ and $\underline{x}_3^+$, we find that all $\underline{\omega}_m^{min}$ which are equal to $C\underline{x}$, with $\underline{x} \in D$, are elements of $\Omega(F_m)$.

The difference between the sets Λ and Ω is similar to the difference between the two ways to derive efficient points; i.e. by means of weights and by minimum values. Λ is related to the weight method as it is the set of all weights leading to a certain corner solution. Ω is connected with the second method as it is the set of all minimum standards leading to a certain facet. Theorem 5 states that Λ is a convex polyhedron. The same can be proved for Ω.

Theorem 6.

The set $\Omega(F_m)$ is a convex polyhedron.

Proof.

Let T_{mj} be the set of minimum values $\underline{\omega}_m^{min}$ corresponding to facet F_m such that for every $\underline{\omega}_m^{min} \in T_{mj}$ there exists an $\underline{\omega}_m \in F_m$ with the property that

$$
\begin{cases}
\omega_{mj}^{min} \leq \omega_{mj} & \text{for a certain } j \\
\omega_{mj'}^{min} = \omega_{mj'} & \text{for all } j' \neq j.
\end{cases}
\qquad (6.54)
$$

T_{mj} is a convex polyhedron which can be generated by means of the vertices of the facet F_m and the direction $-\underline{\varepsilon}_j$:

$$
\qquad (6.55)
$$

$$
T_{mj} = \{\underline{\omega}_m^{min} \mid \underline{\omega}_m^{min} = \sum_k n_k \underline{\omega}_{m_k}^+ + \xi(-\underline{\varepsilon}_j); \sum_k n_k = 1, \; n_k \geq 0 \text{ for all } k, \; \xi \geq 0\}
$$

Consider the intersection S_m of the sets T_{mj}:

$$S_m = T_{m1} \cap T_{m2} \cap \ldots \cap T_{mJ} \qquad (6.56)$$

Since the intersection of several convex polyhedra is a convex polyhedron, we conclude that S_m is a convex polyhedron.

We first show that when $\underline{\omega}_m^{min} \in S_m$, then $\underline{\omega}_m^{min} \in \Omega(F_m)$

Consider the set of efficient solutions satisfying:

$$\begin{cases} \max! & \underline{\omega} = C\underline{x} \\ \text{s.t.} & A\underline{x} \leq \underline{b} \\ & \underline{x} \geq \underline{0} \\ & \underline{\omega} \geq \underline{\omega}_m^{min} \end{cases} \qquad (6.57)$$

where $\underline{\omega}_m^{min} \in S_m$. It follows from the definition of S_m that this set of efficient solutions is non-empty. According to Theorem 3, for every j and $\tilde{\omega}$, the optimal solution of:

$$\begin{cases} \max! & \omega_j = \underline{\varepsilon}_j' C\underline{x} \\ \text{s.t.} & A\underline{x} \leq \underline{b} \\ & \underline{x} \geq \underline{0} \\ & \underline{\omega} \geq \underline{\omega}_m^{min} \\ & \underline{\omega} \geq \underline{\tilde{\omega}} \end{cases} \qquad (6.58)$$

is an efficient solution of (6.57).

Let $\underline{\tilde{\omega}} = (\tilde{\omega}_1, \tilde{\omega}_2, \ldots, \tilde{\omega}_J)'$ be defined as:

$$\tilde{\omega}_j = \max (\omega_{mj}^{min}, \tilde{\omega}_j) \qquad (6.59)$$

so that $\underline{\tilde{\omega}} \geq \underline{\omega}_m^{min}$. It follows from (6.55) that either $\underline{\tilde{\omega}} \in S_m$, or $\underline{\tilde{\omega}}$ is infeasible. The latter possibility can be excluded, however, since (6.58) would otherwise not have a feasible solution. It follows from the definition of S_m that for any j and for any $\underline{\tilde{x}} \in S_m$ the optimal solution of (6.58) is an element of the facet F_m. By means of Theorem 3 we may conclude, therefore, that for all $\underline{\omega}_m^{min} \in S_m$, the resulting efficient solutions of (6.57) are elements of the facet F_m. Thus, when $\underline{\omega}_m^{min} \in S_m$ then $\underline{\omega}_m^{min} \in \Omega(F_m)$.

In the second part of the proof we show that when $\underline{\omega}_m^{min} \notin S_m$
then $\underline{\omega}_m^{min} \notin \Omega(F_m)$. Suppose that $\underline{\omega}_m^{min} \notin S_m$. Then there exists
a j so that there is no $\underline{\omega}_m \in F_m$ with the property described in
(6.54). For this j, assuming that $\underline{\tilde{\omega}} = \underline{\omega}_m^{min}$, the solution of
(6.58) is no element of F_m. By means of Theorem 3 we may con-
clude in this case that when $\underline{\omega}_m^{min} \notin S_m$ then $\underline{\omega}_m^{min} \notin \Omega(F_m)$.

The conclusion is that $\Omega(F_m) = S_m$ which is a convex polyhedron. Q.E.D.

The set Ω may contain relevant information for the DM. It
draws the attention to the fact that there are many different
minimum standards, which yet result in an efficient solution
corresponding to one certain combination of weights. So, in a
way, similar to Λ, it may provide insight into the insensitivi-
ties involved in the decision problem.

If one wants to find all the vertices of the polyhedron
$\Omega(F_m)$, one of the algorithms mentioned earlier in this section
can be employed. In general it is imposible to predict how
many vertices will be found. There is one interesting excep-
tion, however, because when the combination of weights $\underline{\lambda}_m$ contains a non-positive element, it can be shown analytically that
$\Omega(F_m)$ is empty in the sense that the only elements of $\Omega(F_m)$ are
the elements of the facet F_m itself.

Theorem 7.

If at least one element of $\underline{\lambda}_m$ is non-positive, $\Omega(F_m) - F_m$
is empty.

Proof.

Suppose that the j-th element of $\underline{\lambda}_m$ is non-positive.

In the proof of Theorem 6 we have shown that every $\underline{\omega}_m^{min} \in \Omega(F_m)$
satisfies the condition that there exists an $\underline{\omega}_m \in F_m$ such that

$$\begin{cases} \omega_{mj}^{min} \leq \omega_{mj} & \text{for a certain j} \\ \omega_{mj'}^{min} = \omega_{mj'} & \text{for all } j' \neq j \end{cases} \qquad (6.60)$$

From the definition of a facet it follows that for all $\underline{\omega}_m \in F_m$,
the equality holds:

$$\underline{\lambda}'_m \underline{\omega}_m = c_m \qquad (6.61)$$

Given the information that the j-th element of $\underline{\lambda}_m$ is non-positive, we conclude from (6.60) and (6.61) that for every

$\underline{\omega}_m^{min} \in \Omega(F_m)$:

$$\underline{\lambda}_m' \, \underline{\omega}_m^{min} \geq c_m \qquad\qquad (6.62)$$

Let us suppose now that the j'-th element of $\underline{\lambda}_m$ is positive.
Then we find along the same line of reasoning that for every
$\underline{\omega}_m^{min} \in \Omega(F_m)$

$$\underline{\lambda}_m' \, \underline{\omega}_m^{min} \leq c_m \qquad\qquad (6.63)$$

The conclusion which may be drawn from (6.62) and (6.63) is
that for every $\underline{\omega}_m^{min} \in \Omega(F_m)$

$$\underline{\lambda}_m' \, \underline{\omega}_m^{min} = c_m \qquad\qquad (6.64)$$

Hence $\Omega(F_m) = F_m$ Q.E.D.

Theorem 7 is in accordance with our earlier observation that
when the vector $\underline{\lambda}_m$ characterizing a facet F_m has some non-positive weights, the interior points of F_m are dominated. These
findings are important for practical purposes since many facets
may be expected to have vectors $\underline{\lambda}_m$ with some non-positive
weights. When J = 2, it is guaranteed that the weights are
positive, but when J $\geq$ 3 negative weights can be expected.
In Section 11.3 an example is shown in which only 6 of the 13
facets have positive weights. For faces with less than J - 1
dimensions, similar observations can be expected. Therefore
these findings suggest that for practical purposes it is a good
way to start the analysis with efficient vertices and to proceed with higher dimensional faces only when no satisfactory
results can be obtained.

6.8   Conclusion

A number of concepts have been introduced - among others:
compromise solution, half-compromise solution, conflict measure
- by means of which one can reveal important aspects of the
structure of MOD problems. These concepts will appear to play
an important role in a well-structured information provision
scheme, as discussed in Chapter 9 and applied in Chapters 11
and 12. Especially, procedures for linear MOD problems are
well-developed thus far, as has been shown in Section 6.7.

Footnotes

1. It may occur that the DM wants to minimize ω_j rather than to maximize it. This can easily be dealt with by considering $-\omega_j$, instead of ω_j

2. A numerical example of the concepts defined in this and following equations may be helpful for understanding the subject matter.
    A pay-off matrix P

    $$P = \begin{pmatrix} 100 & 70 & 50 \\ 3 & 5 & 0 \\ -15 & -13 & -5 \end{pmatrix}$$

    implies ideal values

    $$\overset{*}{\underline{\omega}} = (100, 5, -5)'$$

    and minimum attainable values

    $$\underline{\bar{\omega}} = (50, 0, -15)'$$

    for the three objectives.
    The normalized version of P is equal to

    $$Q = \begin{pmatrix} 1 & .4 & 0 \\ .6 & 1 & 0 \\ 0 & .8 & 1 \end{pmatrix}$$

    which gives rise to a conflict measure $\gamma_1 = .7$ (see (6.4) and (6.5)).

3. One should realize that $\bar{\omega}_j$ defined in (6.3) is not in all cases the minimum attainable level for the j-th objective. It may be that this objective attains smaller values for alternatives which are not included in P. For example, when $J = 3$ a coalition between ω_1 and ω_2 aiming at the maximization of $\lambda_1 \omega_1 + \lambda_2 \omega_2$ may bring about a smaller value for ω_3 than that which arises from the maximization of ω_1 or ω_2 separately. Only when $J = 2$, this problem does not arise. In practice it appears that $\bar{\omega}_j$ gives a usable indication of the minimum attainable level of objective j in most cases.

4. Of course, one should first check whether the pair of objectives is globally non-conflicting or only locally non-conflicting.

5. An example of a linear separable decision problem is:

    $$\begin{cases} \max! & \underline{\omega} = C\underline{x} \\ \text{s.t.} & A\underline{x} \leq \underline{b} \end{cases}$$

where the matrices A and C have a corresponding block-diagonal structure.

6.   In the context of fuzzy sets of feasible solutions, the requirement to consider only efficient points is less evident (cf. Blin [1977]). Blin also points to the fact that dominated solutions which are very close to non-dominated solutions and which may be very reasonable alternatives are yet excluded from consideration.

7.   The extra condition implies that the points A and B in the figure are not properly efficient. Note that A and B give rise to arbitrary large trade-offs. See also Awerbuch and Wallace [1976]. The use of the concept of proper efficiency appears in Theorem 2. For linear problems efficiency and proper efficiency are equivalent.

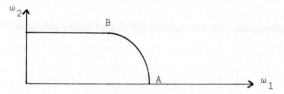

8.   See also Dauer [1978] for a comparison of (6.9) and (6.10).

9.   The proof that for $J = 2$, $\underline{\lambda}_2 = \underline{\lambda}_3$ can be found in Appendix I. The equality of $\underline{\lambda}_1$ and $\underline{\lambda}_2$ can be shown as follows:
Let "α" denote the expression "is proportional to". Then:

$$\underline{\lambda}_2 \ \alpha \ \begin{pmatrix} \overset{*}{\omega}_1 & \bar{\omega}_2 \\ \bar{\omega}_1 & \overset{*}{\omega}_2 \end{pmatrix}^{-1} \begin{pmatrix} 1 \\ 1 \end{pmatrix},$$

hence, by means of Cramer's rule (cf. Apostol [1971])

$$\underline{\lambda}_2 \ \alpha \ \begin{pmatrix} \overset{*}{\omega}_2 - \bar{\omega}_2 \\ \overset{*}{\omega}_1 - \bar{\omega}_1 \end{pmatrix}$$

For $\underline{\lambda}_1$, (6.18) implies:

$$\underline{\lambda}_1 \ \alpha \ \begin{pmatrix} \dfrac{1}{\overset{*}{\omega}_2 - \bar{\omega}_1} \\ \dfrac{1}{\overset{*}{\omega}_2 - \bar{\omega}_2} \end{pmatrix}$$

so that indeed $\underline{\lambda}_1 \ \alpha \ \underline{\lambda}_2$
For $\underline{\lambda}_4$ we find the same outcome since the symmetry condi-

tion for $\hat{\lambda}Q$ means that

$$\lambda_{41}(\overset{*}{\omega}_1 - \bar{\omega}_1) = \lambda_{42}(\overset{*}{\omega}_2 - \bar{\omega}_2), \text{ hence}$$

$$\underline{\lambda}_4 \; \alpha \begin{pmatrix} \dfrac{1}{\overset{*}{\omega}_1 - \bar{\omega}_1} \\[2ex] \dfrac{1}{\overset{*}{\omega}_2 - \bar{\omega}_2} \end{pmatrix}$$

10. For $J = 2$ and $p = 1$, γ_3 reads

$$\gamma_3 = \frac{\overset{*}{\omega}_1 - \omega_1(\underline{x}^c)}{\overset{*}{\omega}_1 - \bar{\omega}_1} + \frac{\overset{*}{\omega}_2 - \omega_2(\underline{x}^c)}{\overset{*}{\omega}_2 - \bar{\omega}_2}$$

For γ_4 we find when $J = 2$:

$$\gamma_4 = \frac{\lambda_1(\overset{*}{\omega}_1 - \omega_1(\underline{x}^e)) + \lambda_2(\overset{*}{\omega}_2 - \omega_2(\underline{x}^e))}{\lambda_1(\overset{*}{\omega}_1 - \bar{\omega}_1) + \lambda_2(\overset{*}{\omega}_2 - \bar{\omega}_2)}$$

From (6.18) we derive:

$$\lambda_1 = \frac{\overset{*}{\omega}_2 - \bar{\omega}_2}{(\overset{*}{\omega}_1 - \bar{\omega}_1) + (\overset{*}{\omega}_2 - \bar{\omega}_2)} \quad \text{and}$$

$$\lambda_2 = \frac{\overset{*}{\omega}_1 - \bar{\omega}_1}{(\overset{*}{\omega}_1 - \bar{\omega}_1) + (\overset{*}{\omega}_2 - \bar{\omega}_2)}$$

After substitution of λ_1 and λ_2, γ_4 can be expressed as

$$\gamma_4 = \frac{\overset{*}{\omega}_1 - \omega_1(\underline{x}^e)}{\overset{*}{\omega}_1 - \bar{\omega}_1} + \frac{\overset{*}{\omega}_2 - \omega_2(\underline{x}^e)}{\overset{*}{\omega}_2 - \bar{\omega}_2}$$

Since for $p = 1$ and $J = 2$, $\underline{x}^c = \underline{x}^e$ we may conclude that $\gamma_3(p=1) = \gamma_4$ when $J = 2$.

11. There are more similarities between measures for these fields. The measures for the compromise solutions, are very similar to the measures for the average of an income distribution.

12.

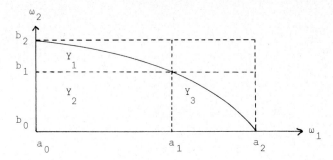

Let (a_1, b_1) in the Figure be the compromise solution $\underline{\omega}^a$. Then the conflict measure γ_2 as defined in (6.29) is:

$$\gamma_2 = \frac{4}{3}\left[\frac{(a_2-a_0)(b_2-b_0) - (a_1-a_0)(b_1-b_0)}{(a_2-a_0)(b_2-b_0)}\right]$$

The measure γ_5 as defined in (6.33) equals:

$$\gamma_5 = 2\left[\frac{(a_2-a_0)(b_2-b_0) - \text{size}(Y_1 \cup Y_2 \cup Y_3)}{(a_2-a_0)(b_2-b_0)}\right]$$

Because of the convexity of K and the concavity of $\underline{\omega}$, we know:

$$\text{size}(Y_1 \cup Y_2 \cup Y_3) \geq (a_1-a_0)(b_1-b_0)+\frac{1}{2}(a_1-a_0)(b_2-b_1)+\frac{1}{2}(a_2-a_1)(b_1-b_0)$$

and

$$(a_1-a_0)(b_2-b_1)+(a_2-a_1)(b_1-b_0) \geq \frac{2}{3}\left[(a_2-a_0)(b_2-b_0)-(a_1-a_0)(b_1-b_0)\right]$$

Substitution of these two inequalities in the expression of γ_5 yields: $\gamma_5 \leq \gamma_2$

13. For the $\underline{x}^{c4}$ compromise (6.40) does not produce new information. The reason is that for $p \to \infty$ the weights $\underline{q}$ do not influence the outcome of (6.38). For each vector $\underline{q}$ with non-zero weights the same solution $\underline{x}^{c4}$ will be found.

14. Contrary to the fact that for $J = 2$, $\underline{x}^{c1} = \underline{x}^{e3}$, it cannot be shown that for $J = 2$ holds: $\underline{y}_j^{c1} = \underline{y}_j^{e3}$. $\underline{y}_1^{c1}$ is based on a linear utility function with weights

$$\underline{\mu} \propto \begin{pmatrix} \dfrac{3}{\overset{*}{\omega}_1 - \bar{\omega}_1} \\[2em] \dfrac{1}{\overset{*}{\omega}_2 - \bar{\omega}_2} \end{pmatrix}$$

(cf. (6.38) and (6.40)), and hence

$$\underline{\mu} \propto \begin{pmatrix} 3(\overset{*}{\omega}_2 - \bar{\omega}_2) \\ (\overset{*}{\omega}_1 - \bar{\omega}_1) \end{pmatrix}$$

The weights of the linear utility function underlying $\underline{y}_1^{e3}$ are equal to

$$\underline{q}_1 = \begin{pmatrix} \dfrac{(\overset{*}{\omega}_2 - \bar{\omega}_2)}{(\overset{*}{\omega}_1 - \bar{\omega}_1)+(\overset{*}{\omega}_2 - \bar{\omega}_2)} + 1 \\[2em] \dfrac{(\overset{*}{\omega}_1 - \bar{\omega}_1)}{(\overset{*}{\omega}_1 - \bar{\omega}_1)+(\overset{*}{\omega}_2 - \bar{\omega}_2)} \end{pmatrix}$$

(cf. (6.41) and (6.43)), so that

$$\underline{q}_1 \propto \begin{pmatrix} 2(\overset{*}{\omega}_2 - \bar{\omega}_2) + (\overset{*}{\omega}_1 - \bar{\omega}_1) \\ (\overset{*}{\omega}_1 - \bar{\omega}_1) \end{pmatrix}$$

The conclusion is that in general $\underline{q}_1 \neq \underline{\mu}$. The only exception arises when $(\overset{*}{\omega}_1 - \bar{\omega}_1) = (\overset{*}{\omega}_2 - \bar{\omega}_2)$.

15. Another interesting contribution to the generation of a
     representative subset of alternatives is contained in
     Sandee [1977]. Sandee's approach can be sketched in the
     following way. First a large number of alternatives is
     generated by varying the values of the parameters in the
     objective function systematically (cf. Section 6.3). To
     improve the tractability of the data obtained, the number
     of dimensions is reduced by means of principal components
     analysis (cf. Section 8.10). The representative subset of
     alternatives to be found form together a convex polyhedron
     (cf. Section 6.7). Sandee proposes to select the elements
     of the subset in such a way that the corresponding poly-
     hedron is as large as possible within the set of feasible
     alternatives. Sandee presents a numerical illustration of
     this approach, based on data derived from Van Eijk and
     Sandee [1959].

16. It can be shown that when K is bounded, the directions $\underline{v}^r$
     are equal to $\underline{0}$ (cf. Rockafellar [1970]).

17.   This procedure bears a certain resemblance to Bayesian
       approaches in statistical inference (cf. Zellner [1971]).
       In Bayesian terms, a prior distribution of weights has
       been assumed which is uniform. When more prior infor-
       mation is available, also other distributions can be
       used.

APPENDIX 6.I

GAME THEORY AND COMPROMISE WEIGHTS

This appendix is devoted to an elaboration of a game theoretic approach to derive compromise weights. The reason for this elaboration is that the approach, described in (6.19) is not completely satisfactory. The compromise weights vector $\underline{\lambda}_2$, defined in (6.19) has the disadvantage that there is no guarantee of it containing only non-negative elements. Hence, one is not certain that $\underline{\lambda}_2$ gives rise to an efficient solution, which is one of the criteria for compromise solutions.

It is not difficult to give a numerical illustration of the pertaining problem. Let the pay-off matrix P be defined as:

$$P' = \begin{pmatrix} 10 & 0 & 0 \\ 7,5 & 100 & 0,65 \\ 0 & 0 & 1 \end{pmatrix} \qquad (I.1)$$

In this case for $\underline{\lambda}_2$, defined as:

$$\underline{\lambda}_2 = \frac{(P')^{-1}\underline{\imath}}{\underline{\imath}'(P')^{-1}\underline{\imath}} \qquad (I.2)$$

will be found:

$$\underline{\lambda}_2 \; \alpha \; (\frac{1}{10}, - \frac{0,4}{100}, 1)' \qquad (I.3)$$

where "α" means "is proportional to".

Only when the number of alternatives J is equal to 2, can it be ascertained that $\underline{\lambda}_2 \geq \underline{0}$. Let P be

$$P' = \begin{pmatrix} \overset{*}{\omega}_1 & \bar{\omega}_2 \\ \bar{\omega}_1 & \overset{*}{\omega}_2 \end{pmatrix} \qquad (I.4)$$

then, after substitution in (I.2) we have:

121

$$\underline{\lambda}_2 \; \alpha \begin{pmatrix} \overset{*}{\omega}_2 - \bar{\omega}_2 \\ \overset{*}{\omega}_1 - \bar{\omega}_1 \end{pmatrix} \tag{I.5}$$

so that we may conclude that both elements of $\underline{\lambda}_2$ are non-negative.

We will prove in this appendix that there is an alternative approach to derive compromise weights, which is very similar to (6.19), but which lacks its weak characteristic. Consider the following game theoretical problem:

$$\begin{cases} \text{min!} & c \\[2mm] \text{s.t.} & Q'\underline{\mu} \le c\underline{\iota} \\[2mm] & \underline{\iota}'\underline{\mu} = 1 \\[2mm] & \underline{\mu} \ge \underline{0} \end{cases} \tag{I.6}$$

where Q is the normalized pay-off matrix (see (6.4)):

$$Q = (\overset{*}{\omega} \overset{\frown}{-} \bar{\omega})^{-1} (P - \underline{\bar{\omega}}\underline{\iota}') \tag{I.7}$$

Indeed, (I.6) is very similar to the original definition of $\underline{\lambda}_2$:

$$\begin{cases} P'\underline{\lambda}_2 = c\underline{\iota} \\[2mm] \underline{\iota}'\underline{\lambda}_2 = 1 \end{cases} \tag{I.8}$$

Apart from the replacement of P by Q, the only difference between the two expressions is that essentially the former includes a non-negativity constraint on $\underline{\mu}$, which necessitates the introduction of an inequality sign for the first part of (I.7).

Two questions can be raised about (I.6):

a. how can it be interpreted?

b. how can it be solved?

The interpretation of (I.6) departs from the customary interpretation of games, because in this case, the columns of P have different dimensions. (See for another treatment of this type of problem Zeleny [1976c]). In spite of this problem, it is not difficult to give a game theoretical interpretation of (I.6). It pertains to a game between two participants A and B. Participant B chooses an alternative from Q. Before B express-es his choice, A has to fix a vector $\underline{\mu}$, where each element of $\underline{\mu}$ indicates the amount of money he must pay B per unit of each normalized objective. So if B selects the j-th alternative, A must pay him $\underline{q}_j'\underline{\mu}$ units of money, where $\underline{q}_j$ is the j-th column of Q. Two conditions hold for $\underline{\mu}$: its elements should be non-neg-ative and should sum up to 1 unit of money. As A does not know beforehand which alternative will be chosen by B, he has to make a decision under uncertainty. Let us assume that A wants to minimize the loss, such that whatever may be the choice of B, the total amount of money paid is as low as possible. This strategy is represented by (I.6) in a formal way.

For the solution of (I.6), we can make use of the finding that game-theoretic problems can be transformed to LP problems (cf. Luce and Raiffa [1957] and Allen [1960]). Notice that when $\underline{\mu}^0 = \frac{1}{c}\underline{\mu}$ and $\underline{\imath}'\underline{\mu} = 1$, we find that $\frac{1}{c} = \underline{\imath}'\underline{\mu}^0$, so that (I.6) can be written as:

$$
\left\{
\begin{array}{ll}
\text{max!} & \underline{\imath}'\underline{\mu}^0 \\[2ex]
\text{s.t.} & Q'\underline{\mu}^0 \leq \underline{\imath} \\[2ex]
& \underline{\mu}^0 \geq \underline{0} \\[2ex]
& \underline{\mu} = (\underline{\imath}'\underline{\mu}^0)^{-1}\underline{\mu}^0
\end{array}
\right.
\tag{I.9}
$$

An assumption underlying (I.8) is that c > 0. Otherwise, the inequality sign in $Q'\underline{\mu} \leq \underline{\imath}$ must be reversed. From (I.6) we know that indeed c > 0, because all elements of Q and $\underline{\mu}$ are non-negative. The solution $\underline{\mu}^0$ of (I.8) can be conceived of as a vector of weights for the normalized alternatives described in Q. The vector of weights we are looking for, $\underline{\lambda}_3$, pertains to the non-normalized alternatives and can be calculated by:

$$
\underline{\lambda}_3 \; \alpha \; (\overset{*}{\omega} \overset{\wedge}{-} \overline{\omega})^{-1}\underline{\mu}^0
\tag{I.10}
$$

In the next theorem, the conditions are stated on which $\underline{\lambda}_2$ and $\underline{\lambda}_3$ are equal.

Theorem I.1. If $(Q)^{-1}\underline{\imath} \geq \underline{0}$ and $(Q')^{-1}\underline{\imath} \geq \underline{0}$, then $\underline{\lambda}_3 = \underline{\lambda}_2$.

Proof. The proof consists of two parts. First, we show that the conditions stated in the theorem are sufficient for opti-mality of the solution $\underline{\mu}^0 = (Q')^{-1}\underline{\imath}$. In the second part we

show that when $\underline{\mu}^0 = (Q')^{-1}\underline{\imath}$, $\underline{\lambda}_3 = \underline{\lambda}_2$.
After the introduction of J slack variables $\underline{s}$, (I.9) reads:

$$
\begin{cases}
\text{max!} & \underline{\imath}'\underline{\mu}^0 \\[2mm]
\text{s.t.} & (Q' \; I)\left(\dfrac{\underline{\mu}^0}{\underline{s}}\right) = \underline{\imath} \\[2mm]
& \underline{\mu}^0, \; \underline{s} \geq \underline{0}
\end{cases}
\tag{I.11}
$$

After pre-multiplication of both sides of the equality relationship in (I.11) by $(Q')^{-1}$, we have:

$$
\underline{\mu}^0 = (Q')^{-1}\underline{\imath} - (Q')^{-1}\underline{s}
\tag{I.12}
$$

so that we find:

$$
\frac{1}{c} = \underline{\imath}'\underline{\mu}^0 = \underline{\imath}'(Q')^{-1}\underline{\imath} - \underline{\imath}'(Q')^{-1}\underline{s}
\tag{I.13}
$$

$\underline{s} = \underline{0}$ and $\underline{\mu}^0 = (Q')^{-1}\underline{\imath}$ is the optimal solution of (I.11) if:
a. the non-negativity constraints are satisfied for $\underline{\mu}^0$;
b. $\frac{1}{c}$ attains its maximum, so $\underline{\imath}'(Q')^{-1} \geq \underline{0}'$.
Hence, a sufficient requirement for optimality of the solution
mentioned above is:

$$
\begin{cases}
(Q')^{-1}\underline{\imath} \geq \underline{0} \\[2mm]
Q^{-1}\underline{\imath} \geq \underline{0}
\end{cases}
\tag{I.14}
$$

We proceed now with the second part of the proof. After
substitution of Q and $\underline{\mu}^0$ in (I.10), we find for $\underline{\lambda}_3$

$$
\underline{\lambda}_3 \; \alpha \; (P' - \underline{\imath}\,\overline{\underline{\omega}}')^{-1}\underline{\imath}
\tag{I.15}
$$

Cramer's rule provides a useful method to simplify (I.15).
As to the rule, the j-th element of $\underline{\lambda}_3$ can be obtained by re-
placing the j-th column of $(P' - \underline{\imath}\,\overline{\underline{\omega}}')$ for $\underline{\imath}$ and calculating the
determinant of the resulting matrix. The final step is the
multiplication of each element of $\underline{\lambda}_3$ by a constant to ensure
that $\underline{\imath}'\underline{\lambda}_3 = 1$. Consider the determinant d_j:

$$d_j = \left| \underline{p}_1 - \bar{\omega}_1 \underline{\iota}, \ \underline{p}_2 - \bar{\omega}_2 \underline{\iota}, \ldots, \underline{p}_{j-1} - \bar{\omega}_{j-1} \underline{\iota}, \underline{\iota}, \ \underline{p}_{j+1} - \bar{\omega}_{j+1} \underline{\iota}, \ldots, \ \underline{p}_J - \bar{\omega}_J \underline{\iota} \right| \tag{I.16}$$

where $\underline{p}_j$ is the j-th column of P'.

As the value of the determinant of a matrix remains unchanged when a column of the matrix is added to or substracted from other columns, (I.16) can be simplified to:

$$d_j = \left| \underline{p}_1, \underline{p}_2, \ldots \underline{p}_{j-1}, \ \underline{\iota}, \ \underline{p}_{j+1}, \ldots, \underline{p}_J \right| \tag{I.17}$$

From (I.17) we may conclude that:

$$\underline{\lambda}_3 \ \alpha \ (P')^{-1} \underline{\iota} \tag{I.18}$$

and hence $\underline{\lambda}_3 = \underline{\lambda}_2$.   Q.E.D.

Corollary. If J=2, $\underline{\lambda}_3 = \underline{\lambda}_2$.

Proof. If J=2, we have Q=I so that the conditions of Theorem I.1 are satisfied. Q.E.D.

The conclusion is that we have developed an alternative compromise weight concept $\underline{\lambda}_3$, which is related to and superior to $\underline{\lambda}_2$. In some cases, when $\underline{\lambda}_2$ is satisfactory, its outcome is identical to it. When $\underline{\lambda}_2$ fails, however, it gives a good outcome. For example, $\underline{\lambda}_2$ proves to be unacceptable when P is defined according to (I.1). The vector $\underline{\lambda}_3$ avoids the problem of the negativity of a weight. In this case, the outcome is:

$$\underline{\lambda}_3 \ \alpha \ (\tfrac{1}{10}, \ 0, \ 1)' \tag{I.19}$$

Some final remarks can be made about the way of normalization of P. In addition to (I.7), there is another way of normalization, proposed by Belenson and Kapur [1973]. They introduce a normalized matrix R, defined as:

$$R = (\overset{*}{\omega} - d\underline{\iota})^{-1} (P - d\underline{\iota}\,\underline{\iota}') \tag{I.20}$$

where d is defined as:

$$\begin{cases} d = 0 & \text{if } \overset{*}{\omega}_j \geq 0 \qquad j=1,\ldots J \\[2mm] d = \min_{jj'} \ p_{jj'}, & \text{if some } \overset{*}{\omega}_j < 0 \end{cases} \tag{I.21}$$

The difference between Q and R is that in the former $\bar{\omega}$ has been replaced by $d\underline{\iota}$. So, to all elements of P the same number d is added in the normalization procedure.

Q and R do not produce in general identical results for λ_3, as will be found after solving (I.9) for Q and R. Only in some cases may the same outcomes arise, i.e. when in (I.9) the same restrictions are active for Q and R. The proof of this state- ment is essentially similar to the second part of the proof of Theorem I.1.

Compared to Q, R has two drawbacks, however.

1. It is not granted that all elements of R are non-negative. This produces difficulties for the derivation of (I.9) from (I.6).

2. It is less easy to interpret R since in the calculation procedure for R, all elements of P have been raised with the same amount, irrespective of their dimension.

Therefore, Q should be preferred to R.

EFFICIENCY OF MIN-MAX SOLUTIONS

Consider the min-max solution $\underline{x}^c$ of:

$$\begin{cases} \text{min!} & \max_{j} \dfrac{\omega^*_j - \omega_j(\underline{x})}{\omega^*_j - \bar{\omega}_j} \\ \\ \text{s.t.} & \underline{x} \in K \end{cases} \qquad (\text{II.1})$$

We wonder whether $\underline{x}^c$ is efficient. The following theorem can be proved to be true.

<u>Theorem II.1</u>. If $\underline{x}^c$ is the only solution of (II.1), it is an efficient solution.

<u>Proof</u>. The proof is very similar to the proof of Theorem 4. Let us assume, therefore, that $\underline{x}^c$ is not efficient. Then a solution $\underline{\tilde{x}} \in K$ exists, such that:

$$\begin{cases} \omega_j(\underline{\tilde{x}}) \geq \omega_j(\underline{x}^c) & \text{for all } j \\ \\ \omega_j(\underline{\tilde{x}}) > \omega_j(\underline{x}^c) & \text{for at least one } j \end{cases} \qquad (\text{II.2})$$

A consequence of (II.2) is:

$$\begin{cases} \dfrac{\omega^*_j - \omega_j(\underline{\tilde{x}})}{\omega^*_j - \bar{\omega}_j} \leq \dfrac{\omega^*_j - \omega_j(\underline{x}^c)}{\omega^*_j - \bar{\omega}_j} & \text{for all } j \\ \\ \dfrac{\omega^*_j - \omega_j(\underline{\tilde{x}})}{\omega^*_j - \bar{\omega}_j} < \dfrac{\omega^*_j - \omega_j(\underline{x}^c)}{\omega^*_j - \bar{\omega}_j} & \text{for at least one } j. \end{cases} \qquad (\text{II.3})$$

and hence:

$$\min_{j}! \ \max_{j} \ \frac{\overset{*}{\omega}_j - \omega_j(\overset{\sim}{\underline{x}})}{\overset{*}{\omega}_j - \overline{\omega}_j} \leq \min_{j}! \ \max_{j} \ \frac{\overset{*}{\omega}_j - \omega_j(\underline{x}^c)}{\overset{*}{\omega}_j - \overline{\omega}_j} \qquad (II.4)$$

which implies that $\overset{\sim}{\underline{x}}$ is a solution with a performance equal to or better than $\underline{x}^c$. By contradiction we may conclude that the theorem is true. The step from (II.3) to (II.4) makes clear why it is necessary that $\underline{x}^c$ is the only solution of (II.1). As we do not know for which $\overline{j}$ (II.1) attains its mimumum, we may not conclude that a strict inequality sign holds for (II.4).

   This complication can also graphically be analyzed. See Figure II.1.

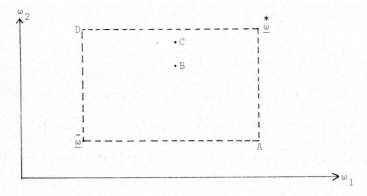

Fig. II.1.   A decision problem with four alternatives

As to the min-max criterion, B is equally remote from $\overset{*}{\underline{\omega}}$ as C. Therefore C, as well as B, are solutions of problem (II.1). B is, however, dominated by C.

   In addition to Theorem (II.1), the following theorem can be proved:

Theorem II.2.   If there are several solutions of (II.1), at least one of them is efficient.

Proof.   Let the set $S = \left\{\underline{x}_1^c, \ldots, \underline{x}_N^c\right\}$ be a set of solutions of (II.1). We will prove the equivalent theorem: If no element of S is efficient, S is not the complete set of solutions of (II.1).

   Suppose that no element of S is efficient; i.e. for each $\underline{x}_n^c \in S$ a vector $\overset{\sim}{\underline{x}}_n \in K$ exists, such that:

$$\begin{cases} \dfrac{\overset{*}{\omega}_j - \omega_j(\overset{\sim}{\underline{x}}_n)}{\overset{*}{\omega}_j - \bar{\omega}_j} \leq \dfrac{\overset{*}{\omega}_j - \omega_j(\underline{x}_n^c)}{\overset{*}{\omega}_j - \bar{\omega}_j} \qquad \text{for all } j \\[6mm] \dfrac{\overset{*}{\omega}_j - \omega_j(\overset{\sim}{\underline{x}}_n)}{\overset{*}{\omega}_j - \bar{\omega}_j} < \dfrac{\overset{*}{\omega}_j - \omega_j(\underline{x}_n^c)}{\overset{*}{\omega}_j - \bar{\omega}_j} \qquad \text{for at least one } j \end{cases} \qquad \text{(II.5)}$$

In principle, two cases may occur now: either

$$\min_{} \max_j \frac{\overset{*}{\omega}_j - \omega_j(\overset{\sim}{\underline{x}}_n)}{\overset{*}{\omega}_j - \bar{\omega}_j} = \min_{} \max_j \frac{\overset{*}{\omega}_j - \omega_j(\underline{x}_n^c)}{\overset{*}{\omega}_j - \bar{\omega}_j} \qquad \text{for all } n \qquad \text{(II.6)}$$

or:

$$\min_{} \max_j \frac{\overset{*}{\omega}_j - \omega_j(\overset{\sim}{\underline{x}}_n)}{\overset{*}{\omega}_j - \bar{\omega}_j} < \min_{} \max_j \frac{\omega_j - \omega_j(\underline{x}_n^c)}{\overset{*}{\omega}_j - \bar{\omega}_j}$$

$$\text{for at least one } n \qquad \text{(II.7)}$$

(II.7) is contrary to the assumption that S is a set of solutions of (II.1), however. Therefore, only (II.6) can arise as a consequence of (II.5). (II.6) implies that $\{\underline{x}_1^c, \ldots, \underline{x}_N^c\}$ as well as $\{\overset{\sim}{\underline{x}}_1, \ldots, \overset{\sim}{\underline{x}}_N\}$ are solutions of (II.1)

However, Lemma II.1 states that there exists always at least one element of $\{\overset{\sim}{\underline{x}}_1, \ldots, \overset{\sim}{\underline{x}}_N\}$ which is not an element of $\{\underline{x}_1^c, \ldots, \underline{x}_N^c\}$. Therefore, we may conclude that $\{\underline{x}_1^c, \ldots, \underline{x}_N^c\}$ is not the complete set of solutions of (II.1). Q.E.D.

Lemma II.1. If there are given two sets $S = \{\underline{x}_1, \ldots \underline{x}_N\}$ and $\tilde{S} = \{\overset{\sim}{\underline{x}}_1, \ldots, \overset{\sim}{\underline{x}}_N\}$ with the property that $\underline{x}_n$ is dominated by $\overset{\sim}{\underline{x}}_n$ for $n = 1, \ldots, N$, then $\tilde{S}$ is not a subset of S.

Proof. Let D_n be the set of points, dominating $\underline{x}_n$

$\underline{x}_1$ is dominated by $\overset{\sim}{\underline{x}}_1 \qquad \rightarrow$ either a. $\overset{\sim}{\underline{x}}_1 \in \{\underline{x}_2, \ldots, \underline{x}_N\}$

$\qquad\qquad\qquad\qquad$ or $\qquad$ b. $\overset{\sim}{\underline{x}}_1 \in D_1 - \{\underline{x}_2, \ldots, \underline{x}_N\}$

In the case of b, the lemma is proved. In the case of a, assume without loss of generality that $\overset{\sim}{\underline{x}}_1 = \underline{x}_2$ and continue with:

$\underline{x}_2$ is dominated by $\overset{\sim}{\underline{x}}_2 \qquad \rightarrow$ either a. $\overset{\sim}{\underline{x}}_2 \in \{\underline{x}_3, \ldots, \underline{x}_N\}$

$\qquad\qquad\qquad\qquad$ or $\qquad$ b. $\overset{\sim}{\underline{x}}_2 \in D_2 - \{\underline{x}_3, \ldots, \underline{x}_N\}$

In the case of b, the lemma is proved (as $\underline{x}_1, \underline{x}_2 \notin D_2$)

In the case of a, assume that $\underline{x}_2 = \underline{x}_3$ and continue for
n=3,...,N-1:

$\underline{x}_n$ is dominated by $\overset{\sim}{\underline{x}}_n$ → either a. $\overset{\sim}{\underline{x}}_n \in \{\underline{x}_{n+1},...,\underline{x}_N\}$

$\qquad\qquad\qquad\qquad\qquad\qquad$ or b. $\overset{\sim}{\underline{x}}_n \in D_n - \{\underline{x}_{n+1},...,\underline{x}_N\}$

If for n=1,...,N-1 case a prevails, we finally have:

$\underline{x}_N$ is dominated by $\overset{\sim}{\underline{x}}_N$ → $\overset{\sim}{\underline{x}}_N \in D_N$

As $S \cap D_N = \emptyset$, we conclude that at least one element of $\tilde{S}$ is no
element of S. Q.E.D.

The reason why the min-max solution $\underline{x}^{c3}$ of (II.1) is not in
all circumstances efficient is that this criterion does not
distinguish between alternatives which are equally attractive
with respect to the most important objective but which differ
for other objectives. It seems valuable, therefore, to look
for a refinement of the min-max concept. A lexicographic criterion seems a good substitute for it, as it considers all objectives in order of importance. Actually, it is the result of a
repeated application of the min-max criterion.

The first step is:

$$\begin{cases} \text{min!} \quad \max_{j=1,...J} \dfrac{\omega_j^* - \omega_j(\underline{x})}{\omega_j^* - \bar{\omega}_j} \\[2ex] \underline{x} \in K \end{cases} \qquad\qquad (II.8)$$

with the solution $\underline{x}^c$ for $j=j_1$.

The second step is:

$$\begin{cases} \text{min! } \max_{\substack{j=1,...J \\ j \neq j_1}} \dfrac{\omega_j^* - \omega_j(\underline{x})}{\omega_j^* - \bar{\omega}_j} \\[2ex] \omega_{j_1}(\underline{x}) = \omega_{j_1}(\underline{x}^c) \\[1ex] \underline{x} \in K \end{cases} \qquad\qquad (II.9)$$

In any further step, a new constraint is added until the final
solution $\underline{x}^{c4}$ is found. As is proved in Theorem II.3, this solution is efficient.

Theorem II.3. If $\underline{x}^c$ is the solution of (II.8), (II.9) etc.,
then it is an efficient solution.

Proof. The first part of the proof is identical to that of
Theorem II.1. As (II.3) says that for at least one j, $\overset{\sim}{\underline{x}}$ is
strictly preferred to $\underline{x}^c$, while for the other objectives $\overset{\sim}{\underline{x}}$ is
at least as good as $\underline{x}^c$, we may conclude that $\overset{\sim}{\underline{x}}$ is preferred to
$\underline{x}^c$ lexicographically. Hence, we proved the theorem by contra-

diction.   Q.E.D.

   This lexicographic min-max procedure will be applied in
Section 12.4

CHAPTER 7

PREFERENCES IN MULTIPLE OBJECTIVE DECISION METHODS

7.1   Introduction

In the preceding chapter attention was focused on the analyst's task of generating information about alternatives assuming no information whatsoever about the DM's priorities among
objectives. In the present chapter we will focus on the latter
aspect: in which ways the DM can express his priorities and how
the analyst can assist him in this activity.

Utility functions form a means to summarize preferences in a
concise way. In Section 7.2 we present a number of specifications for utility functions which have been used for practical
purposes. Utility functions can be estimated by means of two
sources: data of decisions taken in the past (Section 7.3) and
interview data (Section 7.4). Especially for the latter type
many proposals have been made. We distinguish:

direct methods in which the DM directly tries to explicate the
parameters of the utility function;
indirect methods in which the analyst estimates the parameters,
given the preference statements of the DM;
interactive methods in which the interview questions of the analyst depend in a structured way on the DM's answers to preced-
ding questions.

We will also pay special attention to the fact that in the
literature relative weights seem to be interpreted in two different ways, namely as trade-offs and as indicators of relative
importance. The relationship between these two interpretations
will be clarified by means of dimension analysis. In Sections
7.5 - 7.7 we will discuss some special forms of preference
statements, namely goal programming, lexicographic statements
and minimum levels.

7.2   The Specification of Utility Functions

In Chapter 4 we have shown how utility functions can be used
to represent preference relations. In this section we will
present a series of utility functions which are often employed
in decision analysis. As Table 7.1 shows, there are many ways
to specify a utility function.

Some of the utility functions mentioned here have already

1. $U^1 = \sum\limits_{j} \lambda_j \omega_j$ $\qquad\qquad$ $\underline{\lambda} \geq \underline{0}$ $\quad \underline{1}'\underline{\lambda} = 1$

2. $U^2 = \sum\limits_{j} \lambda_j f(\omega_j)$ $\qquad\qquad$ idem

3. $U^3 = \pi\limits_{j} \{1 + c\lambda_j f(\omega_j)\}$ $\quad \{1 + c = \pi\limits_{j} (1 + c\lambda_j);$
    $\qquad\qquad\qquad\qquad\qquad\qquad\quad \underline{\lambda} \geq \underline{0} \qquad \underline{1}'\underline{\lambda} = 1\}$

4. $U^4 = \pi\limits_{j} \omega_j^{\lambda_j}$ $\qquad\qquad\qquad$ $\underline{\lambda} \geq \underline{0}$ $\quad \underline{1}'\underline{\lambda} = 1$

5. $U^5 = (\sum\limits_{j} \lambda_j \omega_j^{-p})^{-\frac{1}{p}}$ $\qquad\quad$ $\underline{\lambda} \geq \underline{0}$ $\quad \underline{1}'\underline{\lambda} = 1$ $\quad p \geq -1$

6. $U^6 = (\underline{\omega} - \underline{\overset{o}{\omega}})' B (\underline{\omega} - \underline{\overset{o}{\omega}})$

7. $U^7 = \sum\limits_{j} \left(\dfrac{\overset{o}{\omega}_j - \omega_j}{\overset{o}{\omega}_j - \overline{\omega}_j} \right)^p$ $\qquad\qquad$ $p \geq 1$

Table 7.1.   Alternative specifications for utility functions

been dealt with in this study. The linear form U^1 plays a central role in Chapter 6. U^6 and U^7 have also been employed in the same chapter. U^2 is one of the simplest forms used in multiple attribute utility theory (MAUT). It is discussed, for example, in Fishburn [1967], Huber [1974], Keeney [1975], and Farquhar [1977]. U^3 is a multiplicative utility function and is discussed in Keeney [1975] and Farquhar [1977]. U^4 and U^5 are analogues of the Cobb-Douglas function and the constant elasticity of substitution function which are widely used in production theory. Examples of their application in a utility context can be found in Miller and Starr [1960], Fano [1973], and Gum, Roefs and Kimball [1976].

The choice of a certain specification of a utility function depends on the assumed structure of the preferences and on the available data on preference statements.

There are in principle two ways to determine the parameters of a utility function (see Table 7.2). The first way is most appropriate when the DM has already made previous decisions in similar situations (case a). The second way is most appropri-

```
┌─────────────────────────────────────────────────────────────────┐
│  a.   DM:       has revealed preferences by previous choices      │
│       Analyst: derives a utility function                         │
│                calculates optimal alternative                     │
│                                                                   │
│  b.   Analyst: designs a list of questions about preferences      │
│                or indifferences                                   │
│       DM:       answers the questions                             │
│       Analyst: derives a utility function                         │
│                calculates optimal alternative                     │
└─────────────────────────────────────────────────────────────────┘
```

Table 7.2.   Activities involved in the process of priority
                        formulation

ate when a decision problem is virtually new (case b). The two
approaches will be discussed in Sections 7.3 and 7.4, respectively.

    One should be aware that in many cases it will be impossible
to achieve an exact determination of parameters. It follows
(referring to Fig. 1.3) that then the analyst's task cannot end
with the unambiguous selection of the optimal solution. His
task will be more elaborate. He must (1) evaluate the extent
to which the DM's information leads to a reduction of the set
of relevant alternatives and (2) present information about the
reduced set according to the rules delineated in Chapter 6.

    The first task deserves some attention. We shall discuss it
by means of a numerical example, represented in Fig. 7.1.

    Figure 7.1 (a) describes a simple linear MOD problem with
three vertices. Assuming a linear utility function U^1, Fig.
7.1 (c) presents the sets Λ corresponding to the vertices (cf.
Section 6.7). If we assume that it is impossible to determine
the weights λ of the utility function, but that we know that
$\lambda_1 \geq \frac{1}{3}$, we can then conclude from Fig. 7.1 (c) that only the
points on the edge BC remain candidates for a final solution.

    It appears that there are at least three ways to conceptual-
ize the information content of priority statements. These
statements:

1) reduce the set of relevant values for the parameters of the
   utility function;
2) reduce the set of potential solutions;
3) change the probabilities that certain alternatives are optimal.

Each of these consequences gives rise to a certain measure of
information content σ, as will be shown below.

1. The statement reduces the set of relevant values for the
parameters of the utility function. A measure σ_1 for the content of the statement can be defined, therefore, as the propor-

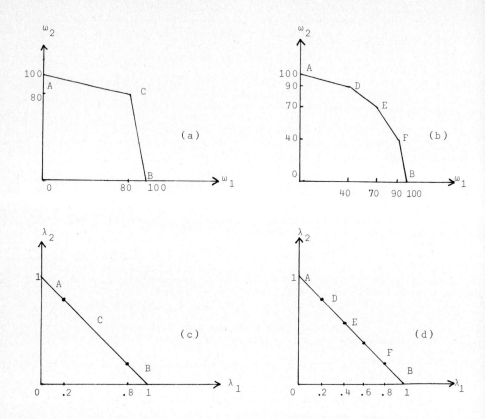

Figure 7.1.   Corner points and corresponding weights of a
               MOLP problem

tion of the space of weights which is eliminated by the state-
ment. In our numerical example when $\lambda_1 \geq \frac{1}{3}$, we find $\sigma_1 = \frac{1}{3}$.
Characteristic for σ_1 is that it only depends on the informa-
tion about the weights, and not on the structure of the pertaining decision problem. That is the reason why in Figure 7.1
(a) and (b) yield the same value for σ_1. This result, however,
does not apply to the next measures.

2. The statement reduces the set of relevant _solutions_. The
second measure σ_2 for the information content of the statement
is defined accordingly as the proportion of the set of efficient solutions which is eliminated. In Figure 7.1 (a), σ_2 is
equal to 0.50, because half of the length of ACB is eliminated
when $\lambda_1 \geq \frac{1}{3}$. In Figure 7.1 (b), only the piece AD of the set
of efficient points is eliminated; hence, σ_2 will attain a

smaller value (i.e.,.27).

3. The statement changes the <u>probability that an efficient so-</u>
<u>lution</u> ultimately <u>is</u> the <u>optimal</u> one. This formulation is
closely related to information theoretic notions about the
evaluation of the content of messages (1) (cf. Theil [1967] and
Mitroff and Mason [1974]). Information theory suggests the
following apporach:
Let $p_1, \ldots, p_N$ be the probabilities that the solutions $\underline{\omega}_1, \ldots, \underline{\omega}_N$
are optimal before the message, and let $q_1, \ldots, q_N$ be the corre-
sponding probabilities after the message. Then, the content of
the information of the message is:

$$\sigma_3 = \sum_{n=1}^{N} \left(q_n \ln \frac{q_n}{p_n} \right) / \ln N \qquad (7.1)$$

(Note that when the message contains no information, namely
when $q_n = p_n$, (7.1) indeed implies that $\sigma_3 = 0$).

In Section 6.7, it has been suggested how p_n can be calcu-
lated. If $\Lambda(\underline{x}_n)$ is the set of weights $\underline{\lambda}$ leading to the solution $\underline{\omega}_n$, then p_n is the ratio of the size of $\Lambda(\underline{x}_n)$ and
$\Lambda(\underline{x}_1) \cup \ldots \cup \Lambda(\underline{x}_N)$. The results of this definition for the example of Figure 7.1 can be found in Table 7.3.

		vertices			
(a)	A	C	B		
Probability before message (p)	.2	.6	.2		
Probability after message (q)	.0	.7	.3		
(b)	A	D	E	F	B
Probability before message (p)	.2	.2	.2	.2	.2
Probability after message (q)	.0	.1	.3	.3	.3

Table 7.3.   Information and the probabilities of alternatives

Application of (7.1) on the data of Table 7.3 yields:

$$\sigma_3(a) = .21 \quad \text{and} \quad \sigma_3(b) = .18$$

Actually, the three measures consider various aspects of the
information content of a message (2). A message is most infor-
mative when it enables the analyst to find the optimal solution.
An example of such a message is: $0.65 \leq \lambda_1 \leq 0.75$.
For case (a), it implies: $\sigma_1 = .90 \quad \sigma_2 = 1.00 \quad \text{and} \quad \sigma_3 = .46$.

For case (b), we find: σ_1 = .90 σ_2 = 1.00   and σ_3 = 1.00 .

After this excursion about the information content of preference statements, we will discuss in the subsequent sections
the two ways to derive utility functions by means of these
preference statements.

7.3   Utility Functions Based on Previous Choices

Past decisions of the DM may contain relevant information
when they have been made in situations similar to the present
problem, and when it may be assumed that the DM's priorities
did not change in the meantime. A clear advantage of this kind
of information (compared with interview data) is that it is
based on real decisions and not on preference statements in artificial conditions. A disadvantage is that the analyst's task
becomes very extensive, because he has to find the whole set of
options among which the DM could choose. Hence, he has to find
the set K as well as the impact functions ω_j, as they were interpreted when the DM made his decision. (Note that for our
purpose it is more important to know how the DM perceived the
problem, than how the problem really was.)

Once the elements of the old decision problem are known, the
analyst may try to estimate the parameters of the utility function U. It is not always possible to derive the parameters un-
ambiguously. Depending on the number of decisions considered
and the number of parameters specified in the utility function,
the parameters may be only partially determinable or, on the
other hand, overdetermined. Table 7.4 shows a number of cases
which will be discussed in this section.

Number of Decisions Considered	Number of Parameters	Determination of Parameters		
		Partial	Full	Over-
1	few	2	1	
1	many	3		
>1	few	4		5
>1	many			6

Table 7.4.   Determinability of parameters of utility functions

When we assume that the utility function has a small number
of parameters (for example, that it is linear), the situation
may arise that the parameters can be fully determined (case 1).
Theorem 2 is relevant in this respect. It states that for every efficient decision taken, the corresponding parameters in λ
can be found. This combination of parameters, however, is not
always unique, as in case 2. When, for example, the decision
problem is completely linear, for each corner point $\underline{x}$, a whole

set of corresponding weights $\Lambda(\underline{x})$ can be derived (cf. Section 6.7). Then an _interval statement_ rather than a point statement is the result.

Another set of circumstances leading to an interval statement about parameters arises when the number of parameters is large compared with the number of decisions considered (i.e. case 3). It is clear that as the J parameters of a linear utility function can be determined exactly, the number of degrees of freedom (defined as the number of observations minus the number of parameters) is equal to zero. A quadratic utility function U^6 which contains J^2 parameters will certainly yield a negative number of degrees of freedom, which implies that the parameters can only be determined partially. Nijkamp [1974] indicates that second order conditions for an optimum solution may provide some additional constraints on the parameters; but in many cases, ultimately no fully specified utility function can be derived. Hence, no complete ordering can be obtained for the set of alternatives of the new decision problem. The analyst is then unable to find the optimal solution, so that he has to resort to the activities mentioned in Section 7.2.

When a series of decisions $\underline{x}_1,\ldots,\underline{x}_T$ has been made, other conclusions may be obtained. When a linear utility function may be assumed to prevail, λ may be derived by analyzing $\Lambda(\underline{x}_1) \cap \Lambda(\underline{x}_2) \cap \ldots \cap \Lambda(\underline{x}_T)$. So here again an interval statement may be obtained (i.e. case 4). When the DM has changed his preferences during the series of decisions, or when the linear specification of the utility function is not realistic for the whole decision space, this intersection may be empty. Hence, the parameters are overdetermined (i.e. case 5). A reasonable way to proceed in this case is to analyze the series of sets:

$$\Lambda(\underline{x}_T)$$

$$\Lambda(\underline{x}_T) \cap \Lambda(\underline{x}_{T-1})$$

$$\Lambda(\underline{x}_T) \cap \Lambda(\underline{x}_{T-1}) \cap \Lambda(\underline{x}_{T-2})$$

.

.

.

The intersections are subsequently examined to find out whether or not they are empty. As soon as an empty set is found, λ can be considered as a member of the last non-empty set.

Another way to overcome the problem of overdetermination of parameters may be to conceive the parameters as stochastic rather than deterministic. Nijkamp [1970] and Nijkamp and Somermeyer [1971] contain an example of a stochastic interpretation of the parameters of a quadratic utility function (i.e. case 6). This enables the analyst to introduce a _probability statement_ about the parameters in the analysis of efficient points.

7.4   Utility Functions Based on Interview Data

Besides information about previous choices, an analyst can
use interview data to derive utility functions. A considerable
amount of work has been carried out in this field. Fishburn,
[1967], for example cites no less than 24 different types of
interview questions which have been used to derive the parameters of the utility function

$$U^2 = \sum_j \lambda_j f(\omega_j)$$

In this section we will pay special attention to the estimation of the weights λ_j of U^1 and U^4. We will deal respectively
with

1. direct estimation
2. indirect estimation
3. interactive estimation
4. methodological considerations

ad 1   The most direct approach to find the weights is asking
the DM questions of the type:
"How large is b when a loss of 1 unit of ω_2 is equally disagreeable as a loss of b units of ω_1?"
For U^1 it follows directly (3) that

$$\frac{\lambda_2}{\lambda_1} = b \tag{7.2}$$

For U^4 the same result can be found when the question is
slightly reformulated as follows:
"How large is b when a loss of 1 percent of ω_2 is equally disagreeable as a loss of b percent of ω_2?"

In many cases, the DM will be uncertain about the values to
be assigned to the λ_j. Hence, it will be difficult to express
unique values for the weights. Fortunately, there are various
ways to present information about weights without the use of
unique values. We shall mention four of them.
a. Interval statements. An example of an interval statement is
   $\lambda_2 \geq .3$ Steuer [1976] discusses its application in linear
   MOD models.
b. Ranking. The DM gives the order of importance of the objectives. If, for example, for three objectives the order is
   1, 2, 3, then the conclusion is $\lambda_1 \geq \lambda_2 \geq \lambda_3$ (cf. Eckenrode
   [1965]) (4). Figure 7.2 shows that this message contains a
   considerable amount of information. Of the original set of
   weights, only 1/6 obeys the ranking indicated above. Hence,
   we find $\sigma_1 = 5/6$
c. (Subjective) probability statements. In Bayesian statistics, interview methods have been developed for the assess-

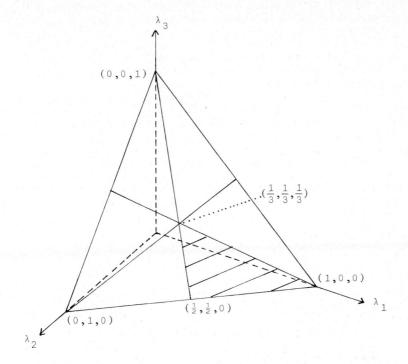

Figure 7.2.   Weights of a three-dimensional utility function

ment of (subjective) prior distributions of parameters (cf.
Raiffa [1968]). Similar methods can be applied to the distribution of the weights of the DM's utility function.
d. Fuzzy set statements. The fuzzy set theory is also important for statements about weights (cf. Blin [1977]). It can
   be used for a systematic analysis of expressions such as "λ_2
   is far greater than λ_1".

No matter how different the four methods may be, they share
one characteristic; i.e. they give rise to preference relations
which are incomplete. The comparability of all alternatives
which arises in the case of known unique values for the weights
does not apply here. At most, part of the alternatives is mutually comparable. It is therefore impossible to assess the
optimal solution by means of them. The measures of information
σ which have been defined in Section 7.2 may be useful in this
case.

An interesting way to derive relative weights has been developed by Saaty [1977]. He proposes to ask the DM for all
pairs (j,j') where objective j is more important than objective
j' to present a value $b_{jj'}$ indicating the measure in which the
j-th objective is more important than the j'-th objective. The

values of $b_{jj'}$ are integers from 1 to (say) 9. When $b_{jj'} = 1$, the objectives are equally important, when $b_{jj'} = 9$, the first objective is more important than the second in the strongest possible sense. Be aware that $b_{jj'} = 1/b_{j'j}$ and $b_{jj} = 1$. Saaty proposes to interpret the $b_{jj'}$ as relative weights: $b_{jj'} = \lambda_j/\lambda_{j'}$. When the $b_{jj'}$ are used to form together a JxJ matrix B, each row j of B consisting of the elements $b_{j1},...,b_{jJ}$ can be used to derive the relative weights. Since, in general, the DM will not reach complete consistency, a (slightly) different weight vector will be found for each row of B. It can easily be shown that when the DM was completely consistent (i.e. every row of B gives rise to the same vector of relative weights) then

$$B\underline{\lambda} = J\underline{\lambda} \qquad\qquad\qquad (7.3)$$

Therefore, Saaty proposes to approximate the vector $\underline{\lambda}$ as the largest eigenvector of the matrix B. Applications of this approach in the field of regional planning can be found in Blair [1979].

ad 2 The former methods have in common that the DM directly provides information about the weights. There are also indirect methods, however, which have close links with the external variant of multidimensional scaling techniques (cf. Nijkamp and Van Veenendaal [1978]). In these techniques, the DM is asked to give a complete ordering of a number of alternatives, such as $\underline{\omega}_1 \gtrsim \underline{\omega}_2 \gtrsim \cdots \gtrsim \underline{\omega}_N$. Let $U_1,...,U_N$ be the unknown values of the utility function which guided the DM in his preference statements. This function is approximated by the linear utility function $\lambda'\underline{\omega}$. Nievergelt [1971] suggests solving the following quadratic programming problem in order to derive the relevant weights:

$$\left\{ \begin{array}{ll} \text{min!} & \sum_{n=1}^{N} (U_n - \underline{\lambda}'\underline{\omega}_n)^2 \\[2em] \text{s.t.} & U_1 \geq U_2 \\[0.5em] & U_2 \geq U_3 \\ & \quad\vdots \\ & U_{N-1} \geq U_N \\[1em] & \underline{\iota}'\underline{\lambda} = 1 \\[0.5em] & \underline{\lambda} \geq \underline{0} \end{array} \right. \qquad (7.4)$$

A similar approach is suggested by Pekelman and Sen [1974], who also take account of the possibility of intransitivities in the preference statements. Huber [1974] discusses a simplification of (7.4) by assuming that the DM has been able to give values for $U_1,\ldots,U_N$ directly. This implies that (7.4) is transformed into an ordinary least squares estimation problem.

ad 3 A common characteristic of the interviews discussed above is that all questions have been devised beforehand. The analyst does not reserve room for feedback on the DM's answers. Frisch [1976] proposes to introduce an <u>interactive</u> element in the interviews so that question no. n is no longer independent from the answers to the preceding (n-1) questions. This approach to estimate the utility function $U^1 = \underline{\lambda}'\underline{\omega}$ can be delineated as follows:

1. Ask the DM to fix the most preferred and most deferred value for each of the objectives $\underline{\omega}^p$ and $\underline{\omega}^d$.

2. Ask the DM for each pair (j,j') which of the two alternatives he prefers: $(\omega_j^p , \omega_{j'}^d)$ or $(\omega_j^d , \omega_{j'}^p)$. If the DM selects the first alternative, ask him to choose between $(\tfrac{1}{2}\omega_j^p + \tfrac{1}{2}\omega_j^d , \omega_{j'}^d)$ and $(\omega_j^d , \omega_{j'}^p)$. If the DM selects the second alternative, present him with a choice between $(\omega_j^p , \omega_{j'}^d)$ and $(\omega_j^d , \tfrac{1}{2}\omega_{j'}^p + \tfrac{1}{2}\omega_{j'}^d)$. Suppose that in the first choice the DM preferred alternative 1, and in the second choice alternative 2, then the third choice is between $(\tfrac{3}{4}\omega_j^p + \tfrac{1}{4}\omega_j^d , \omega_{j'}^d)$ and $(\omega_j^d , \omega_{j'}^p)$. Figure 7.3 shows how this procedure ultimately leads to the formulation of two alternatives between which the DM is indifferent. When a pair of alternatives has been found between which the DM is indifferent, the relative weight $\lambda_j/\lambda_{j'}$ is equal to the absolute value of the slope of the line indicated in Figure 7.3.

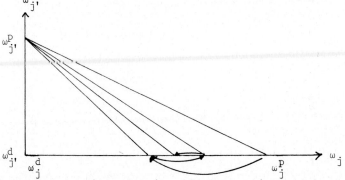

Figure 7.3.   List of pairs of alternatives to be compared in order to assess a utility function

In principle, a series of J-1 interviews is sufficient to determine all relative weights. Some additional interviews may be performed to check consistency   (5).

Another example of an interactive determination of the parameters of a utility function is contained in Haimes and Hall [1974]. First, they generate a series of efficient solutions and the corresponding shadow prices s_{jj}, by means of (6.10). Then they propose to ask the DM for each efficient solution whether he prefers s_{jj}, marginal units of ω_j over 1 marginal unit of ω_j, given the values of all objectives implied by that solution. If the answer is affirmative, the DM may indicate on a scale ranging from 0 to 10 the strength of this preference, which is denoted by w_{jj}, . If the answer is negative, the DM may indicate the strength of his non-preference w_{jj}, on a scale from -10 to 0. Obviously, a value of w_{jj}, equal to 0 means that the DM is indifferent between the two options.

The results of this interview can be used to estimate the values of the weights of a utility function for which all values of w_{jj}, equal 0. These weights can be further refined by a new series of interview questions concerning efficient solutions in the neighbourhood of the one, implied by the estimated weights. This procedure can be repeated until the weights have been determined in a sufficiently accurate way. The result may also be a certain "indifference band" of weights.

ad 4 Finally, we would like to pay some attention to a methodological issue which arises especially with direct interview methods, namely the interpretation of the relative weights λ_j/λ_j, . In certain cases they are interpreted as indicators of trade-offs between variables j and j'; and in other cases, as indicators of the relative importance of objective j compared with j'. How can this difference be explained?

Consider a linear utility function $U = \lambda_1\omega_2 + \lambda_2\omega_2$. Let $[x]$ denote the dimension of variable x and let U, ω_1 and ω_2 be measured in U-, ω_1- and ω_2- units, respectively. Then we find (see De Jong [1967]):

$$\begin{cases} [\lambda_1] = [U]/[\omega_1] \\ [\lambda_2] = [U]/[\omega_2] \\ [\lambda_1/\lambda_2] = [\omega_2]/[\omega_1] \end{cases}$$

When ω_1 and ω_2 are measured in different units, the result for $[\lambda_1/\lambda_2]$ clearly points to the trade-off character of λ_1/λ_2. It indicates how much of ω_2 has to be added to compensate for a

certain loss in ω_1 in order to attain the same utility level.
A change in the dimension of ω_1 (e.g., when length is measured
in meters instead of kilometers) causes a change in $[\lambda_1]$ and
$[\lambda_1/\lambda_2]$ (they should be multiplied by 0.001). This also implies that when $\lambda_1 > \lambda_2$, it is impossible to draw the conclusion that ω_1 is more important than ω_2; a change in the dimension of one of the objectives may reverse the inequality.

When ω_1 and ω_2 are measured in the same units, the "trade-
off interpretation" of λ_1/λ_2 can be maintained, while also the
"relative importance interpretation" is valid. The reason is
that in this case $[\omega_2]/[\omega_1] = 1$ so that the value of λ_1/λ_2
does not depend on the unit of measurement of the objectives.
When, for example, $\lambda_1/\lambda_2 = 2$, this implies that an increase in
ω_1 has an effect on utility which is twice the effect of a same
increase in ω_2. This is what is meant by: ω_1 is twice as important as ω_2.

There are several reasons for being very careful with this
relative importance interpretation (see also Lichfield et. al.
[1975]). It is possible that the DM has another concept of
relative importance than that of the analyst. The DM may have
in mind a multiplicative form of a utility function such as U^4
in Table 7.1. Then his statements about the relative importance of weights are not applicable to linear utility functions
(6).

Another reason concerns the question of how it is possible
to find the same units of measurement for ω_1 and ω_2. In some
cases, the identity of dimensions is reached beforehand; for
example, when ω_1 and ω_2 are the income of group 1 and 2, respectively. In most cases, however, a normalization has to be
applied to remove the difference in dimensions. As there are
several reasonable ways to produce a normalization (7) (see
Table 7.5), a certain amount of arbitrariness is introduced,
because the results of the analysis may depend on the way in
which the normalization has been executed. It is improbable
that the DM can correct this by diversifying his statements
about the importance of the objectives according to the type of
normalization used.

The conclusion is that the trade-off interpretation of relative weights is the most general one. Relative importance interpretations are only meaningful when the dimensions of the
objectives are identical, which may be attained by normalization. One should be aware, however, that in many cases the
concept or relative importance is used in a rather vague way.
Consequently, statements made by a DM about his priorities in

$$\frac{\omega_j}{\omega_j^*}$$

$$\frac{\omega_j - \bar{\omega}_j}{\omega_j^* - \bar{\omega}_j}$$

$$\frac{\omega_j}{\omega_j^g} \qquad\qquad \omega_j^g \text{ is a target value of } \omega_j$$

$$\frac{\omega_j}{\sum\limits_{j'=1}^{J} p_{jj'}} \qquad\qquad \text{see (6.2) for the definition of } p_{jj'}$$

$$\frac{\omega_j}{\left(\sum\limits_{j'=1}^{J} p_{jj'}^2\right)^{\frac{1}{2}}}$$

Table 7.5.   Alternative ways to normalize the variable ω_j

terms of relative importance can be used by analysts in different ways, yielding different results.

7.5   Goal Programming

The preceding sections in this chapter have been devoted to a general discussion about the assessment of various types of utility functions. In the present section and in subsequent ones, we shall deal with some specific types of priority functions and priority structures. We shall begin with a discussion about goal programming.

Goal programming is closely related to the concept of aspiration levels discussed in Chapter 3. Since the publication of Charnes and Cooper [1961], a large number of studies arose about this subject (cf. Ijiri [1965], Lee [1972], Nijkamp and Spronk [1977]). Actually, goal programming is a special case of the utility approach, discussed in the preceding sections. Its characteristic is that a series of goals or aspiration levels $\omega_1^g, \ldots, \omega_J^g$ appear as arguments in the utility function.

It is assumed that the DM aims at attaining the goals. Three cases can accordingly be distinguished for a goal: it can be under-attained, exactly-attained, or over-attained. Let ω_j^+ and ω_j^- denote the level of over-attainment and under-attainment, respectively. Then we have:

$$
\left\{
\begin{array}{l}
\left.
\begin{array}{l}
\omega_j - \omega_j^+ = \omega_j^g \\[2ex]
\omega_j^- = 0
\end{array}
\right\} \text{if } \omega_j \geq \omega_j^g \\[6ex]
\left.
\begin{array}{l}
\omega_j + \omega_j^- = \omega_j^g \\[2ex]
\omega_j^+ = 0
\end{array}
\right\} \text{if } \omega_j \leq \omega_j^g
\end{array}
\right.
\qquad (7.5)
$$

Therefore, either $\omega_j^- = 0$ or $\omega_j^+ = 0$ or both are zero. This is equivalent to:

$$
\left\{
\begin{array}{l}
\omega_j - \omega_j^+ + \omega_j^- = \omega_j^g \\[2ex]
\omega_j^+ \cdot \omega_j^- = 0 \\[2ex]
\omega_j^+ , \omega_j^- \geq 0
\end{array}
\right.
\qquad (7.6)
$$

Analogous to the definition of the vector maximum problem in Section 6.3, a <u>vector minimum problem</u> can be defined:

$$
\left\{
\begin{array}{l}
\text{min!} \quad \underline{\omega}^+ , \underline{\omega}^- \\[2ex]
\text{s.t.} \quad \underline{\omega}(\underline{x}) - \underline{\omega}^+ + \underline{\omega}^- = \underline{\omega}^g \\[2ex]
\qquad \underline{x} \in K \\[2ex]
\qquad \underline{\omega}^+ , \underline{\omega}^- \geq \underline{0} \\[2ex]
\qquad \omega_j^+ \cdot \omega_j^- = 0 \qquad j=1,\ldots,J
\end{array}
\right.
\qquad (7.7)
$$

The vector minimum problem and the vector maximum problem do not always give rise to the same set of efficient solutions (cf. Isermann [1974] and [1977]). This is illustrated in Figure 7.4. Figure 7.4(a) shows a case where only a part (namely AB) of the set of ordinary efficient points (ABC) remains efficient from the point of view of the vector minimization. In (b) the only efficient point as to the goal programming approach ($\underline{\omega}^g$ itself)

is not even efficient in the traditional sense. Only in (c),
where $\underline{\omega}^g \geq \underline{\omega}^*$ the two sets of efficient points are equal. Case
(a) is especially interesting, because it implies that the for-
mulation of (unattainable) goals may reduce the set of relevant

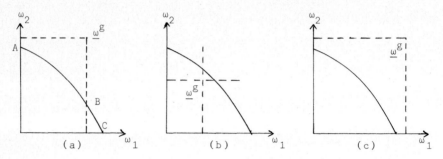

Figure 7.4.   Efficient points in goal programming

efficient points. Hence, such a message contains information
which can be computed in principle by means of the information
measures σ.

    Just as the vector maximum problem can be transformed by the
introduction of a utility function, the vector minimization can
be developed further. The difference is only that in the latter case, a utility function is used with under- and over-at-
tainments of goals as arguments, $f = f(\omega_1^-,\ldots,\omega_J^- , \omega_1^+,\ldots,\omega_J^+)$,
rather than the values of the objectives themselves.
Figure 7.5 shows a number of possible forms for f when J = 1.

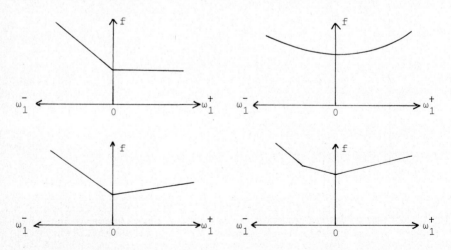

Figure 7.5.   Utility functions in goal programming

A rather general expression for f is the following CES-type function:

$$f(\omega_1^-,\ldots,\omega_J^-, \omega_1^+,\ldots,\omega_J^+) = \left[\sum_j \lambda_j^-\left(\frac{\omega_j^-}{\omega_j^g}\right)^p + \lambda_j^+\left(\frac{\omega_j^+}{\omega_j^g}\right)^p\right]^{\frac{1}{p}} \qquad (7.8)$$

Note the resemblance between this expression and the utility function U^5 in Table 7.1.

For the application of (7.8), a considerable amount of information is needed, as the values of no less than 3J + 1 parameters should be determined: $\omega_1^g,\ldots,\omega_J^g$, $\lambda_1^-,\ldots,\lambda_J^-$, $\lambda_1^+,\ldots,\lambda_J^+$, p. Compared with some of the utility functions discussed in Section 7.2, this number of parameters is large. This implies an aggravation of the DM's task, and therefore, one may doubt whether the DM can accomplish that (cf. Isermann [1977]).

A consequence of specification (7.8) is that the DM must make a choice for p (p $\geq$ 1). It is interesting to consider the question of how sensitive the final solution is for the choice of this rather technical parameter. Figure 7.6 shows that this sensitivity may be considerable.

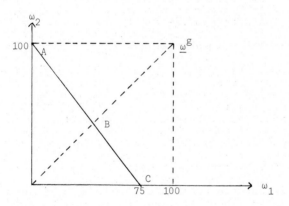

Figure 7.6.   Sensitivity of the final solution for the value of p

If in Figure 7.6 the weights λ_j^- and λ_j^+ are equal for all j, A would be the final solution for p = 1, whereas B would be the final solution when p $\to$ ∞. For intermediate values of p, a final solution between A and B will be found. So, more than half of the set of efficient points is still a candidate for the final solution when all but one parameter have been fixed. This sensitivity for p is also illustrated by the relatively low values for the information measures of the message of the 3J parameters:

$\sigma_1 = 3/7$, $\sigma_2 = 3/7$ and $\sigma_3 = .81$.

From a practical point of view, the choice for p = 1 or
p → ∞ is most attractive, because it enables the analyst to apply LP routines. The choice for p = 2 also deserves special
attention. The arising quadratic programming problem has the
characteristic that it obeys the certainty equivalence rule (cf.
Theil [1964]).

Goal programming has many variants. It may contain stochastic elements (cf. Donckels [1975]). More than one aspiration
level may be defined for a certain objective (cf. Charnes et
al. [1975]). The formulation of goals by the DM may be accomplished in an interactive way during the programming phase (cf.
Nijkamp and Spronk [1978]). Finally, pre-emptive priorities
may be assumed in a goal programming context. The last subject
will be elaborated in the next section dealing with lexicographic statements.

7.6   Lexicographic Statements

There are situations in which a DM feels that the objectives
are clearly hierarchically ordered. It will be impossible for
him to give information about trade-offs, because the one objective is so important compared with the other that they cannot be traded-off against one another. In this situation, a
lexicographic order of alternatives can be used. It implies
that an objective of order j is only considered when the more
important objectives have reached satisfactory or equal levels.

Lexicographic orders have received relatively little attention in economics. The reason is probably that the representation of such an ordering by means of a utility function is only
possible in certain respects (cf. Section 4.2, Day and Robinson
[1973] and Fishburn [1974]). However, a number of economists
have stressed the importance of this ordering (cf. Menger
[1968] and Georgescu-Roegen [1954]). It should also be noted
that the lexicographic ordering is in accordance with the psychological notion of a hierarchy of wants (cf. Maslow [1954]).

There are various ways to elaborate a lexicographic order.
The simplest case arises when one ignores the possibility of a
satiation level for the objectives. Let the objectives be num-
bered in decreasing order of importance: 1,...,J. Then an al-
ternative $\underline{\omega}^1$ is lexicographically preferred to $\underline{\omega}^2$ if one of the
following J cases applies:

$$
\begin{cases}
\text{case 1}: & \omega_1^1 > \omega_1^2 \\[2ex]
\text{case 2}: & \left(\begin{array}{c} \omega_1^1 = \omega_1^2 \\[2ex] \omega_2^1 > \omega_2^2 \end{array}\right) \\[4ex]
\quad\vdots & \\[2ex]
\text{case J}: & \left(\begin{array}{cc} \omega_j^1 = \omega_j^2 & \quad j=1,\dots J-1 \\[2ex] \omega_J^1 > \omega_J^2 & \end{array}\right)
\end{cases}
\qquad (7.9)
$$

In Appendix II of section 6, this type of lexicographic order
has also been employed. The distinguishing characteristic of
the order is that the choice between two alternatives is only
determined by the most important objective for which they are
unequal. Subsequent objectives do not influence the choice in
any way.

A more refined order is obtained when satiation levels are
introduced (cf. Fishburn [1974]). When the two alternatives
are compared in this case, two situations may arise: (a) both
alternatives are satisfactory according to all objectives and
(b) at least one alternative is unsatisfactory according to at
least one objective. In situation (a) statement (7.9) is rele-
vant again to describe the choice between $\underline{\omega}^1$ and $\underline{\omega}^2$. In situation (b) the choice depends on the first unsatisfactory objec-
tive for which the alternatives are unequal. In a formalized
way, these statements read:

$\underline{\omega}^1$ is preferred to $\underline{\omega}^2$ if one of the following cases applies:

$$
\begin{cases}
\text{a.} \quad \underline{\omega}^1, \underline{\omega}^2 \geq \underline{\omega}^s \\[3ex]
\quad \text{case 1}: \omega_1^1 > \omega_1^2 \\[2ex]
\quad \text{case 2}: \left(\begin{array}{c} \omega_1^1 = \omega_1^2 \\[2ex] \omega_2^1 > \omega_2^2 \end{array}\right) \\[4ex]
\qquad\vdots \\[2ex]
\quad \text{case J}: \left(\begin{array}{cc} \omega_j^1 = \omega_j^2 & \quad j=1,\dots J-1 \\[2ex] \omega_J^1 > \omega_J^2 & \end{array}\right)
\end{cases}
\qquad (7.10a)
$$

b. for at least one j ω_j^1 or $\omega_j^2 \leq \omega_j^s$

case 1 : $\omega_1^1 > \omega_1^2$, $\omega_1^2 < \omega_1^s$

case 2 : $\begin{pmatrix} \omega_1^1 , \omega_1^2 \geq \omega_1^s \\ \\ \omega_2^1 > \omega_2^2 , \omega_2^2 < \omega_2^s \end{pmatrix}$

$\vdots$

case J : $\begin{pmatrix} \omega_j^1 , \omega_j^2 \geq \omega_j^s \qquad j=1,\dots J-1 \\ \\ \omega_J^1 > \omega_J^2 , \omega_J^2 < \omega_J^s \end{pmatrix}$

$\qquad\qquad\qquad\qquad\qquad\qquad\qquad\qquad (7.10b)$

Consider, for example, the following alternatives:

$$(\underline{\omega}^1 , \underline{\omega}^2 , \underline{\omega}^3) = \begin{pmatrix} 100 & 100 & 80 \\ 80 & 40 & 50 \\ 7 & 12 & 13 \end{pmatrix} \qquad (7.11)$$

When no satiation levels are introduced, the lexicographic or-
der implies: $\underline{\omega}^1 \ominus \underline{\omega}^2 \ominus \underline{\omega}^3$. When, however, satiation is present,
denoted by the levels (70, 30, 10), we have because of (a):
$\underline{\omega}^2 \ominus \underline{\omega}^3$ and because of (b): $\underline{\omega}^2 \ominus \underline{\omega}^1$ and $\underline{\omega}^3 \ominus \underline{\omega}^1$, hence
$\underline{\omega}^2 \ominus \underline{\omega}^3 \ominus \underline{\omega}^1$.

Lexicographic orders can be used fruitfully in combination
with the methods discussed earlier in this chapter. In the
context of goal programming, for example, it may make sense to
divide the objectives in M priority classes (M $\leq$ J) such that
the objectives in class m-1 have a pre-emptive priority above
the objectives in class m (m=2,...,M). This formulation gives
rise to a sequential analysis of M goal programming problems.
In the first run, the optimal values of the objectives of the
first priority class are determined. The second run is used to
find the values of the second priority objectives under the
condition that the first class objectives attain their optimal
values (cf. Nijkamp and Spronk [1977]). The analysis is concluded when the space for the optimization of low priority objectives has become empty due to the proliferation of side-conditions.

For this method, it is required that the satiation values
are determined before the procedure starts. Van Delft and
Nijkamp [1977] propose an alternative method in which the satiation levels are not filled in beforehand but rather during the
procedure. They show that is is possible to conquer some of
the rigidity of lexicographic orders. Their method can be delineated as follows:
Assume that each priority class contains one objective (M = J).
Then proceed by maximizing the first objective:

$$\begin{cases} \text{max!} \quad \omega_1(\underline{x}) \\ \text{s.t.} \quad \underline{x} \in K \end{cases} \qquad (7.12)$$

On the basis of the optimal outcome ω_1^* the DM is requested to give information about the satiation level for ω_1. Thus the DM tries to express a tolerance limit β_1, for the second run ($\beta_1 \leq 1$):

$$\begin{cases} \text{max!} \quad \omega_2(\underline{x}) \\ \text{s.t.} \quad \underline{x} \in K \\ \qquad \omega_1(\underline{x}) \geq \beta_1 \omega_1^* \end{cases} \qquad (7.13)$$

In the third run, another constraint is added which specifies the tolerance limit for ω_2. Proceeding in this way, the set of alternatives is restricted more and more for low priority objectives. After J runs, the optimal solution is found.

Evaluating, we may say that in certain situations lexicographic statements may be a useful means for the DM to express priorities. The rigidity which is built in can be relaxed to a certain extent by the introduction of satiation levels and tolerance limits.

7.7   Minimum Standards

A straightforward way to express priorities among objectives is the statement of minimum requirements which an alternative should satisfy. These minimum standards ω^{ms} should not be conceived of as _sufficient_ conditions for an alternative to be acceptable. They only specify _necessary_ conditions for acceptability and can be used to eliminate irrelevant alternatives. Hence, minimum standards and aspiration levels (goals) should not be confused. A discussion of minimum standards can be found in MacCrimmon [1973], and Fandel and Wilhelm [1976].

Minimum standards have already been discussed in Chapter 6 in the context of the generation of efficient points by means of parametric programming (cf. Cohon and Marks [1973] and Miller and Byers [1973]). Minimum standards have also links with the various forms to express priorities discussed earlier in this section. The shadow prices of side-conditions can, for example, be interpreted as the weights of the linear utility function, discussed in Section 6.2.

The information $\underline{\omega} \geq \omega^{ms}$ is insufficient to reach a complete ordering of objectives. For example, in Figure 7.7 which is similar to Figure 7.2, the set of efficient points is reduced from A-C-D-E-G to B-C-D-E-F. Hence, we find for the information measures $\sigma_1 = .40$, $\sigma_2 = .33$, and $\sigma_3 = .32$.

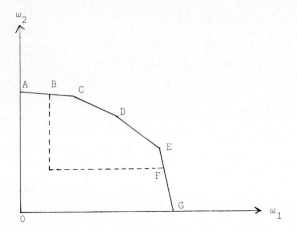

Figure 7.7.   Minimum standards in MOLP

   The minimum standards also play a central role in a number
of interactive methods, discussed in Chapter 9.

7.8   Conclusion

   This chapter has been devoted to the presentation of a number of ways in which the DM's preferences can be modelled in a
mathematical programming framework. The conclusion is that
there are several types of information about priorities which
can be handled and that there is a large variety of forms of
utility functions to represent preference relations.

   Special attention has been paid to the interpretation of
weights of utility functions as indicators of relative importance. The conclusion has been that in certain circumstances,
this interpretation is only valid when the objectives have been
normalized. This produces another difficulty, however, because
a normalization is always to a certain extent arbitrary.

   It appears that in many cases the available information
about preferences is insufficient to achieve a complete ordering of alternatives. Consequently, we need measures for the
information content of a certain statement about priorities.
Several reasonable measures have been developed in this chapter,
each stressing a different aspect of the information content.

Footnotes

1.   In information theory (which has close links with the en-
     tropy concept in physics) a message is conceived of as a
     statement about the probability that certain events will

occur. A message has a minimum information content when
all possible events are judged as equi-probable. A message has a maximum information content when one possible
event receives a probability equal to 1 which means that
the alternative events receive a probability equal to zero.
In equation (7.1) a conceptualization is presented of the
information content of a certain message compared with a
preceding message. Obviously, when both messages assign
the same probabilities to the events, the information content of the last message is equal to zero.

2. The measures have been defined such that the higher the
content of a message the higher the value of σ. The minimum attainable level for σ_i is 0 for i = 1, 2, 3. The
maximum attainable level for σ_1 and σ_2 is 1. Notice that
σ_3 = 1 when for a certain n, $p_n = \frac{1}{N}$ and $q_n = 1$.
In certain cases σ_3 may attain values higher than 1, for
example when $p_n < \frac{1}{N}$ and $q_n = 1$ for a certain n.

3. Note that in both interpretations the values of λ_j are not
determined themselves, but only the ratios. Thus, one of
the weights can be chosen as a 'numéraire'. Unique values
of the weights can also be obtained by adding the constraint that the sum of the weights equals 1.

4. Eckenrode [1965] also discusses other direct methods such
as rating.

5. Thus one may check whether the estimated relative weights
$\left(\frac{\lambda_1}{\lambda_2}\right)$, $\left(\frac{\lambda_2}{\lambda_3}\right)$ and $\left(\frac{\lambda_1}{\lambda_3}\right)$ really satisfy $\left(\frac{\lambda_1}{\lambda_2}\right) \cdot \left(\frac{\lambda_2}{\lambda_3}\right) = \left(\frac{\lambda_1}{\lambda_3}\right)$.
Note the relationship with the method of Saaty [1977] dis-
cussed above.

6. Realize that statement (7.2) : λ_2/λ_1 = b can be based on a
linear utility function, but also on a multiplicative one.

7. In Appendix II of Chapter 6 we already discussed an alternative way of normalization.

CHAPTER 8

DISCRETE MULTI-OBJECTIVE DECISION PROBLEMS

8.1 Introduction

In the preceding chapters we dealt with convex decision problems, characterized by a <u>divisibility</u> of instrument variables. This means that when two alternatives are feasible, any convex combination of them is feasible. In the present chapter we will disregard the divisibility assumption since there are many decision problems in which the indivisibility of resources is essential. This also holds true for the field of regional planning. For example, in decisions concerning physical infrastructure, it is only meaningful to consider a discrete number of bridges or lanes. The number of feasible locations of a new town or an atomic reactor is also in general discrete.

Discreteness means for MOD problems that some characteristic difficulties arise which require special treatment. To present some examples:

(a) The set of alternatives is no longer convex and consequently parametric programming yields only a part of the set of efficient solutions.

(b) Sometimes discreteness implies that only a very limited number of alternatives is available. As a result the main emphasis of the methods should no longer be on presenting a good summary of a large number of objectives. Much more relevant here is the presentation of detailed information about the relative advantages and disadvantages of the alternatives. Analysis of rankings among objectives would be one way to carry this out.

(c) Discrete problems often contain only ordinal information about objectives. Many of the methods discussed before cannot, however, be applied to ordinal data. Alternative methods such as concordance analysis are more appropriate in this case.

These reasons are sufficiently important to justify a separate discussion of the discrete case (1). The decision methods for discrete problems will be classified according to three dimensions (see Table 8.1):

- the availability of priority information (cf. Chapter 6 versus Chapter 7);

- the size of the problem ("many" versus "few" alternatives;
  see for an explanation of "many" and "few" Sections 8.2 and
  8.3);

- the type of information (cardinal versus ordinal; cf. Section
  4.3).

The chapter closes with a discussion on the possibilities of
reducing the size of discrete decision problems (Section 8.10).

is information available about the DM's priorities?	number of alternatives	type of information about objectives	
		cardinal	ordinal
no	many	8.2	8.6
	few	8.3	8.7
yes	many	8.4	8.8
	few	8.5	8.9

Table 8.1.   Subject of Sections 8.2 - 8.9

Although no less than eight types of discrete problems will
be dealt with, this chapter does not claim to be an exhaustive
survey of methods for discrete problems. For more complete
surveys we refer to Bernard and Besson [1971], Guigou [1974],
Bertier and Bouroche [1975], Van Delft and Nijkamp [1977] and
Sinden and Worrell [1979]. The methods will be presented such
that the links with Chapters 6 and 7 become as clear as possible. This means for example that the main attention will be
devoted to the insight into the structure of the decision problem which can be obtained by means of the decision methods.

8.2   Alternatives: many; Measurement: cardinal; Availability
       of Priority Information: no

This section deals with the case of many discrete alternatives. The word "many" will be used in a rather loose sense.
It refers to a situation in which the number of alternatives is
so large that the DM is unable to comprehend them. Thus the
number indicated by "many" depends on the complexity of the
problem and the skills of the DM. In certain problems, therefore, the lower limit of "many" may be 10 alternatives while
for other problems it may be 50 alternatives. The number of
alternatives will be called "few" when it is not "many".

First a formal representation of the discrete decision problem will be given. Let the number of alternatives be
$N(n=1,\ldots,N)$. The outcomes for the objectives of alternative n
will be denoted by $\underline{\omega}^n$. When the number of objectives is equal
to J, the N alternatives form together a $(J \times N)$ matrix
$R = (\underline{\omega}^1,\ldots,\underline{\omega}^N)$. R will be called the project effect matrix.

Then the vector maximum problem reads:

$$\begin{cases} \max! & R\,\underline{\delta} \\ \text{s.t.} & \underline{\imath}'\underline{\delta} = 1 \\ & \underline{\delta} \geq \underline{0} \\ & \delta_n = 0,1 \end{cases} \qquad (8.1)$$

so that $\underline{\delta}$ is an N vector with N-1 zero entries. Expression (8.1) simply states that one of the N alternatives must be selected and that it should be evaluated according to J objectives.

A number of the concepts and methods discussed in Chapter 6 can be applied straightforwardly to the discrete case, although one should be aware of some difficulties which may arise. We give some examples of these difficulties.

The pay-off matrix P contains J columns of the matrix R. These columns can be found by solving for $j=1,\ldots,J$:

$$\begin{cases} \max! & \underline{\varepsilon}'_j\,R\,\underline{\delta} \\ \text{s.t.} & \underline{\imath}'\underline{\delta} = 1 \\ & \underline{\delta} \geq \underline{0} \\ & \delta_n = 0,1 \end{cases} \qquad (8.2)$$

which yields a series of solutions $\overset{*}{\underline{\delta}}_1,\ldots.\overset{*}{\underline{\delta}}_J$. Thus the relationship between P and R can be written as:

$$P = R\,(\overset{*}{\underline{\delta}}_1,\ldots,\overset{*}{\underline{\delta}}_J) \qquad (8.3)$$

Especially when N is not too large compared to J it is probable that P will contain two or more identical columns of R. This would mean that the pertaining objectives are in harmony instead of conflicting.

Another difficulty arises when methods are used to generate efficient solutions. As essential assumption in Theorem 2 (which is the basis of the weights-method to find efficient solutions) is that the set of feasible solutions is convex. Fig. 8.1 shows that non-convexity due to a discrete set of alternatives will reduce the use of the weights-method. Six alternatives have been depicted in it, four of which can be found as

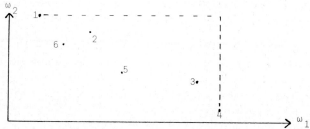

Fig. 8.1.   A discrete set of alternatives

the solution of the parametric programming problem:

$$
\begin{cases}
\max! & \underline{\lambda}' \, R \, \underline{\delta} \\
\text{s.t.} & \underline{\imath}' \, \underline{\delta} = 1 \\
& \underline{\lambda}, \underline{\delta} \geq \underline{0} \\
& \delta_n = 0,1
\end{cases}
\tag{8.4}
$$

The alternatives 5 and 6 are, however, not a solution of (8.4). Yet, alternative 5 is not dominated by any other feasible solution. The conclusion is that in the discrete case no longer all efficient alternatives are a solution of (8.4). Fortunately, other methods are available to generate the set of efficient solutions. The method based on side-conditions (see Theorem 3) does not, for example, break down by the non-convexity. Another method has been proposed by Bowman [1976]. He proves that all efficient solutions can be generated by a parametrization on $\underline{\lambda}$ in:

$$
\begin{cases}
\min! & \max_{j} \, \hat{\lambda} \, (\underline{\overset{*}{\omega}} - R \, \underline{\delta}) \\
\text{s.t.} & \underline{\lambda}, \underline{\delta} \geq \underline{0} \\
& \underline{\imath}' \underline{\delta} = 1 \\
& \delta_n = 0,1
\end{cases}
\tag{8.5}
$$

where $\hat{\lambda}$ is the diagonal matrix with the vector $\underline{\lambda}$ on the main diagonal.

A third consequence of discreteness which should be discussed is its influence on the compromise solutions in Section 6.4. One problem is that compromise e_2 may break down because in (6.19) P may be singular so that it is impossible to proceed with (6.20). Another problem pertains to all compromise solutions, because the non-convexity of the set of feasible solutions caused by the discreteness may lead to a violation of the non-extremity requirement for compromise solutions. A careful analysis of the compromise concepts teaches that most of them will have a tendency to select the rather extreme alternatives 2 or 3 in Figure 8.1, rather than the central alternative 5. The only compromises which meet the non-extremity condition are the min-max solution c_3 and its lexicographic refinement c_4. As to the different measures of conflict and the half-compromises which are introduced in Sections 6.5 and 6.6, the conclusion is that they can be applied in the discrete case as far as the corresponding compromise concepts can be maintained in this context.

8.3 Alternatives: few; Measurement: cardinal; Availability of Priority of Information: no

Decision problems with a small number of alternatives need

another approach than problems with many alternatives. The
main emphasis should no longer be on reducing the redundancy of
information but on gathering as much relevant information as
possible. The extreme case arises when only two alternatives
are distinguished. This occurs, for example, when the question
is whether a bridge should be built or not. There are two obvious responses to such a problem. One is to increase the intensity of the information by collecting data on as many relevant objectives as possible. The other is to increase the ex-
tensity of the information by taking more alternatives into account. In our example this would mean that different types of
bridges and different ferry systems will be included.

Let us now assume that the total number of alternatives and
objectives is fixed. It cannot be expected that all the concepts discussed in the preceding section are useful in the context of small numbers of alternatives. Therefore, other methods which focus more on a detailed analysis of pros and cons of
alternatives should be introduced. We discuss three methods
here based on (a) probabilities, (b) rankings and (c) concordance analysis.

(a) In Section 6.7 we discussed the linear MOD problem. One of
the concepts introduced there was the probability that a vertex
is optimal. The same concept may be effectively applied in the
discrete case. We need the following definition. Let $\Lambda(\underline{\omega}^n)$ be
the set of all weights $\underline{\lambda}$ of a linear utility function which
yields $\underline{\omega}^n$ as the best one of all columns of R (after normalization):

$$\Lambda(\underline{\omega}^n) = \{\underline{\lambda} \mid \underline{\lambda}' \ (\overset{*}{\omega} \overset{\frown}{-} \overline{\omega})^{-1}(\underline{\omega}^n\underline{1}' - R) \geq \underline{0}', \ \underline{\lambda} \geq \underline{0}, \ \underline{1}'\underline{\lambda} = 1\}$$

$$(8.6)$$

then the probability that $\underline{\omega}^n$ is optimal is equal to the ratio
of the size of $\Lambda(\underline{\omega}^n)$ and the size of $\Lambda(\underline{\omega}^1) \cup \Lambda(\underline{\omega}^2) \cup \ldots \cup \Lambda(\underline{\omega}^N)$.

Consider as a numerical example a set with 3 alternatives to be
evaluated according to 3 criteria:

$$(\underline{\omega}^1, \underline{\omega}^2, \underline{\omega}^3) = \begin{pmatrix} 1 & .7 & .0 \\ 80 & 100 & 50 \\ 6 & 4 & 0 \end{pmatrix}$$

After normalization these alternatives are:

$$\begin{pmatrix} 1 & .7 & 0 \\ .6 & 1 & 0 \\ .5 & 0 & 1 \end{pmatrix}$$

The sets $\Lambda(\underline{\omega}^n)$ appear in Figure 8.2.

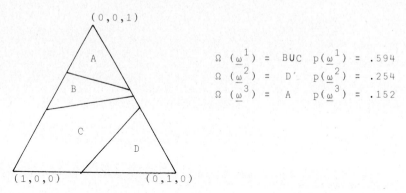

$$\begin{aligned}
\Omega\ (\underline{\omega}^1) &= \text{BUC} & p(\underline{\omega}^1) &= .594 \\
\Omega\ (\underline{\omega}^2) &= D' & p(\underline{\omega}^2) &= .254 \\
\Omega\ (\underline{\omega}^3) &= A & p(\underline{\omega}^3) &= .152
\end{aligned}$$

Fig. 8.2.   Sets of weights associated with three alternatives

In this example, the probability that $\underline{\omega}^1$ is optimal is larger than the probability that one of the other alternatives is optimal.

(b) Another way to analyze small data sets is by studying the rank orders in which the alternatives can be arranged. It is not only important to know that an alternative has a good probability of reaching the first position, because the probability of reaching the second or last position may also be of interest.

When N alternatives are given, they can be arranged in N! different orders. When these orders are given the interpretation of preference orders, a considerable number of them may be excluded on a priori reasons. This may be illustrated by Figure 8.1. The alternatives 1, 2 and 3 can be arranged in 6 different orders. Two of these orders can be excluded beforehand, however, when it is assumed that the utility function $U(\omega_1, \omega_2)$ is concave, namely (1,3,2) and (3,1,2). The conclusion is therefore that number 2 is never the least attractive of the three alternatives. See for a further discussion on the elimination of rank orders Appendix I. An even more detailed study of rank orders can be executed by calculating the probability of each rank order along the same lines as in (a). Instead of $\Lambda(\underline{\omega}^n)$, one has to introduce the concept of a set of weights of a linear utility function which yields a certain rank order of alternatives. Let this set be denoted by $\Lambda(\underline{\omega}^1, \underline{\omega}^2,\ldots,\underline{\omega}^N)$ for the rank order $(\underline{\omega}^1, \underline{\omega}^2,\ldots,\underline{\omega}^N)$.
Then $\Lambda(\underline{\omega}^1, \underline{\omega}^2,\ldots,\underline{\omega}^N)$ can be expressed as follows:

$$\Lambda(\underline{\omega}^1,\underline{\omega}^2,\ldots,\underline{\omega}^N) = \{\underline{\lambda}\,|\,\underline{\lambda}'(\overset{*\frown}{\omega-\omega})^{-1}(\underline{\omega}^1-\underline{\omega}^2,\underline{\omega}^2-\underline{\omega}^3,\ldots,\underline{\omega}^{N-1}-\underline{\omega}^N) \geq \underline{0}'$$

$$\underline{\lambda} \geq \underline{0}\ ,\ \underline{\iota}'\,\underline{\lambda} = 1\}$$

$$(8.7)$$

Along the lines set out in Section 6.7, the set described in
(8.7) can be used to calculate the probabilities of the rankings.   Table 8.2 shows the outcomes of the numerical example
presented above for six potential rankings.

ranking	Λ	probability
$\underline{\omega}^1, \underline{\omega}^2, \underline{\omega}^3$	C	.452
$\underline{\omega}^1, \underline{\omega}^3, \underline{\omega}^2$	B	.142
$\underline{\omega}^2, \underline{\omega}^1, \underline{\omega}^3$	D	.254
$\underline{\omega}^2, \underline{\omega}^3, \underline{\omega}^1$	$\emptyset$	.0
$\underline{\omega}^3, \underline{\omega}^1, \underline{\omega}^2$	A	.152
$\underline{\omega}^3, \underline{\omega}^2, \underline{\omega}^1$	$\emptyset$	.0

Table 8.2.   Probabilities of rankings of alternatives

The conclusion is that owing to the structure of the data, two
rankings out of six can be excluded.   In no case is alternative 1 the least attractive of the three.   This can also be
concluded from Table 8.3.

alternative (n)	position in ranking (r)		
	1	2	3
$\underline{\omega}^1$	.594	.406	–
$\underline{\omega}^2$	.254	.452	.294
$\underline{\omega}^3$	.152	.142	.706

Table 8.3.   Probability that alternative n attains position r
              when ranked in order of attractivity

(c) The third method to be discussed is <u>concordance analysis.</u>
The roots of this method, in which pairwise comparisons of alternatives play a central role, can be found in Benayoun et al.
[1966] (ELECTRE).   It has been further developed by Roy [1972].
An extensive list of applications can be found in Van Delft and
Nijkamp [1977].   A central concept in the method is the concordance set $C_{nn'}$, which is the set of all objectives according
to which alternative n is at least as large as alternative n'
(we assume that for all objectives, high values are preferred
to small values):

$$C_{nn'} = \{j \,|\, \omega_j^n \geq \omega_j^{n'}\}$$ (8.8)

Most of the applications of concordance analysis assume that
certain a priori information about priorities among objectives
is available. This will be dealt with in Section 8.5. Here we
will give a variant in which such an assumption has not been
made. Once a concordance set has been defined, we introduce
the concept of a concordance index $c_{nn'}$, which is an indicator
of the strength or intensity of the viewpoints in favour of the
statement that n is preferred to n'. It can be defined, for
example, as (2):

$$c_{nn'} = \sum_{j \in C_{nn'}} \left(\frac{\omega_j^n - \omega_j^{n'}}{\overset{*}{\omega}_j - \bar{\omega}_j} \right)$$ (8.9)

There are different ways to proceed with the concordance index.

1) One may compare the values of the $c_{nn'}$ with some mean value
    $\bar{c}$. If it is true that:

$$\begin{cases} c_{nn'} > \bar{c} \\ c_{n'n} < \bar{c} \end{cases}$$ (8.10)

the conclusion may be that alternative n is preferred to n'.

2) Compare $c_{nn'}$ and $c_{n'n}$ directly and conclude that n is pre-
    ferred to n' when $c_{nn'} > c_{n'n}$.

3) Compare $\sum_n c_{nn'}$ with $\sum_n c_{n'n}$ and conclude that the best al-
    ternative is that one with the largest positive difference
    between the first and second term. It is interesting to
    note that the third way yields the same result as the cal-
    culation of compromise c_1 in Section 6.4.

These three ways may produce different results which consequently should be interpreted carefully. It is also useful to consider the sensitivity of the outcomes for a small change in the
definition of the concordance set (8.8), namely by replacing
the $\geq$ by a $>$ sign.

Concluding this discrete case with a small number of alternatives,
we find that the main reason for it being impossible to use
methods similar to those in Chapters 6 and 7 is that the idea
of finding a compromise between opposing views is not applicable. It is not surprising, therefore, that several concordance
analyses end up with the recommendation to generate additional
alternatives by combining some of the original alternatives
(cf. Duckstein and David [1976]). Obviously, this is an indica-

tion that such MOD problems actually have a continuous character instead of a discrete one. It may be appropriate to formulate such problems in advance as continuous (3).

8.4   Alternatives: many; Measurement: cardinal; Availability
      of Priority Information: yes

     The subject of this section is very similar to that of
Chapter 7. All concepts and methods discussed there will also
be applicable in this section. One important complication
should be mentioned concerning Section 7.6, which deals with
the imposition of side-conditions on the set of alternatives.
In the continuous case, the shadow-prices of the side-conditions
can be interpreted as the weights of a utility function. In
the discrete case, the derivation of shadow-prices is, however,
problematic. Figure 8.3 gives an example of this problem. What
is the effect of the imposition of a constraint $\omega_1 > \bar{\omega}_1$ on the

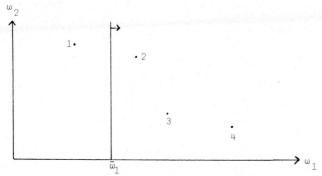

Fig. 8.3.   Shadow-prices in discrete problems

maximum attainable level of ω_2 ? It gives rise to a choice of
alternative 2 instead of 1. Yet the shadow-price of the con-
straint is zero, because $\Delta\omega_2/\Delta\bar{\omega}_1$ is zero for small changes in
$\bar{\omega}_1$. Gomory and Baumol [1960] attempt to solve the problem in
the following way. The original integer programming problem is
translated into an ordinary LP problem by deleting the integer
conditions and adding a number of constraints in such a way
that the problems have the same solution. They propose to conceive the shadow-prices of the derived problem as the prices of
the original problem. A weak point in this procedure is that
there are many ways to accomplish the transformation, each
yielding different values of the shadow-prices. Hence the numerical outcomes are to a certain extent arbitrary (4).

8.5   Alternatives: few; Measurement: cardinal; Availability of
      Priority Information: yes

     Many methods have been developed to deal with this type of
problem. For example, cost-benefit analysis and many related
methods (cf. Sinden and Worrell [1979]) fall under this heading.

Also the main applications of concordance analysis have been in this context. In this section we will pay special attention to the last mentioned method.

The assumption commonly made in concordance analysis is that the DM has expressed his priorities by a series of weights $(\lambda_1,\ldots,\lambda_J)$, indicating the importance he attaches to the J objectives. The analysis then proceeds along the lines discussed in Section 8.3. First the concordance set $C_{nn'}$ is derived.

Then the concordance indices can be calculated. In the context of given priority statements one of the following formulations can be used:

$$c_{nn'} = \sum_{j \in C_{nn'}} \lambda_j \qquad\qquad (8.11a)$$

$$c_{nn'} = \sum_{j \in C_{nn'}} \lambda_j \left(\frac{\omega_j^n - \omega_j^{n'}}{\omega_j^* - \bar{\omega}_j} \right) \qquad (8.11b)$$

Comparing these formulations with (8.9), it is interesting to note that (8.9) only contains information about the project effect matrix R, while (8.11a) deals only with weights. In (8.11b) these two elements are combined. Note that as we distinguished

- two ways to define a concordance set (with $\geq$ and $>$);

- three ways to define concordance indices given information about priorities (see (8.9), (8.11a) and (8.11b));

- three ways to draw conclusions about rankings or optimality;

eighteen different outcomes can, in principle, be obtained. This is a favourable starting point for a nuanced conclusion about the desirability of alternatives.

A comment should be made concerning the meaning attached to the weights λ_j in concordance analysis. In Section 7.4 we established that relative weights have a meaningful interpretation for additive as well as multiplicative utility functions. Obviously (8.11b) is based on an additive utility function but it is not certain whether the DM has determined the weights with this specification in mind. Consequently, the analyst must consider the possibility that the weights are used in a way which is not completely in accordance with the DM's intention.

8.6   Alternatives: many; Measurement: ordinal; Availability of Priority Information: no

An essential assumption in the preceding sections is that the objectives are cardinally measured. In many decision situations this assumption does not however hold true. The reason may be that (a) the nature of some objectives hinders the con-

struction of a satisfactory cardinal operationalization (e.g.
"beauty of landscape") or (b) the objective is cardinally measurable in principle, but it is measured ordinally for practical reasons such as lack of time to collect sufficient data.

   The ordinal project effect matrix R can be constructed as
follows. If, according to objective j, there are k alternatives worse than alternative n, the element r_j^n is equal to k+1.
Thus, for the worst alternative we have r_j^n = 1 and for the best
one we find r_j^n = N. If some alternatives (say $n_1, \ldots, n_L$) are
equally attractive according to objective j, while they dominate k alternatives, we set:

$$r_j^{n_1} = k + \tfrac{1}{2} (L + 1) \qquad \text{for } l = 1, \ldots, L \qquad (8.12)$$

The result of (8.12) is that the sum of the elements in each
row of R is equal to $\tfrac{1}{2}N (N+1)$, irrespective of the fact that
ties may occur. It is obvious that an ordinal project effect
matrix R contains less specific information than a cardinal
one. The consequence is that the information provided by the
analyst about R is less specific.

   Especially when only some of the objectives are ordinal
(while the others are cardinal) it is tempting to treat them as
if they have cardinal properties. Thus it is sometimes assumed
that when $r_j^n - r_j^{n'} = r_j^n - r_j^{n''}$, the difference between n
and n' is as large as that between n and n'' (according to objective j). Although this assumption may be the most appropriate when no more information is available, it may obviously
be completely beside the truth. In a more general context, it
is therefore worthwhile to study the possibility to transform
ordinal data into cardinal data (5). Let ω_j^n be a cardinal value assigned to the j-th objective of alternative n. Then every
function f which maps a rank number to a number in R satisfying:

$$\begin{cases} f (r_j^n) > f (r_j^{n'}) & \text{if} & r_j^n > r_j^{n'} \\[2ex] f (r_j^n) = f (r_j^{n'}) & \text{if} & r_j^n = r_j^{n'} \end{cases} \qquad (8.13)$$

produces a series of cardinal figures $(\omega_j^1, \ldots, \omega_j^N)$ which is consistent with the ordinal figures $(r_j^1, \ldots, r_j^N)$.

   Clearly, there are many functions f which do this job. For
practical purposes it may be sufficient to use only some representative ones, for example, those depicted in Figure 8.4. The
linear function (no. 1) has already been discussed. Function 2

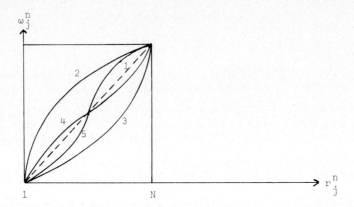

Fig. 8.4.   Alternative transformations of ordinal to cardinal
data

implies that higher ranked alternatives are closer to each other than lower ranked ones. With no. 3 it is exactly vice
versa. The 4th function has the characteristic that the alternatives are closer to each other around the median than at the
ends. Function no. 5 shows the reverse pattern. In Appendix
II some analytical expressions for the transformation functions
are discussed.

    For each of the five (or more) functions a cardinal analysis,
along the lines shown earlier in this chapter, can be executed.
Widely divergent results would point at the necessity to collect
more specific data. If the results are rather similar, the
conclusion may be that ordinal data contain sufficient information. One should always realize, however, that the "real" f
function may be very dissimilar to those depicted in Figure 8.4
and therefore this method is not completely satisfactory (6).

    Cardinalization of the ordinal project effect matrix R is
not the only way to proceed with the analysis. An alternative
way is to respect its ordinality and to develop methods appropriate to ordinal data. Some of the concepts dealt with in
Section 8.2 can still be used for ordinal data. The pay-off
matrix P as well as the set of non-dominated alternatives can
still be derived. Most of the compromise concepts assume data
of a cardinal nature, but the min-max solution c_3 and its lexicographic extension c_4 can be maintained in an ordinal context.

Consider for example the following R matrix, consisting of 6
alternatives, evaluated according to 3 objectives.

$$R = \begin{pmatrix} 4 & 1 & 5 & 2 & 6 & 3 \\ 2 & 3 & 4\frac{1}{2} & 1 & 4\frac{1}{2} & 6 \\ 4 & 5 & 3 & 6 & 1 & 2 \end{pmatrix} \qquad (8.14)$$

The min-max alternative can be found by registering for each column the smallest element and then selecting the column with the highest value of these minima. For (8.14) the min-max compromise is therefore the 3rd alternative, because for each objective it dominates at least two alternatives, which cannot be said of the other alternatives.

Half-compromises can also be derived for ordinal data. The half-compromise with respect to the third objective can be found as follows. Discard the alternatives from R which are worse than the min-max compromise with respect to objective 3 and reorder the ranks accordingly. Thus the last two columns of R have to be deleted and we find:

$$R_3 = \begin{pmatrix} 3 & 1 & 4 & 2 \\ 2 & 3 & 4 & 1 \\ 2 & 3 & 1 & 4 \end{pmatrix} \qquad (8.15)$$

Alternative 1 which turns out to be the min-max solution of the matrix R_3 can be conceived of as the half-compromise with respect to objective 3.

8.7   Alternatives: few; Measurement: ordinal; Availability of Priority Information: no

The subject of this section is analogous to Section 8.3, the difference being that in the present section only ordinal information is available on the project effect matrix. Due to this difference, the methods presented in Section 8.3 cannot be applied unmodified in the present context, since they assume the availability of cardinal information. In the present section we will first show how a stochastic analysis of the ordinal data can be employed to derive statements about the probability that (a) a certain objective is optimal or (b) a certain ranking occurs. Next, we will show how the concordance analysis can be adapted to the ordinal case.

The stochastic approach is based on the assignment of stochastic cardinal numbers to the ordinal data such that the given rank orders in the project effect matrix are satisfied. A crucial assumption is that the cardinal numbers form a sample which is drawn from a certain probability distribution. Assume for example that the (unknown) cardinal numbers $(\omega_j^1, \ldots, \omega_j^N)$ are drawn from a uniform distribution with a probability density function:

$$\begin{cases} f_j(\omega_j) = 1 & 0 \leq \omega_j \leq 1 \\ = 0 & \text{elsewhere} \end{cases} \qquad (8.16)$$

Let $(\nu_j^1,\ldots,\nu_j^N)$ denote the series of order statistics related to $(\omega_j^1,\ldots,\omega_j^N)$ such that ν_j^1 is the smallest of $(\omega_j^1,\ldots,\omega_j^N)$, ν_j^2 is the next in order of magnitude and ν_j^N is the largest ω_j^n. Then the theory of order statistics (cf. Hogg and Craig [1970]) can be used to derive the joint probability density function of $(\nu_j^1,\ldots,\nu_j^N)$:

$$
\begin{cases}
g_j\,(\nu_j^1,\ldots,\nu_j^N) = N! & 0 \le \nu_j^1 \le \nu_j^2 \le \ldots \le \nu_j^N \le 1 \\[2ex]
\qquad\qquad = 0 & \text{elsewhere}
\end{cases}
\tag{8.17}
$$

The joint density function g_j can be used to derive probability density functions for individual ν_j^n and for differences $\eta_j^{nn'}$ between two individual values ($\eta_j^{nn'} = \nu_j^n - \nu_j^{n'}$, $n > n'$):

$$
\begin{cases}
g_j^n\,(\nu_j^n) = \dfrac{N!}{(n-1)!\,(N-n)!} \cdot (\nu_j^n)^{n-1}\,(1 - \nu_j^n)^{N-n} & 0 \le \nu_j^n \le 1 \\[2ex]
\qquad\qquad = 0 \qquad \text{elsewhere}
\end{cases}
\tag{8.18}
$$

and

$$
\begin{cases}
g_j^{nn'}(\eta_j^{nn'}) = \dfrac{N!}{(n-n'-1)!\,(N-n+n')!}\,(\eta_j^{nn'})^{n-n'-1}(1-\eta_j^{nn'})^{N-n-n'} \\[2ex]
\qquad\qquad\qquad\qquad\qquad\qquad\qquad\qquad\qquad 0 \le \eta_j^{nn'} \le 1 \\[2ex]
\qquad\qquad = 0 \qquad \text{elsewhere}
\end{cases}
\tag{8.19}
$$

Note that the ordinal information contained in the data set enables one to establish which of the $(\omega_j^1,\ldots,\omega_j^N)$ is represented by ν_j^n.

For the derivation of the probability that a certain alternative is optimal we also need information about the probability distribution of the weights. When no definite a priori information is available, it is reasonable to assume a uniform distribution for the weights λ_j:

$$
\begin{cases}
h\,(\lambda_1, \lambda_2,\ldots,\lambda_{J-1}) = (J-1)! & 0 \leq \lambda_1 \leq 1 - \lambda_2 - \lambda_3 - \ldots - \lambda_{J-1} \\[2mm]
 & 0 \leq \lambda_2 \leq 1 - \lambda_3 - \ldots - \lambda_{J-1} \\[2mm]
 & \qquad \vdots \\[2mm]
 & 0 \leq \lambda_{J-2} \leq 1 - \lambda_{J-1} \\[2mm]
 & 0 \leq \lambda_{J-1} \leq 1 \\[2mm]
= 0 & \text{elsewhere}
\end{cases}
\tag{8.20}
$$

and where $\lambda_J = 1 - (\lambda_1 + \ldots + \lambda_{J-1})$.

We will now show how the density functions (8.19) and (8.20) can be used to derive the probability that a certain alternative m is preferred to another alternative m'. Let the ranks of m and m' for a certain objective j be denoted by n_j and n'_j.

It is reasonable to assume that $\eta_1^{n_1 n'_1},\ldots,\eta_J^{n_J n'_J}$ are stochastically independent from $\lambda_1,\ldots,\lambda_J$. Then the joint distribution of these variables can be represented by the density function:

$$
\begin{cases}
gh^{mm'}\,(\lambda_1,\ldots,\lambda_{J-1};\, \eta_1^{n_1 n'_1},\ldots,\, \eta_J^{n_J n'_J}) = h\,(\lambda_1,\ldots\lambda_{J-1})\cdot \prod_j g_j^{n_j n'_j}(\eta_j^{n_j n'_j}) \\[2mm]
\qquad \text{for the appropriate values of } \lambda_j \text{ and } \eta_j^{n_j n'_j} \\[4mm]
= 0 \text{ elsewhere}
\end{cases}
\tag{8.21}
$$

By means of transformations-of-variables techniques (cf. Hogg and Craig [1970]) the density function of $\delta = \sum_j \lambda_j\, \eta_j^{n_j n'_j}$ can can be derived from (8.21). Then Prob $[\delta>0]$ is the probability that alternative m is preferred to m'.

The probability that a certain alternative is preferred to all other alternatives, or the probability that a certain ranking occurs can be calculated in a similar manner. In principle, the sensitivity of the outcomes to the assumption of a uniform distribution $f_j(\omega_j)$ can be tested by repeating the whole analysis for alternative probability distributions, for example, the exponential distribution.

For practical purposes one should realize that techniques dealing with transformations of variables are tedious to apply. Therefore, one may also resort to numerical methods since generators of random samples for the stochastic variables are available. When a sufficiently large number of samples has been generated, one can directly calculate the demanded probabilities.

We will now proceed with a discussion on concordance analysis for ordinal data. The starting point of the analysis, the
concordance set C_{nn}' , is relevant in both ordinal and cardinal
cases. As to the concordance indices, two formulations can be
suggested:

$$
\begin{cases}
c_{nn'} = \sum_{j \in C_{nn'}} 1 & (8.22a) \\[2em]
c_{nn'} = \sum_{j \in C_{nn'}} r^n - r^{n'} - 1 & (8.22b)
\end{cases}
$$

The first index represents the number of objectives for which
alternative n is at least as good as alternative n'. The second index counts the number of alternatives which are ranked
between n and n' for all objectives in $C_{nn'}$. Thus the difference
between (8.22a) and (8.22b) is that the former only registers
whether n is better than n', while the latter also takes account of the size of the difference between n and n'. Both indices can be used in the concordance analysis presented earlier,
although one should be aware of their ordinal background.

Obviously, an alternative way to make the use of concordance
analysis possible is by transforming the ordinal data into cardinal data along the lines presented in this section. In Van
Delft and Nijkamp [1977] a numerical example of such an approach is given.

8.8   Alternatives: many; Measurement: ordinal; Availability of
       Priority Information: yes

In this section we will discuss how various types of information about priorities can be used for ordinal problems (cf.
Chapter 7).
(a) Lexicographic information. This type of information can be
handled almost as easily in ordinal as in cardinal contexts,
because it does not involve comparisons of differences between
values of objectives. For this type it is only important to
know that r_j^m is larger than $r_j^{m'}$, but not to what extent it is
larger. Cardinal information about R may be superfluous to
reach conclusions. This statement should be relaxed if the
lexicographic statement also deals with satiation levels (see
Section 7.6).
(b) Minimum standards. In many problems the number of values which
can be attained by r_j^n is smaller than N. This occurs for example when for the value of a certain objective only three
classes are distinguished: high, medium, and low. When this
type of classification is used, the introduction of minimum
standards and also of satiation levels or goals is straightforward.
(c) Goal programming. One of the necessary ingredients of goal

programming is the fixation of a set of goals. As mentioned in
(b) this may be simple in ordinal problems. Confrontation of R
with goal levels yields two derived ordinal matrices: one with
over-attainments and one with under-attainments for all objectives and alternatives. The way in which these matrices can be
used to produce information is discussed in (d), because it is
actually identical to the problem on how to employ utility
functions for ordinal data.
(d) Utility functions. The use of utility functions in ordinal
problems yields some difficulties which are related to the discussion in Section 7.4 about the interpretation of relative
weights in the utility function. Two alternative interpretations have been dealt with: the "trade-off interpretation"
which is the more general one, and the "relative importance interpretation" which is more restricted in scope. Which of the
two is the most appropriate in an ordinal context?

First the "trade-off interpretation" will be considered.
According to this interpretation the relative weight λ_j / λ_j, indicates the increase in the number of units of ω_j, which is
necessary to compensate for a loss of one unit of ω_j. In the
ordinal context this interpretation is of little use because
the units of measurement are not clearly defined, or, if they
are defined, no data are available. The "relative importance
interpretation" looks more promising because it is intended for
situations in which all objectives have the same units of measurement, which includes the case in which all objectives have
been normalized. When one wants to take the problems concerning
the determination of the most appropriate way of normalization
into the bargain, the "relative importance interpretation" can
be applied to ordinal problems.

Suppose that the weights $\lambda_1, \ldots, \lambda_J$ are given. One can then
proceed in the following way. In Section 8.6 the possibility
to try out several transformations of the ordinal R matrix into
a cardinal one has been mentioned. Then for each cardinal R
matrix the optimal solution or the ranking of all alternatives
can be found. After a sensitivity analysis one can try to select the best alternative(s). A special case arises when not
only R is ordinal, but also the information on the importance
of the objectives (see Pearman [1979] and Werczberger [1978]).
One of the ways to deal with this type of information is to try
out several series of cardinal weights, similar to the way in
which cardinal values for alternatives have been found. Again
the functions mentioned in Figure 8.4 can be of help. We con-
jecture that functions of type 3 are the most common for
weights, while functions of type 2 are the most common for the
project effect matrix.

8.9   Alternatives: few; Measurement: ordinal; Availability of
       Priority Information: yes

A number of interesting contributions has been presented on
this subject. We choose Holmes [1971] as a point of departure.
He assumes an ordinal project effect matrix R and a limited

number (say L) of importance classes of objectives. The weight
of the objectives in the least important class is equal to 1
and of the one but least important class equal to 2 , and so
forth. Thus the highest weight is equal to L. The score q_j^n
of alternative n with respect to objective j is equal to:

$$q_j^n = r_j^n + \lambda_j \hspace{5cm} (8.23)$$

Holmes proposed to select the best alternative by means of a
max-max procedure applied to the q_j^n scores. Let q^* be the highest attainable value of the q_j^n ($q^* \leq L + N$), then the best alternative is the one with the largest number of scores equal to
q^*. The next best alternative is the one with the largest number but one which is equal to q^*. When two alternatives have an
equal number of scores equal to q^*, the number of scores equal
to q^*-1 is decisive and so forth.

   Note that in this approach the ordinal information about R
and $\underline{\lambda}$ is treated in a rather unsophisticated way. The additive
structure of (8.23) implies that a ranking on the n-th position
according to an objective in importance class l is valued equal
to a ranking on the (n+1)-th position according to an objective
in importance class l-1.

   There are also methods which imply a more refined treatment
of ordinal data. Van Delft and Nijkamp [1977] discuss some
methods based on concordance analysis. One of these is based
on the assumption that:
1) the difference in the project effects of a pair of alternatives j,j' according to a certain objective can be classified
in a limited number of classes of significance (for example:
j is much better, slightly better, equal,...than j');
2) the objectives can be classified in a limited number of
classes of importance (for example, very important, rather important, rather unimportant...).

   The concordance analysis can be executed now for each class
of importance and significance separately. Let $C_{nn'}(s)$ be the
set of criteria j for which alternative n is preferred to n'
according to class of significance s. Then $c_{nn'}(s,t)$ can be
defined as the concordance index for the pair of alternatives
(n,n') based on $C_{nn'}(s)$ for the criteria of importance-class t,
measured as in (8.22a). Thus $c_{nn'}(s,t)$ measures the number of
criteria of importance-class t for which n has a better performance than n' as far as significance-class s is concerned. When
the number of classes of significance and importance are S and
T, respectively, the total number of concordance indices for
each pair (n,n') is equal to S.T. These indices can be dealt

with along the lines discussed in Section 8.3.

Another approach has been presented by Paelinck [1975] (see
also Mastenbroek and Paelinck [1976]). He assumes that ordinal
information is available about R and the importance of objectives. He aims at determining the set of rankings of the alternatives which are as much as possible in accordance with
this information.

Each potential ranking ρ of alternatives ($\rho=1,\ldots N!$) is confronted with the ranking of alternatives according to the data
in each of the J rows of the project effect matrix R. Thus a
series of $J \times N!$ rank order correlation coefficients τ_j^ρ can be
obtained, defined as follows (see Kendall [1955]):

$$\tau_j^\rho = \frac{S_j^{\rho+} - S_j^{\rho-}}{\frac{1}{2} N (N-1)} \qquad (8.24)$$

where $S_j^{\rho+}$ and $S_j^{\rho-}$ are the number of pairs of alternatives for
which the rankings ρ and the ranking in row j of R are in accordance and discordance, respectively.

Let the τ_j^ρ form together a $(J \times N!)$ matrix T. Then the aim
of the analysis is the determination of the set of rankings ρ
which have the largest weighted sum $\sum_j \lambda_j \tau_j^\rho$ where the λ_j are
the weights assigned to the J objectives ω_j. These weights
cannot however be precisely determined, since there is only ordinal information available. Given that the objectives have
been ranked in order of importance, Paelinck concludes that $\underline{\lambda}$
is an element of the set:

$$S = \{\underline{\lambda} \mid \lambda_j \leq \lambda_{j+1} , \ j=1,\ldots J-1, \ \underline{\imath}'\underline{\lambda} = 1\} \qquad (8.25)$$

Let the vector $\underline{\delta}$ contain N! elements. Then the decision problem can be formalized as follows. Find the solutions $\underline{\delta}$ of:

$$\begin{cases} \max! & \underline{\lambda}' \ T \ \underline{\delta} \\ \text{s.t.} & \underline{\delta} \geq \underline{0} \\ & \underline{\imath}'\underline{\delta} = 1 \\ & \delta_\rho = 0,1 \end{cases} \qquad (8.26)$$

where $\underline{\lambda} \in S$

Paelinck shows that this problem is equivalent to the determination of the solutions $\underline{\delta}$ of:

$$
\left\{
\begin{array}{lll}
\text{max!} & \underline{\lambda}' \text{ T } \underline{\delta} & \\
\text{s.t.} & \underline{\delta} \geq \underline{0} & \\
& \underline{\iota}'\underline{\delta} = 1 & \\
& \delta_\rho = 0,1 & \\
& \lambda_j = 0 & j=1,\ldots,N-k \\
& \lambda_j = \dfrac{1}{k} & j=N-k+1,\ldots,N
\end{array}
\right. \tag{8.27}
$$

for $k=1,\ldots,N$. This means that the set of best rankings can be found by computing $\underline{\lambda}'T$ for $\underline{\lambda}' = (0,\ldots,0,1)$, $(0,\ldots,0,\tfrac{1}{2},\tfrac{1}{2})$, $(0,\ldots,0,\tfrac{1}{3},\tfrac{1}{3},\tfrac{1}{3}),\ldots,$ $(\tfrac{1}{J},\tfrac{1}{J},\ldots,\tfrac{1}{J})$ and by selecting for each $\underline{\lambda}$ the ranking with the highest value for $\underline{\lambda}'T$. See Pearman [1979] for a similar method. Paelinck and Mastenbroek [1976] further discuss a number of refinements, such as how to take the occurrence of ties into account and ways to alleviate the computational burden of the method to ensure its practical applicability.

A comment can be made here concerning the use of the weights λ_j which is similar to that made in Section 8.5, namely that the analyst should envisage the possibility that he is capable of using the information on the relative importance of the objectives in a way which does not completely agree with the DM's intentions. Note that in (8.26), the weights λ_j are attached to the variables τ_j^ρ which denote the rank order correlation coefficients between a certain ranking ρ of the alternatives and the ranking of the alternatives according to objective j. This use obviously differs from the more convential use such as in (8.4), where the weights are directly attached to the outcomes for the objectives.

8.10   Reduction of the Size of Decision Problems

Large problems imply, in general, a heavier computational burden and a harder interactive process between analyst and DM than small problems. It may therefore be worthwhile to reduce the size of decision problems. The number of elements in the project effect matrix R (J x N) is a good measure of this size. Consequently, a reduction of the size can be attained by a reduction in the number of alternatives N, or in the number of objectives J. The first possibility has already been dealt with in the discussion about the elimination of dominated alternatives (see Section 6.3). In this section we will, therefore, pay attention to the possibility of reducing the number of objectives. Note that different phases of decision processes may call for different amounts of information about alternatives. In the first phases when a pre-selection of promising alternatives is pursued, the information does not need to be as specific as in later phases when the ultimate selection takes place. Consequently, project effect matrices with a re-

duced number of objectives may be especially helpful in the
first phases of decision processes (see also Sandee [1977]).

There is yet another reason why an analysis of the number of
objectives is relevant. In many decision problems one will experience that it is easier to find data on effects of some
classes than on other classes. For example: short-term effects
may be easier to quantify than long-term effects; it may be
easier to find data on economic effects than on social effects.
The consequence is that the distribution of objectives among
the classes of objectives is more an indication of the availability of data for these classes than of the preferential importance of the classes. This state may have disadvantageous
consequences for some of the methods discussed earlier. For
example, the compromise concepts assume equal importance of all
objectives. When a certain class of objectives is under-repre-
sented due to lack of data, this gives rise to a bias against
this class when a compromise is calculated.

An obvious possibility to reduce the number of objectives
arises when there is an objective which attains the same value
for all alternatives (see also Zeleny [1974]). Another opportunity to reduce the number of rows of R without much loss of
information arises when two objectives are non-conflicting, so
that one of them may be deleted. A pair of objectives j, j'
is non-conflicting when for all n and n' :

$$
\begin{cases}
\omega_j^n > \omega_j^{n} \Rightarrow \omega_{j'}^{n} > \omega_{j'}^{n'} \\[2ex]
\omega_j^n = \omega_j^{n'} \Rightarrow \omega_{j'}^{n} = \omega_{j'}^{n'}
\end{cases}
\tag{8.28}
$$

One should realize, of course, that although objectives deleted
in this way are not very essential for the structure of the decision problem, they may yet contain useful information for the
image formation by the decision-maker.

In more general terms, a reduction of the number of objectives can be analyzed as follows. Let L be the number of objectives after the reduction of R (L $\leq$ J), and let S denote the
reduced R matrix. If we assume that the reduction is carried
out by linear transformations, then for S the following expression can be found:

$$
S = A R \tag{8.29}
$$

where A is an (L x J) matrix. How can A be determined? We
distinguish three modes, to be discussed below.

1) A is determined on a priori grounds, independent of the data
in R. Sometimes A is based on a definition; for example, when
in R the effects on the income in certain regions are described,
while in S we only have the effect on national income. In oth-

er cases the elements in A have the character of coefficients
of utility functions. This occurs, for instance, when a number
of objectives in R are pollution levels of various materials to
be summarized in one index of environmental quality in S.
There are also intermediate cases such as the definition of the
net present value of incomes during a series of periods, which
depends on a certain rate of discount.

One example deserves special attention. Suppose that the J
objectives can be classified in L exclusive subprofiles (for
example, subprofiles with economic, environmental, and infra-
structural variables). Then A has the form:

$$
A = \begin{pmatrix}
a_{1,1}, \ldots, a_{1,j} & 0 & \ldots & 0 & \ldots & 0 \\
0 & \ldots & 0\, a_{2,j+1}, \cdots\, a_{2,k} & & & \vdots \\
\vdots & & & \ddots & & \vdots \\
0 & \ldots & & 0 & a_{L,m}, \ldots, a_{L,J}
\end{pmatrix}
$$

$$(8.30)$$

Thus, in each column of A there are L-1 elements equal to zero.
2) The objectives in S are a subset of the objectives in R.
For example, when the objectives ω_1, ω_3 and ω_4 are selected
from a set of five objectives, we find for A:

$$
A = \begin{pmatrix}
1 & 0 & 0 & 0 & 0 \\
0 & 0 & 1 & 0 & 0 \\
0 & 0 & 0 & 1 & 0
\end{pmatrix}
$$

$$(8.31)$$

A possible way to arrive at a selection of L variables out of a
set of J is through interdependence analysis (see Boyce et al.
[1974]). By interdependence analysis the selection is performed such that the selected variables contain as much information of the original set as possible. More precisely stated,
interdependence analysis proceeds in the following way. Take
a selection of L variables. Compute the J-L correlation coefficients of the regression with the L selected variables as the
independent ones and each of the J-L remaining variables as the
dependent variables, successively. Retain the minimum value of
this series of correlation coefficients. Repeat this procedure
for all $\binom{J}{L}$ selections of variables. The most appropriate selection can be determined by the max-min principle: it is the
one with the highest value of the minima of the correlation coefficients.

In Blommestein et al. [1980] a number of extensions and
variants of interdependence analysis are suggested. One may
use, for example, other decision criteria than the max-min
principle. Another variant is that simple correlations are employed instead of multiple correlations. Interdependence analysis can also be applied to certain subsets of objectives. In
this way it may help in solving the problem of under and over-
representation of certain classes of objectives, mentioned earlier in this section. Some of these extensions enable one to
deal with cardinal as well as ordinal project effect matrices.
In the latter case, interdependence analysis will be performed
in terms of rank correlation coefficients.

3) A third way to reduce the size of R by means of a linear
transformation is the method of principal components. This
method aims at deriving new variables which are weighted sums
of the original ones in such a way that they describe the matrix R as well as possible. In formal terms, the principal
component method consists of finding the solution of a series
of eigenvalue problems such as:

$$(R \ R' - c \ I) \ \underline{a} = \underline{0}$$ (8.32)

The eigenvectors $\underline{a}$ are vectors of weights which are placed in
the rows of the matrix A. Principal components may have two
weak points. They are often very difficult to interpret, which
would be disadvantageous to the communication between decision-
maker and analyst. The other problem likely to arise is that
there is no guarantee that the sign of the elements of A is
positive. This may be a strange result when one assumes that
all J objectives must be maximized.

It is interesting to note that a reduction in the number of
objectives J may also give rise to a reduction of the number of
alternatives N. The reason is that S may contain a number of
dominated alternatives which may be excluded.

A very important question is: how far should one proceed
with reducing J? The extremes are: L = J and L = 1. In the
first case, all information in R is judged to be essential, in
the second case all information can be reduced to one dimension, which means that the MOD problem has actually been solved. Sometimes L can be fixed on a priori reasons, for example, when a number of subprofiles has been determined. In other cases L depends very much on the structure of the R matrix.
Principal component analysis is a good example here. Figure
8.5 gives a picture of the problem how to determine L. L is
the result of weighing the importance of the aims to have a
tractable problem and to use as much information as possible.
The optimal value of L depends on the form of the curves and
the weights attached to them.

We conclude this section with a brief discussion on methods
to obtain clusters of objectives. These methods are related to
some of the reduction methods dealt with above and they may

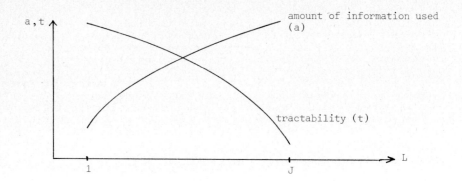

Fig. 8.5.   The relationship between the number of variables
             retained on the one hand and the tractability and
             amount of information used on the other hand.

provide insight into the structure of objectives. From the
many clustering algorithms which have been developed (cf.
Hartigan [1975] and Fisher [1978]) we mention the following hierarchical one, based on a max-min principle. Assume that
M ($1 \leq M \leq N$) clusters have been determined, each cluster m
having elements l_m ($1_m, \ldots, L_m$), such that $L_m \geq 1$ and $\sum_m L_m = N$.

Each cluster m has a certain level of homogeneity h_m, which is
measured by means of the correlations among the objectives in
the cluster:

$$h_m = \min_{(l_m, l'_m)} r_{l_m, l'_m} \qquad\qquad (8.33)$$

where r_{l_m, l'_m} denotes the correlation coefficient between the
objectives l_m and l'_m. Thus all internal correlations in a
cluster m are larger than or equal to h_m.

   A sensible mode to reduce the number of clusters from M to
M-1 in a hierarchical way is to combine two clusters such that
the internal homogeneity decreases as little as possible. Consequently, a pair of clusters (m,m') is looked after which is
the solution of:

$$g_{M-1} = \max_{(m,m')} \min_{(l_m, l'_{m'})} r_{l_m, l'_{m'}} \qquad\qquad (8.34)$$

Obviously, when the algorithm is applied for M = N, N-1,...,1, a decreasing series for the values of g_M will be found, indicating the decreasing homogeneity of the clusters. An application of this algorithm is contained in Section 12.3.

8.11   Conclusion

An important difference between MOD methods for continuous problems (Chapters 6 and 7) and for discrete problems is that the former aim at the <u>design</u> as well as the <u>selection</u> of alternatives, while the latter only deal with selection. This difference appears especially clear when in discrete problems the number of alternatives is small. For example, the aims and contents of concordance analysis differ substantially from the methods in the preceding chapters. Another important aspect of discrete problems is that ordinal data can occur. We discussed two approaches to ordinal data. In the first approach the ordinal data are directly transformed into cardinal data, so that all methods for cardinal data become applicable (see for example Sections 8.6 and 8.7). In this approach an analysis of the sensitivity of the outcomes for the way of cardinalization is necessary. In the second approach a transformation is not directly necessary since concepts are used which do not presuppose cardinal data (see Section 8.9). It appears, however, that in order to reach definite conclusions, these methods can seldom avoid a cardinal interpretation of ordinal data in the last phase of computations.

Finally, we discussed in this chapter some reasons for it being wise to reduce the number of dimensions in an MOD analysis: it may improve the tractability of decision problems, and one may avoid the situation where the objectives of a certain class are over-represented compared to other classes of objectives. Several multivariate techniques are presented to achieve such a reduction: interdependence analysis, principal component analysis, and cluster analysis.

Footnotes

1.   The importance of discrete MOD methods may also be reflected by the fact that there is a tendency to reserve a special name for them, viz. multi-criteria decision methods. The convention to use the term "criterion" in the discrete case and the term "objective" in the continuous case is not, however, followed by all workers in the field.

2.   One should realize that this definition means a departure from the terminology of ELECTRE, where next to concordance indices, discordance indices are also used. We will show here that:
     (a) one can do without the discordance concept without losing any information;
     (b) the way in which discordance indices are used is, to a certain extent, confusing.
     These statements can be shown in the following way. A discordance set $D_{nn'}$ can be defined as the set of criteria

j according to which alternative n is worse than alternative n'. Taking into account the possibility that different alternatives attain equal values for certain objectives, the following definitions can be given:

$$C_{nn'}(\geq) = \{j \mid \omega_j^n \geq \omega_j^{n'}\}$$

$$C_{nn'}(>) = \{j \mid \omega_j^n > \omega_j^{n'}\}$$

$$D_{nn'}(\leq) = \{j \mid \omega_j^n \leq \omega_j^{n'}\}$$

$$D_{nn'}(<) = \{j \mid \omega_j^n < \omega_j^{n'}\}$$

Between these discordance and concordance sets the following relationships exist: $C_{nn'}(\geq) = D_{n'n}(\leq)$ and

$C_{nn'}(>) = D_{n'n}(<)$. A concordance index has been defined as an indicator of the strength or intensity of the viewpoints (criteria) in favour of the statement that n is preferred to n'. A discordance index can be defined analogously as an indicator of the strength or intensity of the criteria which are in favour of the statement that alternative n is deferred to n'. The definitions of the concordance and discordance sets give rise to the definitions of concordance and discordance indices:

$$c_{nn'}(\geq) = \sum_{j \in C_{nn'}(\geq)} f_j(n,n')$$

$$c_{nn'}(>) = \sum_{j \in C_{nn'}(>)} f_j(n,n')$$

$$d_{nn'}(\leq) = \sum_{j \in D_{nn'}(\leq)} f_j(n,n')$$

$$d_{nn'}(<) = \sum_{j \in D_{nn'}(<)} f_j(n,n')$$

where different forms can be proposed for $f_j(n,n')$:
(a) in (8.9) and (8.22) $f_j(n,n')$ depends on the performance of the alternatives n and n' with respect to criterion j.

(b) in (8.11a) the function depends on the weight λ_j attached to objective j.

(c) in (8.11b) the function depends on both elements mentioned above.

Given the relationships between discordance and concordance sets, we find that $c_{nn'}(\geq) = d_{n'n}(\leq)$ and $c_{nn'}(>) = d_{n'n}(<)$, which means that discordance indices do not add anything new, once the concordance indices have been introduced.

Our second statement is related to the convention that concordance indices are always used when $f_j(n,n')$ is of type (b), while for discordance indices $f_j(n,n')$ is always of type (a) or (c). In our opinion this is a confusing convention, since it suggests that it is essential for the concept of "concordance" that $f_j(n,n')$ is of type (b), while for the concept of "discordance" $f_j(n,n')$ should be of type (a) or (c). Obviously, this would be a misconception.

3.   This also applies to many so-called scenario analyses (cf. Memorandum on Urbanization (Verstedelijkingsnota) [1976]) which are often executed for a very limited number of policy alternatives.

4.   Recent developments in dual integer programming theory (cf. Shapiro [1976]) may yield useful results for the derivation of shadow-prices.

5.   Multidimensional scaling techniques are a good example of a transformation of ordinal data into cardinal data (cf. Voogd [1978] and Nijkamp [1979]). Another method to deal with ordinal data - a stochastic analysis - will be discussed in Section 8.7.

6.   The theory of order statistics forms another way to achieve the conversion of ordinal into cardinal data. This idea will be elaborated in Section 8.7, where it is used in the context of a small number of alternatives to compute the probability that certain alternatives are optimal. It may also be useful for the present section dealing with many alternatives, for example, if one interprets the mean values of the order statistics as cardinal representations of ordinal data. A sensitivity analysis concerning the assumed probability density function (uniform, exponential,...) is, of course, a necessary ingredient for well-balanced conclusions.

RANKINGS OF ALTERNATIVES

Consider a set of N non-dominated alternatives. The <u>poten-tial</u> number of rankings is equal to N! The <u>actual</u> number may, however, be considerably less. Consider for example Figure I.1a, where three alternatives have been depicted.

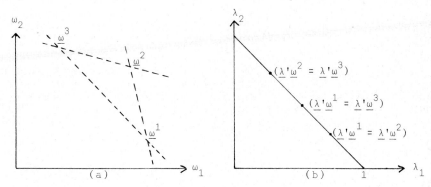

Fig. I.1.   Feasible rankings of alternatives

The six potential rank orders are $(\underline{\omega}^1, \underline{\omega}^2, \underline{\omega}^3)$, $(\underline{\omega}^2, \underline{\omega}^1, \underline{\omega}^3)$ $(\underline{\omega}^2, \underline{\omega}^3, \underline{\omega}^1)$, $(\underline{\omega}^3, \underline{\omega}^2, \underline{\omega}^1)$, $(\underline{\omega}^1, \underline{\omega}^3, \underline{\omega}^2)$ and $(\underline{\omega}^3, \underline{\omega}^1, \underline{\omega}^2)$. The last two rankings are in conflict with the assumption that the utility function is concave, so only four of the six potential rankings are feasible.

If it is assumed that the utility function is linear, a for-mula for the number of feasible rankings can be found as fol-lows. Consider an arbitrary pair of alternatives, $(\underline{\omega}^n, \underline{\omega}^m)$. When J=2, to this pair a weight vector $\underline{\lambda} = (\lambda_1, \lambda_2)'$ can be as-signed such that:

$$\underline{\lambda}'\underline{\omega}^n = \underline{\lambda}'\underline{\omega}^m \qquad\qquad (I.1)$$

For all pairs of alternatives, such a weight vector can be de-termined. These vectors can be depicted in Figure I.1b as points on the line $\lambda_1 + \lambda_2 = 1$. On the one side of each point we have $\underline{\lambda}'\underline{\omega}^n < \underline{\lambda}'\underline{\omega}^m$, on the other side $\underline{\lambda}'\underline{\omega}^n > \lambda'\underline{\omega}^m$.

Starting from a certain point in Figure I.1b and moving along the line $\lambda_1 + \lambda_2 = 1$, the ranking of alternatives remains unchanged until a next point is reached, resulting from the equality $\underline{\lambda}'\underline{\omega}^k = \underline{\lambda}'\underline{\omega}^l$. Thus the conclusion is that the feasible number of rankings is equal to the number of pieces into which the line $\lambda_1 + \lambda_2 = 1$ is split up between the extremes (1,0) and (0,1). The number of pieces q is equal to the number of pairs of alternatives + 1, so we have:

$$q = \binom{N}{2} + 1 \qquad\qquad (I.2)$$

which is considerably smaller than N! In some cases q may even be less than indicated in (I.2), namely when two pairs of alternatives give rise to the same vector $\underline{\lambda}$.

When J is larger than 2, essentially the same type of reasoning can be applied. Consider for example the case when J = 3. Every subset of three alternatives n, m, k implies a certain weight vector $(\lambda_1, \lambda_2, \lambda_3)$ such that:

$$\underline{\lambda}'\underline{\omega}^n = \underline{\lambda}'\underline{\omega}^m = \underline{\lambda}'\underline{\omega}^k \qquad\qquad (I.3)$$

which can be depicted as a point in the plane $\lambda_1 + \lambda_2 + \lambda_3 = 1$. When N = 4, four triads of alternatives can be formed, giving rise to four weight vectors which are depicted in Fig. I.2.

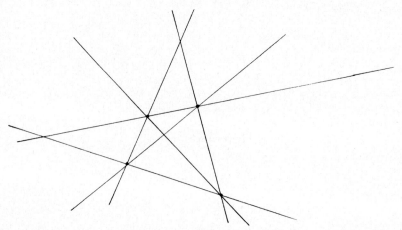

Fig. I.2.   Points and lines in the plane $\lambda_1 + \lambda_2 + \lambda_3 = 1$

Again for each pair of alternatives (ω^m, ω^n), the weight vector λ can be determined for which (I.1) holds true. When $J = 3$, this is not a point, but a line which can be depicted in Figure I.2 as a line through two of the points determined previously. The number of rankings is equal to the number of pieces into which the plane $\lambda_1 + \lambda_2 + \lambda_3 = 1$ is cut by the lines.

   This number can be determined as follows. Assume that there are ρ lines in a plane such that 1) there are no parallel lines and 2) there are no points in which three or more lines intersect. Then the number of pieces q into which the plane is cut is equal to:

$$q = \binom{\rho+1}{2} + 1 \qquad\qquad (I.4)$$

which can be shown by induction. In our case there are however triads of lines intersecting in one point. The number of triads is equal to $\binom{N}{3}$. For every triad, q as defined in (I.4) should be reduced with 1. As ρ, the number of lines, is equal to $\binom{N}{2}$, the formula we are looking for is:

$$q = \binom{\binom{N}{2} + 1}{2} + 1 - \binom{N}{3} \qquad\qquad (I.5)$$

Table I.1 shows to which extent a reduction of the number of potential rankings is achieved for $J = 2$ and 3. The higher the value of J, the larger the number of feasible rankings. When $J \geq N$, the number of feasible rankings is, in general, equal to the number of potential rankings.

   In some cases, the number of feasible rankings may be less than stated in Table I.1. The reasons are: 1) the possibility of coinciding points, parallel lines and so forth in Figure I.2 and 2) the imposition of constraints $\lambda > 0$. If these constraints are imposed in Figure I.2, a considerable number of pieces into which the plane has been cut may have to be excluded.

N: number of alternatives	2	3	4	5	6	7	 10
number of feasible rankings (J=2)	2	4	7	11	16	22	 46
number of feasible rankings (J=3)	2	6	18	46	101	197	916
number of potential rankings	2	6	24	120	720	5040	3628800

Table I.1.   Numbers of feasible and potential rankings

It is interesting to note that there exist close links between
the subject of this appendix and the discussion on the possibi-
ty to derive a meaningful collective preference ordering of alternatives by means of aggregating individual orderings (cf.
Arrow [1951] and Section 9.9). One of the topics involved is
the question whether it is reasonable to assume that for a certain individual all rankings of alternatives may occur. An affirmative answer would seriously hinder the possibility to derive a collective ordering (cf. Mueller [1976]). In the present context we find that when an arbitrary linear utility function is assumed by means of which N alternatives are evaluated
according to J criteria, the feasible number of rankings is
smaller than the potential number as soon as N > J. See also
Black [1971], who elaborated the case for J = 2.

APPENDIX 8.II

TRANSFORMATIONS OF ORDINAL DATA

The aim of this appendix is to develop a set of functions which can be used in assigning cardinal values to ordinal data along the lines depicted in Figure 8.4.

Let f be a function assigning a value ω to r ($\omega = f(r)$) such that:

$$
\begin{cases}
f(r_1) > f(r_2) & \text{if } r_1 > r_2 \\
f(r_1) = f(r_2) & \text{if } r_1 = r_2 \\
f(1) = 1 \\
f(N) = N
\end{cases}
\tag{II.1}
$$

Consider the following function:

$$
f(r) = (N-1) \left(\frac{r-1}{N-1}\right)^a + 1 \quad (a > 0)
\tag{II.2}
$$

If $a = 1$ the function is linear (type 1), if $a < 1$ the function is concave (type 2) and for $a > 1$ the function is convex (type 3).

Types 4 and 5 have a more complicated form. One possible mode to express them in an analytical way is:

$$
\begin{cases}
f(r) = \left[\left(\tfrac{1}{2}\right)^{1-a} \left(\frac{r-1}{N-1}\right)^a\right] (N-1) + 1 & \text{if } 1 < r \leq \tfrac{1}{2}(N+1) \\[2ex]
f(r) = \frac{\tfrac{1}{2}(N-1)}{1-\left(\tfrac{1}{2}\right)^b} \left[\left(\frac{r-1}{N-1}\right)^b - 1\right] + N & \text{if } \tfrac{1}{2}(N+1) \leq r \leq 1
\end{cases}
$$

$$\tag{II.3}$$

This function satisfies the condition: $f(\tfrac{1}{2}(N+1)) = \tfrac{1}{2}(N+1)$. Type 4 occurs when $a < 1$ and $b > 1$, type 5 can be obtained when $a > 1$ and $b < 1$. When we impose the requirement that for

$r=\frac{1}{2}(N+1)$ the derivative of $f(r)$ is continuous, the parameters
a and b should satisfy the following condition:

$$a = \frac{b}{2^{b} - 1}$$

(II.4)

CHAPTER 9

INTERACTIVE DECISION METHODS

9.1   Introduction

In Chapters 6-8, elements of the information exchange between
the DM and analyst have been discussed. We paid much attention
to the modes in which analysts can construct relevant information for DMs and how DMs can provide information about their
priorities among objectives. In the present chapter, we will
show how these elements can be integrated in a communication
structure between analyst and DM, enabling them to carry out a
repeated exchange of information (see also Figure 1.3).

By means of this structure, it may be possible to solve one
of the main problems in decision-making in complex situations.
This problem concerns the dilemma the analyst faces when he presents information to the DM about choice possibilities. The
quantity of information should be: (1) so extensive that it contains a sufficiently complete picture of the decision problem
and (2) so limited that the DM will be able to digest it. By
means of a step by step provision of information, one may satisfy both requirements. Another important advantage of such a
structure is that it enables one to do justice to results of
psychological research concerning decision-making behaviour. An
example is the search for alternatives, described in Chapter 3.

Of course, one should realize that a certain communication
structure is neither a necessary nor a sufficient condition for
a fruitful conversation between analyst and DM. For example,
when the two parties can communicate well together, it may be
possible to reach satisfactory decisions without an agreement
on a certain communication structure. On the other hand, a certain structure is no guarantee of a successful communication,
because a structure implies a number of "rules of communication"
to be respected. These rules reduce the number of possible
types of questions and answers, which may hinder the parties
(especially the DM) during the conversation. This does not,
however, alter the fact that, if the rules are chosen in an adequate way, a certain communication structure may prove to be
a powerful tool in decision-making.

The discussion in this chapter is set out in the following
way. We shall begin with a survey of interactive methods
(Section 9.2). Then, we shall describe in a more detailed way
a special interactive procedure which is based on the setting

191

of side-conditions (Section 9.3). After the presentation of a
proof of convergence of the method (Section 9.4), we shall discuss how the method takes shape with regard to the comparability of alternatives (Section 9.5) and how the results can be interpreted in terms of shadow-prices (Section 9.6). Sections
9.7 - 9.9 will be devoted to some extensions of the interactive
methods. It will be shown that the method described in Section
9.3 can also be employed for discrete decision problems. It is
also possible to extend the method such that it can be used for
the determination of both unique solutions and ranges of acceptable solutions. Finally, some variants of the interactive
procedure are presented which can be used by decision-making
bodies consisting of several DMs. The last section will be devoted to an evaluation of the interactive procedures and to
drawing some conclusions.

9.2   A Survey of Interactive Methods

   A considerable number of authors have contributed to the
study of interactive MOD methods. Of course, these methods
differ in many respects, but their basic structure is very similar. They share the characteristic that the interaction consists of a number of steps, while in each step two elements are
present:

(a) The analyst presents a provisional solution to the DM and

(b) The DM expresses his opinion about the provisional solution.

In this section we will give a concise survey of a number of
interactive methods. More elaborate surveys can be found in
Hwang and Masud [1979], Winkels [1979a] and Isermann [1979].

ad a. One of the ways in which provisional solutions are determined is by making use of the various compromise concepts discussed in Chapter 6. Distance metrics, for example, have
   been used by Benayoun et al. [1971], Fichefet [1974] and
   Nijkamp and Rietveld [1977]. Compromise weights have been
   applied by Fandel [1972], Monarchi et al. [1973], Nijkamp and
   Rietveld [1976a] and Zionts and Wallenius [1976]. Belenson
   and Kapur [1973] and again Fichefet [1974] used compromise
   weights derived from game-theoretic approaches.

   There are also interactive methods in which the provisional solution is not based (implicitly or explicitly) on a compromise concept. In the context of hierarchical models,
   Nijkamp [1977] proposed to proceed as follows. Let the objectives $(\omega_1, \ldots \omega_J)$ be ranked in order of importance. Then,
   in step 1, the provisional solution is obtained by maximizing
   ω_1. In step 2, the provisional solution is obtained by maximizing ω_2, given a certain side-condition on ω_1, etc.

   In some methods, the provisional solutions are not even necessarily efficient. Geoffrion, Dyer, and Feinberg [1972]
   propose to start the procedure with an arbitrary feasible solution. Then, a new provisional solution can be determined
   by the application of the Frank-Wolfe [1956] algorithm to the

DM's statements about the trade-offs between objectives. Another example of a procedure with provisional solutions which are in general not efficient is presented in Nijkamp and Spronk [1978]. In their "Interactive Multiple Goal Programming" method, the vector of minimum attainable levels serves as a provisional solution.

In addition to the provisional solution, a number of other possible and meaningful solutions may be presented in order to provide a frame of reference for the DM. Most authors quoted above present the pay-off matrix or the vector with maximum attainable values. Zionts and Wallenius [1976] propose to calculate in the linear case all adjacent corner solutions.

ad b. As to the reaction of the DM, most authors propose to ask him which of the objectives in the provisional solution is certainly unsatisfactory. In addition, the DM may be enabled to specify minimum achievement levels for other objectives, indicating how far he allows reductions for these objectives in order to improve the unsatisfactory objectives. Monarchi et al. [1973] let the analyst ask the DM to fix a desired value for a certain objective. Zionts and Wallenius [1976] advocate another approach. They do not want to compare the performance of each of the objectives of the provisional solution, but they want to compare the provisional solution with each of the adjacent corner solutions. For each solution the DM must indicate whether he prefers it to the provisional solution or not. In the interactive hierarchical model (Nijkamp [1977]), the DM reacts by means of a certain relaxation of the levels attained for the objectives with high ranks. In this way, certain scope for improvement of the lower ranked objectives is created.

The answer of the DM can easily be integrated into mathematical programming models in the form of additional constraints, so that the next provisional solution may reflect the DM's preferences in a more satisfactory way. In some cases (e.g. Monarchi et al. [1973]) it may appear that the added constraints make the feasible area empty. Then the DM should be asked to revise his reaction. The method of Nijkamp and Spronk [1978] includes a similar possibility for the DM to revise formerly specified satisfactory levels. All methods share the property that they lead to a converging communication between analyst and DM. Difficulties may, of course, arise when a DM wants to abandon constraints, formulated in former steps. Then, convergence cannot be proved.

An exception to this rule forms the method of Geoffrion, Dyer and Feinberg [1972]. This method does not make any use of additional constraints but only of direct expressions by the DM about the weights to be attached to the objectives. This is a disadvantage of the method, because DMs appear to have great difficulties in specifying weights explicitly (cf. Wallenius [1975]).

9.3   Interactive Programming by Imposing Side-Conditions

This section will be devoted to the presentation of a certain variant of interactive MOD-making. The core of the procedure can be delineated as follows:

Stage (a) - The analyst solves J mathematical programming prob-
            lems in order to find the pay-off matrix P and the
            vectors with minimum and maximum attainable levels
            for the objectives $\bar{\underline{\omega}}$ and $\overset{*}{\underline{\omega}}$ (see Section 6.2). He
            calculates one of the compromise solutions $\overset{o}{\underline{\omega}}$ of
            Section 6.4. This solution is presented to the DM.

Stage (b) - The DM mentions the objectives with unsatisfactory
            levels in $\overset{o}{\underline{\omega}}$. If all objectives are satisfactory,
            the procedure can be terminated. If all objectives
            in $\overset{o}{\underline{\omega}}$ are unsatisfactory, the problem does not allow
            an acceptable solution. If only some objectives
            are unsatisfactory, the analyst must add con-
            straints to the mathematical program, indicating
            that the performance of these objectives should be
            better than in $\overset{o}{\underline{\omega}}$. Then return to stage 1.

In Figure 9.1, the essential characteristics of the procedure
can be found. In the first step, the analyst identifies the
pay-off matrix, consisting of the vectors $\overset{*}{\underline{\omega}}_1$ and $\overset{*}{\underline{\omega}}_2$. Let us
denote $\overset{*}{\underline{\omega}}, \bar{\underline{\omega}}, \overset{o}{\underline{\omega}}$ for step s as $\overset{*}{\underline{\omega}}(s)$, $\bar{\underline{\omega}}(s)$, $\overset{o}{\underline{\omega}}(s)$; then the rectangle
with cornerpoints $\bar{\underline{\omega}}^{(1)}$ and $\overset{*}{\underline{\omega}}^{(1)}$ contains all efficient solu-
tions. One of these solutions ($\overset{o}{\underline{\omega}}^{(1)}$) is selected as a provisional solution (see Section 6.4).

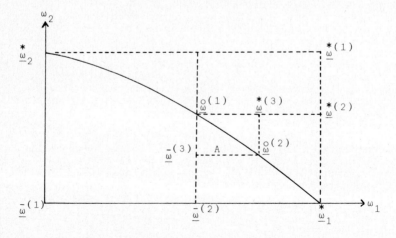

Fig. 9.1. Steps in an interactive procedure

In the second phase of the first step, the DM tries to answer the question of whether he prefers an improvement of the first objective or of the second one. An improvement of the two objectives is impossible, because $\overset{o}{\underline{\omega}}{}^{(1)}$ is an efficient solution. Hence, an improvement for one of the objectives causes a poorer performance for the other one. If the DM prefers an improvement of the first objective, the side-condition $\omega_1 \geq \overset{o}{\omega}{}_1^{(1)}$ is imposed on the original mathematical program. In the other case, the side-condition would be $\omega_2 \geq \overset{o}{\omega}{}_2^{(1)}$.

Say that the DM prefers an improvement of $\overset{o}{\omega}{}_1^{(1)}$, then in the second step vectors $\overset{-}{\underline{\omega}}{}^{(2)}$ and $\overset{*}{\underline{\omega}}{}^{(2)}$ are found which imply a smaller maximum attainable value for ω_2 and a larger minimum value for ω_1. The new provisional solution $\overset{o}{\underline{\omega}}{}^{(2)}$ shows a larger value for ω_1, as was required by the DM. If, in this case, the DM prefers an improvement of the second objective, the side-condition is added: $\omega_2 \geq \overset{o}{\omega}{}_2^{(2)}$.

Thus, in the third step, values for $\overset{-}{\underline{\omega}}{}^{(3)}$ and $\overset{*}{\underline{\omega}}{}^{(3)}$ are found which form together a square which is only a small part of the of the square implied by $\overset{-}{\underline{\omega}}{}^{(1)}$ and $\overset{*}{\underline{\omega}}{}^{(1)}$. This forms an illustration of the fact that the procedure does converge. After a certain number of steps, so little room for improvement of the objectives is left that a further search is pointless. This can be included in the procedure as a stopping rule: when the distance between $\overset{*}{\underline{\omega}}{}^{(s)}$ and $\overset{-}{\underline{\omega}}{}^{(s)}$ is below a certain pre-specified level, the interaction can be stopped.

This example with two objectives has a special characteristic which does not hold for $J \geq 3$. Departing from a certain compromise solution $\overset{o}{\underline{\omega}}$ one may choose between two mutually exclusive options: an improvement of ω_1 or of ω_2. In the first case, the final solution will attain values such that $\omega_1 \geq \overset{o}{\omega}{}_1$ and $\omega_2 \leq \overset{o}{\omega}{}_2$ while in the second case it is just vice versa. Consequently, as Figure 9.1 shows, the set of potential solutions is split into two parts by a compromise solution. The conclusion is that for $J=2$, the decision problem has a dichotomous character. Figure 9.2 shows that for $J=3$, this dichotomy disappears. Imposing the side conditions $\omega_j \geq \overset{o}{\omega}{}_j$ ($j=1,2,3$) splits the set of potential solutions into six parts. This means, for example, that the imposition of the constraint $\omega_1 \geq \overset{o}{\omega}{}_1$ does not imply that both $\omega_2 \leq \overset{o}{\omega}{}_2$ and $\omega_3 \leq \overset{o}{\omega}{}_3$ (surface A). It is also possible to arrive at a solution with $\omega_1 \geq \overset{o}{\omega}{}_1$ as well as $\omega_2 \geq \overset{o}{\omega}{}_2$ (surface B) or with $\omega_1 \geq \overset{o}{\omega}{}_1$ as well as $\omega_3 \geq \overset{o}{\omega}{}_3$ (surface C).

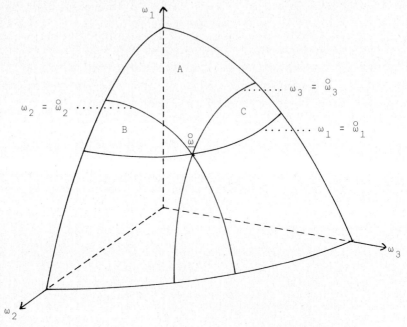

Fig. 9.2.   The effects of imposing restrictions on the set
of feasible solutions

The importance of this observation is that when J $\geq$ 3, the DM
may give different answers to the analyst, which may yet lead to
the same final solution. Therefore, if the DM is uncertain how
to answer in the first steps, this may not be detrimental to the
whole interactive method.

   Another important conclusion is that when there are many objectives, the interactive method is less demanding to the DM
than when there are few objectives (say J = 2). When J = 2,
the imposition of a side-condition for the objective to be improved also means the determination of the objective to be made
worse. When J > 2, no judgement is made as to which objective
must be made worse off. It is only stated that one or more of
the objectives on which no side-conditions are imposed must be
made worse off, but not which one.

9.4   Convergence of the Interaction

   The convergence of the interactive procedure has already been
made plausible by means of Figure 9.1. However, it must still
be proved in a formal way. The convergence can be described by
a series of minimum attainable levels
$\underline{\omega}^{(1)}$, $\underline{\omega}^{(2)}$,...,$\underline{\omega}^{(s)}$,... and of maximum attainable levels

$\underline{\omega}^{*(1)}$, $\underline{\omega}^{*(2)}$,...,$\underline{\omega}^{*(s)}$,... . The following relationships follow directly from the structure of the interactive procedure:

$$\underline{\omega}^{-(s-1)} \leq \underline{\omega}^{-(s)} \leq \underline{\omega}^{o(s)} \leq \underline{\omega}^{*(s)} \leq \underline{\omega}^{*(s-1)} \qquad s = 2,3,.... \qquad (9.1)$$

As indicated by Figure 9.3, the course of the procedure can be depicted on J bars, one bar for each objective. A proof of convergence of the procedure means that it has to be shown that

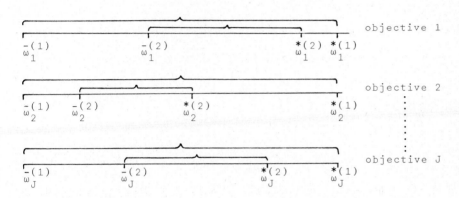

Fig. 9.3.   Minimum and maximum attainable levels during the interaction

after a finite number of steps, the distance between $\omega_j^{-(s)}$ and $\omega_j^{*(s)}$ has been reduced to some arbitrarily chosen small level for all j = 1,2,...J.

This proof consists of two parts (1):
- first, we show that $\omega_j^{-(s)}$ and $\omega_j^{*(s)}$ converge towards certain

  values ω_j^{un} and ω_j^{up} for all j (Lemma 1);
- then, we show that $\omega_j^{un} = \omega_j^{up}$ for all j (Lemma 2).

Lemma 1. $\exists\, \omega_j^{un}$ and ω_j^{up} such that $\forall\, \varepsilon > 0$

$$\exists\, S_\varepsilon \text{ such that } \omega_j^{un} - \omega_j^{(s)} < \varepsilon$$

$$\qquad (9.2)$$

$$\omega_j^{*(s)} - \omega_j^{up} < \varepsilon$$

for all $s \geq S_\varepsilon$ and for j=1,...J.

Proof. As (9.1) states, the vectors $\underline{\omega}^{-(1)}$, $\underline{\omega}^{-(2)}$,... form a monotone increasing series. Since for every s there exists an efficient compromise solution $\underline{\omega}^{o(s)}$ such that $\underline{\omega}^{-(s)} \leq \underline{\omega}^{o(s)}$, the series is bounded by a vector, which is an element of

the set of feasible solutions. Since the set of feasible
solutions is compact and consequently also bounded, the se-
ries $\underline{\omega}^{-(1)}$, $\underline{\omega}^{-(2)}$,... is monotone increasing and bounded. Every monotone bounded series converges towards a certain val-
ue (see, for example, Apostol [1971]) which completes the
proof for the $\underline{\omega}^{-(s)}$ series. The proof for the $\underline{\omega}^{*(s)}$ series
can be given in a completely similar way. Q.E.$\overline{\text{D}}$.

Lemma 2. If, in the interactive procedure, the compromise solution is determined in such a way that:

$$\underline{\omega}^{o(s)} \geq \underline{\omega}^{-(s)} + \alpha(\underline{\omega}^{*(s)} - \underline{\omega}^{-(s)}) \qquad (0 < \alpha \leq \frac{1}{J}) \qquad (9.3)$$

and if the decision problem is inseparable, then $\underline{\omega}^{up} = \underline{\omega}^{un}$.

Proof. We will first prove that there exist feasible solutions
satisfying (9.3). This can be shown by the following chain
of equations and inequalities:

$$\underline{\omega}^{-(s)} + \alpha(\underline{\omega}^{*(s)} - \underline{\omega}^{-(s)}) = (1 - \alpha)\,\underline{\omega}^{-(s)} + \alpha\underline{\omega}^{*(s)} \qquad (9.4)$$

$$(1 - \alpha)\,\underline{\omega}^{-(s)} + \alpha\underline{\omega}^{*(s)} \leq \frac{(J - 1)}{J}\,\underline{\omega}^{-(s)} + \frac{1}{J}\,\underline{\omega}^{*(s)} \qquad (9.5)$$

$$(\frac{J - 1}{J})\,\underline{\omega}^{-(s)} + \frac{1}{J}\,\underline{\omega}^{*(s)} \leq \sum_{j=1}^{J} \frac{1}{J}\,\underline{\omega}(\underline{x}_{-j}^{*(s)}) \qquad (9.6)$$

$$\sum_{j=1}^{J} \frac{1}{J}\,\underline{\omega}(\underline{x}_{-j}^{*(s)}) \leq \underline{\omega}(\sum_{j=1}^{J} \frac{1}{J}\,\underline{x}^{*(s)}) \qquad (9.7)$$

Equation (9.4) follows by definition, while (9.5) holds true
as $\alpha \leq \frac{1}{J}$. Inequality (9.6) is the result of the definition
of the pay-off matrix P, and (9.7) follows from the concavity
of $\underline{\omega}$. As $\underline{x}_{-j}^{*(s)}$ is feasible, $\sum_{j=1}^{J} \frac{1}{J}\,\underline{x}_{-J}^{*(s)}$ is also feasible, because of the convexity of K. Combining this with (9.4)-(9.7)
we may conclude that there are feasible solutions satisfying
(9.3).

We turn now to the main part of the proof. Since we know
that $\underline{\omega}^{up} \geq \underline{\omega}^{un}$ three cases can be distinguished:

(a) $\underline{\omega}_{j}^{un} < \underline{\omega}_{j}^{up}$ $\forall_{j}$

(b) $\underline{\omega}_{j}^{un} = \underline{\omega}_{j}^{up}$ $\forall_{j} \in S_{j}$

           $\underline{\omega}_{k}^{un} < \underline{\omega}_{k}^{up}$ $\forall_{k} \in S_{k}$

           where $S_{j} \cup S_{k} = \{1,...J\}$ and $S_{j} \cap S_{k} = \emptyset$

(c) $\overset{un}{\omega}_j = \overset{up}{\omega}_j$ $\forall\, j$

First, it will be shown that (a) is at variance with Lemma 1, so that it can be excluded. Then, we show that (b) only arises for separable problems. Then only (c) remains as a conclusion.

<u>Case (a)</u>. If $\overset{un}{\omega}_j < \overset{up}{\omega}_j$ for all j, then a $\delta > 0$ exists such that $\overset{up}{\omega}_j - \overset{un}{\omega}_j > \delta$, which implies:

$$\overset{*}{\omega}_j(s) - \overset{-}{\omega}_j(s) > \delta \qquad \forall\, s,\ \forall_j \qquad\qquad (9.8)$$

We have shown previously in this section that for each s a compromise solution $\underset{-}{\overset{o}{\omega}}(s)$ exists with:

$$\overset{o}{\omega}_j(s) \geq \overset{-}{\omega}_j(s) + \alpha(\overset{*}{\omega}_j(s) - \overset{-}{\omega}_j(s)) \qquad \forall\, j \qquad\qquad (9.9)$$

It is a characteristic of the interactive procedure that in step (s + 1) a new side condition will be imposed on some j, such that:

$$\overset{-}{\omega}_j(s+1) \geq \overset{o}{\omega}_j(s) \qquad\qquad (9.10)$$

After substitution of (9.8) in (9.9) and of (9.9) in (9.10), we find:

$$\overset{-}{\omega}_j(s+1) \geq \overset{-}{\omega}_j(s) + \alpha\delta \quad \text{for some j} \qquad\qquad (9.11)$$

This result is at variance with Lemma 1, because it implies that the series $\underset{-}{\overset{-}{\omega}}(1)$, $\underset{-}{\overset{-}{\omega}}(2)$,... does not converge. The contradiction can be shown straightforwardly when ε is set equal to $\alpha\delta$. Then Lemma 1 says that:

$$\overset{un}{\omega}_j - \overset{-}{\omega}_j(s) < \alpha\delta \qquad \forall\, s \geq S_{\alpha\delta},\ \forall\, j \qquad\qquad (9.12)$$

and hence,

$$\overset{-}{\omega}_j(s+1) < \overset{-}{\omega}_j(s) + \alpha\delta \qquad \forall\, s \geq S_{\alpha\delta},\ \forall\, j \qquad\qquad (9.13)$$

which is in conflict with (9.11).

<u>Case (b)</u>. There are given two non-empty sets S_j and S_k
$$(S_j \cap S_k = \emptyset,\ S_j \cup S_k = \{1,...J\})$$

$\forall \, \epsilon' > 0, \; \exists \; S_{\epsilon'} \quad$ such that:

$$\omega_j^{*(s)} - \bar{\omega}_j^{(s)} < \epsilon' \qquad \forall_j \in S_j, \quad \forall \, s \geq S_{\epsilon'} \qquad (9.14)$$

For the remaining objectives, we know that $\exists \, \delta > 0$ such that:

$$\omega_k^{*(s)} - \bar{\omega}_k^{(s)} > \delta \qquad \forall \, k \in S_k \qquad \forall \, s \qquad (9.15)$$

Let us study the effect on an ω_j of the imposition of a constraint on ω_k:

$$\omega_k \geq \bar{\omega}_k^{(s)} + \alpha(\omega_k^{*(s)} - \bar{\omega}_k^{(s)}) \geq \underline{\omega}_k^{(s)} + \alpha\delta \qquad \forall \, s \quad (9.16)$$

Let $M_{jk}^{(s)}$ denote $\dfrac{\Delta \, \omega_j^{*(s)}}{\Delta \, \bar{\omega}_k^{(s)}}$.

Then we find:

$$\omega_j^{*(s+1)} - \omega_j^{*(s)} \geq M_{jk}^{(s)} \cdot \alpha\delta \qquad \forall \, s \qquad (9.17)$$

From (9.14) one may derive, however, that:

$$\omega_j^{*(s+1)} - \omega_j^{*(s)} \leq \epsilon' \qquad \forall \, s \geq S_{\epsilon'} \qquad (9.18)$$

The conclusion which can be drawn from (9.17) and (9.18) is that:

$$\lim_{s \to \infty} M_{jk}^{(s)} = 0 \qquad \forall \, j \in S_j \text{ and } k \in S_k \qquad (9.19)$$

which means that our problem is separable. Consequently, case (c) is the only remaining possibility. Q.E.D.

Theorem 8. If, in the interactive procedure, the compromise solution is determined according to (9.3) and if the decision problem is inseparable, then

$\forall \, \epsilon > 0 \quad \exists \; S_{\epsilon} \quad$ such that:

$$\omega_j^{*(s)} - \bar{\omega}_j^{(s)} < \epsilon \qquad \forall \, j, \, \forall \, s > S_{\epsilon}$$

Proof. The theorem follows directly from Lemmas 1 and 2.   Q.E.D.

A crucial point in the procedure is the determination of the
compromise solution. Condition (9.3), which is imposed on compromise solutions has been clarified in Figure 9.4. The conse-
quence is that the compromise solution $\underset{\sim}{\overset{o}{\omega}}(s)$ yields better values for all objectives than the minimum attainable levels $\underset{\sim}{\overset{-}{\omega}}(s)$:
$\underset{\sim}{\overset{o}{\omega}}(s) > \underset{\sim}{\overset{-}{\omega}}(s)$. This is essential for the interaction, otherwise
it may happen that $\overset{o}{\omega}_j(s) = \overset{-}{\omega}_j(s)$ for some j, which causes prob-
lems when the DM wants to improve the j-th objective. In that
case, the new side condition $\omega_j \geq \overset{o}{\omega}_j(s) = \overset{-}{\omega}_j(s)$ would yield the
same compromise in the next step. The interaction would stop
because the analyst is unable to find a better compromise and
convergence would be impossible.

The condition $\alpha \leq \frac{1}{J}$ in (9.3) is necessary to ensure that
there are feasible solutions satisfying (9.3). In Figure 9.4,
the extreme case $\alpha = \frac{1}{2}$ has been depicted. For $\alpha > \frac{1}{2}$, there may
be feasible solutions, but it is not certain.

Do all compromise solutions discussed in Section 6.4 satisfy
constraint (9.3)? The min-max compromise (c4) certainly does,
but one cannot be sure about the others. It depends on the
form of K and $\underline{\omega}$ on the one hand, and α on the other. If no
certainty exists, the obvious thing to do is to calculate the
compromise under the constraint (9.3).

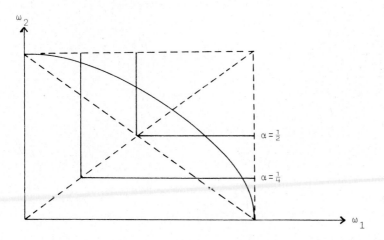

Fig. 9.4.   Conditions on the compromise solution

Next to convergence there is another important property of
the interactive procedure which must be mentioned: the procedure is non-manipulating. It can be shown that it is impossible

for the analyst to influence the outcome of the decision process by presenting very special provisional solutions. Consequently, the outcome only reflects the preferences of the DM
and not those of the analyst.

This property can be shown as follows. Let the set of feasible solutions at the beginning of step s be denoted by
$F^{(s)}$. Say that the DM aims at reaching the feasible and effi-
cient solution $\tilde{\underline{\omega}} \in F^{(1)}$. In step 1 the analyst presents an arbitrary efficient solution $\overset{o}{\underline{\omega}}{}^{(1)} \in F^{(1)}$ satisfying (9.3). Since
$\tilde{\underline{\omega}}$ and $\overset{o}{\underline{\omega}}{}^{(1)}$ are efficient, a non-empty set $S^{(1)}$ exists with a
certain number of elements n ($1 \leq n \leq J-1$) so that:

$$\overset{o}{\omega}{}^{(1)}_{j} < \tilde{\omega}_{j} \qquad \forall \; j \in S^{(1)}$$

The response of the DM will be that one or several objectives
ω_{j} where $j \in S^{(1)}$ have to be improved:

$$\omega_{j} \geq \overset{o}{\omega}{}^{(1)}_{j} \text{ for at least one } j \in S^{(1)} \qquad (9.20)$$

Obviously, $\tilde{\underline{\omega}}$ satisfies the conditions stated in (9.20). Since
$F^{(2)}$ is the intersection of $F^{(1)}$ and the set of solutions satisfying (9.20), and since $\tilde{\underline{\omega}}$ is an element of both last mentioned
sets, $\tilde{\underline{\omega}}$ is also an element of $F^{(2)}$. The same line of reasoning
yields also for the following steps that $\tilde{\underline{\omega}}$ remains a feasible
solution. Given the proof that the procedure converges, we may
conclude that the point of convergence is $\tilde{\underline{\omega}}$ and that this point
can be reached, irrespective of the values of the provisional
solutions, as long as condition (9.3) is satisfied. The rules
of the interaction do not offer the opportunity to the analyst
to manipulate the DM.

9.5   Comparability of Alternatives

At the beginning of the interaction, no information is available to the analyst about the DM's preferences. Except in the
case of dominance, every pair of alternatives is judged as incomparable. Hence, the corresponding preference relation is
incomplete. In this section, we will have a closer look at the
comparability of alternatives during the interaction.

Let X be the set of alternatives. Let the preference relation
$\gtrsim$ ("is preferred to") have the following properties:

reflexivity : $\underline{\omega} \gtrsim \underline{\omega} \qquad \forall \; \underline{\omega} \in X$

transitivity: if $\underline{\omega}_{1} \gtrsim \underline{\omega}_{2}$ and $\underline{\omega}_{2} \gtrsim \underline{\omega}_{3}$, then $\underline{\omega}_{1} \gtrsim \underline{\omega}_{3}$, $\forall \; \underline{\omega}_{1}, \underline{\omega}_{2}, \underline{\omega}_{3} \in X$

dominance : $\underline{\omega}_{1} \gtrsim \underline{\omega}_{2}$ if $\underline{\omega}_{1} \geq \underline{\omega}_{2} \qquad \forall \; \underline{\omega}_{1}, \underline{\omega}_{2} \in X$

This is the only information available about $\gtrapprox$ at the beginning of the procedure. During the procedure, more information about $\gtrapprox$ is provided by the DM as he is allowed to impose side-conditions on some objectives.

There are at least two ways in which these statements can be interpreted in terms of preference relations. Let X_1 denote the set of all elements of X which satisfy the minimum standards, and let X_2 be the set of alternatives which do not satisfy one or more of these standards:

$$
\begin{cases}
X_1 = \{\underline{\omega} \mid \underline{\omega} \in X, \ \underline{\omega} \geq \underline{\omega}^{ms}\} \\
\\
X_2 = X - X_1
\end{cases}
\tag{9.21}
$$

A lexicographic interpretation of imposing minimum standards is:

$$
\underline{\omega}_1 \gtrapprox \underline{\omega}_2 \quad \forall \ \underline{\omega}_1 \in X_1 \quad \text{and} \quad \forall \ \underline{\omega}_2 \in X_2
\tag{9.22}
$$

In Figure 9.1, this means that after the imposition of $\underline{\omega} \geq \underline{\omega}^{-(3)}$, all elements in A are preferred to all remaining feasible alternatives. The levels ω^{ms} are satiation levels. They are increased during each step so that the interaction terminates when the satiation levels form together an efficient solution.

Another interpretation of the imposition of minimum standards is:

$$
\exists \ \underline{\omega}_1 \in X_1 \ \text{such that} \ \underline{\omega}_1 \gtrapprox \underline{\omega}_2 \quad \forall \ \underline{\omega}_2 \in X_2
\tag{9.23}
$$

This formulation means for the third step in Figure 9.1 that there is an element of A which is preferred to all feasible alternatives outside A. As the interaction proceeds, A becomes smaller and smaller; the set of potential best solutions can be reduced as far as one wishes.

Is it possible to find representations of the preference relations by means of utility functions? As to the lexicographic interpretation (9.22), the answer is negative, because of the difficulties discussed in Section 4.2 about the representation of lexicographic orderings. As to interpretation (9.23), this difficulty does not arise. One should be aware, however, that (9.23) only allows a representation by means of a partially representing utility function and not a faithful one because of the lack of the completeness property (see Section 4.5).

Any utility function $U = \underline{\lambda}'\underline{\omega}$ ($\underline{\lambda} > \underline{0}$ and $\underline{\iota}'\underline{\lambda} = 1$) is partially representing the preference relation $\underset{\sim}{\geq}$ before the interaction. Given the standards $\underline{\omega}^{ms}$ imposed during the interaction, (9.23) can be partially represented by the same utility function if $\underline{\lambda}$ is a member of:

$$V(\underline{\lambda} \mid \underline{\omega}^{ms}) = \{\underline{\lambda} \mid \underline{\iota}'\underline{\lambda} = 1, \underline{\lambda} > \underline{0}, \exists \underline{\omega}_1 \in X_1 \text{ such that:}$$

$$\underline{\lambda}'\underline{\omega}_1 \geq \underline{\lambda}'\underline{\omega}_2 \quad \forall \underline{\omega}_2 \in X_2\} \tag{9.24}$$

It can be proved in a straightforward way that (9.24) implies:

$$V(\underline{\lambda} \mid \underline{\omega}^{ms}) = \{\underline{\lambda} \mid \underline{\iota}'\underline{\lambda} = 1, \underline{\lambda} > \underline{0} \; \exists \underline{\omega}_1 \in X_1 \text{ such that:}$$

$$\underline{\lambda}'\underline{\omega}_1 \geq \underline{\lambda}'\underline{\omega} \quad \forall \underline{\omega} \in X\} \tag{9.25}$$

The proof reads in the following way:

(a). If $\underline{\lambda}$ satisfies the conditions in (9.25), then also those of (9.24) are satisfied, because the conditions in (9.25) are an extension of those in (9.24).

(b). If $\underline{\lambda}$ does not satisfy the conditions in (9.25), it implies that no $\underline{\omega}_1 \in X_1$ exists such that $\underline{\lambda}'\underline{\omega}_1 \geq \underline{\lambda}'\underline{\omega}$, $\forall \underline{\omega} \in X$, hence, no $\underline{\omega}_1 \in X_1$ exists such that both $\underline{\lambda}'\underline{\omega}_1 \geq \underline{\lambda}'\underline{\omega}_2, \forall \underline{\omega}_2 \in X_2$ and $\underline{\lambda}'\underline{\omega}_1 \geq \underline{\lambda}'\underline{\omega}_3$, $\forall \underline{\omega}_3 \in X_1$. The latter condition is always satisfied when we set $\underline{\omega}_3 = \underline{\omega}_1$. So, if $\underline{\lambda}$ does not satisfy (9.25), it it also does not satisfy (9.24). This completes the proof.

By means of (9.25) we know that if $\underline{\lambda}$ has been determined at the end of the procedure, that vector cannot be used to generate a complete ordering of alternatives. It is only possible to determine the optimal solution $\overset{o}{\underline{\omega}}$ for which the value of $\underline{\lambda}'\underline{\omega}$ is maximal. Since $U = \underline{\lambda}'\underline{\omega}$ is partially representing, one should not conclude from $\underline{\lambda}'\underline{\omega}_1 \geq \underline{\lambda}'\underline{\omega}_2$ that $\underline{\omega}_1 \underset{\sim}{\geq} \underline{\omega}_2$. Thus, all alternatives, except for the optimal solution, remain incomparable during the interaction.

9.6   Shadow Prices and Interactive Decision-Making

In this section we shall discuss in more detail the relationship between the minimum standards $\underline{\omega}^{ms}$ and the set of weights $V(\underline{\lambda} \mid \underline{\omega}^{ms})$ of the linear utility function. For this purpose, the shadow price concept appears to be helpful.

Suppose that K can be written in the following form:

$$K = \{x \mid g_n(\underline{x}) \leq 0 \quad \text{for } n=1,\ldots,N\} \qquad (9.26)$$

where the functions $g_n(\underline{x})$ are convex and have continuous derivatives $\dfrac{\delta g_n(\underline{x})}{\delta x_i}$. Then the set of potential solutions during the interaction can be described as the set of solutions of:

$$\begin{cases} \text{max! } \underline{\nu}'\underline{\omega}(\underline{x}) \\[2mm] \text{s.t. } g_1(\underline{x}) \leq 0 \\ \qquad \vdots \\ \qquad g_N(\underline{x}) \leq 0 \\[2mm] \underline{\omega}(\underline{x}) \geq \underline{\omega}^{ms} \\[2mm] \underline{\nu} \in \{\underline{\nu} \mid \underline{1}'\underline{\nu} = 1, \ \underline{\nu} \geq \underline{0}\} \end{cases} \qquad (9.27)$$

In accordance with (9.25), another way to describe the set of potential solutions is:

$$\begin{cases} \text{max! } \underline{\lambda}'\underline{\omega}(\underline{x}) \\[2mm] \text{s.t. } g_1(\underline{x}) \leq 0 \\ \qquad \vdots \\ \qquad g_N(\underline{x}) \leq 0 \\[2mm] \underline{\lambda} \in V(\underline{\lambda} \mid \underline{\omega}^{ms}) \end{cases} \qquad (9.28)$$

The Kuhn-Tucker conditions for an optimum of (9.27) read:

$$\begin{cases} \underline{\nu}' \dfrac{\partial \underline{\omega}}{\partial x_i} + \sum_{n=1}^{N} \xi_n \dfrac{\partial g_n}{\partial x_i} - \underline{\mu}' \dfrac{\partial \underline{\omega}}{\partial x_i} = 0 & i=1,\ldots,I \\[4mm] \xi_n g_n(\underline{x}) = 0 & n=1,\ldots,N \\[4mm] \mu_j(\omega_j(\underline{x}) - \omega_j^{ms}) = 0 & j=1,\ldots,J \end{cases} \qquad (9.29)$$

The vector $\underline{\mu}$ contains the J shadow prices of the constraints $\underline{\omega}(\underline{x}) \geq \underline{\omega}^{ms}$.

The Kuhn-Tucker conditions for an optimum of (9.28) read:

$$
\begin{cases}
\underline{\lambda}' \dfrac{\partial \omega}{\partial x_i} + \displaystyle\sum_{n=1}^{N} \gamma_n \dfrac{\partial g_n}{\partial x_i} = 0 & i = 1, \ldots, I \\[4mm]
\gamma_n\, g_n(\underline{x}) = 0 & n = 1, \ldots, N
\end{cases}
\tag{9.30}
$$

If $\overset{o}{\underline{x}}$ is a solution of (9.29), it is also a solution of (9.30) if we set:

$$
\underline{\lambda} = \underline{\nu} - \underline{\mu}
\tag{9.31}
$$

Hence, for every $\underline{\lambda}$ satisfying (9.31) holds: $\underline{\lambda} \in V(\underline{\lambda} \mid \underline{\omega}^{ms})$. On the other hand, if $\overset{o}{\underline{x}}$ is a solution of (9.30) then it is also a solution of (9.29) when $\underline{\nu} = \underline{\lambda}$ and $\underline{\mu} = \underline{0}$. Consequently, the set $V(\underline{\lambda} \mid \underline{\omega}^{ms})$ can be found by varying the values of $\underline{\nu}$ in (9.27) in a systematic way and by subtracting the values of the shadow prices $\underline{\mu}$.

Simultaneously with the convergence of the series $\{\overline{\underline{\omega}}^{(s)}\}$ and $\{\overset{*}{\underline{\omega}}^{(s)}\}$, there is also a certain convergence in the set $V(\underline{\lambda} \mid \underline{\omega}^{ms})$. If the decision problem is linear, it is even possible that the weights have converged before the series $\overline{\underline{\omega}}^{(s)}$ has converged. In the following theorem (2), this is stated in a more formal way.

__Theorem 9.__ Let $\overset{\wedge}{\underline{x}}_k$ and $\overset{\wedge}{\underline{x}}_1$ be the solutions of the linear programming problem:

$$
\begin{cases}
\text{max!}\ (c_{j1}, \ldots, c_{jI})\ \underline{x} \\[3mm]
\text{s.t.}\ \begin{pmatrix} a_{11}, \ldots, a_{1I} \\ \vdots \\ a_{N1}, \ldots, a_{NI} \end{pmatrix} (\underline{x}) \leq \underline{b} \\[8mm]
(c_{11}, \ldots c_{1I})\underline{x} \geq \omega_1^{ms} \\
\qquad\vdots \\
(c_{J1}, \ldots c_{JI})\underline{x} \geq \omega_J^{ms}
\end{cases}
\tag{9.32}
$$

for $j = k$ and $j = 1$, respectively.

These solutions share the same subset T of active restrictions
from the set $A \underline{x} \leq \underline{b}$, where A is the N x I matrix in (9.32).
Let S_k and S_l be the sets of active restrictions in $C \underline{x} \geq \underline{\omega}^{ms}$,
such that:

$$
\begin{cases}
S_k \cap S_l = S \\
\\
S_k \cup S_l = S \cup \{k,l\}
\end{cases}
\tag{9.33}
$$

Let $\underline{\xi}_j$ and $\underline{\mu}_j$ denote the shadow prices of the side-conditions
of $A \underline{x} \leq \underline{b}$ and $C \underline{x} \geq \underline{\omega}^{ms}$, respectively, when the j-th objective is maximized. Then:

$$
\begin{pmatrix} \underline{\xi}_k \\ \\ \underline{\varepsilon}_k - \underline{\mu}_k \end{pmatrix} = c \begin{pmatrix} \underline{\xi}_l \\ \\ \underline{\varepsilon}_l - \underline{\mu}_l \end{pmatrix}
\tag{9.34}
$$

where $\underline{\varepsilon}_j$ is the basic vector with J-1 zero elements and an element 1 on the j-th position: c is an arbitrary non-zero constant
factor.

Proof.   The Kuhn-Tucker conditions for an optimum of (9.32) are:

$$
\begin{cases}
c_{ji} + \sum\limits_{n=1}^{N} \xi_{jn} a_{ni} - \sum\limits_{j'=1}^{J} \mu_{jj'} c_{j'i} = 0 & i=1,\ldots,I \\
\\
\xi_{jn} (\sum\limits_{i} a_{ni} x_i - b_n) = 0 & n=1,\ldots,N \\
\\
\mu_{jj'} (\sum\limits_{i} c_{j'i} x_i - \omega_{j'}^{ms}) = 0 & j'=1,\ldots,J
\end{cases}
\tag{9.35}
$$

Given the information about active restrictions, we may conclude
that $\xi_{jn} = 0$ if $n \notin T$, and $\mu_{jj'} = 0$ if $j' \notin S_j$ so that (9.35) can
be written for $\hat{\underline{x}}_k$ and $\hat{\underline{x}}_l$ respectively as:

$$
\begin{cases}
c_{ki} - \sum\limits_{j' \in S_k} \mu_{kj'} c_{j'i} + \sum\limits_{n \in T} \xi_{kn} a_{ni} = 0 & i=1,\ldots,I \\
\\
(\sum\limits_{i} a_{ni} x_i - b_n) = 0 & n \in T \\
\\
(\sum\limits_{i} c_{j'i} x_i - \omega_{j'}^{ms}) = 0 & j' \in S_k
\end{cases}
\tag{9.36}
$$

and

$$\begin{cases} c_{li} - \sum_{j' \in S_l} \mu_{1j'} + \sum_{n \in T} \xi_{ln} \, a_{ni} = 0 & i=1,\ldots,I \\[2em] \sum_{i} a_{ni} \, x_i - b_n = 0 & n \in T \\[2em] \sum_{i} c_{j'i} \, x_i - \omega_{j'}^{ms} = 0 & j' \in S_l \end{cases} \qquad (9.37)$$

Condition (9.33) implies that
$\mu_{kj'} \neq 0 \ \forall_{j'} \in S$, $\mu_{1j'} \neq 0 \, \forall_{j'} \in S$, $\mu_{kk} = \mu_{11} = 0$ and
$\mu_{kl} \neq 0$, $\mu_{1k} \neq 0$. Hence, the first equations in (9.36) and
(9.37) can be written as:

$$\sum_{j' \in S \cup \{k,l\}} (\epsilon_{kj'} - \mu_{kj'}) \, c_{j'i} + \sum_{n \in T} \xi_{kn} \, a_{ni} = 0 \quad i=1,\ldots,I \quad (9.38)$$

and

$$\sum_{j' \in S \cup \{k,l\}} (\epsilon_{1j'} - \mu_{1j'}) \, c_{j'i} + \sum_{n \in T} \xi_{ln} \, a_{ni} = 0 \quad i=1,\ldots,I \quad (9.39)$$

Therefore, the conclusion may be that if $(\underline{\xi}'_k, \underline{\epsilon}'_k - \underline{\mu}'_k)$ is a solution of (9.38), any vector with the form $c(\underline{\xi}'_k, \underline{\epsilon}'_k - \underline{\mu}'_k)$ is a
solution of (9.39). Q.E.D.

Corollary. If the conditions of the theorem are satisfied,

then $\mu_{1k} = \dfrac{1}{\mu_{kl}}$.

Proof. This follows straightforwardly from the result (9.34):
$\underline{\epsilon}_k - \underline{\mu}_k = c(\underline{\epsilon}_1 - \underline{\mu}_1)$. Q.E.D.

Theorem 9 states that the weights corresponding with certain
solutions may be converged, even before the solutions have converged. Moreover, it enables one to calculate immediately the
consequences of the imposition of new side conditions for some
columns of the pay-off matrix. One should realize that in linear MOD problems, it may also be just vice versa: the optimal
solution may be determined with certainty, while yet the corresponding weights cannot be determined in a unique way (see
Section 6.7).

9.7   An Interactive Procedure for Discrete Problems

   The preceding sections have been devoted to interactive
methods for continuous problems. In the literature, little attention has been paid to interactive methods for discrete problems. This may be due to the fact that discrete problems often
include only a limited number of alternatives, but this is not
always the case.

Discussions about interactive decision-making for discrete
problems can be found in Zionts [1977], Nijkamp and Rietveld
[1977] and Nijkamp and Spronk [1978]. Zionts [1977] presents
an adaptation of the interactive method of Zionts and Wallenius
[1976] mentioned in Section 9.2 for integer linear problems.
He shows that it is possible to integrate well-developed integer linear programming algorithms (such as the branch-and-
bound-algorithm) in the interactive method. A drawback of the
method is that when the underlying utility function is generally concave, certain potential solutions may be overlooked. For
example, solution C in Figure 9.5 will not be generated as a
potential solution by the Zionts algorithm since this algorithm
only deals with the vertices of the convex polyhedron generated
by the feasible integer solutions (cf. Section 6.7).

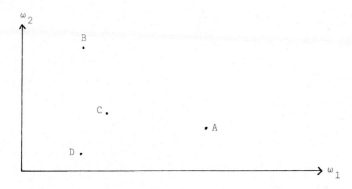

Fig. 9.5.   Discrete alternatives

The interactive procedure of Nijkamp and Rietveld [1977] for
discrete problems is also based on an interactive procedure for
continuous problems, namely that discussed in Section 9.3. This
procedure can be formulated in the following way.

stage (a): The analyst calculates $\bar{\omega}$ and $\overset{*}{\omega}$. Next, he calculates
           the generalized min-max solution (see Chapter 6,

           Appendix I) as a provisional solution $\overset{o}{\omega}$. He presents
           these solutions to the DM and asks him which element

           of $\overset{o}{\omega}$ must be improved.

stage (b): The DM answers that a certain objective j must be
           improved ($\omega_j \geq \overset{o}{\omega}_j$) or strictly improved ($\omega_j > \overset{o}{\omega}_j$). The
           analyst applies this information to reduce the set
           of feasible alternatives and returns to stage (a).

This procedure differs from that in Section (9.3) in two respects. First, the provisional solution should be of the min-
max type. Second, the DM can choose between a strict improvement and an ordinary improvement of an objective. Both differences can be understood when the convergence of the procedure
is studied for the discrete case. At the beginning of the procedure, the number of alternatives equals N. Assume that N is

"large" (cf. Section 8.2), otherwise it does not make much
sense to apply this type of interactive method. For the convergence of the procedure, the relationship between $\underset{\omega}{o}(s)$ and
$\underset{\omega}{-}(s)$ plays a crucial role. We can distinguish four cases concerning this relationship:

$$1. \quad \underset{j}{\overset{o}{\omega}}(s) > \underset{j}{\overset{-}{\omega}}(s) \qquad\qquad \forall\; j \qquad\qquad\qquad (9.40)$$

$$2. \quad \begin{cases} \underset{j}{\overset{o}{\omega}}(s) = \underset{j}{\overset{-}{\omega}}(s) & \forall\; j \in\; J_1 \neq \emptyset \\[2mm] \underset{j}{\overset{o}{\omega}}(s) > \underset{j}{\overset{-}{\omega}}(s) & \forall\; j \in\; J_2 \end{cases} \qquad (9.41)$$

2a.   The DM imposes a side-condition on an element of
      J_2.

2b.   The DM imposes a strict side-condition on an ele-
      ment of J_1.

2c.   The DM imposes a non-strict side-condition on an
      element of J_1.

In case 1, every step of the procedure implies the rejection of
a number of elements from the set of feasible solutions. Consequently, as long as (9.40) holds, the procedure converges
within a finite number of steps. Figure 9.5 illustrates the
importance of the condition that the provisional solution is of
the min-max type when the number of objectives is equal to two.
Other compromise concepts might lead to the selection of A or B
as the provisional solution which would imply that (9.40) is no
longer satisfied. Then (9.41) would hold, which may hinder the
convergence as we shall show now.

   It is obvious that cases 2a and 2b do not hinder the convergence of the interaction when (9.41) holds, because in each
step one or more alternatives are rejected. In the case of 2c,
however, the convergence is impossible. If, for example, the
project effect matrix R contains four alternatives for J=3:

$$R = \begin{pmatrix} 1 & 0 & 0 & .2 \\ 0 & 1 & 0 & .6 \\ 0 & 0 & 1 & 0 \end{pmatrix} \qquad (9.42)$$

then the fourth alternative will be selected as the provisional
solution. Case 2c arises when the DM imposes a non-strict side-
condition on the third objective. The convergence stops because this side-condition does not lead to the rejection of any
of the feasible alternatives.

   The conclusion may be that the procedure does not guarantee
the selection of a unique alternative. The result may also be

a set of potential attractive alternatives. In spite of this
conclusion, it is not necessary to reject the interactive method. As shown in Chapter 12, the problem of an incomplete convergence did not arise at all in an application of this method.
Another argument in favour of the procedure is that if the convergence stops at a certain step, it is probable that the number of feasible alternatives is not large compared to the number of objectives J. Then it is possible to use one of the
methods in Chapter 8 to make a final selection.

The interactive method can also be used for problems with
ordinal or mixed data. Consider the following vector maximization problem:

$$
\begin{cases}
\max! & \underline{\omega}\left(\dfrac{x}{y}\right), \ \underline{v}(\underline{y}) \\[2ex]
\text{s.t.} & \left(\dfrac{x}{y}\right) \in K \\[2ex]
& \underline{y} \in L \ , \ \underline{y} \text{ contains integer variables} \qquad (9.43) \\[2ex]
& \underline{\omega} \ : \ \text{cardinal measurable} \\[2ex]
& \underline{v} \ : \ \text{ordinal measurable}
\end{cases}
$$

This may be the formalization of a highway planning problem.
For example, three different routes for a certain connection
may be devised (y = 1,2,3), each influencing the beauty of the
landscape ($v(1)$, $v(2)$, $v(3)$), which is only measurable in an
ordinal way. The vector $\underline{x}$ concerns the materials and techniques
used, ω_1 denotes the costs of the construction (for which a
minimum value is aimed at) and ω_2 is the employment generated
by the construction. Figure 9.6 gives a graphical explanation
of this three-dimensional example.

In Section 8.6, we discussed the possibility of finding compromise solutions for ordinal data. The result was that this
is indeed possible. Hence, the interactive method can also be
applied to ordinal or mixed problems, although one should be
aware of the character of ordinal data. In Figure 9.6, for example, (a) and (b) represent the same mixed problem in two considerably varying cardinal ways.

9.8   An Interactive Method for Selecting a Range of
      Alternatives

The interactive methods, discussed in Sections 9.2 and 9.3,
share the property that a unique alternative can be selected if
at least the DM and the analyst obey the communication rules.
In certain situations, however, the determination of a whole

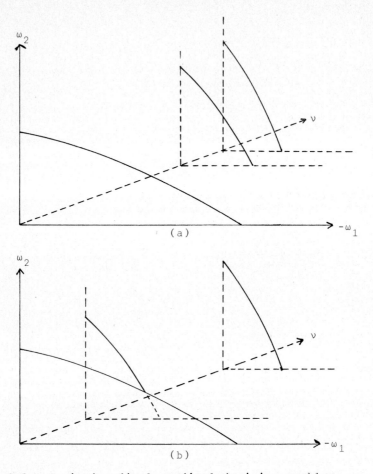

Fig. 9.6.   A mixed ordinal-cardinal decision problem

range of alternatives instead of only one seems to be more appropriate. We will give some examples:

(a) When a decision problem is very complicated, it may be
worthwhile to use a "mixed scanning" approach (cf. Faludi
[1973]). Then, first a set of promising alternatives is selected, based on a limited amount of information. Only in the
second stage is the final decision selected from this set,
based on all available information.

(b) A politician who must take a decision needs a certain
space for bargaining with the various groups concerned. It
will be wise for him to reserve some options.

In (a) and (b), it is <u>undesirable</u> to select a unique alternative. In the next example, it is even <u>impossible</u>.

(c) The objectives involved in the problem may be so diverse,
that the DM is unable to rank or specify his priorities in the
course of the interaction (3).

There are several ways to define a range R of alternatives.
Two obvious ways are: a definition by means of a series of minimum standards $\underline{\omega}^{min}$, or by means of a set of corresponding
weights. In the context of this chapter, the former is the
most adequate one, because the minimum standards have a central
position in the interactive procedure. Thus:

$$R = \{\underline{x} \in K \mid \underline{x} \text{ is efficient, } \underline{\omega}(\underline{x}) \geq \underline{\omega}^{min}\} \qquad (9.44)$$

One might expect that the determination of R is less time con-
suming than the determination of a unique alternative, but this
is not the case. It may even take much more time to approxi-
mate the J elements of $\underline{\omega}^{min}$ sufficiently, compared to the approximation of a unique alternative.

The range R can be determined in two phases:
(a) Proceed with the interactive procedure described in
Section 9.3. Let the analyst ask in every step whether the
provisional solution $\overset{o}{\underline{\omega}}$ is in the range, or outside it. As long
as the latter situation prevails, the vector $\overline{\underline{\omega}}$ may serve as a
first approximation of $\underline{\omega}^{min}$. Once the provisional solution $\overset{o}{\underline{\omega}}$
is inside the range, go to phase (b).
(b) The refinement of $\underline{\omega}^{min}$ is based on the generation of provisional solutions which are outside the range so that new
side-conditions can be imposed on the least satisfactory elements of these solutions. When compromise solutions can no
longer be used as provisional solutions because they are in the
range, the half-compromises (which are more eccentric) may be
useful as provisional solutions. As there are J half-compromises, it must first be established in which direction
the largest improvement can be expected. If the generated
half-compromise is still in the range, then by means of (6.37')
another half-compromise can be found which is more eccentric
than the original one.

The flow chart of the procedure is shown in Figure 9.7. The
first six elements form together the interactive procedure, described in Section 9.3. The elements 7 and 8 are devoted to
the determination of the vector in P for which the generation
of a corresponding half-compromise is most promising. The value of h is of importance for (6.37'). The elements 9-11 of the
procedure lead to the determination of a provisional solution
outside the range. The doubling of h means for (6.37') that a
more eccentric half-compromise will be generated. The elements
12-14 are identical to the elements 4-6: they result in the imposition of new side-conditions and hence in a more refined de-

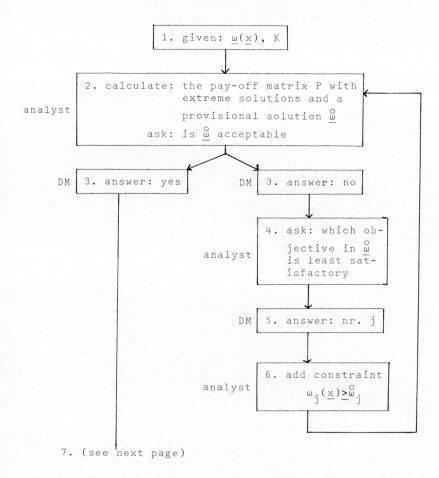

1. given: $\underline{\omega}(\underline{x})$, K

2. calculate: the pay-off matrix P with extreme solutions and a provisional solution $\underline{\overset{o}{\omega}}$

   ask: is $\underline{\overset{o}{\omega}}$ acceptable

analyst

DM 3. answer: yes

DM 3. answer: no

4. ask: which objective in $\underline{\overset{o}{\omega}}$ is least satisfactory

analyst

DM 5. answer: nr. j

6. add constraint
   $\omega_j(\underline{x}) \geq \overset{o}{\omega}_j$

analyst

7. (see next page)

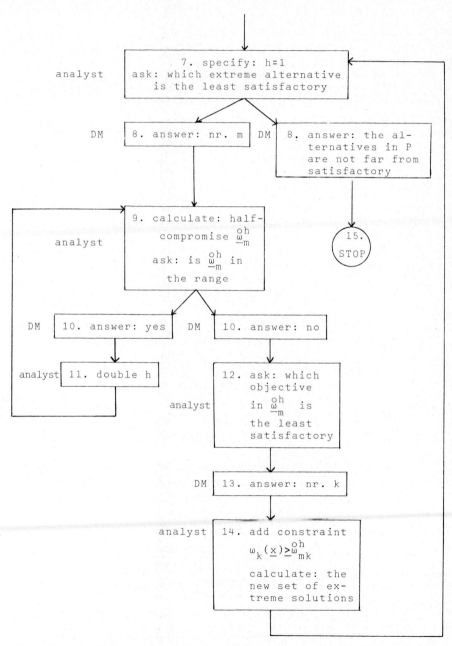

Fig. 9.7.   Flow chart of an interactive procedure to determine
             a range of potential alternatives

termination of $\underline{\omega}^{min}$. The procedure stops when the DM feels
that all elements of the pay-off matrix P are not far from
being satisfactory (element 15).

Figure 9.8 gives a graphical illustration of the procedure
involved. Let R be the yet unknown range and $\underline{\omega}^{min}$ the corresponding vector of minimum achievement levels. The first com-
promise solution C is outside the range. Hence, a constraint
on ω_2 is added. In the second step the compromise D is in R.
Consequently, we turn to the second phase of the procedure:
the evaluation of the elements of the pay-off matrix B and C.
Since B is the least satisfactory solution, the half-compromise
$\underline{\omega}_2^{oh}$ is calculated (E), which is still unsatisfactory. Hence,
another constraint is added. The new P matrix consists of the
alternatives E and C. E is less satisfactory than C. Again a
half-compromise $\underline{\omega}_2^{oh}$ is calculated (F), which falls inside the
range. After a redoubling procedure, we find the alternative
G, which falls outside the range. Note that in a limited num-
ber of steps, the minimum levels $\underline{\omega}$ have risen from M_1 to M_4,
which is already relatively close to $\underline{\omega}^{min}$.

One final comment should be made about the appropriate
starting value of h. This value of h depends inter alia on the
number of steps which has already been passed through in the
procedure. When h is held constant during the procedure, the
probability rises that a half-compromise is in the range R. As
the procedure is most rapid when $\underline{\omega}_j^h$ is just outside R, it is
better to increase h continuously during the interaction.

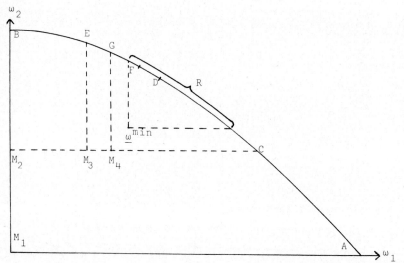

Fig. 9.8. Illustration of range-aiming interactive procedure

The proof that this interactive procedure is convergent and non-manipulating proceeds along the lines set out in Section 9.4. Concerning the convergence it is obvious that the range-aiming procedure does not converge in the sense that the minimum and maximum attainable levels of the objectives can be brought arbitrarily close together. For the range-aiming procedure only Lemma 1 (see Section 9.4) holds, stating that the series of minimum attainable levels converges towards some limit point. For the proof that the procedure is non-manipulating we find that condition (9.3) must not only apply to compromise solutions, but also to half-compromise solutions (4).

9.9   Interactive Decision-Making by Groups

Relatively little attention has been paid in the literature to MOD-making in groups of decision-makers. In this section, we will show that the interactive procedures developed in this chapter form a good base for group decision-making.

Let us start with the assumption that a group of decision-makers $(DM^1, \ldots DM^N)$ aims at <u>unanimous decisions</u>. Then it is only possible to achieve agreement when the intersection of the ranges R^n of the N persons is non-empty. Consequently, unanimity about the alternative to be selected can seldom be reached. This does not imply that in the case of a unanimity requirement no progress can be made in decision-making. For example, if it is impossible to agree on the alternative to be selected, it may still be possible to agree on the alternatives to be rejected.

If the N members of the group have found their final efficient solution by means of the procedure described in Section 9.3 or the minimum attainable levels for a range of acceptable solutions (Section 9.8), then it is possible in principle to reach agreement on the rejection of some of the feasible solutions. This can be shown as follows. Let $\bar{\omega}^n$ denote the minimum levels for the J objectives established by person n. Then, for the whole group, minimum levels $\bar{\bar{\omega}}$ can be found in the following way:

$$\bar{\bar{\omega}}_j = \min_n \bar{\omega}_j^n \qquad (9.45)$$

All members of the group are unanimous about the statement that the final solution ω should satisfy $\omega \geq \bar{\bar{\omega}}$, which means that all alternatives which do not satisfy this condition may be rejected. Figure 9.9 presents an illustration of the definition of $\bar{\bar{\omega}}$. It also shows that the number of alternatives rejected is greater when (1) the number of DMs is less, (2) the range of uncertainty is less for each DM, and (3) the conflict among DMs is less. An extreme case arises when the conflict between two DMs is complete, so that no alternatives can be rejected. This

would occur, for example, if one DM were to express that, in
his opinion, the desirable solution is A, while another DM
would propose B as the best solution.

It is not necessary to determine $\bar{\underline{w}}$ as the result of N interactive procedures with individual DMs. It is also possible to
find it by means of one interactive group-procedure, which bears
a close resemblance to the procedure discussed in Section 9.8.

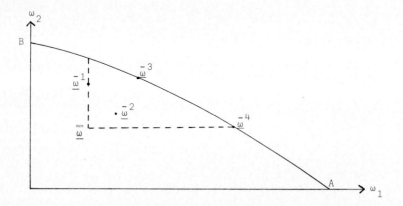

Fig. 9.9.   The determination of minimum standards when there
                are several decision-makers present

Figure 9.10 contains the flow-chart of the procedure. The elements 1-6 are similar to the corresponding elements in Figure
9.7.   If all DMs agree that certain objectives in the provisional
solution must be improved, constraints can be imposed accordingly. If such an agreement cannot be reached, one has to continue with the elements 7-15. This means that first the J extreme solutions in the pay-off matrix P must be considered. If
unanimity about the undesirability of any of these cannot be
reached, the procedure terminates (element 9b). If unanimity
arises, the introduction of half-compromises may eventually result in the imposition of a new constraint (element 14b). The
interactive group decision procedure is convergent and non-manipulating, as can be shown along the lines set out in Section
9.4 (cf. also Section 9.8).

The conclusion is that a procedure can be developed to construct a range of potential alternatives upon which all members
of the group agree. If the group wishes to make a final selection, however, it must set aside the unanimity requirement so
that also majority voting can become an element of the decision
procedure. Then the following decision-making strategy could
be used:

1.   Delete the irrelevant alternatives by means of the inter-
     active group decision procedure.

2.   Generate a representative set of alternatives along the

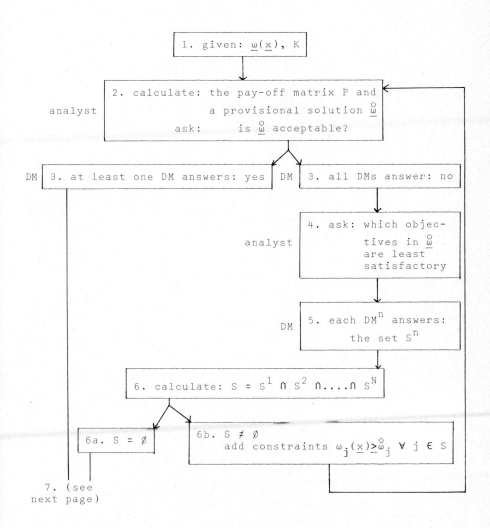

1. given: $\underline{\omega}(\underline{x})$, K

2. calculate: the pay-off matrix P and
              a provisional solution $\overset{o}{\underline{\omega}}$
   ask: is $\overset{o}{\underline{\omega}}$ acceptable?

analyst

DM 3. at least one DM answers: yes   DM 3. all DMs answer: no

4. ask: which objec-
        tives in $\overset{o}{\underline{\omega}}$
        are least
        satisfactory

analyst

5. each DM^n answers:
   the set S^n

DM

6. calculate: $S = S^1 \cap S^2 \cap \ldots \cap S^N$

6a. $S = \emptyset$

6b. $S \neq \emptyset$
    add constraints $\omega_j(\underline{x}) \geq \overset{o}{\underline{\omega}}_j \ \forall \ j \in S$

7. (see
next page)

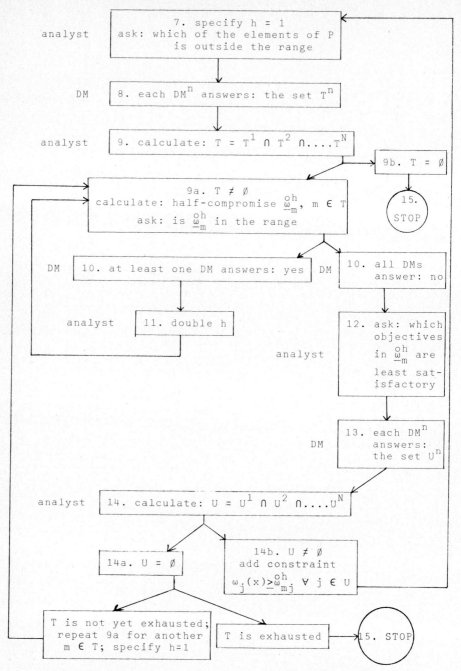

Fig. 9.10. Flow chart of the interactive decision procedure for groups

lines of Chapter 6.

3. Select the final solution by means of a voting procedure.

One should realize that there is no guarantee that this procedure satisfies the Arrow conditions (cf. Arrow [1951]). For
example, majority voting may give rise to an intransitive collective preference relation, which means that the alternative
ultimately selected depends on the order in which the alternatives have been put to the vote. It is worthwhile to deal with
these questions in more detail. Consider Figure 9.11 where for

$N=5$ DMs the ranges R^n of admissible solutions have been represented in a bi-criterion case.

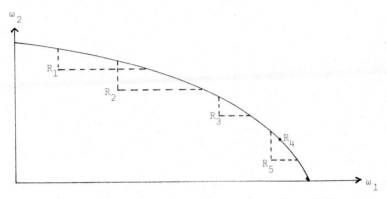

Fig. 9.11. Ranges of admissible solutions for 5 DMs

Assume that the 5 DMs have agreed upon the following interactive voting procedure:

1) an efficient alternative is generated;

2) by means of majority voting it is determined in which direction a more attractive alternative can be found: either by
   improving ω_1 or by improving ω_2. If no majority exists for
   any option: stop the procedure; otherwise: return to 1, taking into account the newly found side-condition.

Obviously, the outcome of this procedure in the case of Figure
9.11 is that an arbitrary element of R_3 is selected. This result can easily be generalized in the bi-criterion case where
N DMs participate (N is odd), namely that the outcome is a certain element of the range of the voter in the median position.

We conclude that when $J = 2$, no difficulties arise with intransitivities in this voting procedure. This conclusion is in
accordance with the finding of Black [1971] that when only two
dimensions are involved in the alternatives, majority voting
yields a transitive collective preference ordering.

We will show now that the situation changes when the number
of dimensions is larger than two. Consider Figure 9.12 where

for J=3 the admissible ranges for N=3 DMs have been depicted.

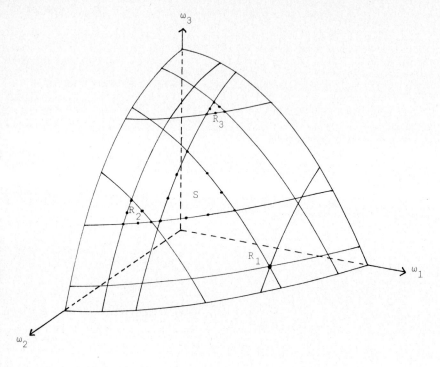

Fig. 9.12.   Ranges of admissible solutions when J= 3

Every range R^n is characterized by a set of minimum levels $\underline{\omega}^{min}$. Let ω_j^m be the median value of the ω_j^{min} of all DMs. Consider the set S which is defined as follows:

$$S = \left\{ \underline{\omega} \mid \underline{\omega} \geq \underline{\omega}^m \ ; \ \underline{\omega} \text{ is efficient} \right\} \qquad (9.46)$$

Obviously, S is empty when $\underline{\omega}^m$ is not feasible (5). When J=2, $\underline{\omega}^m$ is always feasible, but when J>3 this does not necessarily hold true by definition. It is easy to draw a similar figure as Figure 9.12 such that S is empty. In the latter case we find that S', defined as:

$$S' = \left\{ \underline{\omega} \mid \underline{\omega} \leq \underline{\omega}^m \ ; \ \underline{\omega} \text{ is efficient} \right\} \qquad (9.47)$$

is not empty. How does the interactive voting procedure operate when J$\geq$3? We distinguish two cases: S$\neq\emptyset$ and S=$\emptyset$.

a. We begin with the case that S≠∅. As long as the provision-
    al solution $\overset{o}{\underline{\omega}}$ is not an element of S, voting results in the
    imposition of side-conditions to the set of potential so-
    lutions. When $\overset{o}{\underline{\omega}}$ ∈ S, however, no majority can be achieved
    for the imposition of any additional side-condition. There-
    fore, when J≥3 and S≠∅, the procedure has to be reformula-
    ted as:
    1. Generate a provisional efficient solution $\overset{o}{\underline{\omega}}$.
    2. Determine by means of majority voting which elements of
       $\overset{o}{\underline{\omega}}_j$ of the provisional solution must be improved.
       - if no majority can be reached for any improvement, re-
         turn to 1 in order to generate another efficient solu-
         tion for which a majority can be found. If, after a
         systematic presentation of provisional solutions still
         no majority is feasible: stop the procedure;
       - if a majority can be found, return to 1,having added
         the newly determined side-conditions.
    The result of this procedure is a vector of minimum levels
    $\underline{\omega}^{min}$ being near to $\underline{\omega}^m$ which yields a good approximation of
    the set S. The element of S to be selected must be deter-
    mined by another method such as bargaining (6).

b. When S=∅ the voting procedure fails because it gives rise
    to intransitivities which means that the ultimate solution
    depends on the way in which the provisional alternatives
    have been selected. This can be illustrated when $\overset{o}{\underline{\omega}}$ is an
    element of S'. In that case a majority can be reached for
    imposing side-conditions in all directions, which obvious-
    ly is inconsistent with the fact that $\overset{o}{\underline{\omega}}$ is already effi-
    cient. Consequently the interactive majority voting pro-
    cedure does not yield meaningful results when S=∅. Other
    methods such as bargaining are more appropriate in this
    case.

   We may conclude that the principles of the interactive decision method presented in Section 9.3 can also be employed for
group decision-making. When the group aims at unanimous decisions, an interactive decision method is available to derive a
range of potential solutions, such that each group member
agrees that the most preferred solution is inside this range.
Under certain conditions this set can be further reduced by
means of an interactive majority voting procedure. We have
shown, however, that voting may sometimes give rise to arbitrary outcomes, related to the so-called Arrow paradox. Therefore, in many group decisions additional procedures are necessary in order to reach a final decision. Among these procedures are: bargaining; coalition formation and the expression
of the intensities of preferences.

9.10   Conclusion

   Interactive methods form a well-developed part of MOD methods. There is a considerable variety of methods, most of which

seem to be sound from the internal consistency viewpoint: they
are convergent and yield efficient solutions. As to the DM's
ability and willingness to co-operate with the analyst by means
of an interactive method, less definite inferences can be drawn,
because most of the methods presented have not yet been applied
in many real decision situations.

One method has received special attention in this chapter:
that method characterized by the imposition of side-conditions.
This method appears very general in its range of potential applications. It can be used in situations which require the
determination of a unique solution, as well as that of a range
of solutions. It can be employed with individual DMs as well
as with groups of DMs. It is applicable to both continuous and
discrete problems and to linear as well as non-linear problems.
Combined with the fact that this method does not seem too demanding with respect to the DM's abilities to co-operate, we
may conclude that this method is a promising candidate for application.

Chapter 10 contains a further classification and evaluation
of interactive as well as non-interactive MOD methods.

Footnotes

1.   This proof is related to a proof by Fandel [1972].

2.   See for a similar theorem Nijkamp and Rietveld [1976b],
     which is proved by means of the primal-dual relationships
     in LP.

3.   There appears to be a certain similarity between the con-
     cept of a range of potential solutions developed here, and
     the concept of a confidence interval in econometrics (cf.
     Johnston [1972]).
     Assume e.g. a linear utility function $U = \underline{\lambda}'\underline{\omega}$, where $\underline{\lambda}$ is
     a stochastic variable which has a normal distribution with
     mean $\underline{\lambda}^0$ and a covariance matrix Ω. Let S_ε be a set of
     combinations of weights, which is symmetric around $\underline{\lambda}^0$,
     such that $\Pr[\underline{\lambda} \in S_\varepsilon] = \varepsilon$. Then a range of potential solu-
     tions can be defined as follows:
     $R_\varepsilon = \{\underline{\omega} | \exists$ a certain value of $\underline{\lambda} \in S_\varepsilon$ such that $\underline{\omega}$ is the
     optimal solution corresponding to this value of $\underline{\lambda}\}$.

4.   Note that the value of α in (9.3) should be determined
     carefully in the case of half-compromise solutions. When
     α is too large the half-compromise may fall inside the
     range of potential solutions R which would hinder the con-
     vergence of the procedure. Just as the value of h (cf.
     Figure 9.7) is flexible, is a flexible value of α an ap-
     propriate solution of this problem.

5.   Note that it has been shown by means of inequality (9.7)
     that the mean value of a number of feasible solutions is

feasible. Such a proof cannot be given for the _median
value_. We learn from this that when the median value is
equal to, or smaller than, the mean value, feasibility is
warranted.

6. Note that a low value of $\underline{\omega}^m$ is an indication of a strong
measure of conflict. In an extreme case, ω^m may be equal
to the vector with minimum attainable levels $\underline{\bar{\omega}}$, so that S
is identical to the set of efficient solutions. Obvious-
ly, the interactive voting procedure is pointless in such
an extreme case.

CHAPTER 10

CLASSIFICATION AND EVALUATION OF MULTIPLE

OBJECTIVE DECISION METHODS

10.1   Introduction

Chapters 6-9 have been devoted to a survey of existing MOD methods and also to the development of new concepts and methods in this field. The methods have been classified mainly according to two criteria:

1. The nature of the data, i.e. continuous problems (Chapters 6 and 7; Chapter 9 with the exception of Section 9.7) or discrete problems (Chapter 8; Section 9.7);

2. The amount of information available to the analyst about the DM's priorities, i.e. no information (Chapter 6; Sections 8.2 - 8.5), some information (Chapter 7; Sections 8.6 - 8.9), or interactive provision of information (Chapter 9).

There are, of course, more dimensions according to which the methods can be classified. This will be dealt with in Section 10.2. In Section 10.3 we will discuss the possibility of evaluating the MOD methods. In this section the MOD methods will be confronted with a series of desiderata which have been developed in Chapters 2-5. Consequently, Section 10.3 can be conceived of as the place of integration between the mainly qualitative Chapters 2-5 and the mainly technical Chapters 6-9.

10.2   Classification

A considerable number of surveys on MOD methods have been written, each based on its own classification. Examples are: Roy [1971, 1976, 1977], Bernard and Besson [1971], MacCrimmon [1973], Haimes, Hall and Freedman [1975], van Loon [1975], Wallenius [1975], Nijkamp and Rietveld [1976a, 1977], Nijkamp and Spronk [1977], Starr and Zeleny [1977], Hwang and Masud [1979], Sinden and Worrell [1979] and Winkels [1979b]. There are basically three principles according to which MOD methods can be classified, namely the nature of (1) the input, (2) the throughput and (3) the output. In Table 10.1 we show how these principles can be elaborated. In all, we arrive at a series of 13 characteristics. In Table 10.2 these characteristics are used to typify the methods presented in the various sections of the preceding chapters. In certain sections, methods are dealt with which differ according to one or two characteristics. In such a case an entry of the table contains more than one number.

CHARACTERISTIC	OPTION	CODE (used in Table 10.2)
1. INPUT		
a. Scale of measurement of variables	ordinal mixed cardinal	1 2 3
b. Number of feasible alternatives	finite, small finite, large infinite	1 2 3
c. Are variables stochastic?	yes no	1 2
d. Is information available about priorities among objectives?	yes no	1 2
e. Is information available about comparable choices in the past?	yes no	1 2
f. Number of DMs	one several	1 2
2. THROUGHPUT		
a. Does the method make use of pairwise comparisons of alternatives?	yes no	1 2
b. In which way are preferences modelled?	utility functions (linear or general) goals minimum standards lexicographic	1 2 3 4
c. Is attention restricted to efficient solutions?	yes no	1 2
d. Is the method interactive?	yes no	1 2
3. OUTPUT		
a. Number of alternatives in the final selection presented to the DM	one some	1 2
b. Is information provided on rankings of alternatives?	yes no	1 2
c. Are the probabilities of alternatives calculated?	yes no	1 2

Table 10.1.   Characteristics of MOD methods

Section	Characteristic (see Table 10.1)												
	1a	1b	1c	1d	1e	1f	2a	2b	2c	2d	3a	3b	3c
6.2,6.4,6.6	3	3	2	2	2	1,2	2	1,3	1	2	2	2	2
6.3	3	3	2	2	2	1,2	2	1,3	1	2	3	2	2
6.7	3	3	2	2	2	1,2	2	1,3	1	2	2	2	1
7.2, 7.4	3	3	2	1	2	1	2	1	1	1,2	1	2	2
7.3	3	3	2	1	1	1	2	1	1	2	1	2	2
7.5	3	3	2	1	2	1	2	2	1	2	1	2	2
7.6	3	3	2	1	2	1	2	3	1	2	1	2	2
7.7	3	3	2	1	2	1	2	4	1	2	2	2	2
8.2	3	2	2	2	2	1,2	2	1	1	2	2	2	2
8.3	3	1	2	2	2	1,2	1	1	1	2	2	1	1,2
8.4	3	2	2	1	2	1	2	1	1	2	1	2	2
8.5	3	1	2	1	2	1	1	1	1	2	2	1	2
8.6	1,2	2	2	2	2	1,2	2	1	1	2	2	2	2
8.7	1	1	1	2	2	1,2	1	1	1	2	2	1	1,2
8.8	1	2	2	1	2	1	2	1	1	2	1	2	2
8.9	1	1	2	1	2	1	1	1	1	2	1,2	1	2
9.2	3	3	2	1	2	1	2	1-4	1,2	1	1	2	2
9.3	3	3	2	1	2	1	2	3	1	1	1	2	2
9.7	1,2	2,3	2	1	2	1	2	3	1	1	1	2	2
9.8	3	3	2	1	2	1	2	3	1	1	2	2	2
9.9	3	3	2	1	2	2	2	3	1	1	2	2	2

Table 10.2.   Classification of MOD methods

Table 10.2 reveals certain one-sidedness in the body of MOD
methods (1). The number of methods dealing with stochastic data (1c) and with inefficient solutions (2c) is small. Given
the discussion in Section 6.3, the latter is not alarming, but
in light of Chapter 2 the former is certainly unsatisfactory.
Another underdeveloped area appears from characteristic 1f.
There are only a few methods appropriate for multiple DMs, giv-
en that some information is available about their priorities.
This is obviously a disadvantage in many fields of planning, of
which regional planning is one.

The table also throws light on the relationship between the
characteristics. We find clear links between the characteristics 1b, 2a and 3b: pairwise comparisons of alternatives and
rankings of alternatives are only employed when the number of
alternatives is small. Another cluster of characteristics (1d,
1e and 2d) follows more or less per definition: interactive
methods and methods using information about comparable choices
in the past obviously imply that information on priorities
among objectives is available. Characteristic 3c can largely
be deduced from these two clusters: probabilities of objectives
are only calculated when the number of alternatives is small
and when no (or incomplete) information on priorities is available (1d). The only exception is Section 6.7, which has the
special characteristic that the set of alternatives can be generated by a finite series of alternatives.

These findings give rise to the following conclusions concerning the essential dimensions according to which MOD methods
can be classified. There are at least five relatively independent dimensions according to which MOD methods display considerable variation:

- the number of feasible solutions of the decision problem
  (1b, 2a, 3b);

- the scale of measurement of the data (1a);

- the availability of information about priorities (1d, 1e,
  2d);

- the way in which preferences are modelled (2b);

- the number of alternatives to be presented to the DM in the
  final selection.

There are at least two dimensions according to which MOD
methods are still relatively underdeveloped:

- the uncertainty about data (1c);

- the number of DMs (1f).

10.3   Evaluation

Having traced the most pertinent dimensions in the set of
MOD methods, we turn to a more precise evaluation of these
methods. There have been several attempts to evaluate MOD
methods (cf. Hwang and Masud [1979]). Up to now, however,
agreement about the criteria to be employed has not been

reached.   As an example we mention the criteria proposed by Cohon and Marks [1975], Fandel and Wilhelm [1976] and Voogd [1976].

Cohon and Marks [1975] put forward the following criteria. A MOD method should:

1. be computationally feasible and relatively efficient;

2. foster the explicit quantification of the trade-offs among objectives;

3. provide sufficient information that an informed decision can be made.

Fandel and Wilhelm [1976] mention the following requirements for MOD methods:

1. they should generate only feasible alternatives;

2. if two different combinations of instruments bring about the same outcome for the objectives, and if one of them is selected by the MOD method, then the other should also be selected;

3. they should generate only efficient alternatives;

4. they should generate a non-empty set of alternatives;

5. the outcome should be independent of irrelevant alternatives (2).

Voogd [1976] suggests the following criteria concerning MOD methods.   Relating to the DM, the relevant questions include:

1. Does the DM need much formal insight into the method?

2. Is the structure of the method comprehensible?

3. Is the method applicable to ordinal data?

4. Does the method require many activities of the DM?

Relating to the analyst, the following questions are posed:

5. Does the method require many deeds from the analyst?

6. Does the analyst need a computer?

7. Does the analyst need formal knowledge?

Obviously, the scope of the criteria differs substantially. On the one extreme, Fandel and Wilhelm are concerned mainly with the formal consistency of the method.   On the other extreme, Voogd states a number of factors which are favourable to the disposition of the DM and analyst to start a structured MOD procedure.   The contribution of Cohon and Marks is somewhere in between these two extremes.   Not all criteria mentioned above are very appealing.   For example, Cohon and Marks' second criterion concerning the explicit quantification of the trade-offs among objectives is too restrictive, because it excludes the possibility that conflicts among objectives can be analyzed in other ways.   Another example can be found in Fandel and Wilhelm's criteria, where it can easily be established that the third criterion (efficiency) includes the first one (feasibility).

For the criteria to be employed in this study, we will take
in the results of Chapters 2-5, supplemented with several criteria which are suggested in Chapters 6-9. The criteria will
be arranged in three classes - criteria concerning: (a) the
DM's situation; (b) the analyst's situation; (c) the internal
consistency of the method. In Table 10.3 the criteria are enumerated, together with the finding place in the preceding chapters.

Given the strong links between these criteria and the contents of Chapter 2-5, this section can be conceived of as the
place where the predominantly qualitative contributions to the
theory of MOD-making (Part A) are confronted with the MOD methods surveyed in Part B. Note that some of the desiderata developed in Part A are not represented in Table 10.3. These desiderata pertain to the activities in decision processes which
precede the performance of MOD methods. They are necessary to
ensure that the data which form the starting-point of MOD methods are reliable and useful. Obviously these desiderata are
important for an effective use of MOD methods, but they do not
play a role in the evaluation of the internal structure of
these methods.

The criteria of Table 10.3 will be applied to a representative series of methods, discussed in Chapters 6-9. The pertaining methods are enumerated in Table 10.4. It is important
to note that the evaluation of the methods has largely an ex
ante character. There have been too few applications of most
MOD methods to allow us to make an ex post evaluation. Consequently, the outcomes of the evaluation are not so much based
on experiences and tests, but they reflect tentative results
based on intuition and insight. There are two additional reasons why one should be careful in the interpretation of the
evaluation. First, the MOD methods should not always be seen
as competitive. They can also be used in combination with each
other, as is the case with methods 2 and 11. Different methods
can be employed in different phases of a decision process. The
second reason concerns the dynamic character of MOD methods.
Methods are seldom developed for once and for all; they may go
through several stages of development so as to meet a larger
number of requirements. Thus it may happen that a method at a
given moment does not satisfy some criteria in a strict sense,
while it can yet be adapted in principle to yield a favourable
outcome.

The results of the evaluation can be found in Table 10.5.
The outcome of the valuation according to each criterion has
been performed on an ordinal scale. The possible outcomes are:
-, -0, 0, 0+, +, where "-" indicates an unfavourable outcome
and "+" a favourable one. The other symbols indicate intermediate positions. The valuations of the methods can be derived
more or less directly from the discussions in the finding
places mentioned in Table 10.4 (3). Table 10.5 shows that, according to the majority of the criteria of the first two
classes, there is a considerable variety among the MOD methods.
According to the criteria of the third class - the consistency

CRITERIA	FINDING PLACE section: S desideratum: D
CONCERNING THE DM	
1. The method includes search and learning elements.	S. 3.6, D. 4,5,6 S. 4.9, D. 5
2. It produces adequate (digestible, clarifying) information for a deliberate choice.	S. 2.7, D. 7
3. It recognizes uncertainties in the importance of objectives.	S. 4.9, D. 2, 3
4. It allows a straightforward instruction concerning the interpretation of questions and results.	S. 2.7, D. 8
5. It does not give rise to many activities of the DM.	S. 2.7, D. 9
6. The type of priority information to be presented by the DM is not difficult to provide.	S. 3.6, D. 3
CONCERNING THE ANALYST	
7. The method requires few activities for the analyst.	S. 2.7, D. 9
8. It does not require special formal knowledge.	S. 2.7, D. 9
9. It recognizes uncertainties in impacts and restrictions.	S. 2.7, D. 3, 4
It is flexible as it is applicable to:	
10. all convex forms of problems and not only to linear ones;	S. 6.7
11. arbitrary numbers of DMs and not only individual ones;	S. 2.7, D. 8
12. problems with ordinal or mixed data and not only with cardinal data;	S. 2.7, D. 4
13. problems which require the choice of a range of alternatives, not only a unique alternative;	S. 9.8
14. problems with little alternatives as well as with many alternatives;	S. 8.2
15. continuous problems as well as discrete problems.	S. 8.1
CONCERNING THE INTERNAL CONSISTENCY	
16. The method produces efficient solutions.	S. 4.9, D. 4
17. It produces a non-empty set of solutions.	S. 2.7, D. 7
18. The procedures of which the method consists are convergent.	S. 2.7, D. 8
19. It does not depend on an (arbitrary) normalization of objectives.	S. 7.4
20. It does not depend on a questionable interpretation of weights.	S. 7.4 S. 2.7, D. 6
21. An appropriate utility scale is employed.	S. 4.9, D. 1

Table 10.3.   Criteria for the evaluation of MOD methods

METHOD	FINDING PLACE
1. Generation of a large set of efficient alternatives by means of parametric programming.	Section 6.3
2. Computation of P, compromises, half-compromises and conflict measures.	Section 6.2, 6.4 - 6.6
3. Computation of vertices and corresponding probabilities and of facets and corresponding sets of minimum standards.	Section 6.7, 8.3
4. Estimation of utility function by means of information about former choices, followed by computation of the optimum.	Section 7.3
5. Estimation of utility function by means of interview questions, followed by computation of the optimum.	Section 7.4
6. Interactive determination of utility function, followed by computation of the optimum (Frisch).	Section 7.4
7. Concordance analysis without priority information.	Section 8.3, 8.7
8. Concordance analysis with priority information.	Section 8.5, 8.9
9. Permutation rank order correlation method (Paelinck).	Section 8.9
10. Interactive method by means of revision of minimum standards.	Section 9.3 - 9.9
11. The interactive method of Zionts and Wallenius for linear problems.	Section 9.2
12. The surrogate worth trade-off method of Haimes and Hall.	Section 6.3, 7.4
13. The interactive method of Geoffrion, Dyer and Feinberg.	Section 9.2

Table 10.4.   A list of MOD methods.

criteria (see Table 10.3)	MOD methods (see Table 10.4)												
	1	2	3	4	5	6	7	8	9	10	11	12	13
1	-	-	-	-	-	0+	-	-	-	+	+	+	+
2	-0	0	0	0	0+	0+	0	+	+	+	+	+	+
3	+	+	+	-0	-0	0+	+	0	0+	+	+	+	+
4	+	0+	-0	+	0+	0	0	0	0	0	0	0	0
5	+	+	+	+	-0	-0	+	0+	0+	0	-	-0	0
6	+	+	+	+	0	0	+	0	0	0	0	0	-0
7	-	0	-	-	-	-	+	+	0+	-0	-	-	-0
8	-	-	-	-	-	-	0+	0+	0+	-	-	-	-
9	-	-	-	-	-	-	0	0	0	-	-	-	-
10	+	+	-	+	+	+	+	+	+	+	-	+	+
11	+	+	+	-	-	-	+	-	-	0+	-0	0+	-0
12	+	+	-	-0	-0	-0	+	+	+	+	-	-	-
13	+	+	+	-	-	-	+	+	+	+	+	+	-0
14	-	0	+	+	+	+	-	-	-	-	-	-	-
15	+	+	0	+	+	+	-	-	-	+	+	-	-
16	+	+	+	+	+	+	+	+	+	+	+	+	0+
17	+	+	+	+	+	+	+	+	+	+	+	+	+
18	+	+	+	+	+	+	+	+	+	+	+	+	+
19	+	0+	0+	+	+	+	0	0	+	+	+	+	+
20	+	+	+	+	+	+	+	0	0	+	+	+	+
21	+	+	+	+	+	+	+	+	+	+	+	+	+

Table 10.5.   Evaluation of 13 MOD methods by means of 21 criteria

of methods - the methods are largely acceptable. Only in certain cases should some of these methods be queried. The table
also illustrates a basic feature of MOD methods: the value of
the information produced by a decision method (criterion 2) is
positively related to the precision and extent of the DM's priority information (cf. criteria 5 and 6). Thus we may conclude
that MOD methods only yield a valuable output when the quality
of the inputs (priority information) is in keeping with it.

   Four clusters of methods can be distinguished in the table.

a. For methods 1-3, derived from Chapter 6, the analyst needs
    little information from the DM; his computational activi-
    ties are extensive and the methods are rather flexible.

b. Methods 4-6, derived from Chapter 7, are in general rather
    demanding with regard to the DM as well as the analyst.
    The methods are less flexible.

c. Methods 7-9, found in Chapter 8, require relatively few ac-
    tivities from both DM and analyst.

d. The interactive methods are the only ones which really in-
    clude search and learning elements. As a consequence, the
    load of the activities of the DM and the analyst are con-
    siderable.

   The choice of a certain method depends on the importance attached to the evaluation criteria. This importance cannot be
indicated in general, but depends on the specific situation.
For example, the flexibility criteria (10-15) will be judged to
be more important when one foresees the application of the
method to several divergent types of problems than when a method has only to be applied to a special case. The requirements
on the DM (criteria 4-6) form another example. The importance
of these criteria depend on the DM's willingness and ability to
be engaged in the decision-making process.

   Obviously, it is less difficult to draw conclusions about
the relative attractivity of MOD methods when they are in the
same cluster than when they are in different clusters, since in
the former case they are more similar. We turn therefore to a
discussion of the attractivity of the methods per cluster.

   In cluster (a), method 2 has a performance which is equal to,
or better than, method 3 according to all criteria but one
(number 14). Consequently, we may conclude that when there are
many alternatives in a decision problem, method 2 is, in general, more appropriate than method 3. Of course, this does not
mean that method 3 cannot be employed meaningfully in combination with other methods.

   In cluster (b), the methods are equivalent according to the
criteria concerning the situation of the analyst and the internal consistency. Comparing methods 4 and 5, we find that when
a DM wants to take the possibly less precise outcomes of method
4 into the bargain, the former should be preferred to the latter. Methods 5 and 6 are similar in most respects. Method 6

includes a procedure for arriving at priority statements in an interactive way, which is not the case with method 5. Therefore, method 6 is more appropriate than method 5 when the DM is uncertain about the importance to be attached to the various objectives. The disadvantage of method 6 is that the instructions for the DM may be more difficult to understand.

In cluster (c), method 7 has a better performance than methods 8 and 9 according to several criteria (3, 5, 6, 11, 20). Yet it would be premature to conclude that method 7 should be preferred, since criterion 2 indicates that methods 8 and 9 yield an output which is considerably more valuable than method 7. Methods 8 and 9 are very similar. Method 9 has the advantage that it is more suitable for ordinal information about the importance of objectives (criterion 3) and that it does not entail more or less arbitrary choices concerning the way of normalization (criterion 19). When the number of alternatives is not too large so that the extent of the computations remains reasonable (criterion 7), we may conclude that method 9 seems slightly better than method 8.

For cluster (d) we find that the interactive method based on side-conditions (method 10) dominates the other interactive methods discussed here. The most important reasons are that it is relatively easy to operate for the DM as well as the analyst, and that it is flexible with regard to the number of DMs and the occurrence of ordinal or mixed data and discrete decision problems. For the other methods (11-13), no such clear dominance relationships exist.

We repeat that one should be cautious in considering these outcomes as definite. The evaluation performed in this section has an ex ante tentative and preliminary character and it is applied to methods which are still in the process of development. Ex post evaluations of the methods have been very rare so far, and therefore the conclusions are provisional. Ultimately "the proof of the pudding is in the eating". Therefore we will discuss some applications of the methods in the following chapters.

10.4   Conclusion

In this chapter we have carried out a classification of MOD methods. We traced five relatively independent dimensions according to which the methods display considerable variation:

- the number of feasible solutions of the decision problem;
- the scale of measurement of the data;
- the availability of information about priorities;
- the way in which preferences are modelled;
- the number of alternatives to be presented to the DM in the final selection.

There are also some dimensions according to which MOD methods are still relatively underdeveloped:

- the uncertainty about data;
- the number of DMs.

We have, in this chapter, also performed an evaluation of a
representative set of methods (13) according to 21 criteria developed in earlier chapters (see Tables 10.3 - 10.5). With
this evaluation we have reached answers to the two research
questions formulated in Chapter 1. The outcome of the evaluation - which has an ex ante character - is that there is a considerable variety of methods, and that for many types of decision problems well-developed MOD methods are available. In
Section 10.3 we also performed a comparative evaluation of the
methods. The outcomes are formulated at the end of that section. One of the conclusions is that the interactive method
based on side-conditions - which was the main subject of Chapter
9 - is a very attractive alternative in the set of interactive
methods.

Footnotes

1.   One might also infer from Table 10.2 that the set of meth-
      ods dealing with information about comparable choices in
      the past (characteristic 1e) is insufficiently developed.
      The contents of Section 7.3, however, show that this in-
      ference is incorrect.

2.   The condition of independence of irrelevant alternatives
      can be formalized in the following way. Let K_1 be a sub-
      set of the set of alternatives K. Let s(K) be the set of
      solutions selected by means of a certain method from the
      set of alternatives K. Then a method meets the above con-
      dition if s(K) $\cap$ K_1 is either empty or identical to s(K_1).

3.   The rather favourable outcome of the surrogate worth
      trade-off method (number 12) according to criterion 11
      (applicability for multiple DMs) deserves explanation.
      The reason is that Hall and Haimes [1976] show that this
      method can, in principle, also be employed in relation to
      multiple DMs.

PART C

APPLICATIONS OF MULTIPLE OBJECTIVE DECISION

METHODS IN REGIONAL PLANNING

The aim of Part C is to illustrate the importance of MOD methods for regional planning. Chapter 11 contains a treatment of a transportation model with several types of transportation costs for various kinds of modal split. The main emphasis is on illustrating the concepts and methods of Part B (see Table B.1 for the most important links between Parts B and C). Chapter 12 deals with the application of MOD methods in the preparation of policies aiming at a so-called selective industrial growth. This application has been carried out with real data and in co-operation with a person actually involved in decision-making. Chapter 13 illustrates the use of MOD methods to analyze conflicting objectives in a hierarchical decision framework in which a central policy unit co-ordinates the decisions of several regions. The applications show that regional planning is a very appropriate field for the use of MOD methods.

It is important to note that MOD methods are not only useful for planning purposes itself, but also for the development of a sound theory underlying regional planning. The multi-dimensionality paradigm appears, for example, very useful for (cf. Nijkamp [1979]):

- theories concerning modal choice in transportation;

- migration theories and theories on residential choice;

- the analysis of regional welfare inequalities;

- methods of regional demarcation.

Another interesting field in which MOD methods appear useful is formed by the statistical methods of testing and estimation (cf. Kockelhorn [1979] and Narula and Wellington [1979]). MOD methods enable researchers to select an estimation, taking into account several statistical criteria (such as the sum of the squared errors and the sum of the absolute errors).

This wide scope of MOD methods is an additional argument in favour of further developments and applications of this body of methods.

CHAPTER 11

A TRANSPORTATION PROBLEM

11.1   Introduction

This chapter will be devoted to the use of MOD methods for
transportation problems. Applications of MOD methods and related methodologies, such as Cost-Benefit Analysis, to the
evaluation of _investment_ projects in the transportation sector
are not rare: for example, Roy and Jacquet-Lagreze [1977] mention several detailed Cost-Benefit Analyses of airport locations. However, the number of studies which focus in an MOD
context on the _exploitation_ of transport networks (instead of
on the investment itself) is small.

Transportation models of the latter category have mainly
been applied to single-objective problems, such as the minimization of transport costs or the maximization of entropy (cf.
Nijkamp [1975]). In some cases, the conclusion was that such
an approach is not satisfactory, because in transportation
problems, multiple optimal solutions are likely to occur (cf.
Barr and Smillie [1972]). Consequently, one needs additional
criteria in order to discriminate between these solutions (cf.
Leinbach [1976]). This would actually lead to a decision by
means of a lexicographic ordering, as discussed in Chapter 7,
which is a very specific form of an MOD method. It is more in-
clusive, therefore, to formulate the transportation problem as
a general MOD problem, as will be done in the present chapter.

We shall first give a formal presentation of a transportation model dealing with home-to-work trips (Section 10.2).
Next, a number of concepts and methods from Chapter 6 will be
applied to the model (Section 10.3). In Section 10.4, we shall
give a numerical illustration of the interactive method, as
discussed in Chapter 9. The transportation model used in this
chapter is not based on a real decision problem. It is only
used to present instructive numerical examples of MOD methods.

11.2   Formulation of the Problem

The decision problem to be dealt with concerns the determination of the optimal pattern of home-to-work trips in a certain region. In the region, several locations can be distinguished with unbalanced local labour markets. With respect to
the resulting commuting pattern, the following questions must
be answered:

- In which location(s) will the labour force working in a certain location find employment?

- By means of which mode(s) of transport will commuting take
  place?

- Along which routes will commuting take place?

The alternative commuting patterns will be evaluated according to three criteria (J = 3):

(1) total private transport cost (measured in units of money);

(2) total damage to the urban environment (measured in appro-
    priate units of urban environmental quality);

(3) total damage to the natural environment (measured in appro-
    priate units of natural environmental quality).

Obviously, these objectives, which must be minimized, are of a
composite nature. The first objective, for example, reflects
several aspects of trips, such as costs, duration and comfort.
We shall assume here that one of the methods to reduce the number of objectives discussed in Section 8.10 may have been used
to achieve this concise formulation with only three objectives.

The structure of the transportation model used in this chapter is as follows. We assume a closed region with K different
locations (k=1,...,K) and M modes of transport (m=1,...,M).
Some locations show labour shortages; others show surpluses.
For the total region, the balance of labour indicates a certain
amount of unemployment. Some locations on the transportation
network are directly connected. The set S^m with elements (k,l)
indicates the pairs of locations between which a direct connection exists with respect to transport mode m. The costs (category j) of transport by means of mode m between the directly
connected locations k and l for one person will be denoted by
$c_{k,l}^{m,j}$. Let $x_{k,l}^m$ denote the number of persons travelling by mode
m from k to l (1).

The objectives of the programming problem can be formulated
as:

$$
\left\{
\begin{array}{l}
\min! \; \omega_1 = \sum\limits_m \sum\limits_{k,l \in S^m} c_{k,l}^{m,1} \, x_{k,l}^m \\
\qquad\qquad \vdots \\
\min! \; \omega_J \quad \sum\limits_m \sum\limits_{k,l \in S^m} c_{k,l}^{m,J} \, x_{k,l}^m
\end{array}
\right.
\tag{11.1}
$$

The constraints of the problem are of various kinds:

(a) capacity constraints:

$$
x_{k,l}^m \leq \bar{x}_{k,l}^m \qquad \forall m, \; \forall (k,l) \in S^m
\tag{11.2}
$$

(b) constraints related to the situation on the labour market
    in each location:

$$\sum_m \sum_{k,n \in S^m} x^m_{k,n} - \sum_m \sum_{n,k \in S^m} x^m_{n,k} - u_n + v_n = s_n \quad \forall n, \tag{11.3}$$

where u_n, v_n and s_n represent unemployment, vacancies and net local labour demand on location n, respectively.

(c) a constraint indicating the number of vacancies allowed in the whole region:

$$\sum_n v_n \leq V \tag{11.4}$$

(d) non negativity constraints:

$$\begin{cases} x^m_{k,1} \geq 0 & \forall m, \quad (k,1) \in S^m \\ \\ u_n, v_n \geq 0 & \forall n \end{cases} \tag{11.5}$$

We now turn to the description of the data of the transportation network. The network has been visualized in Figure 11.1.

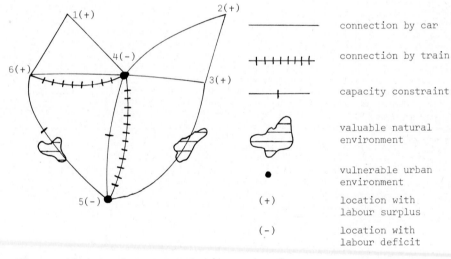

Figure 11.1.   A transportation network

The network consists of six nodes (K = 6), while two modes of transport have been distinguished (M = 2), namely car and train. There are nine connections by car and two by train. For two connections, capacity constraints have been specified. The situation on the labour market has been described in Table 11.1.

The total region shows a certain excess labour supply. One of the interesting characteristics of a multiple objective transportation model is that the localization of the unemployment in one of the excess-supply nodes (1,2,3,6) depends on

location	1	2	3	4	5	6	Σ
employment 1)	1,500	2,500	5,000	20,000	65,000	5,000	99,000
labour supply 1)	5,000	3,000	10,000	15,000	50,000	17,000	100,000
net labour demand 1)	-3,500	-500	-5,000	5,000	15,000	-12,000	-1,000

1) All figures indicate numbers of persons.

Table 11.1.   Labour demand and supply

the weights attached to the various transportation cost categories.   These costs per person can be found in Table 11.2 for
both modes of transport.   In addition, Table 11.2 presents the
capacity constraints $\bar{x}^m_{k,1}$ mentioned previously.

mode (m)	1									2	
traject (k,1)	(1,4)	(1,6)	(2,3)	(2,4)	(3,4)	(3,5)	(4,5)	(4,6)	(5,6)	(4,5)	(4,6)
$c^{m,1}_{k,1}$ 1)	23	14	16	30	18	34	25	21	30	27	24
$c^{m,2}_{k,1}$ 1)	10	9	5	9	11	14	18	14	16	7	6
$c^{m,3}_{k,1}$ 1)	20	15	10	13	12	35	8	9	40	3	3
$\bar{x}^m_{k,1}$ (number of persons)	-	-	-	-	-	-	7,000	-	10,000	14,000	

1) measured in the units mentioned above.

Table 11.2.   Transportation costs per person and capacity
                              constraints

    It has been assumed that the connections are symmetric, so
that:

$$\begin{cases} c^{m,j}_{k,1} = c^{m,j}_{1,k} \\ \\ \bar{x}^m_{k,1} = \bar{x}^m_{1,k} \end{cases} \quad m=(1,2) \quad \forall(k,1)\in S^m \quad j=(1,2,3) \qquad (11.6)$$

For only two connections by car, capacity constraints have been
included into the model.   The capacity constraint on transport
by train means that only 14,000 persons can travel by train from
a certain location to a subsequent one during their trip from
home to work.

    Finally, it has been assumed that no vacancies exist in the
region (V=0).

The programming problem (11.1)-(11.6) is a linear one.
This is to a certain extent unrealistic, because then it is
impossible to deal with a problem like congestion in a satisfactory way. Given the purpose of the model, however, - viz.
to illustrate the possibilities of a multiple objective transportation model - this approach may be satisfactory. In addition to its simplicity, it has the advantage that some of the
concepts in Section 6.7 can be applied.

11.3   Analysis of Conflicts and Compromises

In this section, we will present a number of numerical illustrations of the concepts (2) and methods of Chapter 6.

Our point of departure is the pay-off matrix P associated
with the above-mentioned model:

$$P' = \begin{pmatrix} 629.0 & 336.0 & 584.0 \\ 716.5 & 253.5 & 433.5 \\ 826.5 & 395.5 & 265.5 \end{pmatrix} \tag{11.7}$$

From this matrix we conclude that:

$$\begin{cases} \overset{*}{\underline{\omega}} = (629,0,\ 253.5,\ 265.5)' \\ \overline{\underline{\omega}} = (826.5,\ 395.5,\ 584.0)' \end{cases} \tag{11.8}$$

The least attractive value of ω_1 is obtained when ω_3 is minimized. The same holds true the other way round, which reflects
a mutual conflict between the first and third objective. This
intensity of conflict between ω_1 and ω_3 can also be shown by
means of the normalized pay-off matrix Q.

$$Q' = \begin{pmatrix} 1 & .419 & 0 \\ .557 & 1 & .472 \\ 0 & 0 & 1 \end{pmatrix} \tag{11.9}$$

The zero elements of Q indicate the most intense conflicts between pairs of objectives.

The aggregate conflict measure γ_1, which is based on this
matrix, is equal to .758 which is considerably high. It is
interesting to analyze further the nature of this conflict by
means of the measures γ_2-γ_5 for the various pairs of alternatives (cf. Section 6.5). Its results have been summarized in
Table 11.3.

When we compare the elements of Table 11.3 horizontally, the
conclusion may be drawn that the values of the five measures of
conflict are rather close to one another. They all show the
same picture of the intensity of conflict. This unanimity does
not necessarily arise for all types of decision problems, however. It can be imagined that for other decision problems, the
conflict measures are themselves conflicting (3).

measures of conflict	γ_2	$\gamma_3(p=1)$	$\gamma_3(p=2)$	$\gamma_3(p\to\infty)$	γ_5
ω_1 versus ω_2	.360	.355	.376	.415	.320
ω_1 versus ω_3	.931	.929	.931	.932	.909
ω_2 versus ω_3	.843	.842	.843	.843	.781

Table 11.3.   Measures of conflict for various pairs of
objectives (4)

Comparing the elements of Table 11.3 vertically, we notice
an intense conflict between the quality of natural environment
(ω_3) on the one hand, and the quality of urban environment (ω_2)
as well as the private transport costs (ω_1) on the other. The
conflict between private transportation costs (ω_1) and the urban environmental quality (ω_2), however, is far more moderate.
This can be made plausible by means of Figure 11.1, where we
find that the least cost connections between the largest labour demanding location (5) and the four locations with excess
supply of labour (1,2,3, and 6) all avoid the rather vulnerable
location 4. Owing to this, however, the routes (3,5) and (6,5)
will be used more intensively, giving rise to a considerable
damage to the natural environment.

When the decision has to be made by a group, rather than by
a single person, Table 11.3 may shed light on the formation of
coalitions. For example, suppose that the group consists of
three persons j, advocating respectively the minimization of
objective j (j = 1,2,3). Then, the table suggests that a coalition between the persons 1 and 2 is far more probable than
the other two possibilities.

There is still another way to study the probabilities of the
formation of coalitions. For that purpose we have to determine
the compromise alternative on which both parties in the coalition would agree. When both parties are equally powerful, this
compromise alternative will probably be near one of the compromise concepts defined in Chapter 6. The outcomes for the various compromise concepts can be found in Table 11.4.

Our conclusion is that per coalition the compromise concepts
lead to very similar outcomes. The table shows that both 1 and
2 reach the best results by a coalition with each other. Person 3 will prefer a coalition with 2 above that with 1. These
results are completely in accordance with the finding in Table
11.3, that the conflict between 1 and 3 is greater than that
between 2 and 3.

The conclusion may be drawn that when the decision procedure
is majority voting, an alternative near (650, 263, 539) will
probably be selected by the group.

Owing to the linear structure of the transportation model, we can illustrate a number of concepts mentioned in Section 6.7. It appears that the set of efficient solutions can be represented by means of 15 efficient corner solutions, which can be found in Table 11.5. For each corner solution we present:

- the values of the objectives;

- the intensity of the traffic on the various routes;

- the unemployment arising in the various locations;

- the probability that the pertaining solution is optimal.

coalition	compromise		
	ω_1	ω_2	ω_3
(1,2)	$\underline{\omega}^a$ 650.0	263.0	539.0
	$\underline{\omega}^{c1}$ 650.0	263.0	539.0
	$\underline{\omega}^{c2}$ 650.0	263.0	539.0
	$\underline{\omega}^{c4}$ 647.1	270.6	544.7
(1,3)	$\underline{\omega}^a$ 715.8	281.7	421.6
	$\underline{\omega}^{c1}$ 715.5	281.5	422.0
	$\underline{\omega}^{c2}$ 716.5	282.3	420.6
	$\underline{\omega}^{c4}$ 721.0	286.3	413.9
(2,3)	$\underline{\omega}^a$ 781.4	312.8	337.0
	$\underline{\omega}^{c1}$ 776.5	305.5	345.5
	$\underline{\omega}^{c2}$ 781.5	312.9	336.8
	$\underline{\omega}^{c4}$ 781.7	313.4	336.3

Table 11.4. Compromise solutions given various coalitions

The use of routes (1,6) and (2,3) for home-to-work trips appears to be inefficient. Therefore, these routes have been deleted from the table. It is interesting to consider the sets of weights $\Lambda(\underline{x}_1)$ corresponding to corner solution $\underline{x}_1^+$ (l=1,...,15). These sets have been depicted in Figure 11.2. From these sets, the probabilities have been computed that the pertaining solution is optimal. As the last column in Table 11.5 shows, these probabilities vary largely in magnitude. The three most probable corner solutions (1, 2, and 7) account for

number of corner	ω_1	ω_2	ω_3	$x^1_{1,4}$	$x^1_{2,4}$	$x^1_{3,4}$	$x^1_{3,5}$	$x^1_{4,5}$	$x^1_{6,4}$	$x^1_{6,5}$	$x^2_{4,5}$	$x^2_{6,4}$	u_1	u_2	probability of optimality
	measured in thousands of the appropriate units			measured in numbers of persons											
1	817.5	368.5	274.5	2500	500	5000	--	1000	12000	--	14000	--	1000	--	.169
2	716.5	253.5	433.5	2500	500	--	5000	--	--	4000	6000	8000	1000	--	.206
3	826.5	395.5	265.5	2500	500	5000	--	10000	3000	--	5000	9000	1000	--	.125
4	776.5	305.5	345.5	2500	500	--	5000	--	8000	--	10000	4000	1000	--	.038
5	808.5	353.5	289.5	2500	500	4000	1000	--	12000	--	14000	--	1000	--	.025
6	629.0	336.0	584.0	3000	500	--	5000	3000	5000	7000	--	--	500	500	.044
7	650.0	263.0	539.0	3000	--	--	5000	--	--	7000	3000	5000	500	500	.240
8	705.0	283.0	439.0	3000	--	5000	--	--	--	7000	8000	5000	500	500	.003
9	798.0	353.0	301.0	3000	--	5000	--	--	11000	1000	14000	--	500	500	.003
10	715.5	281.5	422.0	3000	--	5000	--	--	--	6500	8500	5500	500	500	.016
11	635.0	303.0	569.0	3000	--	--	5000	--	5000	7000	3000	--	500	500	.047
12	713.0	254.0	437.0	3000	--	5000	--	--	--	4000	6000	8000	500	500	.070
13	814.0	369.0	278.0	3000	--	5000	--	1000	12000	--	14000	--	500	500	.013
14	773.0	306.0	349.0	3000	--	5000	--	--	8000	--	10000	4000	500	500	.001
15	805.0	354.0	293.0	3000	1000	1000	--	--	12000	--	14000	--	500	500	.001

Table 11.5.   Efficient corner solutions

more than 60 percent of the size of the weights triangle.

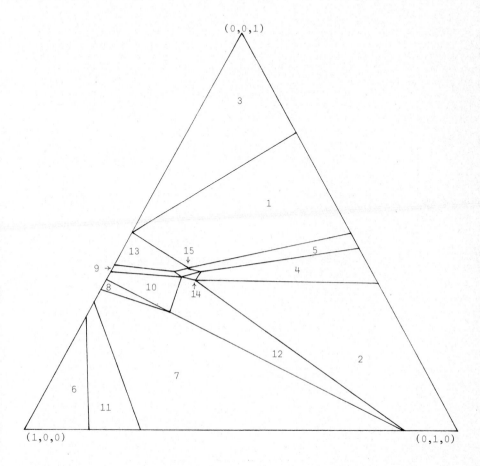

Fig. 11.2. Representation of the sets of weights $\Lambda(\overset{+}{\underline{x}}_l)$ with
elements $(\lambda_1, \lambda_2, \lambda_3)$ corresponding to the 15 cor-
ner solutions $(l=1,\ldots,15)$

Comparing Table 11.5 with Figure 11.2, we find that the corner solutions with the largest weight for the private transport
costs (ω_1) also appear to be the alternatives with the most restricted use of public transport $(x^2_{6,5} + x^2_{4,5})$. It also appears
that the distribution of the unemployment among the locations
depends upon the priorities attached to the various cost categories. For example, high priorities to avoid the environmental costs lead to a concentration of unemployment in location
2 (see corner solutions 1-5), whereas a priority to avoid pri-

vate transport costs results in a more equal unemployment distribution.

As discussed in Chapter 6, the set of efficient solutions in
MOLP problems can be generated by means of the efficient vertices. In our case the efficient vertices appear to generate
14 facets, which have been depicted in Table 11.6. Most of the
facets consist of three corner points. It is a striking characteristic of this decision problem that the facets 1, 2, 4, 5,
6 and 7 correspond to a vector of weights with a negative element. It has been proved in Chapter 6 that the interior points
of these facets are not efficient.

facet	constituent corners	corresponding weights		
		λ_1	λ_2	λ_3
1	8,9,10	.653	-.062	.409
2	8,9,13	.667	-.077	.410
3	2,7,12	.125	.875	0
4	7,8,11	.662	-.022	.360
5	6,8,11	.675	-.046	.371
6	6,8,13	.706	-.120	.414
7	3,6,13	.721	-.142	.421
8	1,3,13	.500	0	.500
9	1,5,13,15	.435	.152	.413
10	4,5,14,15	.422	.181	.397
11	2,4,12,14	.422	.183	.396
12	9,10,12,14,15	.427	.177	.396
13	7,8,10,12	.546	.128	.326
14	9,13,15	.449	.141	.410

Table 11.6. Facets of the decision problem and corresponding
weights

There is still another conclusion which can be drawn from
Chapter 6. In Theorem 7, it has been proved that the set of
minimum standards $\Omega(F_m)$ corresponding to the face F_m is empty
when any element of the pertaining vector of weights $\underline{\lambda}_m$ is non-
positive. Consequently, in this case, these sets are empty for
the majority of faces (m=1,...,8). Only the facets 9-14 give
rise to non-empty sets $\Omega(F_m)$. In Theorem 6, it has been
proved that these sets are convex polyhedra. As an example, we
present $\Omega(F_{14})$ in Table 11.7, which is a tetrahedral set. Any
side-condition which is an element of this tetrahedron and

which is imposed on the set of efficient solutions yields such
a reduction of this set that only elements of F_{14} remain efficient.

corner	value of objectives		
	ω_1	ω_2	ω_3
1	798.0	353.0	301.0
2	814.0	369.0	278.0
3	805.0	354.0	293.0
4	805.0	358.6	293.0

Table 11.7.   Corner points of the polyhedron $\Omega(F_{14})$

We shall complete the present section with a presentation of
some half-compromise solutions. These solutions, together with
the J extreme solutions and a compromise solution, are useful
in giving a concise image of the feasible alternatives. The
results can be found in Table 11.8. Notice the identity of
$\overset{*}{\underline{\omega}}_2$ and $\underline{\omega}(\underline{y}_2^{c1})$. In linear problems of moderate size, the occur-
ence of such identities is probable.

type of solution	defined in equation	ω_1	ω_2	ω_3
$\overset{*}{\underline{\omega}}_1$	(6.1)	629.0	336.0	584.0
$\overset{*}{\underline{\omega}}_2$	(6.1)	716.5	253.5	433.5
$\overset{*}{\underline{\omega}}_3$	(6.1)	826.5	395.5	265.5
$\overset{*}{\underline{\omega}}(\underline{x}^{c1})$	(6.14)	713.0	254.0	437.0
$\overset{*}{\underline{\omega}}(\underline{y}_1^{c1})$	(6.40)	650.0	263.0	539.0
$\overset{*}{\underline{\omega}}(\underline{y}_2^{c1})$	(6.40)	716.5	253.5	433.5
$\overset{*}{\underline{\omega}}(\underline{y}_3^{c1})$	(6.40)	776.5	305.5	345.5

Table 11.8.   A number of representative solutions of the
                transportation problem

11.4   Application of the Interactive Method

In this section we will present the results of a simulated
application of the interactive decision procedure to the trans-

portation model, as described in Section 9.3. The information
is contained in Table 11.9. It shows for each step the pay-off
matrix P and the provisional compromise solution $\underline{\omega}^{e1}$. In each
step, the DM indicates which element of the provisional solu-
tion must be improved. These values have been encircled. They
function as side-conditions for the calculations in the following steps. Comparing the pay-off matrices in step 1 and 4, we
notice that the convergence towards a unique preferred solution
is considerable. The convergence also appears in the last column of Table 11.8, where the weights corresponding to the generated alternatives have been presented (cf. Section 9.6).

step	procedure	outcomes of objectives ω_1	ω_2	ω_3	weights attached to ω_1	ω_2	ω_3
1	min! ω_1	629.0	336.0	584.0	1	0	0
	min! ω_2	716.5	253.5	433.5	0	1	0
	min! ω_3	826.5	395.5	265.5	0	0	1
	compromise	705.0	283.0	(439.0)	.642	-.034	.392
2	min! ω_1	705.0	283.0	439.0	.645	0	.355
	min! ω_2	716.5	253.5	433.5	0	1	0
	min! ω_3	826.5	395.5	265.5	0	0	1
	compromise	(798.0)	353.0	301.0	.480	.111	.409
3	min! ω_1	705.0	283.0	439.0	.645	0	.355
	min! ω_2	716.5	253.5	433.5	0	1	0
	min! ω_3	798.0	353.0	310.0	.590	0	.410
	compromise	715.5	(281.5)	422.0	.491	.118	.391
4	min! ω_1	705.3	281.5	439.0	.546	.128	.326
	min! ω_2	716.5	253.5	433.5	0	1	0
	min! ω_3	748.8	281.5	386.1	0	.629	.371

Table 11.9.   Outcomes of the interactive procedure

The table also illustrates the potential difficulties of the use of compromise concept $\underline{\omega}^{el}$. As has been shown in Section 6.4, some of the compromise weights corresponding to this concept may be negative, so that there is no guarantee that $\underline{\omega}^{el}$ is efficient. In the first step of the present case, one of the weights is indeed negative, but it appears that the corresponding compromise is efficient. Consequently, the compromise $\underline{\omega}^{el}$ can be used without difficulties in our case.

11.5   Conclusion

In the present chapter, many methods discussed in Chapters 6 and 9 have been illustrated. It appears that for transportation problems, the methods form a flexible set of tools to analyze the structure of the conflicts involved in it as well as to generate attractive alternatives.

The methods also appear appropriate to deal with decisions in which several persons or groups are involved with different interests. For example, it is possible to analyze the probability of the formation of coalitions between groups by means of the MOD methods.

The transportation model served as a numerical illustration. Consequently, there has not been a real DM to participate in the interactive MOD method. Since the active participation of DMs is an essential characteristic of many MOD methods, this chapter does not give an illustration of all aspects of MOD methods. Therefore, in the next chapter we shall present an application of MOD methods to a more real decision problem.

Footnotes

1.   It has not been assumed that k and l are the starting and end points, respectively, of the trips. (k,l) may only be part of the route followed by the commuters.

2.   Notice that in Chapter 6 all objectives must be maximized, whereas in the present chapter they must be minimized. In some cases this gives rise to a straightforward adaptation of the concepts used in Chapter 6.

3.   The conflict measures can be compared with the many measures to describe the inequality of a certain variable in a population. The various measures focus on different aspects of inequality and may, to a certain extent, lead to different pictures of the same phenomenon.

4.   The measure γ_4 has been omitted, due to its being completely identical to $\gamma_3(p=1)$ when only two objectives are considered.

5.   Notice that the outcomes of Table 11.4 have already been implicitly used in Table 11.3.

CHAPTER 12

SELECTIVE GROWTH AND THE COMPOSITION OF AN INDUSTRIAL SITE

12.1   Introduction

   The first decades after the Second World War showed a rapid
industrial expansion in the western countries. Industry dis-
appeared increasingly from the central cities and became concentrated in industrial sites, at the periphery of or outside
the cities. In the governmental policy guiding this industrialization, the central goal was the creation of sufficient employment. Eventually this policy resulted in a situation characterized by a considerable degree of congestion and pollution.
Hence, after the sixties, industrialization policy no longer
aimed at achieving growth (of employment) per se, but at selective growth. Selective growth involves industrialization policies taking into account several aspects such as: environmental
quality, the scarcity of natural resources, and the spatial
pattern of existing activities. Consequently, regional and
sector planning play an important role in selective growth policies.

   In this chapter a case study will be presented of how such a
selective growth policy can be accomplished at the level of the
industrial site. The case under study is an industrial site of
considerable size in the western part of the Netherlands (the
Maasvlakte). We will first discuss the decision problem in
more detail (Section 12.2). Next, a detailed analysis of the
conflicts in the policy objectives will be given, followed by
the presentation of compromise and half-compromise solutions
(Sections 12.3 and 12.4). Finally, in Section 12.5 we will present the results of an interactive decision procedure carried
out with one of the governmental officials involved in the decision.

12.2   Formulation of the Decision Problem

   The problem to be dealt with in this chapter is the determination of the optimal composition of the industrial area the
Maasvlakte. As Figure 12.1 shows, the Maasvlakte is situated
at the southern entrance to the New Waterway (the canal connec-
ting Rotterdam with the North Sea). It was created at the beginning of the seventies and is of considerable size (2460 ha.,
of which approximately 1250 ha. can be used for industrial activities). Part of the area has already been occupied by certain industries, but for the larger part it is still empty. At

the time of the analysis (1976-1977) 900 ha. were still available for new industrial activities (1). Because of its location, the Maasvlakte is especially attractive for industries
requiring accessibility for deep-draught sea vessels.

   The decision to create the Maasvlakte was taken in 1965,
when the main emphasis of economic policy in the Rhine-delta
region was still on rapid industrialization. This situation
changed at the beginning of the seventies.

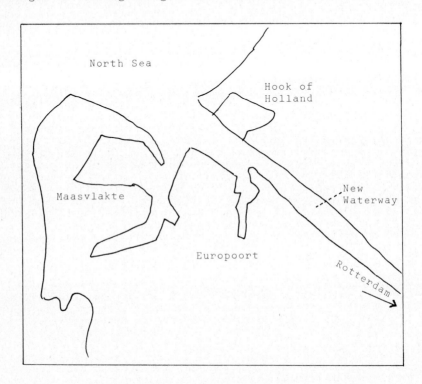

Fig. 12.1.   Situation of the Maasvlakte area

Several pressure groups and authorities concerned with the decision with respect to the Maasvlakte stressed that one has to
take into account that the western part of the Netherlands was
already congested and that the air pollution could not be allowed to increase much further. Consequently, several studies
have been undertaken on the alternative ways in which the area
can be used (see Van Delft and Nijkamp [1977] for a description of these studies). These studies focused on only a small
number of alternatives. The present analysis can be conceived
of as a generalization of these studies, since a much larger
set of alternatives has been envisaged.

Below, we will present a more precise statement of the decision problem. We will consider successively:

- the objectives and the way in which they are measured;
- the candidate activities and their impacts on the objectives;
- the full set of alternative combinations of activities.

The objectives formulated for the use of the area can be divided into the following classes:

- economic objectives;
- labour market objectives;
- spatial-physical objectives;
- environmental objectives.

Three economic variables have been formulated:

ω_1 : value added produced on the industrial site, measured in millions of Dfl.

ω_2 : the differentiation in the regional economic structure which can be attained by the new site, compared with the existing industrial complex in the Rhine-delta region. The oil refineries and petro-chemical industries play a dominant role in the existing industries. Diversification may help to make the region less vulnerable to economic fluctuations.

The diversification can be measured as follows (cf. Czamanski [1972]): Assume that there are I candidate activities. Let e_i^R denote the present employment in sector i (i=1,...I) in the Rhine-delta and let e_i^M denote the employment created in sector i (i=1,...I) on the Maasvlakte. Then ω_2 can be measured as:

$$\omega_2 = \frac{1}{2} \sum_{i=1}^{I} \left| \frac{e_i^M}{\sum_i e_i^M} - \frac{e_i^R}{\sum_i e_i^R} \right| \cdot 100 \qquad (12.1)$$

which means that ω_2 is measured as the sum total of the absolute differences between the employment shares of the combined activities in the Maasvlakte and the employment shares of the same activities in the whole Rhine-delta region. The objective ω_2 has been standardized such that $0 \leq \omega_2 \leq 100$.

ω_3 : amount of port revenues (port charges), measured in millions of Dfl.

The labour market variables are:

ω_4 : total demand for labour created by the industrial activities on the Maasvlakte (measured in man-years).

ω_5 : the discrepancy between the demand for labour of various categories created on the Maasvlakte and the supply of labour in the Rhine-delta region. This variable can be measured in a way which is analogous to ω_2. Assume that three labour categories m have been distinguished; (low-, medium-, and high-skilled; m=1, 2, 3). Let 1_m^R and 1_m^M denote the share of labour supply in category m in the Rhine-delta region and the share of labour demand in category m on the Maasvlakte, respectively. Then ω_5 can be measured as:

$$\omega_5 = \tfrac{1}{2} \sum_m \left| 1_m^R - 1_m^M \right| . 100 \qquad\qquad (12.2)$$

which implies that $0 \leq \omega_5 \leq 100$.

ω_6 : the demand for foreign labour on the Maasvlakte (measured as a percentage of total labour demand on the Maasvlakte). The number of foreign labourers has grown rapidly during the last decade, producing residential problems. In certain quarters of Rotterdam open conflicts arose between the local population and the migrants. Hence, governmental policy aims at reducing the inflow of foreigners.

The spatial-physical variable is:

ω_7 : the occupation rate of the total available area.

The environmental objective is:

ω_8 : total quantity of pollution, measured as the number of tons of particulates and SO_2 per year.

In the analysis, ω_1, ω_2, ω_3, ω_4 and ω_7 have been considered as benefit criteria, whereas the remaining variables are cost criteria (2). In order to simplify the further presentation, the latter variables have been multiplied by -1 so that all variables can be conceived of as benefit criteria.

We turn next to the candidate activities envisaged for the Maasvlakte area. In the studies eight relevant candidate activities have been distinguished:

1. Integrated blast furnaces and steelworks;

2. Medium-sized steelworks;

3. Tank storage plant;

4. Ores and coal trans-shipment and integrated processing plants;

5. Container terminal;

6. Oil refinery;

variable \ activity	1	2	3	4	5	6	7	8
1. Value added per ha. per year (in mln. Dfl.).	1.838	1.838	.480	.450	.163	.957	2.315	.510
2. Percentage share of employment in the main parts of the Rhine Delta region.	8.64	8.64	.36	4.32	.0	26.69	36.89	12.94
3. Port charges per year (in mln. Dfl.).	15.0	7.5	5.0	30.0	15.0	20.0	15.0	5.0
4. Demand for labour (per ha.).	24.0	24.0	1.0	2.0	.48	6.0	20.0	8.0
5. Share of labour demand (3) low-skilled	.40	.40	.00	.49	.15	.48	.48	.50
medium-skilled	.48	.48	.93	.42	.62	.47	.47	.37
high-skilled	.12	.12	.07	.09	.23	.05	.05	.13
6. Percentage foreign workers.	10.0	10.0	1.1	1.1	1.1	4.0	2.8	2.8
7. Land use (in hectares).	500	200	100	200	250	200	100	40
8. Pollution emission (tons per ha. per year).	82.6	124.0	.0	72.4	.0	510.1	42.9	.0

Table 12.1.   Data of individual candidate activities (in prices of 1973)

7. Petro-chemical industry;

8. Ship repair yard and tanker cleaning plant.

The data contained in Table 12.1 may be helpful in clari-
fying the character of these activities. We find that activities 1, 2 and 7 imply a relatively large value added and demand
for labour, in contrast to activities 3 and 5. Activities 6
and 7 are already strongly represented in the region. The oil
refineries (activity 6) create much pollution, as opposed to the
clean activities 3, 5 and 8. Activity 1 (integrated steelworks)
needs the largest amount of space. It also needs the most foreign labour.

We turn now to the third item: the generation of the full
set of alternative combinations of candidate activities. Every
alternative bundle of activities can be written as a vector
$\underline{x}' = (x_1, \ldots x_8)$ with $x_i = 0$ or 1 for $i=1,\ldots 8$. Activity i is
present in the bundle when $x_i = 1$, otherwise it is absent. In
principle, the total number of alternative bundles equals
$2^8 = 256$. There are two types of restrictions on the x_i, however. Firstly, certain types of activities may be incompatible.
This is the case with the first and second activities which are
so similar that it is not sensible to combine them in one bundle. Hence $x_1 \cdot x_2 = 0$. The other constraint concerns the limited amount of available land. Let a_i denote the number of
hectares necessary for activity i. Then the total demand for
land is equal to $\sum_i a_i x_i$, which should not exceed the available
900 ha.

Formulated as a vector maximum problem (cf. Section 6.2),
the occupation problem is to find the vector $(x_1, \ldots x_8)$, which
is the solution of:

$$
\begin{cases}
\text{max!} & \omega_1, \ldots, \omega_8 \\
\text{s.t.} & \omega_j = \omega_j(x_1, \ldots, x_8) \qquad j = 1, \ldots, 8 \\
\sum_i a_i x_i \leqslant 900 \\
x_i = 0 \text{ or } 1 \qquad\qquad i = 1, \ldots, 8 \\
x_1 \cdot x_2 = 0
\end{cases}
\qquad (12.3)
$$

where the $\omega_j(x_1, \ldots x_8)$ are the objectives as defined earlier in
this section. After the imposition of the side-conditions, 151
of the 256 alternatives still remain feasible. These alternatives are presented in Table 12.2. This impact table serves as
a point of departure for the application of several MOD methods,
as discussed in the next sections.

composition of indus-trial site 12 34 5678	values of decision criteria							
	economic objectives			labour market objectives			spatial physical/objective	envi-ronmental objective
	ω_1	ω_2	ω_3	ω_4	ω_5	ω_6	ω_7	ω_8
1 1011 1111	0.0	0.0	0.0	0.0	-91.0	0.0	0.0	0.0
2 0000 0001	20.4	87.1	5.0	320.0	-24.0	-2.8	4.4	0.0
3 0000 0010	231.5	63.1	15.0	2000.0	-18.0	-2.8	11.1	-4.3
4 0000 0011	251.9	50.2	20.0	2320.0	-16.3	-2.8	15.6	-4.3
5 0000 0100	191.4	73.3	20.0	1200.0	-18.0	-4.0	22.2	-102.0
6 0000 0101	211.8	60.4	25.0	1520.0	-18.4	-3.8	26.7	-102.0
7 0000 0110	422.9	36.4	35.0	3200.0	-18.0	-3.3	33.3	-106.3
8 0000 0111	443.3	27.3	40.0	3520.0	-18.2	-3.2	37.8	-106.3
9 0000 1000	40.8	100.0	15.0	120.0	-15.0	-1.1	27.8	0.0
10 0000 1001	61.2	87.1	20.0	440.0	-17.2	-2.3	32.2	0.0
11 0000 1010	272.3	63.1	30.0	2120.0	-16.1	-2.7	36.9	-4.3
12 0000 1011	292.7	50.2	35.0	2440.0	-16.6	-2.7	43.3	-4.3
13 0000 1100	232.2	73.3	35.0	1320.0	-15.0	-3.7	50.0	-102.0
14 0000 1101	252.6	60.4	40.0	1640.0	-16.0	-3.6	54.4	-102.0
15 0000 1110	463.7	36.4	50.0	3320.0	-16.8	-3.2	61.1	-106.3
16 0000 1111	484.1	27.6	55.0	3640.0	-17.1	-3.1	65.6	-106.3
17 0001 0000	90.0	95.7	30.0	400.0	-19.0	-1.1	22.2	-14.5
18 0001 0001	110.4	92.7	35.0	720.0	-21.2	-1.9	26.7	-14.5
19 0001 0010	321.5	58.8	45.0	2400.0	-18.2	-2.5	33.3	-18.8
20 0001 0011	341.9	47.0	50.0	2720.0	-18.4	-2.6	37.8	-18.8
21 0001 0100	281.4	69.0	50.0	1600.0	-18.3	-3.3	44.4	-116.5
22 0001 0101	301.8	56.1	55.0	1920.0	-18.5	-3.2	48.9	-116.5
23 0001 0110	512.9	32.1	65.0	3600.0	-18.1	-3.0	55.6	-120.8
24 0001 0111	533.3	23.9	70.0	3920.0	-18.3	-3.0	60.0	-120.8
25 0001 1000	130.8	95.7	45.0	520.0	-14.4	-1.1	50.0	-14.5
26 0001 1001	151.2	82.7	50.0	840.0	-18.1	-1.8	54.4	-14.5
27 0001 1010	362.3	58.8	60.0	2520.0	-16.6	-2.5	61.1	-18.8
28 0001 1011	382.7	47.5	65.0	2840.0	-17.0	-2.5	65.6	-18.8
29 0001 1100	322.7	69.0	65.0	1720.0	-15.9	-3.1	72.2	-116.5
30 0001 1101	342.6	56.1	70.0	2040.0	-16.6	-3.0	76.7	-116.5
31 0001 1110	553.7	32.1	80.0	3720.0	-17.0	-3.0	83.3	-120.8
32 0001 1111	574.1	24.2	85.0	4040.0	-17.3	-2.9	87.8	-120.8
33 0010 0000	48.0	99.6	5.0	100.0	-32.0	-1.1	11.1	0.0
34 0010 0001	68.4	86.7	10.0	420.0	-10.7	-2.4	15.6	0.0
35 0010 0010	279.5	62.8	20.0	2100.0	-15.7	-2.7	22.2	-4.3
36 0010 0011	299.4	49.8	25.0	2420.0	-16.3	-2.7	26.7	-4.3
37 0010 0100	239.4	73.0	25.0	1300.0	-14.3	-3.8	33.3	-102.0
38 0010 0101	259.8	60.3	30.0	1620.0	-15.4	-3.6	37.8	-102.0
39 0010 0110	470.9	36.1	40.0	3300.0	-16.6	-3.2	44.4	-106.3
40 0010 0111	491.3	27.2	45.0	3620.0	-16.9	-3.2	48.9	-106.3

Table 12.2.   Project effect matrix of the Maasvlakte problem

composition of industrial site 1234 5678	economic objectives			labour market objectives			spatial/ physical objective	environmental objective
	ω_1	ω_2	ω_3	ω_4	ω_5	ω_6	ω_7	ω_8
41 0010 1000	88.8	99.5	20.0	220.0	-21.8	-1.1	38.9	0.0
42 0010 1001	109.2	86.7	25.0	540.0	-8.1	-2.1	43.3	0.0
43 0010 1010	320.3	62.8	35.0	2220.0	-14.1	-2.6	50.0	-4.3
44 0010 1011	340.7	50.2	40.0	2540.0	-14.8	-2.7	54.4	-4.3
45 0010 1100	280.2	73.0	40.0	1420.0	-11.8	-3.6	61.1	-102.0
46 0010 1101	300.6	60.0	45.0	1740.0	-13.3	-3.4	65.6	-102.0
47 0010 1110	511.7	36.1	55.0	3420.0	-15.4	-3.1	72.2	-106.3
48 0010 1111	532.1	27.5	60.0	3740.0	-15.8	-3.1	76.7	-106.3
49 0011 0000	138.0	95.3	35.0	500.0	-9.2	-1.1	33.3	-14.5
50 0011 0001	158.4	82.4	40.0	820.0	-14.7	-1.8	37.8	-14.5
51 0011 0010	369.5	58.4	50.0	2500.0	-16.2	-2.5	44.4	-18.8
52 0011 0011	389.9	47.1	55.0	2820.0	-16.7	-2.5	48.9	-18.8
53 0011 0100	329.4	68.6	55.0	1700.0	-15.4	-3.2	55.6	-116.5
54 0011 0101	349.8	55.7	60.0	2020.0	-16.1	-3.1	60.0	-116.5
55 0011 0110	560.9	31.7	70.0	3700.0	-16.8	-3.0	66.7	-120.8
56 0011 0111	581.3	23.8	75.0	4020.0	-17.1	-3.0	71.1	-120.8
57 0011 1000	178.8	95.3	50.0	620.0	-6.9	-1.1	61.1	-14.5
58 0011 1001	199.2	82.4	55.0	940.0	-12.7	-1.7	65.6	-14.5
59 0011 1010	410.3	58.4	65.0	2620.0	-14.8	-2.4	72.2	-18.8
60 0011 1011	430.7	47.6	70.0	2940.0	-15.4	-2.4	76.7	-18.8
61 0011 1100	370.2	68.6	70.0	1820.0	-13.4	-3.0	83.3	-116.5
62 0011 1101	390.6	55.7	75.0	2140.0	-14.4	-3.0	87.8	-116.5
63 0011 1110	601.7	31.7	85.0	3820.0	-15.8	-2.9	94.4	-120.8
64 0011 1111	622.1	24.0	90.0	4140.0	-16.1	-2.9	98.9	-120.8
65 0100 0000	367.6	91.4	7.5	4800.0	-13.0	-10.0	22.2	-24.8
66 0100 0001	388.0	85.1	12.5	5120.0	-13.7	-9.6	26.7	-24.8
67 0100 0010	599.1	62.0	22.5	6800.0	-13.3	-7.9	33.3	-29.1
68 0100 0011	619.5	58.8	27.5	7120.0	-13.8	-7.7	37.8	-29.1
69 0100 0100	559.0	71.4	27.5	6000.0	-13.2	-8.8	44.4	-126.8
70 0100 0101	579.4	67.3	32.5	6320.0	-13.8	-8.5	48.9	-126.8
71 0100 0110	790.5	51.4	42.5	8000.0	-13.4	-7.3	55.6	-131.1
72 0100 0111	810.9	49.1	47.5	8320.0	-13.4	-7.1	60.0	-131.1
73 0100 1000	408.4	91.4	22.5	4920.0	-12.7	-9.8	50.0	-24.8
74 0100 1001	428.8	85.3	27.5	5240.0	-13.4	-9.4	54.4	-24.8
75 0100 1010	639.9	62.5	37.5	6920.0	-13.1	-7.8	61.1	-29.1
76 0100 1011	660.3	59.3	42.5	7240.0	-13.5	-7.6	65.6	-29.1
77 0100 1100	599.8	71.8	42.5	6120.0	-12.9	-8.7	72.2	-126.8
78 0100 1101	620.2	67.8	47.5	6440.0	-13.5	-8.4	76.7	-126.8
79 0100 1110	831.3	52.0	57.5	8120.0	-13.2	-7.2	83.3	-131.1
80 0100 1111	851.7	49.7	62.5	8440.0	-13.6	-7.0	87.8	-131.1

Table 12.2.   Project effect matrix of the Maasvlakte problem (cont'd)

composition of industrial site 1234 5678	values of decision criteria							
	economic objectives			labour market objectives			spatial/environmental objectives	
	ω_1	ω_2	ω_3	ω_4	ω_5	ω_6	ω_7	ω_8
81 0101 0000	457.6	87.0	37.5	5200.0	-13.5	-9.3	44.4	-39.3
82 0101 0001	478.0	81.2	42.5	5520.0	-14.1	-8.9	48.9	-39.3
83 0101 0010	689.1	59.3	52.5	7200.0	-13.6	-7.5	55.6	-43.6
84 0101 0011	709.5	56.2	57.5	7520.0	-14.1	-7.3	60.0	-43.6
85 0101 0100	649.0	68.3	57.5	6400.0	-13.6	-8.3	66.7	-141.3
86 0101 0101	669.4	64.4	62.5	6720.0	-14.1	-8.1	71.1	-141.3
87 0101 0110	880.5	48.9	72.5	8400.0	-13.7	-7.0	77.8	-145.6
88 0101 0111	900.9	46.7	77.5	8720.0	-14.1	-6.9	82.2	-145.6
89 0101 1000	498.4	87.0	52.5	5320.0	-13.1	-9.1	72.2	-39.3
90 0101 1001	518.8	81.1	57.5	5640.0	-13.8	-8.8	76.7	-39.3
91 0101 1010	729.9	59.7	67.5	7320.0	-13.4	-7.4	83.3	-43.6
92 0101 1011	750.3	56.7	72.5	7640.0	-13.8	-7.2	87.8	-43.6
93 0101 1100	689.8	68.6	72.5	6520.0	-13.3	-8.2	94.4	-141.3
94 0101 1101	710.2	64.6	77.5	6840.0	-13.8	-7.9	98.9	-141.3
95 0110 0000	415.6	91.0	12.5	4900.0	-12.1	-9.8	33.3	-24.8
96 0110 0001	436.0	84.9	17.5	5220.0	-12.8	-9.4	37.8	-24.8
97 0110 0010	647.1	62.0	27.5	6900.0	-12.6	-7.8	44.4	-29.1
98 0110 0011	667.5	58.9	32.5	7220.0	-13.1	-7.6	48.9	-29.1
99 0110 0100	607.0	71.3	32.5	6100.0	-12.5	-8.7	55.6	-126.8
100 0110 0101	627.4	67.3	37.5	6420.0	-13.0	-8.4	60.0	-126.8
101 0110 0110	838.5	51.5	47.5	8100.0	-12.8	-7.2	66.7	-131.1
102 0110 0111	858.9	49.2	52.5	8420.0	-13.3	-7.1	71.1	-131.1
103 0110 1000	456.4	91.0	27.5	5020.0	-11.8	-9.6	61.1	-24.8
104 0110 1001	476.8	85.0	32.5	5340.0	-12.5	-9.2	65.6	-24.8
105 0110 1010	687.9	62.1	42.5	7020.0	-12.4	-7.7	72.2	-29.1
106 0110 1011	708.3	59.4	47.5	7340.0	-12.9	-7.5	76.7	-29.1
107 0110 1100	647.8	71.7	47.5	6220.0	-12.2	-8.5	83.3	-126.8
108 0110 1101	668.2	67.8	52.5	6540.0	-12.8	-8.3	87.8	-126.8
109 0110 1110	879.3	52.1	62.5	8240.0	-12.6	-7.1	94.4	-131.1
110 0110 1111	899.7	49.8	67.5	8540.0	-13.1	-7.0	98.9	-131.1
111 0111 0000	505.6	86.7	42.5	5300.0	-12.6	-9.2	55.6	-39.3
112 0111 0001	526.0	81.0	47.5	5620.0	-13.3	-8.8	60.0	-39.3
113 0111 0010	737.1	59.3	57.5	7300.0	-13.0	-7.4	66.7	-43.6
114 0111 0011	757.5	56.2	62.5	7620.0	-13.5	-7.2	71.1	-43.6
115 0111 0100	697.0	68.2	62.5	6500.0	-12.9	-8.2	77.8	-141.3

Table 12.2.   Project effect matrix of the Maasvlakte problem (cont'd)

composition of industrial site		values of decision criteria							
		economic objectives			labour market objectives			spatial/physical objective	spatial/environmental objective
1234	56 78	ω_1	ω_2	ω_3	ω_4	ω_5	ω_6	ω_7	ω_8
116	0111 0101	717.4	64.4	67.5	6820.0	-13.4	-8.0	82.2	-141.3
117	0111 0110	928.5	49.0	77.5	8500.0	-13.1	-6.9	88.9	-145.6
118	0111 0111	948.9	46.8	82.5	8820.0	-13.5	-6.8	93.3	-145.6
119	0111 1000	546.4	86.7	57.5	5420.0	-13.0	-9.0	83.3	-39.3
120	0111 1001	566.8	81.1	62.5	5740.0	-13.0	-8.6	87.8	-39.3
121	0111 1010	777.9	59.7	72.5	7420.0	-12.8	-7.3	94.4	-43.6
122	0111 1011	798.3	56.7	77.5	7740.0	-13.2	-7.1	98.9	-43.6
123	1000 0000	919.0	91.4	15.0	12000.0	-13.0	-10.0	-55.6	-41.3
124	1000 0001	939.4	88.8	20.0	12320.0	-13.3	-9.8	60.0	-41.3
125	1000 0010	1150.5	77.1	30.0	14000.0	-13.1	-9.0	66.7	-45.6
126	1000 0011	1176.9	75.2	35.0	14320.0	-13.4	-8.8	71.1	-45.6
127	1000 0100	1110.4	82.3	35.0	13200.0	-13.1	-9.5	77.8	-143.3
128	1000 0101	1130.8	80.1	40.0	13520.0	-13.4	-9.3	82.2	-143.3
129	1000 0110	1341.9	70.3	50.0	15200.0	-13.2	-8.6	88.9	-147.6
130	1000 0111	1362.3	68.7	55.0	15520.0	-13.4	-8.5	93.3	-147.6
131	1000 1000	959.8	91.4	30.0	12120.0	-12.9	-9.9	83.3	-41.3
132	1000 1001	980.2	88.8	35.0	12440.0	-13.2	-9.7	87.8	-41.3
133	1000 1010	1191.3	77.2	45.0	14120.0	-13.0	-8.9	94.4	-45.6
134	1000 1011	1211.7	75.3	50.0	14440.0	-13.3	-8.8	98.9	-45.6
135	1001 0000	1009.0	88.1	45.0	12400.0	-13.2	-9.7	77.8	-55.8
136	1001 0001	1029.4	85.7	50.0	12720.0	-13.5	-9.5	82.2	-55.8
137	1001 0010	1240.5	74.7	60.0	14400.0	-13.3	-8.8	88.9	-60.1
138	1001 0011	1260.9	72.9	65.0	14720.0	-13.5	-8.6	93.3	-60.1
139	1001 0100	1200.4	79.6	65.0	13600.0	-13.3	-9.2	100.0	-157.8
140	1010 0000	967.0	91.0	20.0	12100.0	-12.6	-9.9	66.7	-41.3
141	1010 0001	987.4	88.4	25.0	12420.0	-12.9	-9.7	71.1	-41.3
142	1010 0010	1198.5	76.8	35.0	14100.0	-12.8	-8.9	77.8	-45.6
143	1010 0011	1218.9	74.9	40.0	14420.0	-13.1	-8.8	82.2	-45.6
144	1010 0100	1158.4	82.0	40.0	13300.0	-12.8	-9.4	88.9	-143.3
145	1010 0101	1178.8	79.3	45.0	13620.0	-13.0	-9.2	93.3	-143.3
146	1010 0110	1389.9	70.1	55.0	15300.0	-12.9	-8.5	100.0	-147.6
147	1010 1000	1007.8	91.0	35.0	12220.0	-12.5	-9.8	94.4	-41.3
148	1010 1001	1028.2	88.5	40.0	12540.0	-12.8	-9.7	98.9	-41.3
149	1011 0000	1057.0	87.8	50.0	12500.0	-12.8	-9.6	88.9	-55.8
150	1011 0001	1077.4	85.4	55.0	12820.0	-13.1	-9.5	93.3	-55.8
151	1011 0010	1288.5	74.5	65.0	14500.0	-13.0	-8.7	100.0	-60.1

Table 12.2.   Project effect matrix of the Maasvlakte problem (cont'd)

12.3   A Multivariate Analysis of the Alternatives

The matrix with the impacts of the feasible alternatives, as shown in Table 12.2, contains a considerable number of elements (1208). It is worthwhile, therefore, to try and condense the information contained in this matrix. This can be accomplished in two different ways: the selection of a subset of representative objectives, or the selection of a subset of representative alternatives. In this section the first approach will be dealt with.

1.000	.049	.316	.977	.306	-.745	.752	-.388
-.057	1.000	-.469	.204	.351	-.390	-.065	.381
.253	-.379	1.000	.141	.217	.028	.735	-.517
.906	-.053	.177	1.000	.283	-.809	.655	-.255
.343	.352	-.091	.362	1.000	-.373	.373	-.137
-.438	-.420	.149	-.452	-.472	1.000	-.483	.182
.560	-.061	.511	.514	.286	-.270	1.000	-.487
-.475	.255	-.394	-.410	-.056	.169	-.450	1.000

Table 12.3.   Correlation matrix implied by the plan impact
              table based on cardinal data (north-east corner)
              and ordinal data (south-west corner)

Our starting point is the correlation matrix between the objectives, which is presented in Table 12.3. The range of correlations appears to be wide: it varies from -.81 for the pair (4,6) to .98 for the pair (1,4). We will show that in the context of the present chapter, rank correlations which are based on ordinal data are more meaningful, however (cf. Section 8.9). One of our aims is to distinguish slightly conflicting pairs of objectives from other pairs. When we consider, for example, Figure 12.2, we find that by means of the rank correlation coefficient the absence of conflict can be registered in a more accurate way than by means of the ordinary correlation coefficient.

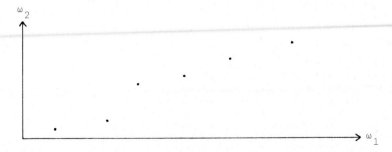

Fig. 12.2.   Absence of conflict for a pair of objectives

The former just attains its maximum value 1, while the latter
is smaller than 1. Hence, conflict may be completely absent,
although the ordinary correlation coefficient does not attain
its maximum value 1. We prefer, therefore, the use of ordinal
data in the remainder of this analysis.

    We have used the information contained in Table 12.3 to per-
form a hierarchical clustering procedure, as suggested in
Section 8.10. The underlying idea of this algorithm is that
clusters of objectives are formed such that the internal mutual
correlations are as high as possible. The computational results of the algorithm can be found in Figure 12.3. For each
number of clusters the corresponding minimum value of the internal correlations has been presented. This value ranges from
1 for eight clusters (each consisting of only 1 element) to
-.475 for one cluster.

    What is the appropriate number of clusters? The answer de-
pends on the evaluation of 1) the need for detailed information
and 2) the need for information of tractable size (cf. Section
8.10), so it cannot be given in general. Given the considerable decrease in r_{min} resulting from a step from three to two
clusters, however, a number of three clusters seems reasonable.

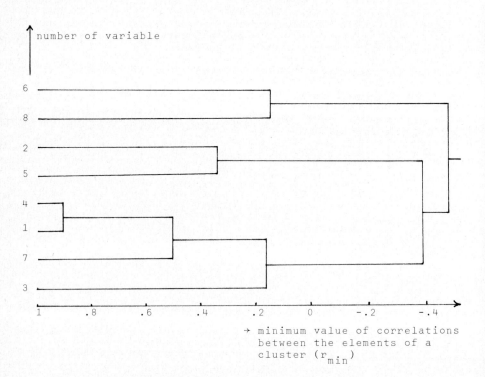

Fig. 12.3.   Results of the clustering algorithm

The clusters can be characterized as follows:

1. The variables 1, 3, 4 and 7 all favour an intensive use of the industrial site (due to economic and labour market considerations).

2. The variables 6 and 8 suggest a limited use of the site (due to environmental quality and the participation of foreign labour).

(a)

1.000	.299	.351	.014	.072	.841	0.000	.412
.347	1.000	.482	.303	.047	.110	.127	0.000
.406	.487	1.000	.329	.110	.289	.011	.341
.020	.317	.400	1.000	.078	.846	.014	.359
.101	.066	.155	.103	1.000	.110	.072	.014
.882	.156	.409	1.115	.156	1.000	.300	0.000
0.000	.150	.016	.020	.100	.409	1.000	.273
.444	0.000	.357	.420	.020	0.000	.370	1.000

(b)

1.000	.360	.556	.028	.143	1.105	0.000	.523
.326	1.000	.556	.348	.094	.220	.180	0.000
.364	.484	1.000	.556	.167	.488	.022	.444
.014	.307	.345	1.000	.143	1.358	.028	.523
.073	.047	.113	.079	1.000	.220	.133	.028
.872	.113	.314	1.129	.113	1.000	.488	0.000
0.000	.130	.011	.014	.073	.323	1.000	.467
.421	0.000	.344	.373	.014	0.000	.291	1.000

(c)

1.000	.221	.171	.000	.101	.887	.000	.429
.221	1.000	.343	.211	.008	.115	.077	.000
.171	.343	1.000	.212	.062	.322	.006	.320
.000	.211	.212	1.000	.106	1.059	.001	.412
.101	.008	.062	.106	1.000	.143	.049	.001
.887	.115	.322	1.059	.143	1.000	.320	.000
.000	.077	.006	.001	.049	.320	1.000	.174
.429	.000	.320	.412	.001	.000	.174	1.000

Table 12.4.   Various conflict measures for all pairs of objectives:

$\gamma_3(p=1)$ (a) north-east corner

$\gamma_3(p=2)$ (a) south-west corner

$\gamma\ (p\to\infty)$ (b) north-east corner

γ_2 (b) south-west corner

γ_5 (c) both corners

3. The variables 2 and 5 point to a <u>differentiated use</u> of the site with respect to economic structure and labour market conditions.

The conclusion can be drawn that from a set of eight variables, three clusters can be derived with maximum internal correlations which can be interpreted in a meaningful way.

After the analysis of correlations we turn to an analysis of the conflict measures γ among the objectives (see Section 6.5). Table 12.4 contains the values of 5 different conflict measures for all pairs of objectives. We find three pairs of objectives which are non-conflicting: (1,7), (2,8) and (6,8). The reason is that for these pairs the ideal solution is also <u>feasible</u> (see the alternatives 146, 9 and 1 from Table 12.2, respectively). Notice that γ assumes values larger than 1 for the pair (4,6) which is contrary to the property formulated in Section 6.5 that γ satisfies: $0 \leq \gamma \leq 1$. One should realize, however, that this property only applies to convex continuous problems. For discrete problems sometimes values of γ can be found which are larger than 1.

Comparing the elements of the matrices we find that for every pair of objectives

$$\gamma_3(p=1) \leq \gamma_3(p=2) \leq \gamma_3(p\to\infty) \qquad\qquad (12.4)$$

The reason is that in the definition of γ_3, a larger value of p implies a heavier weight for the large discrepancies with respect to the ideal situation. The value of γ_2 is in general between $\gamma_3(p=1)$ and $\gamma_3(p=2)$. The contents of Table 12.4 are, to a certain extent, in agreement with the division in clusters as derived heretofore. The internal conflict in the clusters (2,5) and (6,8) is low. This also applies to the cluster (1, 3, 4, 7) with the exception of objective 3 which shows medium levels of conflict with the objectives 1 and 4.

Finally, we present the values of the measures of the overall conflict. See Table 12.5.

measure of conflict	$\gamma_3(p=1)$	$\gamma_3(p=1.5)$	$\gamma_3(p=2)$	$\gamma_3(p=3)$	$\gamma_3(p=4)$	$\gamma_3(p=6)$	$\gamma_3(p=10)$	$\gamma_3(p\to\infty)$	γ_2
value of conflict	.20	.35	.42	.50	.54	.60	.66	.81	.39

Table 12.5.   The conflict among objectives measured for 8 objectives simultaneously

Again we find that $\gamma_3(p) \geq \gamma_3(p')$ if $p \geq p' \geq 1$ and $\gamma_3(p=1) \leq \gamma_2 \leq \gamma_3(p=2)$. The values of the measures range from .29 to .81, which means that one should be careful when interpreting a certain value as high or low. Each measure has its own frame of reference for deeming an outcome as high or low.

12.4   The Selection of Representative Solutions

This section will be devoted to the selection of a representative set of alternatives. We will deal with the elements of the pay-off matrix (Section 6.2), the compromise solution (Section 6.3) and the half-compromise solutions (Section 6.5), respectively.

The pay-off matrix often has some typical features in discrete cases:

1. it may be singular;

2. it may appear that it is not unique.

The cause of the first feature is that more than one objective may attain its maximum value for the same alternative. Then the pay-off matrix will contain identical columns and hence it will be singular. Especially when the number of alternatives is not large compared to the number of objectives, this difficulty will often arise. The second feature means that the maximum level of a certain objective can be attained for more than one alternative.

Table 12.6 shows that both features may arise in our case study. Several alternatives appear twice in the table (1,9 and 146) (4). For some objectives there appear multiple optimal solutions. The last problem can be solved when another criterion can be formulated to select one of the multiple optima.

objective	optimal solutions
max! ω_1	146
ω_2	9
ω_3	64
ω_4	130
ω_5	57
ω_6	1
ω_7	139, 146, 151
ω_8	1, 2, 9, 10, 33, 34, 41, 42

Table 12.6.   Potential candidates of the pay-off matrix

For example, a min-max procedure, similar to that described in Appendix II in Chapter 6 gives rise to the selection of the al-

ternatives 151 and 42 for the objectives 7 and 8, respectively.
The entailing pay-off matrix would be as described in Table
12.7.

objectives	resulting values of objectives							
	ω_1	ω_2	ω_3	ω_4	ω_5	ω_6	ω_7	ω_8
max! ω_1	1389.9	70.1	55.0	15300.0	-12.9	-8.5	100.0	-147.6
ω_2	40.8	100.0	15.0	120.0	-15.0	-1.1	27.8	0.0
ω_3	622.1	24.0	90.0	4140.0	-16.1	-2.9	98.9	-120.8
ω_4	1362.3	68.7	55.0	15520.0	-13.4	-8.5	93.3	-147.6
ω_5	178.8	95.3	50.0	620.0	-6.9	-1.1	61.1	-14.5
ω_6	0.0	0.0	0.0	0.0	-91.0	0.0	0.0	0.0
ω_7	1288.5	74.4	65.0	14500.0	-13.0	-8.7	100.0	-60.1
ω_8	109.2	86.7	25.0	540.0	-8.1	-2.1	43.3	0.0

Table 12.7.   Pay-off matrix for eight objectives

The main diagonal of the pay-off matrix shows the highest
attainable levels of the objectives. Together with the minimun
attainable levels they present the boundaries between which the
solution of the problem must be found (see Table 12.8). The
value of the conflict measure associated with the pay-off table,
γ_1, is equal to .48.

	ω_1	ω_2	ω_3	ω_4	ω_5	ω_6	ω_7	ω_8
maximum attain- able figures	1389.9	100.	90.	15520.	-6.9	0.	100.	0.
minimum attain- able figures	0.0	0.	0.	0.	-91.0	-10.	0.	-157.8

Table 12.8.   Maximum and minimum attainable levels for eight
objectives

The information contained in the pay-off matrix can be supplemented with information about less extreme options by means
of compromise and half-compromise solutions. In Table 12.9 we
present a survey of these solutions. We notice the following
regularities:

1. For $p \to \infty$, the half-compromises $\underline{y}_j^c$ (p) are identical to the
   compromise solution $\underline{x}^c$ (p) for all j.

2. The smaller p, the closer the half-compromises $\underline{y}_j^c$ are to the

corresponding extreme solutions as these can be found in Tables 12.6 or 12.7. For example, when p=1, no less than four half-compromises $\underline{y}_j^c$ (p) are identical to $\underline{x}_j^*$ (j=1,3,7,8).

3. The smaller p, the larger the number of different solutions $\underline{y}_j^c$ (p), j=1,...8.

4. The outcomes for the half-compromise concept $\underline{y}_j^a$ are similar to the outcomes for $\underline{y}_j^c$ (p=1.5).

	definition of (half-) compromise concept								
	c(p=1)	(p=1.5)	c(p=2)	c(p=3)	c(p=4)	c(p=6)	c(p=10)	c(p→∞)	a
compro-mise $\underline{x}$	151	151	151	122	122	122	122	122	151
half-compro-mise $\underline{y}$ for									
j=1	146	151	151	138	138	122	122	122	151
j=2	147	148	150	151	138	122	122	122	151
j=3	64	122	122	122	122	122	122	122	122
j=4	138	138	138	138	138	122	122	122	138
j=5	151	151	151	122	122	122	122	122	151
j=6	57	57	59	60	60	60	47	122	60
j=7	151	151	151	122	122	122	122	122	151
j=8	42	60	59	122	122	122	122	122	60

Table 12.9.   Compromise and half-compromise solutions for different compromise concepts

From these regularities we learn that in discrete problems the potential number of representative solutions (2J+1) will not often be reached. If we constrain ourselves to the compromise and half-compromise concepts $\underline{x}_j^c(p)$ and $\underline{y}_j^c(p)$, we find that for p=1 several half-compromises are identical to the extreme solutions, while for p→∞ they are identical to the compromise solution. Hence an intermediate value of p seems appropriate. When p=2, for example, the maximum number of different solutions can be derived (12), given a potential number of 17 representative solutions (cf. also Steuer and Schuler [1978]).

12.5   Application of the Interactive Method

In the former sections we focused on the generation of meaningful information regarding the decision structure; the main

step	no. of compromise solution from Table 12.2	total number of feasible solutions	type of solution	values of decision criteria							
				ω_1	ω_2	ω_3	ω_4	ω_5	ω_6	ω_7	ω_8
1	122	151	ideal	1389.9	100.0	90.0	15520.0	6.9	0.0	100.0	0.0
			minimum	0.0	0.0	0.0	0.0	91.0	-10.0	0.0	-157.8
			compromise	787.3	56.7	77.5	7740.0	-13.2	-7.1	98.9	-43.6
2	109	41	ideal	1389.9	91.4	82.5	15520.0	-12.5	-6.8	100.0	-41.3
			minimum	790.5	46.7	15.0	8000.0	-14.0	-10.0	55.6	-157.8
			compromise	879.3	52.1	62.5	8220.0	-12.6	-7.1	94.4	-131.1
3	142	21	ideal	1288.5	91.4	65.0	14720.0	-12.5	-8.6	100.0	-41.3
			minimum	919.0	72.9	15.0	12000.0	-13.5	-10.0	55.6	-60.1
			compromise	1198.5	76.8	35.0	14100.0	-12.8	-8.9	77.8	-45.6
4	133	10	ideal	1288.5	88.4	65.0	14720.0	-12.8	-8.6	100.0	-41.3
			minimum	1028.2	72.9	40.0	12500.0	-13.5	-9.7	82.2	-60.1
			compromise	1191.3	77.2	45.0	14120.0	-13.0	-8.9	94.4	-45.6
5	134	7	ideal	1288.5	87.8	65.0	14720.0	-12.8	-8.6	100.0	-45.6
			minimum	1029.4	72.9	50.0	12500.0	-13.5	-9.6	82.2	-60.1
			compromise	1211.7	75.3	50.0	14440.0	-13.3	-8.8	98.9	-45.6
6	136	3	ideal	1077.4	87.8	55.0	12820.0	-12.8	-9.5	93.3	-55.8
			minimum	1029.4	85.4	50.0	12500.0	-13.5	-9.6	82.2	-55.8
			compromise	1029.4	85.7	50.0	12720.0	-13.5	-9.5	82.2	-55.8
7	150	1	compromise	1077.4	85.4	55.0	12820.0	-13.1	-9.5	93.3	-55.8

Table 12.10.   Results of the interactive procedure

emphasis was placed on the analytical aspects of decision-making. In this section we will present the results of an interaction performed with a regional decision-maker, which means that also the political aspects of decision-making will be dealt with.

As in many real world problems, several governmental authorities are involved:

1. The Rotterdam City Council takes the ultimate decision on the use of the Maasvlakte.

Several other authorities have considerable influence in the decision, however, since they have the competence to test the decision according to laws concerning (a) physical planning (b) environmental protection and (c) selective investments (SIR).

2. The Rhine Delta authorities play an important role in the implementation of the SIR. Moreover they advise the province concerning the aspects (a) and (b).

3. The province of South Holland acts as the co-ordinator of physical and environmental planning. It is at this level that the ultimate permission for the investment is granted.

4. The national government serves as an instance of appeal for (a) and (b). Moreover, it may give certain directions in the framework of the SIR.

We have applied the interactive procedure of Section 9.7 with the delegate of economic affairs of the Rhine Delta Council (5). The course of the interaction has been depicted in Table 12.10. After 6 iterations the most desired solution (no. 150) has been determined. This is a rather extensive industrial complex which is favourable for the employment and does not give rise to excessive amounts of pollutants. The complex is a firm contribution to the differentiation of the economic structure. A weak element of the complex is the large number of foreign labourers that must be attracted. This plan comprises the following activities: an extensive steel complex; a tank storage plant; an integrated trans-shipment plant; a ship repair yard; and a tanker cleaning plant.

It appears to be interesting to investigate the sensitivity of the values of the decision criteria with regard to the achievement levels specified by the decision-maker during each step of the interactive procedure. These partial trade-offs are contained in Table 12.11. It can be expected that the introduction of a minimum achievement level for a certain objective induces an increase in the minimum attainable levels of conflicting objectives. For example, the imposition of achievement levels on objectives ω_3 and ω_4 during the third iteration gives rise to higher minimum attainable levels for ω_1 and ω_4, while the maximum attainable levels of ω_2 and ω_5 are decreased.

It did not cause the decison-maker much trouble to join the interaction. A short instruction period appeared to be sufficient to teach the basic principles of the interactive proce-

steps		$\Delta\omega_1$	$\Delta\omega_2$	$\Delta\omega_3$	$\Delta\omega_4$	$\Delta\omega_5$	$\Delta\omega_6$	$\Delta\omega_7$	$\Delta\omega_8$
1 - 2	achievement level	-	-	-	>7740.0	-	-	-	-
	shift in minimum value	790.5	46.7	15.0	8000.0	77.0	0.0	55.6	0.0
	shift in maximum value	0.0	-8.6	-7.5	0.0	5.6	-6.8	0.0	-41.3
2 - 3	achievement level	-	-	-	> 220.0	-	-	-	>26.7
	shift in minimum value	128.5	26.2	0	4000.0	.5	0	0	97.7
	shift in maximum value	-1001.4	0	-17.5	-800.0	0	-1.8	0	0
3 - 4	achievement level	-	-	>20.0	-	-	-	>22.2	-
	shift in minimum value	109.2	0	25.0	500.0	0	.3	26.6	.3
	shift in maximum value	0	-3.0	0	0	-.3	0	0	0
4 - 5	achievement level	-	-	>5.0	-	-	-	-	-
	shift in minimum value	1.2	0	10.0	0	0	.1	0	0
	shift in maximum value	0	-.6	0	0	0	0	0	-4.3
5 - 6	achievement level	-	>2.4	-	-	-	-	-	-
	shift in minimum value	0	12.5	0	0	0	0	0	4.3
	shift in maximum value	-211	0	-10.0	-100	0	-.9	-6.7	-10.2
6 - 7	achievement level	-	-	>0	-	-	-	-	-
	shift in minimum value	48.0	0	5.0	320.0	.4	.1	11.1	0
	shift in maximum value	0	-2.4	0	0	-.3	0	0	0

Table 12.11.   Sensitivity table with partial trade-offs of decision criteria with regard to achievement levels

dure (6). The interaction itself took approximately one hour. Since the decision-maker chose in all cases for strict improvements in the compromise values, the procedure converged directly (cf. Section 9.7). Concerning the course of the procedure, two remarks can be made:

1. It appears difficult to distinguish objectives from instruments. Reconsidering the selected alternative, the decision-maker realized that a container terminal (activity no. 5) was not included. The presence of the container terminal had already been the topic of political debate (7) and the local authorities tended to give permission for the terminal, as opposed to the national government. The decision-maker therefore revised his responses of the last two iterations and eventually selected alternative 124, which is the only feasible alternative out of seven during the fifth iteration which contains the container terminal. Obviously, the presence of a container terminal is for the DM not only a means to reach the 8 objectives, but also an objective itself. We may therefore conclude from this lesson that in the interactive procedure, information must be provided by the analyst about both objectives and instruments.

2. Some objectives are easier to interpret than others. For example, the structure of ω_2 and ω_5 is much more complex than that of ω_3 and ω_4. Complexity is not the only dimension, however, since also the eighth objective may be difficult to handle for the decision-maker although its structure - the quantity of emitted pollutants - is quite simple. It is plausible that these objectives are difficult to interpret for a decision maker, since the way in which these objectives are measured may not be directly related to the intuitive notions he has about the objectives (cf. Section 5.3). For a meaningful co-operation the decision-maker needs a well-developed frame of reference of the objectives. For the objective ω_8 such a frame may be formed, for example, by a number of pollution standards enabling the decision-maker to judge a certain level of emission as more or less harmful. When such a frame of reference is lacking, one should take into account the possibility that the decision-maker leaves certain objectives unmentioned as capable of improvement, not because he deems them unimportant, but because he does not know how to evaluate them. In the present study this holds true for the objectives ω_2, ω_3 and ω_8.

Of course, this procedure has been only a small element of the whole decision-making process concerning the use of the Maasvlakte area. How have further developments been? The course of affairs testifies to the essentially dynamic character of many decision problems. In 1976/77 several new topics arose regarding the Maasvlakte.

- The European steel industry started to display a large overcapacity so that the need for a new steel complex became questionable.

- The growing uncertainty about the oil imports gave rise to
  the evaluation of substitutes. Consequently, the Maasvlakte
  area has been mentioned as a potential location for an atomic reactor (8). Another possibility suddenly recognized was
  the use of the Maasvlakte for the landing and storage of LNG
  or LPG.

- Simultaneously a study group started a feasibility study of
  an artificial industrial island in the North Sea, approximately 60 kilometres from the Maasvlakte.

Due to these developments, no definite large ranging decisions have been taken up to now regarding the use of the
Maasvlakte area.

12.6   Conclusion

This case study shows that several methods and concepts from
Chapters 6, 8 and 9 can be applied in a meaningful way to a
real world decision problem. We mention especially the clustering method to derive the pattern of interdependencies among
the objectives (Section 12.3) and the methods to derive a representative set of alternatives (Section 12.4). The interactive procedure (Section 12.5) appears to be a feasible method
in reaching a structured communication between a decision-maker
and an analyst. Two lessons have been learned from the interaction with the decision-maker. First, it is necessary to be
very careful when distinguishing a variable as an objective or
an instrument. Second, before beginning the procedure one
should ascertain whether the decision-maker can relate the objectives as they are measured to the intuitive notions he has
about them.

Footnotes

1.   In these 900 ha. is also included some empty space of the
      adjacent Europoort area.

2.   With respect to the occupation rate ω_7, it is not comple-
      tely clear whether it should be considered as a benefit or
      a cost-variable. It is a benefit variable when it is con-
      ceived of as an indicator of the efficiency of land use,
      whereas it would be a cost-variable if it were conceived
      of as an indicator of inflexibility with respect to future
      developments. In the analysis we have chosen the first
      interpretation.

3.   The local labour supply is distributed as follows: low-
      skilled 30%; medium-skilled 61%; high-skilled 9%.

4.   Note that these alternatives correspond to the pairs of
      objectives in Table 12.4 with zero-values for the mutual
      conflict.

5.   The author wishes to express his thanks to Mr. P.A. Ruiter
      for his kind co-operation.

6.   This favourable condition may partly be due to the fact
      that the decision-maker holds a degree in Economics, so
      that a certain training in handling these types of proce-
      dures might be assumed to be present.

7.   Cf. Memorandum on Regional Socio-Economic Planning 1977-
      1980 (Nota Regionaal-Sociaal-Economisch Beleid 1977-1980)
      [1977], p.64, where the national government queries the
      local plans to use the Maasvlakte as a container terminal.

8.   Cf. Supplementary Scheme for Electricity Supply (Aanvul-
      lend Structuurschema Electriciteitsvoorziening) [1977].

CHAPTER 13

MULTILEVEL MULTIOBJECTIVE MODELS IN A MULTIREGIONAL SYSTEM

13.1   Introduction

   Harmonized planning strategies for a system divided into a
set of subsystems require methods for the resolution of interest conflicts emerging from the interdependence between the
components of the system at hand. In regional planning these
subsystems can be of various types: districts in a metropolis,
regions in a country, sectors in the national economy etc. In
these subsystems there are decision units whose sphere of influence is generally broader than the subsystem concerned, implying that external effects can occur. For example, the pollution dumped into a river at a certain place may influence regions being located downstream. Another example is that an improvement of the network of roads in a certain region may increase the accessibility of other regions.

   Given the interdependencies between subsystems, it is worthwhile to study the possibility of co-ordination of the actions
in subsystems. The present chapter will be devoted to the development of an analytical framework for such a co-ordination
with the following features:

1. a central decision unit aims at co-ordinating lower-level
   decision units in a number of subsystems;

2. the subsystems are interdependent;

3. each decision unit aims at achieving a number of objectives.
   The objectives may be conflicting within subsystems as well
   as between subsystems;

4. the decision units have not been able to give an explicit
   formulation of their priorities among the objectives;

5. the central decision unit has incomplete information on the
   feasible decisions in the subsystems.

   For the construction of an integrated analytical framework
we will combine two types of methods developed in decision theory: MOD methods (dealing with the elements 1, 2, 3 and 4) and
multilevel planning methods (dealing with the elements 1, 2 and
5). The discussion in this chapter proceeds as follows. In
Section 13.2 an analysis will be given of goal conflicts in a
multiregional system. In Sections 13.3 and 13.4 we give an exposition of certain aspects of multilevel planning. In Section
13.5 the two methods mentioned above are combined with the re-

sult of an integrated multiobjective multilevel planning framework.   Section 13.7 is devoted to a numerical illustration of
multiobjective multilevel planning by means of a multiregional
model, which is presented in Section 13.6.

In light of the conclusions of Chapter 10, this application
of MOD methods is especially interesting because of the occurrence of multiple decision units and the assumed incomplete information on the structure of the decision problem.   The proposed multiobjective multilevel planning method has no preten-
sion of being directly applicable.   Its most important contribution is that it sheds light on the structure of communication
processes in systems.   Two different types of communication are
integrated:

a. communication between decision units to fill up the information gap concerning the structure of the decision problem
   (element 5);

b. communication within decision units between analysts and DMs
   to fill up the information gap concerning the priorities
   among the objectives (element 4).

13.2   Multiple Objectives in a Multiregional System

In the present chapter the traditional assumption of independent decision units will be abandoned.   Instead, a multiregional system composed of R mutually dependent regions will be
assumed; this interdependence emerges from spatial spill-over
effects.   Each region is considered to be a spatially decentralized decision unit aiming at achieving a set of multiple
objectives.   Furthermore, there is a central decision or planning unit which attempts to co-ordinate the various regional
decision strategies.   Assuming J different objectives
($j=1,\ldots,J$), R regions ($r=1,\ldots,R$) and one central unit c, the
following joint matrix Ω of objective functions for the total
spatial system may be assumed:

$$\Omega \; = \; \begin{pmatrix} \omega_{1c} & \omega_{11} & \cdots\cdots\cdots\cdots & \omega_{1R} \\ \vdots & \vdots & & \vdots \\ \vdots & \vdots & & \vdots \\ \vdots & \vdots & & \vdots \\ \omega_{Jc} & \omega_{J1} & \cdots\cdots\cdots & \omega_{Jr} \end{pmatrix} \qquad (13.1)$$

where ω represents a certain objective function (production
growth, environmental quality, equitable distribution, e.g.).
Each objective function ω_{jr} is functionally determined by a set
of state variables $\underline{s}_{jr}$, a set of instrument variables $\underline{t}_{jr}$, a
set of external state and instrument variables $\underline{y}_{jr}$ (from sur-

rounding regions) and a set of exogenous variables $\underline{e}_{jr}$:

$$\omega_{jr} = \omega_{jr} \, (\underline{s}_{jr}, \, \underline{t}_{jr}, \, \underline{y}_{jr}, \, \underline{e}_{jr}) \qquad (13.2)$$

The arguments of ω_{jr} are assumed to be related to each other by means of an underlying functional structure:

$$\underline{s}_{jr} = f \, (\underline{t}_{jr}, \, \underline{y}_{jr}, \, \underline{e}_{jr}) \qquad (13.3)$$

Then the multiobjective program of region r attempts to maximize ω_{jr} (j=1,...,J) subject to (13.3) and other side-conditions (inequalities, e.g.).

The conflicts inherent in a separate optimization of the successive objective functions (either at an individual or at a regional scale) can be represented by means of the following pay-off matrix P (see also Section 6.2 and Nijkamp [1978]).

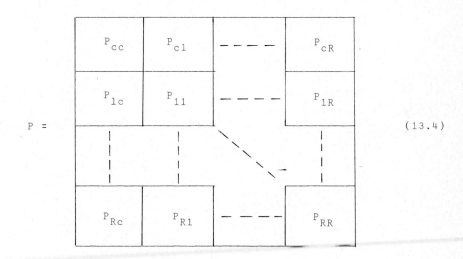

$$P = \qquad\qquad\qquad\qquad\qquad\qquad\qquad (13.4)$$

The elements on the main diagonal of (13.4) represent the absolute maxima of the corresponding functions. The block-diagonal matrices of (13.4) represent the intraregional conflicts: they represent the values of a certain objective function in region r when a competing objective function in region r is maximized. The off-diagonal blocks represent interregional conflicts: they indicate the value of a certain objective function in region r when an objective function in another region is maximized.

In the case of a centralized decision system, the central

unit will indicate the limits within which the successive regional units have to achieve their objectives. In a decentralized system, the successive regions will give signals to the
central co-ordinating unit in order to reconcile the various
interests. This situation implies an extension of traditional
MOD methods: in addition to conflicts between objectives, one
has to deal with conflicts between regions (or decentralized
decision units), so that a double choice conflict has to be
coped with at a higher decision level. This problem of multilevel decision-making and its relationship to MOD-making will
be discussed in the next sections.

13.3   Multilevel Programming: Introduction

Multilevel programming models provide a framework for the
co-ordination of decisions made in the various components of a
multiregional system. It is assumed that the co-ordination has
to be accomplished by a central decision unit which has the
power to give certain directives to the components. The central decision unit has only fragmentary knowledge about the
structure of the decision problems of the components. Therefore, multilevel programming includes a structured learning
process so as to enable the central unit to gather sufficient
information about the structure of the problem.

Multilevel programming models can be delineated as follows:
assume that there are R components. (The words component,
subsystem, and region are interchangeable in this chapter.)
Every component r has a series of J objectives
$\underline{\omega}_r = (\omega_{1r}, \ldots, \omega_{Jr})'$ which have to be maximized and which depend
on the I instrument and state variables $\underline{x}_r = (x_{1r}, \ldots, x_{Ir})'$.
Assume that the system has a linear structure, then $\underline{\omega}_r = C_r \underline{x}_r$,
where C_r is a (JxI) matrix with impact coefficients. We assume
for the moment that the components have solved their interior
goal conflicts. Hence, we may take the existence of a regional
welfare function $\omega_r = \sum_j \lambda_{jr} \omega_{jr}$ for granted, where λ_{jr} is the
weight attached to objective j by region r.

With respect to the restrictions faced by the regions, two
types may be distinguished:

1.   internal restrictions $B_r \underline{x}_r \leq \underline{b}_r$

2.   joint restrictions $\sum_r A_r \underline{x}_r \leq \underline{a}$

Internal restrictions may, for example, pertain to the constraints on regional production, due to the limited supply of
regional labour.

Joint restrictions may pertain inter alia to:

a.   common tasks to be performed by the regions (for example,
     the provision of sufficient outputs);

b. common resources to be distributed among regions (for exam-
    ple, manpower, capital, subsidies, funds);

c. spill-over effects (for example, the immission of pollut-
    ants from surrounding regions).

We conclude that the elements of $\underline{a}$ = $(a_1,\ldots,a_k,\ldots a_K)'$ may have
the character of a resource but also of a liability. For ease
of presentation the a_k's will be termed common resources.

When only internal restrictions prevail, the components are
obviously independent of each other, so that no co-ordination
is necessary. Consequently, the need for co-ordination stems
from the occurrence of joint restrictions. In order to co-ordinate the decisions, the centre has to formulate the objectives that it pursues. In many multilevel studies it is assumed that the central objective ω_c is simply the sum of the
subdivisional objectives: $\omega_c = \sum_r \omega_r$ (see also Togsverd [1976]).
In Sections 13.3 and 13.4 we will follow this assumption, but
in Section 13.5 we will show that the concept of multilevel
planning can be maintained without it.

The central planning problem can be formulated now as:

$$
\begin{cases}
\max! \underline{\lambda}_1' \, C_1\underline{x}_1 + \ldots + \underline{\lambda}_R' \, C_R\underline{x}_R \\[1em]
\text{subject to } A_1\underline{x}_1 + \ldots + A_R\underline{x}_R \leq \underline{a} \\[1em]
\quad B_1\underline{x}_1 \qquad\qquad\qquad \leq \underline{b}_1 \\[1em]
\qquad\qquad \ddots \qquad\qquad \vdots \\[1em]
\qquad\qquad\qquad B_R\underline{x}_R \leq \underline{b}_R \\[1em]
\qquad \underline{x}_r \geq \underline{0} \, , \; r = 1,\ldots,R
\end{cases}
\qquad (13.5)
$$

Problem (13.5) cannot be solved immediately, since it has been
assumed that the centre has limited information on the matrices
B_r and the vectors $\underline{b}_r$. Therefore, multilevel programming aims
at determining the optimal values of $\underline{x}_r$ by the components r
themselves, guided by some co-ordination from the centre.

There are essentially two ways in which this co-ordination
can be accomplished: directly and indirectly.

In the direct methods the distribution of the common resources among the regions plays a central role. The resources
have to be distributed such that an overall optimum will be
reached. This distribution cannot be determined by the centre
instantaneously, due to the lack of information mentioned above.
Therefore, the optimal distribution of resources has to be determined in a stepwise manner. In the first step, the centre

generates a provisional distribution of resources $(\underline{a}_1,\ldots,\underline{a}_R)$, satisfying $\sum_r \underline{a}_r = \underline{a}$, where $\underline{a}_r$ denotes the vector of resources placed at the disposal of region r.   Then each region r solves:

$$\begin{cases} \text{max!} \quad \omega_r = \underline{\lambda}_r' \, C_r \underline{x}_r \\[2mm] \text{subject to } B_r \underline{x}_r \le \underline{b}_r \\[2mm] \qquad\qquad A_r \underline{x}_r \le \underline{a}_r \\[2mm] \qquad\qquad \underline{x}_r \ge \underline{0} \end{cases} \qquad (13.6)$$

and reports the shadow-prices $\underline{\pi}_r$ (productivities) of the common resources back to the centre. Note that we assume that the regional decision unit, in contrast to the central decision unit, has complete information on the B_r, A_r and $\underline{b}_r$. Given the information on the productivities, the centre revises the distribution of the resources to increase the efficiency of the common resources. When all shadow-prices are equal (r=1,...,R), a redistribution does not increase ω_c, so that the optimum has been attained. Examples of direct methods can be found in Kornai [1965], Schleicher [1972], Ten Kate [1972a] and Johansen [1978]. These methods are termed direct, since the centre distributes directly the common resources among the subsystems, which is not the case with the indirect methods to be discussed below.

In the indirect methods the prices of the resources play a central role. The regions have to pay for their use of the common resources to ensure that these resources are used in an optimal way. Just as above, the optimal value of the prices $\underline{\pi} = (\pi_1,\ldots,\pi_K)'$ cannot be determined instantaneously and therefore the centre starts off with the generation of provisional prices $\underline{\pi}$ for the common resources. The regions then solve:

$$\begin{cases} \text{max!} \underline{\lambda}_r' \, C_r \underline{x}_r - \underline{\pi}' \, A_r \underline{x}_r \\[2mm] \text{subject to } B_r \underline{x}_r \le \underline{b}_r \\[2mm] \qquad\qquad \underline{x}_r \ge \underline{0} \end{cases} \qquad (13.7)$$

and report back to the centre the optimal amounts $\underline{a}_r$ they need from $\underline{a}$. If $\sum_r \underline{a}_r = \underline{a}$, the overal optimum has been attained. If not, the centre has to revise the prices such that this equality will ultimately be reached (1). See for examples of indirect methods Dantzig and Wolfe [1960], Dantzig [1963], Baumol and Fabian [1964] and Johansen [1978]. These methods are termed indirect since the centre computes the optimal distribution of resources only after the optimal prices of resources have been determined.

The main distinction between direct and indirect methods is that in the former the centre provides information on quantities to the components and receives in its turn information on prices, while in the latter it is exactly vice versa (see Figure 13.1).

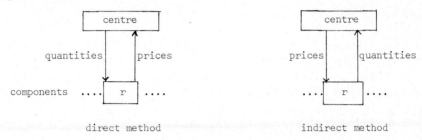

direct method   indirect method

Fig. 13.1.   Communication streams in multilevel planning

In the next section we will go into greater detail with regard to the way in which the centre has to determine the indices in order to guarantee a converging process.

13.4   Computational Aspects of Multilevel Programming

One of the first contributions to the indirect methods of distribution was given by Dantzig and Wolfe [1960]. Its contents can be sketched as follows. Let S_r denote the set of all $\underline{x}_r$ satisfying the regional constraints in (13.5):

$$S_r = \{\underline{x}_r \mid B_r\underline{x}_r \leq \underline{b}_r \; ; \; \underline{x}_r \geq \underline{0}\} \tag{13.8}$$

At the beginning of the procedure, B_r (and consequently also S_r) is unknown to the centre. The Dantzig-Wolfe algorithm aims at a stepwise determination of the relevant part of S_r ($r=1,\ldots,R$), which is a convex polyhedron with a finite number of extreme points (see Section 6.7). Let T_r be the matrix with extreme points of S_r. Then every $\underline{x}_r \in S_r$ can be written as a convex combination of the columns of T_r : $\underline{x}_r = T_r\underline{\mu}_r$ ($\underline{1}'\underline{\mu}_r = 1, \underline{\mu}_r \geq \underline{0}$). Consequently, (13.5) is equivalent to:

$$
\begin{cases}
\max! \quad \underline{\lambda}_1' \, C_1 \, T_1 \, \underline{\mu}_1 + \ldots + \underline{\lambda}_R' \, C_R \, T_R \, \underline{\mu}_R \\[2ex]
\text{subject to} \quad A_1 \, T_1 \, \underline{\mu}_1 + \ldots + A_R \, T_R \, \underline{\mu}_R \leq \underline{a} \\[2ex]
\qquad\qquad \underline{\imath}' \, \underline{\mu}_r = 1 \qquad\qquad r = 1, \ldots R \\[2ex]
\qquad\qquad \underline{\mu}_r \geq \underline{0} \qquad\qquad r = 1, \ldots R
\end{cases}
\qquad (13.9)
$$

The difference between (13.5) and (13.9) is that in the former $\underline{x}_1, \ldots, \underline{x}_R$ are the unknowns to be determined, whereas in the latter the unknowns are $\underline{\mu}_1, \ldots, \underline{\mu}_R$. Obviously, the question is how $T_1, \ldots, T_R$ can be determined. To solve this problem, Dantzig and Wolfe have proposed the following algorithm:

a. in the first step T_r is completely unknown. The centre reports arbitrary prices π to the components;

b. the components solve (13.7) and report one column of T_r back to the centre;

c. the centre solves (13.9) for the T_r matrix, as far as its columns are known. The dual variables related to the common resources $\underline{a}$ are reported to the components.

The iterations must be repeated until the recurrent solution of (13.9) does not yield new outcomes. Dantzig and Wolfe show that the algorithm converges in a finite number of steps. The information reported by the regions is apparently handled in a very efficient way. Related algorithms can be found in Malinvaud [1972] and Johansen [1978].

An attractive procedure for a <u>direct</u> distribution of the common resources has been developed by Ten Kate [1972a]. In fact, his proposal is based on a dualization of the Dantzig-Wolfe algorithm. In its original formulation, the Dantzig-Wolfe algorithm aims at determining in a stepwise way the relevant part of the feasible region implied by (13.7). Ten Kate's algorithm attempts to identify the relevant part of the set of feasible dual variables implied by (13.6) in a stepwise way.

The central programming problem implied by the Ten Kate method reads as follows. Let π_{kr}^i denote the dual variable related to the k-th common resource of component r during iteration i. Let $\underline{v}_r^i$ be the vector with dual variables related to the regional resources $\underline{b}_r$ of region r during iteration i. Then $\eta_r^i = \underline{b}_r' \, \underline{v}_r^i$ represents the value of the resources $\underline{b}_r$ during iteration i. Then the centre has to solve in step i' :

$$\begin{cases} \max! \quad z_c = \sum_r v_r \\[2mm] \text{subject to} \quad v_r \leq \eta_r^i + \sum_k \pi_{kr}^i \, a_{kr} \quad \begin{cases} i=1,\ldots,i'-1 \\ r=1,\ldots,R \end{cases} \quad (13.10) \\[3mm] \qquad\qquad\qquad \sum_r a_{kr} = a_k \qquad\qquad k=1,\ldots,K \end{cases}$$

which is equivalent to:

$$\begin{cases} \max! \quad z_c = \sum_r \min_i (\eta_r^i + \sum_k \pi_{kr}^i \, a_{kr}) \\[3mm] \text{s.t.} \quad \sum_r a_{kr} = a_k \qquad\qquad k=1,\ldots,K \end{cases} \qquad (13.11)$$

Note that the term $\eta_r^i + \sum_k \pi_{kr}^i \, a_{kr}$ indicates the value of the regional objective function ω_r according to the productivities reported in step i, when the region receives the resources $(a_{1r},\ldots,a_{Kr})$. The result of (13.10) is a new distribution of resources $(\underline{a}_1,\ldots,\underline{a}_R)$ based on productivities per component in all preceding steps which is used as an input in (13.6). The algorithm is proved to guarantee a convergence within a finite number of iterations.

Some computational aspects of (13.10) deserve our attention. When i' is small, the number of side-conditions in (13.10) is small which may give rise to unbounded outcomes (2). Ten Kate shows that this can be solved by adding upper and lower bounds for the a_{kr} into (13.10). After a finite number of iterations these bounds will become inactive constraints.

Another aspect of the method is that the distribution of the common resources arising from (13.10) may appear infeasible for one or more subsystems. This problem can be tackled as follows. Let $\underline{a}_r^{i'}$ be the vector of resources for region r in iteration i'. When $\underline{a}_r^{i'-1}$ is feasible and $\underline{a}_r^{i'}$ is infeasible, a new proposal for region r can be calculated as $q\,\underline{a}_r^{i'} + (1-q)\,\underline{a}_r^{i'-1}$ for q < 1. This adaptation should be applied for all regions (r=1,...,R) to ensure that $\sum_r \underline{a}_r = \underline{a}$. The value of q can be reduced step-wise until all regional decision problems are feasible.

Alternative direct methods have also been proposed (see for example Kornai [1965], Schleicher [1971] and Johansen [1978]). These methods do not have the property of converging in a finite number of steps, but they do have the advantage above Ten Kate's method in that their central idea can be explained very easily. This central idea is that when a component r has

reported a relatively high productivity π_{kr}^{i-1} in iteration i-1,
the central objective function can be improved by re-allocating
in iteration i a certain amount of a_k to component r at the ex-
pense of less productive components. Obviously, this idea concerning the <u>direction</u> of a redistribution has to be followed by
a rule to determine the <u>order of magnitude</u> of the redistribution. Such a rule is not easy to find, however, since a small
step size may imply a very slow speed of convergence, while a
large step size may imply no convergence at all. Schleicher
[1971] solves this dilemma by introducing a variable step size,
which can be adapted in each iteration according to the outcomes.

In Nijkamp and Rietveld [1979a] a more extensive analysis of
various aspects of multilevel planning methods is contained,
including: the amount of prior information needed, the size of
the information streams, the number of iterations and the complexity of the computational activities to be performed. It
appeared to be impossible to determine a method which is more
favourable than alternative methods according to all criteria,
although within certain subsets of methods more definite conclusions can be drawn.

In Nijkamp and Rietveld [1979a] some computational results
of the Schleicher and Ten Kate method are also contained. The
conclusion is that the latter method is clearly superior to the
former with regard to the speed of convergence.

13.5   Multiobjective Multilevel Planning

When we compare the contents of Sections 13.3 and 13.4 with
Section 13.2, we find that in the multilevel planning methods
formulated here the multidimensional character of the objectives has not been sufficiently recognized. This can be exem-
plified in at least two respects:

a. the conflicts between the systems components are neglected,
    as witnessed by the fact that the central objective is simply
    the unweighted sum of the objectives of the components;

b. the components can easily determine the weights $\underline{\lambda}_r$ they at-
    tach to the various objectives they pursue. Consequently,
    the internal conflicts receive little attention.

ad a. Apparently, most contributors to multilevel planning
studies have in mind a unidimensional objective for the components, such as the maximization of income, which can be aggre-
gated in a meaningful way. However when other interpretations
of the term $\underline{\lambda}_r' C_r \underline{x}_r$ are introduced (for example, when it denotes
welfare in component r), difficulties may arise. In that case
an aggregation is only meaningful when a consensus has been
reached on a common denominator of welfare in various subdivi-
sions. In indirect methods another problem arises, since the
objective $\underline{\lambda}_r' C_r \underline{x}_r - \underline{\pi}' A_r \underline{x}_r$ in (13.7) essentially assumes the existence of welfare payments from component r to the centre,

which can hardly be imagined.

As we will show in this section, it is yet possible to design multilevel programming models in such a way that they take
account of the various conflicts between objectives. In this
respect, Salih [1975] has given an example for indirect methods.
In the present chapter we will focus on direct methods, especially the method of Ten Kate.

A first step is the following. Let the central objective
function no longer be $\omega_c = \sum_r \underline{\lambda}'_r \underline{\omega}_r$, where $\underline{\lambda}_r$ is the vector with
weights determined by component r, but $\omega_c = \sum_r \underline{\gamma}'_r \underline{\omega}_r$, where the
$\underline{\gamma}_r$ indicate the centre's own priorities with respect to the objectives of subdivision r.

Allowing this divergence of priorities gives rise to some
very interesting phenomena. Assume, for example, that $\underline{a}_1,\ldots,\underline{a}_R$
is the optimal division of resources when no divergence in po-
litical weights exists (i.e., $\underline{\gamma}_r = \underline{\lambda}_r$, r=1,...,R), which would
give rise to the solutions $\underline{x}_1,\ldots,\underline{x}_R$. What will happen when
the distribution $\underline{a}_1,\ldots,\underline{a}_R$ is dealt with by the systems components, if a divergence in political weights does exist? Obvi-
ously, there is no guarantee that the resources will be used
according to the intentions of the centre (3). Hence, one may
wonder whether it is possible for the centre to determine a
distribution $\overset{o}{\underline{a}}_1,\ldots,\overset{o}{\underline{a}}_R$ which yields the best feasible outcome,
given the divergence of priorities.

We will show that such a division $\overset{o}{\underline{a}}_1,\ldots,\overset{o}{\underline{a}}_R$ can, in principle, be determined, although it implies a considerable exten-
sion of the regional computational burden. The former information π_{kr} is inapplicable in the new situation, since the centre
is no longer interested in the productivity of resource k with
respect to the welfare of component r as it is conceived of by
the component itself, but rather with respect to the successive
objectives 1,...,J of component r. Consequently, the subdivi-
sions have to provide information about a J x K matrix Π_r with
elements π_{jkr} instead of a vector $\underline{\pi}_r$ with elements π_{kr}. Unlike
$\underline{\pi}_r$, Π_r cannot be derived directly from the Simplex tableau. A
sensitivity analysis is needed to compute the matrix.

Given this new information, the Ten Kate method for direct
distribution can be adapted as follows in order to compute
$\overset{o}{\underline{a}}_1,\ldots,\overset{o}{\underline{a}}_R$ in an iterative way without violating its convergence
properties:

$$\begin{cases} \text{max! } \sum_r v_r & \quad (13.12) \\[2mm] \text{subject to} \quad v_r \leq \sum_{j,k} \gamma_{jr} \pi^i_{jkr} a_{kr} + \sum_j \gamma_{jr} \eta^i_{jr} \begin{cases} r=1,\ldots,R \\ i=1,\ldots,i'-1 \end{cases} \\[2mm] \hspace{2.5cm} \sum_r a_{kr} = a_k \hspace{3cm} k=1,\ldots,K \end{cases}$$

Note that in (13.12) the priorities of both levels play a role. This is evident for the central weights γ_{jr}, but the regional weights λ_{jr} also play a role, since, according to (13.6), the dual variables π^i_{jkr} depend on the λ_{jr}. Obviously, when $\gamma_{jr} = \lambda_{jr}$ for all j and r, (13.12) is equivalent to (13.10).

The multilevel planning method exposed above is characterized by a certain measure of decentralization. The centre does not instruct the components on which decision $\underline{x}_r$ they should take; it only specifies the boundaries $\underline{a}_r$, within which the components have to operate. This decentralization, in general, yields a lower value of the central objectives when the central and regional authorities do not coincide. Consequently, in the case of conflicting objectives between central and subdivisional objectives, a certain cost of decentralization from the centre's viewpoint will emerge.

Section 13.7 will be devoted to a numerical illustration of the multiobjective multilevel planning method implied by (13.12) and also to the cost of decentralization in a multiregional planning problem.

ad b. The second shortcoming of standard multilevel planning methods is its neglect of conflicting objectives: these methods take uncertainties about the decision structure into account, but not about the priority structure. The MOD methods presented in Chapters 6-9 may be helpful in dealing with the latter type of uncertainties. The interactive MOD methods developed in Chapter 9 are especially interesting in this context since they give rise to a double interactive decision procedure. When interactive MOD methods are applied, multiobjective multilevel planning can be characterized as a decision procedure in which two different learning processes take place simultaneously (i.e. the learning of the priorities and of the decision structure). The following 2R + 2 parties play a role in this procedure:
R   regional policy-making bodies
R   regional bodies for analytical decision aid
1   central policy-making body
1   central body for analytical decision aid.

Fig. 13.2 presents the entailing communication network. It shows how the information exchange between centre and regions (see Fig. 13.1) has been extended with two phases of deliberation at the central and regional level. Steps (a) and (b) are

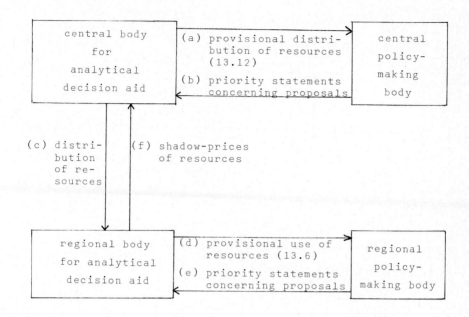

Fig. 13.2.   Communication network implied by a direct multilevel multiobjective planning process

passed through repeatedly at the central level, until the central policy-making body is certain about the distribution of
resources to be reported to the regions (c). Then steps (d)
and (e) are passed through repeatedly, until the regional policy-making body is certain about how the resources should be al-
located. Then the corresponding productivities are reported
back (f) and a new iteration can be started. This procedure
obviously does not converge when the policy-making bodies
change their priorities during each iteration, since (13.12)
only guarantees convergence when the priorities remain unchanged. This double interactive procedure will be illustrated
by means of an interregional model which will be presented in
the next section.

13.6   An Interregional Model

The interregional model discussed in this section is a simple two-region model for the Netherlands and only serves for
the sake of illustration. It is an input-output model with the
following elements:

- 4 sectors   : agriculture, industry, services, transport
                ($s=1,\ldots,4$);

- 2 regions   : Rijnmond (the greater Rotterdam region) and
               the rest of the Netherlands ($r=1,2$);
- 2 objectives: maximization of regional income and minimiza-
               tion of regional pollution ($j=1,2$).

The following variables are distinguished:

$\underline{y}'_r = (y_{1r}, \ldots, y_{4r})$: production levels in sectors $1, \ldots, 4$ in re-
                     gion r;

e_r : emission of pollutants in region r;

m_r : immision of pollutants in region r;

$\underline{i}'_r = (i_{1r}, \ldots, i_{4r})$: productive investments in sectors $1, \ldots, 4$
                     in region r;

v_r : environmental investments in region r
                     (abatement investments, e.g.).

The two objectives are: max! $\omega_{1r} = \underline{c}'_r \underline{y}_r$ and min! $\omega_{2r} = k_r m_r$,
where $\underline{c}_r$ contains the value added coefficients in region r and
k_r denotes the damage per unit of emission in region r.

The model contains 11 common constraints:

1) 8 input-output relationships for the intermediate deliveries
between the 4 sectors in both regions:

$$\begin{pmatrix} -I+A_{11} & A_{12} \\ A_{21} & -I+A_{22} \end{pmatrix} \begin{pmatrix} \underline{y}_1 \\ \underline{y}_2 \end{pmatrix} \leq \underline{a}_1 \qquad (13.13)$$

where the matrices A reflect the input-output matrices and
where $-\underline{a}_1$ indicates the requirements for the final demand in
the various sectors.

2) 1 constraint for the limited amount a_2 for total investments:

$$\underline{\imath}' \, \underline{i}_1 + v_1 + \underline{\imath}' \, \underline{i}_2 + v_2 \leq a_2 \qquad (13.14)$$

3) 2 constraints for the relationships between the immission of
pollutants in a certain region and the emission in both regions.

$$\begin{cases} m_1 - h_{11}e_1 - h_{21}e_2 + f_1v_1 = 0 \\ m_2 - h_{12}e_1 - h_{22}e_2 + f_2v_2 = 0 \end{cases} \qquad (13.15)$$

where the coefficients h denote the multiregional diffusion
pattern of pollution and f_r represents the productivity of pollution abatement investments to reduce the immission of pollutants.

In addition to these 11 constraints, there are for both regions 6 <u>constraints</u> for the components:

1) 4 constraints for the restricted amounts of <u>capital</u> for each
sector:

$$\underline{y}_r - \hat{s}\,\underline{i}_r \leq \hat{s}\,\underline{\bar{K}}_r \qquad (13.16)$$

where $\hat{s}$ is the diagonal matrix with capital productivities and
$\underline{K}_r$ the vector with the amounts of capital available at the beginning of the planning period.

2) 1 constraint for the limited amount of available <u>labour</u>:

$$\underline{1}'\,\hat{L}_r\underline{y}_r \leq b_{2r} \qquad (13.17)$$

where $\hat{L}_r$ is the diagonal matrix with labour productivities and
b_{2r} is the labour force in region r.

3) 1 relationship for the links between the production levels
in a region and the emission of pollution:

$$e_r - \underline{d}'_r\,\underline{y}_r = 0 \qquad (13.18)$$

where $\underline{d}_r$ is a vector with emission coefficients.

For the precise data used, and the units of measurement of the
variables, we refer to Appendix I. Before we discuss a numerical application of the model to multilevel planning, some attention should be paid to the way in which the decomposition
has been accomplished.

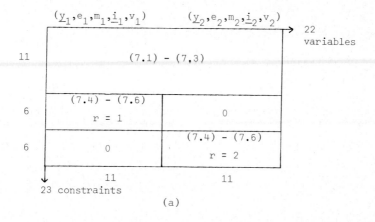

(a)

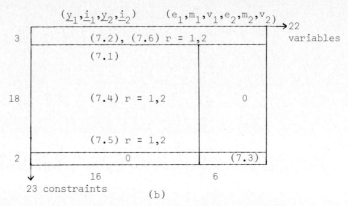

(b)

Figure 13.3.   Alternative ways of decomposition

   Figure 13.3(a) shows the decomposition as proposed above.
The zero-matrices indicate that the two components (regions)
are partly independent of each other. The multilevel planning
procedure aims at a decision on 11 items.

   Figure 13.3(b) shows that another frame of reference can
also be adopted to achieve a decomposition, namely by classi-
fying the variables according to the policy fields: "economic"
and "environmental". According to this decomposition, the multilevel algorithm only faces three common constraints (4).

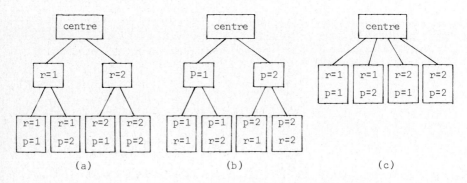

(a)   (b)   (c)

Figure 13.4.   Hierarchical co-ordination of regional and facet
                                policies

In Figure 13.4(a) the regions are first responsible for facet policies, while in (b) the facet agencies are first responsible for regional policies. When the centre is not content
with such a delegation of responsibilities, it may try to
achieve a direct integration of regional and facet policy (c).
In practice, regional and facet policies are frequently a very
complex mixture of (a), (b) and (c).

13.7   A Numerical Illustration

Before presenting the results of the multilevel multiobjective planning process as delineated in Figure 13.2, we will
first pay some attention to the nature of the conflicts between
the objectives formulated above (5). These conflicts can be
illustrated by means of the pay-off matrix (see Table 13.1).

	resulting values of			
	ω_{11}	ω_{21}	ω_{12}	ω_{22}
max! ω_{11}	624	-402	686	-79
max! ω_{21}	63	0	654	-41
max! ω_{12}	105	-140	2863	-316
max! ω_{22}	63	-39	654	-32

Table 13.1.   Pay-off matrix of the interregional model

It follows from the definition of the pay-off matrix that the
best attainable levels of the objectives can be found on the
main diagonal. With the exception of the pair (ω_{21}, ω_{22}), all
pairs of objectives show a considerable degree of conflict.

For the illustration of the interactive multilevel multiobjective planning procedure, we made the following assumptions.

1. The weights attached to the objectives by the centre are
(γ_{11}, γ_{21}, γ_{12}, γ_{22}) = (1, 3, 1, 3). These weights are not
known _explicitly_ by the centre, however, and hence an interac-
tive MOD procedure must be employed to find the desired outcomes. Furthermore, the centre does not know the data on the
regional decision structure (A_r, B_r, $\underline{b}_r$, $\underline{\lambda}_r$). Therefore, an
interactive multilevel planning procedure must be employed.

2. The weights attached to the objectives by the regions differ
from the centre's weights: (λ_{11}, λ_{21}) = (1, 0) and
(λ_{12}, λ_{22}) = (1, 2). These weights are not known _explicitly_
by the regions, so that an interactive MOD procedure must be
used. The regions have reliable information on the data of the
decision structure (A_r, B_r, $\underline{b}_r$).

i step		type of solution	values of objectives ω_{11} ω_{21}		weights corresponding to the compromise	
1	1	ideal minimum compromise	392.7 351.6 368.0	-200.0 -224.0 -209.6	 .368	 .632
1	2	ideal minimum compromise	392.7 368.0 377.9	-209.6 -224.0 -215.4	 .368	 .632
1	3	ideal minimum compromise	392.7 377.9 383.9	-215.4 -224.0 -218.8	 .368	 .632
1	4	ideal minimum compromise	392.7 383.9 387.4	-218.8 -224.0 -220.9	 .368	 .632
1	5	ideal minimum compromise	392.7 387.4 389.5	-220.9 -224.0 -221.1	 .368	 .632
2	1	ideal minimum compromise	323.9 298.5 323.6	-106.4 -159.8 -121.1	 .677	 .323
2	2	ideal minimum compromise	323.9 323.6 323.7	-121.1 -159.8 -136.2	 .990	 .010

Table 13.2.   Results of the interactive MOD procedure for region 1 during the first two iterations i of the multilevel planning procedure

i step		type of solution	values of objectives ω_{12} ω_{22}		weights corresponding to the compromise	
1	1	ideal minimum compromise	1515.6 1515.6 1515.6	-147.5 -147.5 -147.5	 	
2	1	ideal minimum compromise	2793.1 2787.8 2791.0	-237.9 -247.1 -243.4	 .633	 .367
2	2	ideal minimum compromise	2791.0 2787.8 2789.8	-237.9 -243.4 -241.2	 .633	 .367

Table 13.3.   Results of the interactive MOD procedure for region 2 during the first two iterations i of the multilevel planning procedure

i	step	type of solution	ω_{11}	ω_{21}	ω_{12}	ω_{22}	weights corresponding to the compromise
			values of objectives				
2	1	ideal	544	0	28,138	23	
		minimum	238	-366	26,438	-396	
		compromise	392	-32	27,118	-152	.36 .36 .05 .23
2	2	ideal	544	-32	28,138	-146	
		minimum	392	-336	27,118	-396	
		compromise	453	-154	27,526	-250	.35 .21 .07 .37
2	3	ideal	453	-51	28,138	-241	
		minimum	392	-154	27,526	-380	
		compromise	416	-104	27,771	-301	.30 .21 .04 .45
2	4	ideal	416	-63	28,138	-297	
		minimum	392	-104	27,771	-380	
		compromise	402	-86	27,918	-332	.35 .23 .04 .37
2	5	ideal	402	-70	28,138	-331	
		minimum	392	-86	27,918	-380	
		compromise	395	-80	28,006	-351	.41 .26 .03 .30
3	1	ideal	544	0	2913	23	
		minimum	238	-256	2561	-380	
		compromise	392	-17	2645	-81	.24 .30 .17 .29
3	2	ideal	402	0	2645	23	
		minimum	238	-17	2572	-81	
		compromise	392	-4	2590	-20	.13 .50 .15 .22
3	3	ideal	395	0	2580	23	
		minimum	238	-4	2572	-20	
		compromise	392	-1	2577	-5	.05 .67 .15 .12
3	4	ideal	393	0	2577	0	
		minimum	392	-1	2572	-5	
		compromise	392	0	2573	-1	.41 .25 .12 .22

Table 13.4.   Results of the interactive MOD procedure for the
centre during the iterations i=2 and i=3 of the
multilevel planning procedure

In Tables 13.2 and 13.3 we show how the two regions (r=1,2)
use the interactive MOD procedure in order to determine the optimal allocation of the resources a_r^i during the first two iterations (i=1,2) of the multilevel planning procedure. The compromise solutions employed in this case are of type e_4 (cf.
Section 6.4). The weights λ_4 underlying these compromises have
also been represented in the tables. The answers of the regional policy-making bodies to the questions concerning the attractiveness of the compromise solutions have been generated
such that they are consistent with the assumed values of the
regional weights λ_r. The objective of which the value must be
improved in a certain step has been indicated by [   ] .

Given the absolute priority which the policy-making body of
region 1 is assumed to give to objective ω_{11}, it is obvious that
in Table 13.2 only improvements of the value of that objective
are stated. For region 2 we find that during the first iteration the objectives are non-conflicting. The reason is that
the resources a_2^1 for the pertaining region are so restrictive
that the region does not have the opportunity to develop a policy according to its own political views. This is not the case
with the resources a_2^2 during the second iteration, which leave
this region with certain (although modest) scope to trade-off
the importance of the objectives.

Having determined the desired allocation of the resources,
the regions r report the prices π_{jkr}^i to the centre, indicating
the productivity of resource k with regard to objective j during iteration i. This information is used by the centre during
iteration i+1 to determine a new distribution of resources. In
Table 13.4 the interactions to find the new distributions of
resources have been represented for i=2 and 3 (6). The values
for $(\omega_{11},\ldots,\omega_{22})$ represented in the table are not mentioned
explicitly, but only implicitly in (13.12):

$$\omega_{jr} = \min_{i'=1,\ldots i} \left(\sum_k \pi_{jkr}^{i'} a_{kr} + \eta_{jr}^{i'} \right) \tag{13.19}$$

It is important to note that these values of the objectives are
approximations, due to the limited information of the centre
during iteration i. Comparing the results of Table 13.4 with
the pay-off matrix (Table 13.1), we conclude that the additional information available when i=3 enables the centre to reach
more realistic values for ω_{12} than when i=2. We conclude from
Table 13.4 that the range of the various objectives has considerably decreased after 4 or 5 steps of the interactive MOD procedure have been effected.

We will next focus on how the results of the MOD procedures
carried out by the centre and the regions are employed in the
multilevel planning algorithm (communication streams c and f
in Figure 13.2) to find an optimal distribution of resources.
In Table 13.5 we present for each iteration i the distribution
of resources $\underline{a}_r^i$ between the regions and the corresponding productivities reported by the regions. In the last column of the
table we find for every i and r the values of ω_{1r}^i and ω_{2r}^i ,
respectively. It appears that the algorithm converges after 11
iterations. We have two remarks concerning the convergence.
First, for several common resources the reported shadow-prices
are equal to zero for both regions. Obviously there is no need
to revise the distribution of such resources. Second, the algorithm does not guarantee a monotone process of convergence:
the values of the central and regional objectives oscillate to
a certain extent.

It is interesting to compare these results with the situation that the central and regional weights do not diverge
($\gamma_{jr} = \lambda_{jr}$, $\forall$ j, r). When $(\lambda_{11}, \lambda_{21}, \lambda_{12}, \lambda_{22}) = (1, 3, 1, 3)$,
the multilevel planning algorithm yields as a solution for
$\underline{\omega} = (\omega_{11}, \omega_{21}, \omega_{12}, \omega_{22})'$:

$$\underline{\omega} = (295, -59, 2762, -218)' \quad \sum_{j,r} \gamma_{jr}\,\omega_{jr} = 2226$$

(13.20)

When $(\lambda_{11}, \lambda_{21}, \lambda_{12}, \lambda_{22}) = (1, 0, 1, 2)$, however, Table 13.5
shows that the optimal solution is:

$$\underline{\omega} = (195, -43, 2762, -217)' \quad \sum_{j,r} \gamma_{jr}\,\omega_{jr} = 2177$$

(13.21)

We conclude that given the divergence of the weights, the centre
redistributes the resources. This redistribution only slightly
effects region 2, but the outcomes for region 1 change considerably. In the present example with divergent weights the relative autonomy of the regions (they are free to use the resources according to their own views) gives rise to a cost of
decentralization equal to 49 units, measured by means of the
central weights.

13.8   Conclusion

Multilevel planning is an important concept for regional
planning, since it explicitly recognizes that lack of information will induce communication in hierarchical networks. In
this paper it has been shown that the range of multilevel planning methods can be extended when it is placed in the context
if MOD methods, which means that uncertainties about priorities

Common resources (k=1,....11)

i	r	1	2	3	4	5	6	7	8	9	10	11	ω_jr
1	1	-5.000	-80.000	-100.	-5.000	20.000	100.000	75.	5.000	200.000	4000.000	-6000.000	
		0.000	0.000	0.	0.000	0.000	0.000	0.	0.000	.206	0.000	-.019	390.
		0.000	0.000	0.	0.000	0.000	0.000	0.	0.000	0.000	-.008	.032	-221.
1	2	1.000	50.000	35.	3.000	-50.000	-650.000	-550.	-20.000	550.000	-4000.000	6000.000	1516.
		0.000	7.924	0.	165.979	0.000	0.000	0.	2.930	0.000	-.170	-.000	-148.
		0.000	0.000	0.	0.000	0.000	0.000	0.	0.000	.030	.038	-.002	
2	1	-5.000	-146.667	-100.	-70.333	20.000	100.000	75.	2.778	444.444	6322.105	-3412.391	324.
		0.000	1.099	0.	0.000	0.000	0.000	0.	49.795	.001	-.000	-.101	-136.
		0.000	0.000	0.	0.000	0.000	0.000	0.	0.000	0.000	-.008	.032	
2	2	1.000	116.667	35.	68.333	-50.000	-650.000	-550.	-17.778	305.556	-6322.105	3412.391	2790.
		0.000	0.000	0.	0.000	0.000	0.000	0.	0.000	0.000	-.034	0.000	-241.
		0.000	0.000	0.	0.000	0.000	0.000	0.	0.000	.030	.038	-.002	
3	1	-5.000	-94.815	-100.	-70.333	20.000	100.000	75.	5.318	580.247	3515.539	-1895.773	165.
		1.178	3.461	0.	.378	0.000	0.000	0.	0.000	0.000	0.000	-.277	-19.
		0.000	0.000	0.	0.000	0.000	0.000	0.	0.000	.120	-.008	.032	
3	2	1.000	64.815	35.	68.333	-50.000	-650.000	-550.	-20.318	169.753	-3515.539	1895.773	1885.
		0.000	7.777	0.	0.000	0.000	0.000	0.	.005	.115	-.188	0.000	-137.
		0.000	0.000	0.	0.000	0.000	0.000	0.	0.000	0.000	.038	-.002	
4	1	-4.333	-184.938	-100.	-27.881	20.000	100.000	75.	6.431	693.416	2541.748	-3022.749	182.
		1.178	3.461	0.	.378	0.000	0.000	0.	0.000	0.000	0.000	-.277	-34.
		0.000	0.000	0.	0.000	0.000	0.000	0.	0.000	0.000	-.008	.032	
4	2	.333	154.938	35.	25.881	-50.000	-650.000	-550.	-21.431	56.584	-2541.748	3022.749	1673.
		0.000	0.000	0.	0.000	.241	.683	0.	0.000	.048	-.627	0.000	-103.
		0.000	0.000	0.	0.000	0.000	0.000	0.	0.000	0.000	.038	-.002	

Common resources (k=1,...,11)

i	r	k1	k2	k3	k4	k5	k6	k7	k8	k9	k10	k11	ω_{jr}
5	1	-4.235	-186.365	-100.	-21.667	14.074	70.370	75.	6.431	710.181	3000.500	-3053.268	188.
		1.178	3.461	0.	.378	0.000	0.000	0.	0.000	-.000	0.000	-.277	-36.
		0.000	0.000	0.	0.000	0.000	0.000	0.	0.000	.120	-.008	.032	
5	2	.235	156.365	35.	19.667	-44.074	-620.370	-550.	-21.431	39.819	-3000.500	3053.268	1966.
		325.833	0.000	0.	0.000	0.000	0.000	0.	0.000	.135	-.233	0.000	-120.
		0.000	0.000	0.	0.000	0.000	0.000	0.	0.000	0.000	.038	-.002	
6	1	-5.760	-189.754	-100.	-6.908	14.074	70.370	75.	6.431	750.000	4090.035	-3133.789	202.
		1.178	3.461	0.	.378	0.000	0.000	0.	0.000	.000	0.000	-.277	-43.
		0.000	0.000	0.	0.000	0.000	0.000	0.	0.000	.120	-.008	.032	
6	2	1.760	159.754	35.	4.908	-44.074	-620.370	-550.	-21.431	0.000	-4090.035	3133.789	2108.
		0.000	0.000	0.	207.411	0.000	0.000	0.	3.266	.133	-.214	0.000	-162.
		0.000	0.000	0.	0.000	0.000	0.000	0.	0.000	0.000	.038	-.002	
7	1	-5.760	-189.754	-100.	-9.827	14.074	70.370	75.	4.840	750.000	4090.035	-3138.065	202.
		1.178	3.461	0.	.378	0.000	0.000	0.	0.000	.000	0.000	-.277	-43.
		0.000	0.000	0.	0.000	0.000	0.000	0.	0.000	.120	-.008	.032	
7	2	1.760	159.754	35.	7.827	-44.074	-620.370	-550.	-21.840	0.000	-4090.035	3138.065	2182.
		0.000	0.000	0.	21.637	0.000	0.000	0.	0.000	.130	-.233	0.000	-162.
		0.000	0.000	0.	0.000	0.000	0.000	0.	0.000	0.000	.038	-.002	
8	1	-5.760	-189.754	-100.	-34.335	14.074	70.370	75.	6.840	750.000	4090.035	-3173.962	203.
		1.178	3.461	0.	.378	0.000	0.000	0.	0.000	.000	0.000	-.277	-44.
		0.000	0.000	0.	0.000	0.000	0.000	0.	0.000	.120	-.008	.032	
8	2	1.760	159.754	35.	32.335	-44.074	-620.370	-550.	-21.840	0.000	-4090.035	3173.962	2417.
		0.000	0.000	0.	0.000	0.000	0.000	0.	0.000	.135	-.233	0.000	-162.
		0.000	0.000	0.	0.000	0.000	0.000	0.	0.000	0.000	.038	-.002	

i	r	Common resources (k=1,....11)											ω_{jr}
9	1	-4.855	-160.455	-100.	-20.695	14.074	70.370	75.	6.840	750.000	5571.662	-2756.807	195.
		1.178	3.461	0.	.378	0.000	0.000	0.	0.000	-.000	0.000	-.277	-43.
		0.000	0.000	0.	0.000	0.000	0.000	0.	0.000	.120	-.008	.032	
9	2	.855	130.455	35.	18.695	-44.074	-620.370	-550.	-21.840	0.000	-5571.662	2756.807	2759.
		4.415	7.672	0.	0.000	0.000	0.000	0.	0.000	.116	-.189	0.000	-217.
		0.000	0.000	0.	0.000	0.000	0.000	0.	0.000	.000	.038	-.002	
10	1	-5.674	-160.455	-100.	-20.695	14.074	70.370	75.	6.840	750.000	5571.662	-2760.549	195.
		1.178	3.461	0.	.378	0.000	0.000	0.	0.000	-.000	0.000	-.277	-43.
		0.000	0.000	0.	0.000	0.000	0.000	0.	0.000	.120	-.008	.032	
10	2	1.674	130.455	35.	18.695	-44.074	-620.370	-550.	-21.840	0.000	-5571.662	2760.549	2759.
		0.000	7.672	0.	0.000	0.000	0.000	0.	0.000	.116	-.189	0.000	-217.
		0.000	0.000	0.	0.000	0.000	0.000	0.	0.000	.000	.038	-.002	
11	1	-4.855	-160.927	-100.	-20.695	14.074	70.370	75.	6.840	750.000	5571.662	-2763.138	195.
		1.178	3.461	0.	.378	0.000	0.000	0.	0.000	-.000	0.000	-.277	-43.
		0.000	0.000	0.	0.000	0.000	0.000	0.	0.000	.120	-.008	.032	
11	2	.855	130.927	35.	18.695	-44.074	-620.370	-550.	-21.840	0.000	-5571.662	2763.138	2762.
		0.000	7.672	0.	0.000	0.000	0.000	0.	0.000	.116	-.189	0.000	-217.
		0.000	0.000	0.	0.000	0.000	0.000	0.	0.000	.000	.038	-.002	

Table 13.5   Iterations of the multiobjective multilevel algorithm. For every iteration i and region r the distribution of resources $\underline{a}_r^i$ has been given, followed by the corresponding matrix Π_r^i of dual variables with respect to the objectives j=1,2. In the last column, the outcomes for the objectives ω_{1r} and ω_{2r} have been presented for each iteration i and region r.

and conflicts between divergent objectives are taken into consideration.

It is important to note several limitations of the multilevel multiobjective planning method developed in this chapter.

1. It has only been formulated for linear models.

2. It only deals with static models.

3. It does not contain checks to prevent the regions from reporting misleading information.

Further research is necessary to investigate whether it is possible to come to meet these criticisms. The prospects for such a research are not unfavourable (cf. Weitzman [1970] for the first point and Nijkamp and Rietveld [1979b] for the third point).

We conclude that, although not all aspects of the multilevel multiobjective planning method have been fully developed, it is a valuable contribution to planning in hierarchical systems, since it provides a consistent communication network between the the actors in the system.

Footnotes

1.   See Ten Kate [1972b] for a more precise statement of the optimality conditions of the direct and indirect methods.

2.   Note that (13.10) does not include non-negativity constraints on the a_{kr}.

3.   See for a related statement of this problem Leibenstein [1976], Chapter 8.

4.   Since it is our aim to illustrate the multilevel planning method implied by (13.12) for a large number of common constraints, we will use the first decomposition.

5.   For ease of presentation we multiply ω_{21} and ω_{22} with a factor -1, so that min! ω_{2r} can be replaced by max! ω_{2r}.

6.   Note that for $i=1$, this procedure cannot be used, since at the start of it there is no information on the productivities π_{jkr}^i. Therefore, the distribution of resources $\underline{a}_r^1$ has to be determined in another way, for example by basing it on distributions in preceding periods.

APPENDIX 13.I

DATA OF THE INTERREGIONAL MODEL

The interregional model employed in this chapter is based on Mastenbroek and Nijkamp [1977].

The following units of measurement have been used:

$\underline{y}_r, \underline{i}_r, \overline{K}_r, v_r$: units of 10^7 Dfl.

e_r, m_r : units of 10^3 tons SO_2

L_r : units of 10^4 persons.

The values of the coefficients are:

$$A_{11} = \begin{pmatrix} .072 & .006 & .000 & .000 \\ .011 & .173 & .075 & .063 \\ .040 & .036 & .088 & .037 \\ .002 & .003 & .044 & .025 \end{pmatrix}$$

$$A_{12} = \begin{pmatrix} .018 & .004 & .000 & .000 \\ .053 & .003 & .010 & .015 \\ .007 & .016 & .004 & .005 \\ .000 & .000 & .007 & .004 \end{pmatrix}$$

$$A_{21} = \begin{pmatrix} .001 & .000 & .000 & .000 \\ .047 & .007 & .010 & .052 \\ .003 & .001 & .002 & .009 \\ .000 & .000 & .001 & .017 \end{pmatrix}$$

$$A_{22} = \begin{pmatrix} .102 & .073 & .002 & .001 \\ .290 & .283 & .125 & .138 \\ .039 & .051 & .053 & .049 \\ .003 & .007 & .085 & .037 \end{pmatrix}$$

305

$-\underline{a}_1$ = (4 30 65 2 30 550 475 15)'

$\underline{s}$ = (.40 .31 .28 .17)'

$\hat{s}\overline{\underline{K}}_1$ = (15 875 325 140)'

$\hat{s}\overline{\underline{K}}_2$ = (850 5600 1700 360)'

$\underline{L}_1$ = (.078 .026 .050 .062)'

$\underline{L}_2$ = (.065 .034 .074 .072)'

$\underline{d}_1$ = (30.4 55.3 4.4 12.1)'

$\underline{d}_2$ = (17.5 24.0 4.2 13.9)'

$\underline{c}_1$ = (.63 .21 .52 .52)'

$\underline{c}_2$ = (.53 .28 .53 .53)'

$(a_2 \; b_{21} \; b_{22})$ = (750 100 360)

$(h_{11} \; h_{12} \; h_{21} \; h_{22})$ = (.80 .20 .05 .95)

$(f_1 \; f_2 \; k_1 \; k_2)$ = (15 15 .08 .02)

CHAPTER 14

CONCLUSION

The concluding chapter of this study need not be very long, since in several preceding chapters conclusions concerning the central research questions have already been drawn.

The first research question pertains to the criteria to be met by MOD methods. In Part A these criteria have been formulated from the viewpoint of various disciplines. The contribution of planning theory (Chapter 2) has been focused on the co-operation between planners and policy-makers. This co-operation is in continuous danger of failure and therefore a set of criteria has been formulated for MOD methods so that these methods can be employed to achieve a successful co-operation.

The main contribution of psychology (Chapter 3) to the first research question concerns the capability of people in dealing with complex problems. The perceptive and evaluative capacities of people are clearly limited; therefore search and learning form important ingredients of human problem-solving approaches. Consequently, it is an important criterion for MOD methods that they are linked up with these problem-solving approaches.

An important contribution of economics (Chapter 4) to the theory of decision-making is the development of utility concept to represent preferences of several kinds. A criterion stated for MOD methods is that utility should be measured on an appropriate (and not on a too specific) scale. Another criterion is that utility should be formulated such that it leaves room for incomplete preference relations, which means that incomparable alternatives may occur.

In Chapter 5 a number of methodological rules have been formulated for scientific research in order to yield reliable data for MOD methods. Furthermore, certain notions have been derived from philosophy with regard to decision-making in complex situations, i.e. that a scientification of decision-making and an absolutization of only one objective in decision-making should be avoided.

In Chapters 6-9 a survey of MOD methods has been presented. Given the results in Part A, the following two aspects of MOD methods have received special attention:

- MOD methods have been presented as a means of communication between analyst and DM;

- MOD methods enable the analyst to generate digestible amounts of information about decision problems which provide the DM with insight into the structure of these problems.

We conclude from Chapters 6-9 that MOD methods are a promising tool to bridge the gap between the different worlds of policy-makers and planners. MOD methods imply an orientation of sophisticated algorithms developed by scientists towards trial-and-error recipes employed by policy-makers.

In Chapter 10 a classification and evaluation of the MOD methods has been performed (cf. research question 2). We traced five dimensions according to which the methods display considerable variation:

- the number of feasible solutions of the decision problem;

- the scale of measurement of the data;

- the availability of information about priorities;

- the way in which preferences are modelled;

- the number of alternatives to be presented to the DM in the final selection.

There are also some dimensions according to which MOD methods are (still) relatively underdeveloped:

- the uncertainty about data;

- the number of DMs.

The evaluation of the methods has a provisional character since many methods have neither been fully developed nor applied in practice. We conclude that a majority of the methods satisfy the consistency requirements formulated in Chapter 10. Concerning the value of the information produced by the methods, we observe a clear, positive relationship with the precision and extent of the priority information provided by the DM. Consequently we may conclude that when selecting a MOD method, one has to trade-off the pleasure of a valuable output against the pains of providing precise and extensive priority information. The interactive method discussed in Chapter 9 appears to yield a reasonable candidate from these points of view. For more precise conclusions concerning the attractiveness of the methods we refer to Chapter 10.

Part C has been devoted to the application of several MOD methods and concepts to regional planning problems. From Chapter 11 we conclude that these methods form an appropriate tool to analyze commuting patterns according to several types of transportation costs (private costs, damage to the national environment, damage to the urban environment).

In Chapter 12 an interactive MOD method has been applied for the preparation of a policy aiming at a so-called selective industrial growth. For the politician who was involved in the

interaction, the method was manageable. From this application
we learn several lessons:

  - one should be very careful when distinguishing a variable
    as an objective or an instrument;

  - the objectives should be measured in such a way that they
    are comprehensible to the decision-maker;

  - the DM should have the opportunity to revise priority state-
    ments expressed earlier in light of new information obtained
    during the decision process.

Chapter 13 is especially attractive from the viewpoint of the
underdeveloped dimensions in MOD methods traced in Chapter 10.
The chapter provides an analytical framework for an integrated
regional policy in the situation of several regions aiming at
conflicting objectives. These regions have to be co-ordinated
by a central policy-unit which suffers from lack of information
on the regional problems. MOD methods appear useful for the
design of a communication network to reach acceptable outcomes.

In the introduction to Part C it has been noted that MOD
methods are potentially applicable to a wide range of planning
fields besides regional planning, while these methods may also
play a useful role in the development of new theories concerning human choice and new statistical methods. This wide scope
of MOD methods is an important argument for further developments and applications of these methods.

What are the prospects of MOD methods? A tendency can be
observed in research to overrate the possibilities of new methods, while the disadvantages are underrated. This danger is
also present with MOD methods. It is important to realize,
therefore, that MOD methods do not form a magical formula to
solve decision problems. Also with MOD methods, decision-making
in complex situations remains a difficult and sometimes painful
activity. It is the value of MOD methods, however, that they
may enlighten the tasks of the participants in the decision process and that they provide operational tools for a fruitful co-
operation between the participants. Given the expectation that
the complexity of, and the interrelationships between the problems we are facing will increase, MOD methods have a good per-
spective, so that one may expect that these methods will increasingly form part of the standard equipment for solving decision problems.

REFERENCES

Abele, H., From One-Dimensional to Multidimensional Economics:
   "Paradigm" Lost, *Zeitschrift für Nationalökonomie*, vol.31.
   1971, pp.45-62.
Admiraal, P.H., *Besluitvorming in het Consumptieproces*, Sten-
   fert Kroese, Leiden, 1976.
Allen, R.G.D., *Mathematical Economics*, MacMillan, London, 1960.
Apostol, T.M., *Mathematical Analysis*, Addison-Wesley, Reading,
   1971.
Arrow, K.J., *Social Choice and Individual Values*, Wiley, New
   York, 1951.
Aumann, R.J., Subjective Programming , in M.W. Shelley and
   G.L. Bryan (eds.), *Human Judgment and Optimality*, Wiley,
   New York, 1964, pp.217-242.
Awerbuch, S. and W.A. Wallace, *Policy Evaluation for Community
   Development*, Praeger, New York, 1976.
Barr, B. and K. Smillie, Some Spatial Interpretations of Alter-
   native Optimal and Sub-Optimal Solutions to the Transporta-
   tion Problem, *Canadian Geographer*, vol.16, 1972, pp.356-364.
Bator, F., The Simple Analytics of Welfare Economics, *The Amer-
   ican Economic Review*, vol.47, 1957, pp.22-59.
Baumol, W.J. and T. Fabian, Decomposition, Pricing for Decen-
   tralization and External Economies, *Management Science*, vol.
   11, 1964, pp.1-32.
Beckenbach, E. and R. Bellman, *An Introduction to Inequalities*,
   Random House, New York, 1961.
Beckman, N., The Planner as a Bureaucrat, *Journal of the Amer-
   ican Institute of Planners*, vol.30, 1964, pp.323-327.
Belenson, S.M. and K.C. Kapur, An Algorithm for Solving Multi-
   criterion Linear Programming Problems with Examples, *Opera-
   tional Research Quarterly*, vol.24, 1973, pp.65-77.
Benayoun, R., B. Roy and N. Sussman, Manual de Réference du
   Programme Electre, Note de Synthèse et Formation, No.25,
   Direction Scientifique SEMA, Paris, 1966.
Benayoun, R., J. Tergny and D. Keuneman, Mathematical Program-
   ming with Multi-Objective Functions: A Solution by P.O.P.,
   Metra, vol.9, 1970, pp.279-299.
Benayoun, R. , O.I. Larichev, J. de Montgolfier and J. Tergny,
   Mathematical Programming with Multi-Objective Functions: a
   Solution by P.O.P., *Metra*, vol.9, 1971, pp.279-299.
Bergson, A., A Reformulation of Certain Aspects of Welfare Eco-
   nomics, *Quarterly Journal of Economics*, vol.52, 1938, pp.
   310-334.
Bernard, G. and M.L. Besson, Douze Méthodes d'Analyse Multicri-
   tère, *Revue Francaise d'Informatique et de Recherche Opéra-
   tionnelle*, vol.5, 1971, pp.19-66.

Bernouilli, D., Specimen Theoriae Novae de Mensura Sortis, *Commentarii Scientiarum Imperialis Petropolitanae*, 1738, translated by L. Sommer, Exposition of a New Theory on the Measurement of Risk, *Econometrica*, vol.22, 1954, pp.23-36.

Bertier, P. and J. Bouroche, *Analyse des Données Multi-Dimensionelles*, Presses Universitaires de France, Paris, 1975.

Black, D., *The Theory of Committees and Elections*, Cambridge University Press, Cambridge, 1971.

Blair, P.D., *Multiobjective Regional Energy Planning*, Martinus Nijhoff, Boston, 1979.

Blin, J.M., Fuzzy Sets in Multiple Criteria Decision Making, in M.K. Starr and M. Zeleny (eds.), *Multiple Criteria Decision Making*, North-Holland, Amsterdam, 1977. pp.129-146.

Blommestein, H.J., P. Nijkamp and P. Rietveld, A Multivariate Analysis of Spatial Inequalities, in W. Buhr and P. Friedrich (eds.), *Regional Development under Stagnation*, Nomos, Baden-Baden, 1980.

Bowman, V.J., On the Relationship of the Tchebycheff Norm and the Efficient Frontier of Multiple-Criteria Objectives, in H. Thiriez and S. Zionts (eds.), *Multiple Criteria Decision Making, Jony en Josas, 1975*, Springer, Berlin, 1976, pp.76-86.

Boyce, D.E., Planning in Regional Science, *Papers of the Regional Science Association*, vol.34, 1975, pp.187-189.

Boyce, D.E., A.Farhi and R. Weischedel, *Optimal Subset Selection, Multiple Regression, Interdependence and Optimal Network Algorithms*, Springer, Berlin, 1974.

Bruner, J.S., T.J. Goodnow and G.A. Austin, *A Study of Thinking*, Wiley, New York, 1956.

Buit, J., Over de Betekenis van Doelstellingenformulering in de Planologie; Een Inventarisatie van Argumenties, *Stedebouw en Volkshuisvesting*, vol.58, 1977, pp.91-106.

Charnes, A. and W.W. Cooper, *Management Models and Industrial Application of Linear Programming*, Wiley, New York, 1961.

Charnes, A., W.W. Cooper, D. Klingman and R.J. Niehaus, Explicit Solutions in Convex Goal Programming, *Management Science*, vol.22, 1975, pp.438-448.

Charnetski, J.R., Multiple Criteria Decisionmaking with Partial Information: A Site Selection Problem, in M. Chatterji (ed.), *Space Location and Regional Development*, Pion, London, 1976, pp.51-62.

Coats, A.W., Economics and Psychology: the Death and Resurrection of a Research Programme, in S.J. Latsis (ed.), *Method and Appraisal in Economics*, Cambridge University Press, Cambridge, 1976, pp.43-64.

Cohon, J.L., *Multiobjective Programming and Planning*, Academic Press, New York, 1978.

Cohon, J.L. and D.H. Marks, Multiobjective Screening Models and Water Resource Investment, *Water Resource Research*, vol.9, 1973, pp.826-836.

Cohon, J.L. and D.H. Marks, A Review and Evaluation of Multiobjective Programming Techniques, *Water Resources Research*, vol.11, 1975, pp.208-220.

Czamanski, S., *Regional Science Techniques in Practice: The Case of Nova Scotia*, Heath, Lexington, 1972.

Dantzig, G., *Linear Programming and Extensions*, Princeton

University Press, Princeton, 1963.

Dantzig, G. and P. Wolfe, The Decomposition Principle for Linear Programming, *Operations Research Quarterly*, vol.8, 1960, pp.101-111.

Dauer, J.P., Energy and Resource Modelling with Multiple Objectives, Department of Mathematics and Statistics, University of Nebraska-Lincoln, Lincoln, 1978.

Davidoff, P., Advocacy and Pluralism in Society, *Journal of the American Institute of Planners*, vol.31, 1965, pp.331-338.

Davidoff, P., and T. Reiner, A Choice Theory of Planning, *Journal of the American Institute of Planners*, vol.28, 1962, pp. 103-115.

Dawes, R.M., The Robust Beauty of Improper Linear Models in Decision Making, *American Psychologist*, 1980, forthcoming.

Day, R.H. and S.M. Robinson, Economic Decisions with L** Utility, in J.L. Cochrane and M. Zeleny (eds.), *Multiple Criteria Decision Making*, University of South Carolina Press, Columbia, 1973, pp.84-91.

Debreu, G., *Theory of Value*, Wiley, New York, 1959.

Delft, A. van, and P. Nijkamp, *Multicriteria Analysis and Regional Decision-Making*, Martinus Nijhoff, The Hague/Boston, 1977.

Donckels, R., Regional Multi-Objective Planning, Regional Science Research Paper 8, University of Louvain, Louvain, 1975.

Dooyeweerd, H., *A New Critique of Theoretical Thought*, 4 vols., Presbyterian and Reformed Publishing Company, Philadelphia, 1953-1958.

Dror, Y., The Planning Process, A Facet Design, *International Review of Administrative Sciences*, vol.29, 1963, pp.46-58.

Duckstein, L. and L. David, Multi-Criterion Ranking of Alternative Long Range Water Resource Systems, Paper presented at the Annual Meeting of the Operations Research Society of America, Las Vegas, 1975.

Eckenrode, R.T., Weighting Multiple Criteria, *Management Science*, vol.12, 1965, pp.180-192.

Edgeworth, F.Y., The Pure Theory of Taxation, *Economic Journal*, vol.7, 1897, pp.550-571.

Eijk, C.J. van, and J. Sandee, Quantitative Determination of an Optimum Economic Policy, *Econometrica*, vol.27, 1959, pp.1-13.

Einhorn, H.J., The Use of Nonlinear Noncompensatory Models in Decision Making, *Psychological Bulletin*, vol.73, 1970. pp. 221-230.

Evans, J.P. and R.E. Steuer, Generating Efficient Extreme Points in Linear Multiple Objective Programming: Two Algorithms and Computing Experience, in J.L. Cochrane, and M. Zeleny (eds.), *Multiple Criteria Decision Making*, University of South Carolina Press, Colimbia, 1973, pp.349-365.

Faludi, A., *Planning Theory*, Permagom Press, Oxford, 1973.

Fandel, G., *Optimale Entscheidung bei Mehrfacher Zielsetzung* Springer, Berlin, 1972.

Fandel, G. and J. Wilhelm, Zur Entscheidungstheorie bei Mehrfacher Zielsetzung, *Zeitschrift für Operations Research*, vol.20, 1976, pp.1-21.

Fano, P.L., Evaluating Alternative Plan Configurations: a Cost Effectiveness Approach, *Papers of the Regional Science Asso-*

ciation, vol.31, 1973, pp.161-172.

Farquhar, P.H., A Survey of Multiattribute Utility Theory and Applications, in M.K. Starr and M. Zeleny (eds.), *Multiple Criteria Decision Making*, North-Holland, Amsterdam, 1977, pp.59-89.

Festinger, L., *A Theory of Cognitive Dissonance*, Stanford University Press, Stanford, 1957.

Fishburn, P.C., Methods of Estimating Additive Utilities, *Management Science*, vol.13, 1967, pp.435-453.

Fishburn, P.C., Lexicographic Orders, Utilities and Decision Rules: A Survey, *Management Science*, vol.20, 1974, pp.1442-1471.

Fichefet, J., GPSTEM, an Interactive Multi-Objective Optimization Method, in A. Prékopa (ed.), *Progress in O.R., vol.1*, North-Holland, Amsterdam, pp.317-332.

Fisher, M.M., Regional Taxonomy: A Comparison of some Hierarchic and Non-Hierarchic Strategies, Paper presented at the Regional Conference of the International Geographical Union, Lagos, 1978.

Forcese, D.P. and S. Richer, *Social Research Methods*, Prentice Hall, Englewood Cliffs, 1973.

Forrester, J.W., *Urban Dynamics*, MIT Press, Cambridge, 1969.

Forrester, J.W., *World Dynamics*, Wright-Allen Press, Cambridge, 1971.

Frank, M. and P. Wolfe, An Algorithm for Quadratic Programming, *Naval Research Logistics Quarterly*, vol.3, 1956, pp.95-110.

Frisch, R., Co-operation between Politicians and Econometricians on the Formalization of Political Preferences, *Economic Planning Studies*, Reidel, Dordrecht, 1976, pp.41-86.

Friedman, M., *Essays in Positive Economics*, University of Chicago Press, Chicago, 1963.

Friedmann, J. and G. Abonyi, Social Learning: A Model for Policy Research, *Environment and Planning*, vol.8, 1976, pp.927-940.

Friend, J. and N. Jessop, *Local Government and Strategic Choice*, Tavistock, London, 1969.

Friend, J., J. Power and C. Yewlett, *Public Planning, The Inter-Corporate Dimension*, Tavistock, London, 1974.

Gal, T., A General Method for Determining the Set of all Efficient Solutions to a Linear Vectormaximum Problem, Arbeitsbericht 76/12, Institut für Wirtschaftswissenschaften, Aachen, 1976.

Galloway, Th. D. and R.G. Mahayni, Planning Theory in Retrospect: The Process of Paradigm Change, *Journal of the American Institute of Planners*, vol.43, 1977, pp.62-71.

Geoffrion, A.M., Proper Efficiency and the Theory of Vector Maximization, *Journal of Mathematical Analysis and Applications*, vol.22, 1968, pp.618-630.

Geoffrion, A.M., J.S. Dyer and J.S. Feinberg, An Interactive Approach for Multicriteria Optimization, with an Application to the Operation of an Academic Department, *Management Science*, vol.19, 1972, pp.357-368.

Georgescu-Roegen, N., Choice, Expectations and Measurability, *Quarterly Journal of Economics*, vol.68, 1954, pp.503-534.

Gillingwater, D., *Regional Planning and Social Change*, Saxon House, Westmead, 1975.

Gillingwater, D., Regional Planning: Policy, Control or Commu-
    nication?. Paper presented at the Tenth Annual Conference
    of the British Section of the Regional Science Association,
    London, 1977.
Gomory, R.E. and W.J. Baumol, Integer Programming and Pricing,
    Econometrica, vol.28, 1960, pp.521-550.
Grover, R.A., The Ranking Assumption, *Theory and Decision*, vol.
    4, 1974, pp.277-299.
Guigou, J.L., *Analyse des Données et Choix à Critères Multiples*,
    Dunod, Paris, 1974.
Gum, R.L., Th. G. Roefs and D.B. Kimball, Quantifying Societal
    Goals: Development of a Weighting Methodology, *Water Re-
    sources Research*, vol.12, 1976, pp.617-622.
Haan, R.L., *Economie in Principe en Praktijk*, Haan, Groningen,
    1975.
Haimes, Y.Y, and W.A. Hall, Multiobjectives in Water Resources
    Systems Analysis: the Surrogate Worth Trade-Off Method,
    Water Resources Research, vol.10, 1974, pp.615-624.
Haimes, Y.Y., W.A. Hall and H.T. Freedman, *Multi-Objective
    Optimization in Water Resource Systems*, Elsevier, Amsterdam,
    1975.
Hall, W.A. and Y.Y. Haimes, The Surrogate Worth Trade-Off Meth-
    od with Multiple Decision-Makers, in M. Zeleny (ed.),
    Multiple Criteria Decision Making, Kyoto, 1975, Springer,
    Berlin, 1976, pp.207-233.
Hansen, F., *Consumer Choice Behavior, A Cognitive Theory*, The
    Free Press, New York, 1972.
Hartigan, J.A., *Clustering Algorithms*, Wiley, New York, 1975.
Harvey, D., *Explanation in Geography*, Arnold, London, 1969.
Hills, G.A., A Philosophical Approach to Landscape Planning,
    Landscape Planning, vol.1, 1974, pp.339-371.
Hogg, R.V. and A.T. Craig, *Introduction to Mathematical Statis-
    tics*, MacMillan, London, 1970.
Hollnagel, E., Cognitive Functions in Decision Making, in H.
    Jungermann and G. de Zeeuw (eds.), *Decision Making and
    Change in Human Affairs*, Reidel, Dordrecht, 1977, pp.431-
    444.
Holmes, J.C., An Ordinal Method of Evaluation, *Urban Studies*,
    vol.9, 1971, pp.179-191.
Huang, S.C., Note on the Mean Square Strategy for Vector Objec-
    tive Functions, *Journal of Optimization Theory and Appli-
    cations*, vol.9, 1972, pp.364-366.
Huber, G.P., Multi-Attribute Utility Models: a Review of Field
    and Field-Like Studies, *Management Science*, vol.20, 1974,
    pp.1393-1402.
Hwang, C.L. and A.S.M. Masud, *Multiple Objective Decision
    Making - Methods and Applications*, Springer, Berlin, 1979.
Ijiri, Y., *Management Goals and Accounting for Control*, North-
    Holland, Amsterdam, 1965.
Isermann, H., Lösungsansätze zum Entscheidungsproblem des Satis-
    fizieres bei Mehrfacher Zielsetzung, in P. Gessner, R.
    Hein, V. Steinecke and H. Todt (eds.), *Proceedings in Oper-
    ations Research*, vol.3, Physica Verlag, Würzburg, 1974, pp.
    64-74.
Isermann, H., The Relevance of Duality in Multiple Objective
    Linear Programming, in M.K. Starr and M. Zeleny (eds.),

Multiple Criteria Decision Making, North-Holland, Amsterdam, 1977, pp.241-262.

Johansen, L., _Lectures on Macroeconomic Planning_ (ch.2), North-
Holland, Amsterdam, 1978.

Johnsen, E., _Studies in Multi-Objective Decision Models_, Mono-
graph No.1, Economic Research Center in Lund, Lund, Sweden,
1968.

Johnston, J., _Econometric Methods_, McGraw-Hill, Tokyo, 1972.

Jong, F.J. de, _Dimensional Analysis for Economists_, North-
Holland, Amsterdam, 1967.

Kalsbeek, L., _Contours of a Christian Philosophy_, Wedge Publishing Foundation, Toronto, 1975.

Kapteyn, A., _A Theory of Preference Formation_, Pasmans, The
Hague, 1977.

Karlin, S., _Mathematical Methods and Theory in Games, Programming and Economics_, Addison Wesley, Reading, 1959.

Kate, A. ten, Decomposition of Linear Programs by Direct Distribution, _Econometrica_, vol.40, 1972a, pp.883-898.

Kate, A. ten, A Comparison between Two Kinds of Decentralized
Optimality Conditions in Nonconvex Programming, _Management
Science_, vol.18, 1972b, pp.734-743.

Katona, G., _Psychological Analysis of Economic Behavior_,
McGraw-Hill, New York, 1951.

Katona, G., _The Powerful Consumer_, McGraw-Hill, New York, 1960.

Keen, P.G.W., The Evolving Concept of Optimality, in M.K. Starr
and M. Zeleny (eds.), _Multiple Criteria Decision Making_,
North-Holland, Amsterdam, 1977, pp.31-57.

Keeney, R.L., Multiattribute Utility Analysis: A Brief Survey,
Research Memorandum 75-13, International Institute for
Applied Systems Analysis, Laxenburg, 1975.

Kendall, M.G., _Rank Correlation Methods_, Hafner Publishing
Company, New York, 1955.

Keuning, D., _Algemene Systeemtheorie, Systeembenadering en
Organisatietheorie_, Stenfert Kroese, Leiden, 1973.

Kockelhorn, U., How to Order Three Hypotheses According to
their Plausibility, Paper presented at the Third Conference
on Multiple Criteria Decision Making, Köningswinter, 1979.

Koopmans, T.C., Analysis of Production as an Efficient Combi-
nation of Activities, in T.C. Koopmans (ed.), _Activity
Analysis of Production and Allocation_, Yale University
Press, New Haven, 1951, pp.33-97.

Kooy, T.P. van der, De Wetenschap der Economie en de Doelstel-
ling der Universiteit, Diskussienota Onderzoek 1978-8,
Department of Economics, Free University, Amsterdam, 1978.

Kornai, J., _Mathematical Planning of Structural Decisions_,
North-Holland, Amsterdam, 1965.

Kornai, J., A General Descriptive Model of Planning Processes,
Economics of Planning, vol.10, 1970, pp.1-19.

Kornai, J., _Anti-Equilibrium_, North-Holland, Amsterdam, 1971.

Kornbluth, J.S.H., Duality, Indifference and Sensitivity Analysis in Multiple Objective Linear Programming, _Operations
Research Quarterly_, vol.25, 1974, pp.599-614.

Krech, D., R.S. Crutchfield and N. Livson, _Elements of Psycho-
logy_, Knopf, New York, 1974.

Kuhn, H.W. and A.W. Tucker, Non-Linear Programming, in _Proceed-
ings of the Second Berkeley Symposium on Mathematical Sta-_

tistics and Probability, J. Neyman (ed.), University of California Press, Berkeley, 1951, pp.481-493.

Lancaster, K., *Consumer Demand, a New Approach*, Columbia University Press, New York, 1971.

Landry, M., and J.L. Malouin, An Epistemological Comparison of the Scientific Method and the Systems Approach, Research Memorandum, Université Laval, Quebec, 1977.

Lee, S.M., *Goal Programming for Decision Analysis*, Auerbach, Philadelphia, 1972.

Leibenstein, H., *Beyond Economic Man*, Harvard University Press, Cambridge, 1976.

Leinbach, T.R., Transportation Geography, Networks and Flows, *Progress in Geography*, vol.8, 1976, pp.177-207.

Lewin, K., *Principles of Topological Psychology*, McGraw-Hill, New York, 1936.

Lewin, K., T. Dembo, L. Festinger and P.S. Sears, Level of Aspirations, in J. Mc. V. Hunt (ed.), *Personality and the Behavior Disorders*, Ronald Press, New York, 1944, pp.333-378.

Lichfield, N., P. Kettle and M. Whitbread, *Evaluation in the Planning Process*, Pergamon Press, Oxford, 1975.

Lindblom, C., *The Intelligence of Democracy: Decision Making through Mutual Adjustment*, Free Press, New York, 1965.

Lohuizen, C.W.W. van, Mobiliteitsonderzoek in Nederland, in P. Nijkamp and P. Rietveld (eds.), *Het Stuur uit Handen?* Stenfert Kroese, Leiden, 1979, pp.227-259.

Loon, P.J.J.M. van, Beslissingsmethoden bij Meer Doelstellingen, *Maandschrift Economie*, vol.39, 1975, pp.383-416.

Luce, R.D. and H. Raiffa, *Games and Decisions*, Wiley, New York, 1957.

MacCrimmon, K.R., An Overview of Multiple Objective Decision Making, in J.L. Cochrane and M. Zeleny (eds.), *Multiple Criteria Decision Making*, University of South Carolina Press, Columbia, 1973, pp.18-44.

Malinvaud, E., *Lectures on Microeconomic Theory*, North-Holland, Amsterdam, 1972.

Maslow, A.H., *Motivation and Personality*, Harper and Row, New York, 1954.

Mastenbroek, A.P. and P. Nijkamp, A Spatial Environmental Model for an Optimal Allocation of Investments, in P. Nijkamp (ed.), *Environmental Economics*, vol.2, Martinus Nijhoff, The Hague, 1976, pp.19-38.

Mastenbroek, P. and J. Paelinck, Multiple Criteria Decision Making: Information Exhaustion, Uncertainty and Non-Linearities, Netherlands Economic Institute, Foundations of Empirical Economic Research, no.4, 1976.

May, K.O., Transitivity, Utility and the Aggregation of Preference Patterns, *Econometrica*, vol.22, 1954, pp.1-13.

Meehl, P.E., *Clinical versus Statistical Prediction*, University of Minnesota Press, Minneapolis, 1954.

Memorandum on Urbanization (Verstedelijkingsnota), Staatsuitgeverij, The Hague, 1976.

Memorandum on Regional Socio-Economic Planning 1977-1980, (Nota Regionaal Sociaal-Economisch Beleid 1977-1980), Staatsuitgeverij, The Hague, 1977.

Menger, C., *Gesammelte Werke*, Band I, Mohr, Tübingen, 1968.

Miller, D.L. and D.M. Byers, Development and Display of Multiple Objective Project Impacts, *Water Resources Research*, vol.9, 1973, pp.11-20.

Miller, D.W. and M.K. Starr, *Executive Decisions and Operations Research*, Prentice Hall, Englewood Cliffs, 1960.

Miller, G.A., The Magical Number Seven, Plus or Minus Two: Some Limits on our Capacity for Processing Information, *The Psychological Review*, vol.63, 1956, pp.81-97.

Mishan, E.J., *Cost-Benefit Analysis*, Allen & Unwin, London, 1971.

Mitroff, I.I. and R.O. Mason, On Evaluating the Scientific Contribution of the Apollo Moon Missions via Information Theory: A Study of the Scientist-Scientist Relationship, *Management Science*, vol.20, 1974, pp.1501-1513.

Monarchi, D.E., C.C. Kisiel and L. Duckstein, Interactive Multiobjective Programming in Water Resources, *Water Resources Research*, vol.9, 1973, pp.837-850.

Mueller, D.C., Public Choice: A Survey, *Journal of Economic Literature*, vol.14, 1976, pp.395-433.

Narula, S.C. and J.F. Wellington, Linear Regression Using Multiple-Criteria, Paper presented at the Third Conference on Multiple Criteria Decision Making, Köningswinter, 1979.

Naylor, T.H., *Computer Simulation Experiments with Models of Economic Systems*, Wiley, London, 1971.

Neumann, J. von and O. Morgenstern, *The Theory of Games and Economic Behavior*, Princeton University Press, Princeton, 1944.

Nievergelt, E., Ein Beitrag zur Lösung von Entscheidungsproblemen mit Mehrfacher Zielsetzung, *Die Unternehmung*, vol.25, 1971, pp.101-126.

Nijkamp, P., Determination of Implicit Social Preference Functions, Report 7010, Econometric Institute, Netherlands School of Economics, Rotterdam, 1970.

Nijkamp, P., Operational Determination of Collective Preference Parameters, Research Memorandum 17, Department of Economics, Free University, Amsterdam, 1974.

Nijkamp, P., Reflections on Gravity and Entropy Models, *Regional Science and Urban Economics*, vol.5, 1975, pp.205-255.

Nijkamp, P., *Theory and Application of Environmental Economics*, North-Holland, Amsterdam, 1977.

Nijkamp, P., Competition among Regions and Environmental Quality, in W. Buhr and P. Friedrich (eds.), *Competition among Small Regions*, Nomos Verlag, Baden-Baden, 1978, pp. 153-170.

Nijkamp, P., *Multidimensional Spatial Data and Decision Analysis*, Wiley, New York, 1979.

Nijkamp, P. and P. Rietveld, Multi-Objective Programming Models, New Ways in Regional Decision Making, *Regional Science and Urban Economics*, vol.6, 1976a, pp.253-274.

Nijkamp, P. and P. Rietveld, Properties of Multi-Objective Optimization Models, Research Memorandum 57, Department of Economics, Free University, Amsterdam, 1976b.

Nijkamp, P. and P. Rietveld, Impact Analyses, Spatial Externalities and Policy Choices, Research Memorandum 65, Department of Economics, Free University, Amsterdam, 1977.

Nijkamp, P. and P. Rietveld, Methoden voor de Selectie van
    Economische Activiteiten, *Intermediair*, vol.14 (25), 1978,
    pp.39-47.
Nijkamp, P. and P. Rietveld, Multilevel Multiobjective Models
    in a Multiregional System, Research Memorandum 3, Department
    of Economics, Free University, Amsterdam, 1979a.
Nijkamp, P. and P. Rietveld, Multiobjective Multilevel Policy
    Models, Diskussienota Onderzoek 11, Department of Economics,
    Free University, Amsterdam, 1979b.
Nijkamp, P. and W.H. Somermeyer, Explicating Implicit Social
    Preference Functions, *Economics of Planning*, vol.11, 1971,
    pp.101-119.
Nijkamp, P. and J. Spronk, Goal Programming for Decision Making,
    Report 7709/A, Centrum voor Bedrijfseconomisch Onderzoek,
    Erasmus University, Rotterdam, 1977.
Nijkamp, P. and J. Spronk, Interactive Multiple Goal Program-
    ming, Research Memorandum 3, Department of Economics, Free
    University, Amsterdam, 1978.
Nijkamp, P. and W.H. van Veenendaal, Psychometric Scaling and
    Preference Methods in Spatial Analysis, Research Memorandum
    2, Department of Economics, Free University, Amsterdam,
    1978.
Paelinck, J., Qualitative Multiple Criteria Analysis, Environ-
    mental Protection and Multiregional Development, Netherlands
    Economic Institute, Foundations of Empirical Economic
    Research, No.10, 1975.
Paelinck, J.H. and P. Nijkamp, *Operational Theory and Method
    in Regional Economics*, Saxon House, Farnborough, 1976.
Pearman, A., Approaches to Multiple Objective Decison Making
    with Ranked Criteria, in I.G. Cullen (ed.), *Analysis and
    Decision in Regional Policy*, Pion, London, 1979, pp.136-152.
Pekelman, D. and S.K. Sen, Mathematical Programming Models for
    the Determination of Attribute Weights, *Management Science*,
    vol.20, 1974, pp.1217-1229.
Philip, J., Algorithms for the Vector Maximization Problem,
    Mathematical Programming, vol.1, 1971, pp.239-266.
Piaget, J., *The Origins of Intelligence in Children*, Interna-
    tional Universities Press, New York, 1952, originally pub-
    lished in French, 1936.
Pitz, G.F., Decision Making and Cognition, in H. Jungermann and
    G. de Zeeuw (eds.), *Decision Making and Change in Human
    Affairs*, Reidel, Dordrecht, 1977, pp.403-424.
Polenske, K.R., Regional Methods of Analysis for Stagnating
    Regions, in W. Buhr and P. Friedrich (eds.), *Regional
    Development under Stagnation*, Karlsruhe Papers in Regional
    Science 4, 1980.
Quirk, J. and R. Saposnik, *Introduction to General Equilibrium
    Theory and Welfare Economics*, McGraw-Hill, New York, 1968.
Raiffa, H., *Decision Analysis*, Addison Wesley, Reading, 1968.
Reitman, W.R., Heuristic Decision Procedures, Open Constraints,
    and the Structure of Ill-Defined Problems, in M.W. Shelley
    and G.L. Bryan (eds.), *Human Judgments and Optimality*,
    Wiley, New York, 1964, pp.282-315.
Riessen, H. van, *Wijsbegeerte*, Kok, Kampen, 1970.
Rittel, H.W.J. and M.M. Webber, Dilemmas in a General Theory
    of Planning, *Policy Sciences*, vol.4, 1973, pp.155-169.

Roberts, F.S., What if Utility Functions do not Exist?, *Theory and Decision*, vol.3, 1972, pp.126-139.

Rockafellar, R.T., *Convex Analysis*, Princeton University Press, Princeton, 1970.

Roy, B., Problems and Methods with Multiple Objective Functions, *Mathematical Programming*, vol.1, 1971, pp.239-266.

Roy, B., Décision avec Critères Multiples, *Metra*, vol.11, 1972, pp.121-151.

Roy, B., From Optimization to Multicriteria Decision Aid: Three Main Operational Attitudes, in H. Thiriez and S. Zionts (eds.), *Multiple Criteria Decision Making, Jouy en Josas*, Springer, Berlin, 1976, pp.1-32.

Roy, B., A Conceptual Framework for a Prescriptive Theory of Decision-Aid, in M.K. Starr and M. Zeleny (eds.), *Multiple Criteria Decision Making*, North-Holland, Amsterdam, 1977, pp.179-210.

Roy, B. and E. Jacquet-Lagreze, Concepts and Methods Used in Multicriterion Decision Models: Their Applications to Transportation Problems, in H. Strobel, R. Genser and M.M. Etschmaier (eds.), *Optimization Applied to Transportation Systems*, International Institute for Applied Systems Analysis, Laxenburg, 1977, pp.9-26.

Rudner, R.S., *Philosophy of Social Science*, Prentice Hall, Englewood Cliffs, 1966.

Saaty, T.L., Scaling Method for Priorities in Hierarchical Structures, *Journal of Mathematical Psychology*, vol.15, 1977, pp.234-281.

Salih, K., Goal Conflicts in Pluralistic Multi-Level Planning for Development, *International Regional Science Review*, vol.1, 1975, pp.49-72.

Samuelson, P.A., *The Foundations of Economic Analysis*, Harvard University Press, Cambridge, 1953.

Sandee, J., Optimum Policy Alternatives, in C.A. van Bochove, C.J. van Eijk, J.C. Siebrand, A.S.W. de Vries and A. van der Zwan (eds.), *Modeling for Government and Business*, Martinus Nijhoff, Leiden, 1977, pp.149-163.

Schleicher, S., Decentralized Optimization of Linear Economic Systems with Minimum Information Exchange of the Subsystems, *Zeitschrift für Nationalökonomie*, vol.31, 1971 pp.33-44.

Schuurman, I.E., *Techniek, Middel of Moloch?*, Kok, Kampen, 1977.

Second Memorandum on Physical Planning in The Netherlands (Tweede Nota over de Ruimtelijke Ordening), Staatsuitgeverij, The Hague, 1966.

Sengupta, S.S., M.M. Podrebarac and T.D.H. Fernando, Probabilities of Optima in Multi-Objective Linear Programmes, in J.J. Cochrane and M. Zeleny (eds.), *Multiple Criteria Decision Making*, University of South Carolina Press, Columbia, 1973, pp. 217-235.

Shapiro, J.F., Multiple Criteria Public Investment Decision Making by Mixed Integer Programming, in H. Thiriez and S. Zionts (eds.), *Multiple Criteria Decision Making, Jouy en Josas, 1975*, Springer, Berlin, 1976, pp.170-182.

Shepard, R.N., On Subjectively Optimum Selection among Multi-attribute Alternatives, in M.W. Shelley and G.L. Bryan (eds.), *Human Judgments and Optimality*, Wiley, New York, 1964, pp.257-281.

Simon, H.A., *Models of Man*, Wiley, New York, 1957.

Simon, H.A., From Substantive to Procedural Rationality, in S.J. Latsis (ed.), *Method and Appraisal in Economics*, Cambridge University Press, Cambridge, 1976, pp.129-148.

Sinden, J.A. and A.C. Worrell, *Unpriced Values*, Wiley, New York, 1979.

Skull, F.A., A.L. Delbecq and L.L. Cunnings, *Organizational Decision Making*, McGraw-Hill, New York, 1970.

Smit, J.G., De Betrouwbaarheid van Verkeerskundige Prognoses, Paper presented at the Colloquium Vervoersplanologisch Speurwerk, The Hague, 1979.

Somermeyer, W.H., Specificatie van Economische Relaties, *De Economist*, 115, 1967, pp.305-327.

Spier, J.M., *An Introduction to Christian Philosophy*, Craig Press, Nutley, New Jersey, 1966.

Starr, M.K. and M. Zeleny, MCDM - State and Future of the Arts, in M.K. Starr and M. Zeleny (eds.), *Multiple Criteria Decision Making*, North-Holland, Amsterdam, 1977, pp.5-29.

Steiss, A., *Public Budgetting and Management*, Lexington Books, Lexington, 1972.

Steuer, R.E., Linear Multiple Objective Programming with Interval Criterion Weights, *Management Science*, vol.23, 1976, pp.305-316.

Steuer, R.E. and A.T. Schuler, An Interactive Multiple-Objective Linear Approach to a Problem in Forest Management, *Operations Research*, vol.26, 1978, pp.254-269.

Stigler, G.J., The Development of Utility Theory, *Journal of Political Economy*, vol.58, pp.307-327, 373-396, 1950.

Stilwell, F.J.B., *Regional Economic Policy*, MacMillan, London, 1972.

Supplementary Scheme for Electricity Supply (Aanvullend Structuurschema Electriciteits Voorziening), Staatsuitgeverij, The Hague, 1977.

Takayama, A., *Mathematical Economics*, Dryden Press, Hinsdale, 1974.

Tarascio, V.J., *Pareto's Methodological Approach to Economics*, The University of North Carolina Press, Chapel Hill, 1968.

Theil, H., *Optimal Decision Rules for Government and Industry*, North-Holland, Amsterdam, 1964.

Theil, H., *Economics and Information Theory*, North-Holland, Amsterdam, 1967.

Tinbergen, J., *Economic Policy, Principles and Design*, North-Holland, Amsterdam, 1956.

Togsverd, T., Multi-Level Planning in the Public Sector, in H. Thiriez and S. Zionts (eds.), *Multiple Criteria Decision Making, Jouy en Josas, 1975*, Springer, Berlin, 1976, pp.201-212.

Torgerson, W.S., *Theory and Methods of Scaling*, Wiley, New York, 1958.

Tversky, A., Elimination by Aspects: A Theory of Choice, *Psychological Review*, vol.79, 1972, pp.281-299.

Vink, H., Mogelijkheden en Problemen bij de Toepassing van Doelstellingen en de Strategische Keuzebenadering in de Praktijk, *Planning*, vol.3, 1977, pp.2-14.

Voogd, J.H., Methoden en Technieken betreffende Evaluatie, Planologisch Studiecentrum, TNO, Delft, 1976.

Voogd, J.H., On the Principles of Ordinal Geometric Scaling,
    Research Paper 10, Planologisch Studiecentrum, TNO, Delft,
    1978.
Wallenius, J., *Interactive Multiple Criteria Decision Methods*,
    Helsinki School of Economics, Helsinki, 1975.
Walster, E., The Temporal Sequence of Post-Decision Processes,
    in L. Festinger (ed.), *Conflict Decision and Dissonance*,
    Stanford University Press, Stanford, 1964, pp.112-128.
Weitzman, M., Iterative Multilevel Planning with Production
    Targets, *Econometrica*, vol.38, 1970, pp.50-65.
Werczberger, E., Multi-Objective Linear Programming with Ordi-
    nal Ranking of Objective Functions, Working Paper No.50,
    Center for Urban and Regional Studies, Tel Aviv University,
    1978.
Winkels, H.M., Interaktive Lösungsverfahren für Lineare Prob-
    leme mit Mehrfacher Zielsetzung, Arbeitsbericht 7903, Ab-
    teilung für Wirtschaftswissenschaft und Abteilung für Math-
    ematik, Ruhr University, Bochum, 1979a.
Winkels, H.M. Multiparametrische Lösungsansätze für Probleme
    Linearer Vektormaximum-Systeme, Arbeitsbericht 7902, Ab-
    teilung für Wirtschaftswissenschaft und Abteilung für Math-
    ematik, Ruhr University, Bochum, 1979b.
Zellner, A., *An Introduction to Bayesian Inference in Econo-
    metrics*, Wiley, New York, 1971.
Zeleny, M., Compromise Programming, in J.L. Cochrane and M.
    Zeleny (eds.), *Multiple Criteria Decision Making*, University
    of South Carolina Press, Columbia, 1973, pp.262-301.
Zeleny, M., *Linear Multi-Objective Programming*, Springer,
    Berlin, 1974.
Zeleny, M., Multiple Criteria Decision Making Bibliography,
    in M. Zeleny (ed.), *Multiple Criteria Decision Making,
    Kyoto, 1975*, Springer, Berlin, 1976a, pp.292-321.
Zeleny, M., The Theory of Displaced Ideal, in M. Zeleny (ed.),
    Multiple Criteria Decision Making, Kyoto, 1975, Springer,
    Berlin, 1976b, pp.153-206.
Zeleny, M., Games with Multiple Pay-Offs, *International Jour-
    nal of Game Theory*, vol.4, 1976c, pp.179-191.
Zionts, S., *Linear and Integer Programming*, Prentice Hall,
    Englewood Cliffs, 1974.
Zionts, S., Integer Linear Programming with Multiple Objectives,
    Annals of Discrete Mathematics, vol.1, 1977, pp.551-562.
Zionts, S. and Wallenius, J., An Interactive Programming Method
    for Solving the Multiple Criteria Problem, *Management Sci-
    ence*, vol.22, 1976, pp.652-663.

AUTHOR INDEX

Abele, H. 49

Abonyi, G. 21

Admiraal, P.H. 41

Allen, R.G.D. 123

Apostol, T.M. 67,115,198

Arrow, K.J. 50,188,221

Aumann, R.J. 51,60

Austin, G.A. 37

Awerbuch, S. 115

Barr, B. 241

Bator, F. 57

Baumol, W.J. 165,284

Beckenbach, E. 94

Beckman, N. 28

Belenson, S.M. 89,103,125,192

Bellman, R. 94

Benayoun, R. 89,163,192

Bergson, A. 57

Bernard, G. 158,227

Bernouilli, D. 56

Bertier, P. 158

Besson, M.L. 158,227

Black, D. 188,217

Blair, P.D. 142

Blin, J.M. 115,141

Blommestein, H.J. 179

Bouroche, J. 158

Bowman, V.J. 160

Boyce, D.E. 18,178

Bruner, J.S. 37

Buit, J. 35

Byers, D.M. 92,153

Charnes, A. 146,150

Charnetski, J.R. 108

Coats, A.W. 64

Cohon, J.L. 91f,153,227

Cooper, W.W. 146,150

Craig, A.T. 171

Crutchfield, R.S. 40

Cunnings, L.L. 39f

Czamanski, S. 257

Dantzig, G. 284f

Dauer, J.P. 115

David, L. 164

Davidoff, P. 18,28

Dawes, R.M. 45

Day, R.H. 150

Debreu, G. 51f

Delbecq, A.L. 39f

Delft, A. van 58,94,152,158,163,
            172,174,256

Dembo, T. 42

Donckels, R. 150

Dooyeweerd, H. 80

Dror, Y. 17

SUBJECT INDEX

absolutization of objectives
      15,78f,307
activity analysis 62

aspects of reality 77ff

aspiration level 41f,146

Arrow paradox 50,187,221

blueprint planning 22ff,33

bureaucracy 28

clustering algorithm 180,
              266ff

coalition formation 246

cognitive dissonance 44

commuting 242

compromise solution 93ff,
        160,168,177,192ff,
        201,247ff,270f,
        296ff,

computer 46

conceptual system 37f,42f,
        47

concordance analysis 163f,
        166,174

conflict
   interpersonal 2,42ff
   intrapersonal 2
   between regions 282,288

conflict measure 90,99ff,
        245ff,268ff

consistency of choice 46

constant elasticity of substitution (CES) 134,149

convergence 7,196ff,210,217f,
              275,287,289,291,299

co-operation 21ff

co-ordination 279ff

cost-benefit analysis 58,141,
        165,241

Cramer's rule 115,124

decentralization 290

demand theory 55,63

dichotomous problems 195f

discordance index 181ff

dimensional analysis 144f

discrete problems 157,208,260ff

disjointed incrementalism 28,33

distribution function
   uniform 169f,183
   exponential 171,183

diversification 257

divisibility 157

dominance 202

duality theorem 106

economics 49ff

edge 105

efficient solution 62f,90ff,97f,
        127ff,159,192f,231

emission 292

environmental objectives 178,
        242,258

evaluative capacity 45f,93,191